Math Expressions

Volume 2

Developed by
The Children's Math Worlds Research Project

PROJECT DIRECTOR AND AUTHOR
Dr. Karen C. Fuson

This material is based upon work supported by the
National Science Foundation
under Grant Numbers
ESI-9816320, REC-9806020, and RED-935373.

Any opinions, findings, and conclusions, or recommendations expressed in this material are those of the author and do not necessarily reflect the views of the National Science Foundation.

HOUGHTON MIFFLIN HARCOURT

Teacher Reviewers

Kindergarten
Patricia Stroh Sugiyama
Wilmette, Illinois

Barbara Wahle
Evanston, Illinois

Grade 1
Sandra Budson
Newton, Massachusetts

Janet Pecci
Chicago, Illinois

Megan Rees
Chicago, Illinois

Grade 2
Molly Dunn
Danvers, Massachusetts

Agnes Lesnick
Hillside, Illinois

Rita Soto
Chicago, Illinois

Grade 3
Jane Curran
Honesdale, Pennsylvania

Sandra Tucker
Chicago, Illinois

Grade 4
Sara Stoneberg Llibre
Chicago, Illinois

Sheri Roedel
Chicago, Illinois

Grade 5
Todd Atler
Chicago, Illinois

Leah Barry
Norfolk, Massachusetts

Special Thanks
Special thanks to the many teachers, students, parents, principals, writers, researchers, and work-study students who participated in the Children's Math Worlds Research Project over the years.

Credits
© Kerstin Layer/Age Fotostock

Illustrative art: Robin Boyer/Deborah Wolfe, LTD; Dave Clegg, Geoff Smith, Ron Mahoney, Tim Johnson
Technical art: Nesbitt Graphics, Inc.
Photos: Nesbitt Graphics, Inc.; Page 93 © C Squared Studios/Photodisc/Getty Images; Page 455 © Nick Green/Jupiter Images.

Printed in the U.S.A.

ISBN: 978-0-547-06072-9

9 1421 17 16 15 14 13

4500407845

VOLUME 2 CONTENTS

Mini Unit 8 Area and Perimeter

1 Explore Perimeter and Area 285
FAMILY LETTER 289
2 Relate Area and Perimeter 291
3 Formulas for Area and Perimeter . . 294
UNIT 8 Test 297

Unit 9 Multiplication and Division with 6, 7, and 8 and Problem Solving

The Remaining Multiplications

1 Multiply and Divide with 6 301
FAMILY LETTER 303
2 Solve Area Word Problems 305
Study Sheet C 305
Going Further 308
3 Multiply and Divide with 8 309
Check Sheet 8: 6s and 8s 309
4 Write Word Problems and Equations 313
5 Multiply and Divide with 7 317

Multiplication Comparisons and Square Numbers

6 Comparison Word Problems 319
Dashes 5–8 319
Answers to Dashes 5–8 321
Going Further 326
7 More Comparison Word Problems 327
8 Square Numbers 331
Check Sheet 9: 7s and Squares . . . 332
9 Practice with 6s, 7s, and 8s 335
Check Sheet 10: 6s, 7s, and 8s. . . . 335
Check Sheet 11: 0s–10s 336
Dashes 9–12 337
Answers to Dashes 9–12 339
Play *High Card Wins* 341
Going Further 343

Word Problems

10 Solve Mixed Word Problems 345
Going Further 350
11 Solve Multi-Step Word Problems . . . 351
Going Further 354
12 Solve Complex Multi-Step Word Problems 355
Dashes 13–16 355
Answers to Dashes 13–16 357
13 Play Multiplication and Division Games 361
Dashes 17–20 361
Answers to Dashes 17–20 363
Play *Division Three-in-a-Row* 367
14 Use Mathematical Processes 369
Basic Multiplications Test 371
Basic Divisions Test 373
UNIT 9 Test 375

VOLUME 2 CONTENTS (CONTINUED)

Mini Unit 10 Time

1 Tell Time 376A
Paper Clock 376A
FAMILY LETTER 381
2 Elapsed Time 383
3 Clock Angles 389
UNIT 10 Test 391

Unit 11 Explore Fractions, Decimals, Probability, and Division with Remainders

Fraction Concepts

1 Fractions as Parts of a Whole 393
FAMILY LETTER 397
2 Fractions as Parts of a Set 399
3 Unit Fractions of Sets and Numbers. 401
4 Compare with Fractions. 403
5 Practice Fractional Comparisons . . 405

Use Fraction Concepts

6 Find a Fraction of a Set or a Number 407
Going Further 410
7 Fractions on Circle Graphs 411
8 Explore Probability 413

Equivalent Fractions

9 Introduce Equivalence 418A
Fraction Strips 418A
10 Explore Equivalence. 421
Play *Spinning a Whole* 421
Game Board for Halves 423
Game Board for Thirds 424
Spinners for Halves and Thirds . . . 424A
11 Equivalence Patterns 424C
Equivalence Chains 424C
12 Find Equivalent Fractions by Multiplying 427
13 Find Equivalent Fractions by Dividing 429

Compare, Add, and Subtract Fractions, and Relate Fractions and Decimals

14 Add Any Fractions 430A
Equivalent Fraction Strips 430A
15 Compare and Subtract Fractions . . 435
16 Whole Numbers and Fractions on a Number Line 439
17 Fractions and Decimals 443

Mixed Numbers and Division with Remainders

18 Improper Fractions and Mixed Numbers 447
19 Introduce Division with Remainders 449
20 Understand Remainders 451
21 Practice Division with Remainders 453
22 Use Mathematical Processes 455
UNIT 11 Test. 457

Mini Unit 12 Three-Dimensional Figures

1 Explore Cubes 460A
FAMILY LETTER 461
2 Two-Dimensional Pictures of Three-Dimensional Buildings 463
Going Further 468
3 Explore Prisms, Cylinders, and Pyramids 468A
4 Explore Cones 468G
5 Explore Circles and Spheres 471
UNIT 12 Test. 473

Unit 13 Measurement

Length

1 Customary Units of Length 475
FAMILY LETTER 477
2 Inches, Feet, and Yards 479
3 Centimeters, Decimeters, and Meters 481
4 Add Lengths 485

Capacity, Weight, Mass, and Temperature

5 Customary Units of Capacity 487
6 Metric Units of Capacity 491
7 Improper Fractions and Mixed Numbers in Measurement 493
8 Measurement Equivalencies and Fractions 495
9 Customary Units of Weight and Metric Units of Mass 497
10 Temperature 503
11 Use Mathematical Processes 505
UNIT 13 Test 507

Mini Unit 14 Directions and Locations

1 Directions and Maps 509
FAMILY LETTER 513
2 Locate Points on a Coordinate Grid 515
3 Explore Line Segments and Figures on a Coordinate Grid 519
UNIT 14 Test 523

Extension Lessons

1 Place Value through Hundred Thousands 525
2 Multiplication Arrays 527
3 Mental Math and Multiplication with Tens 531
4 Model One-Digit by Two-Digit Multiplication 533
5 Methods of One-Digit by Two-Digit Multiplication 535
6 Discuss Different Methods of Multiplication 537
7 One-Digit by Three-Digit Multiplication 539
8 Practice One-Digit by Three-Digit Multiplication 541
9 Find the Unknown Factor 543
10 Estimate Products and Quotients . 545
11 Different Ways to Solve a Problem 547
12 Line Graphs 549

Glossary S1–S14

8–1 Class Activity

Name ______________________ Date ____________

Vocabulary
perimeter
area

▶ Visualize Perimeter and Area

Find the perimeter and area of each figure.
Remember to include the correct units in your answers.

1.

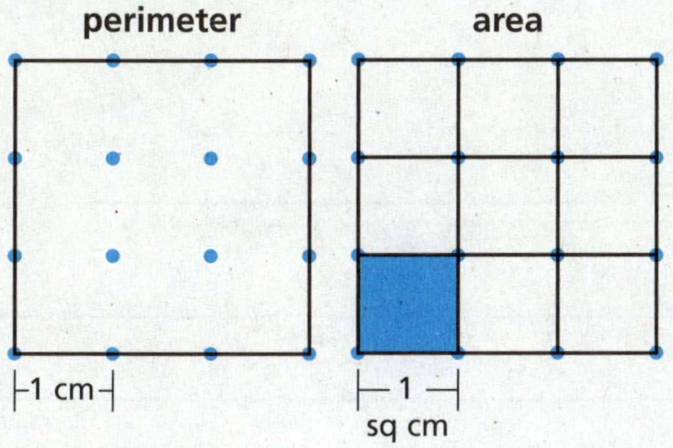

Perimeter = ______________________

Area = ______________________

2.

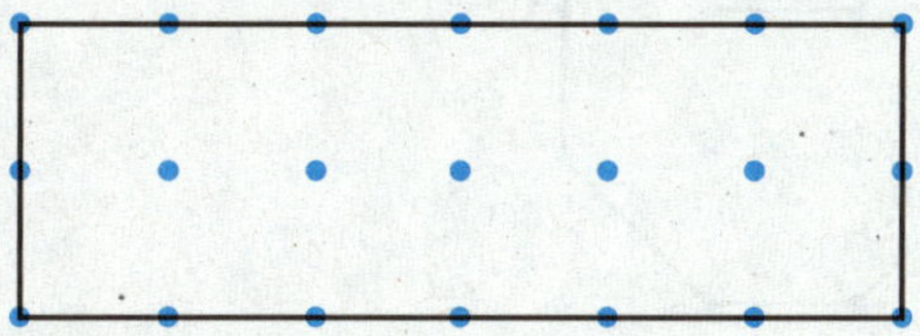

Perimeter = ______________________

Area = ______________________

3.

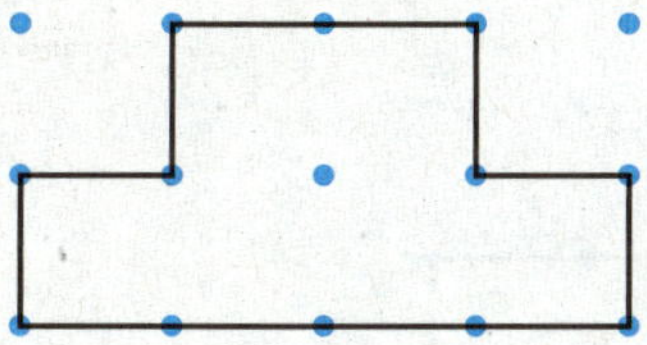

Perimeter = ______________________

Area = ______________________

4.

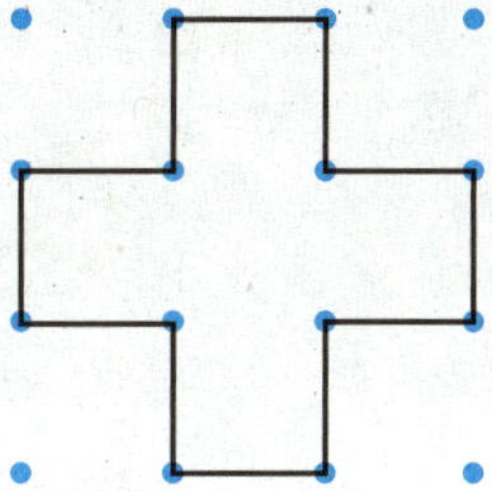

Perimeter = ______________________

Area = ______________________

5.

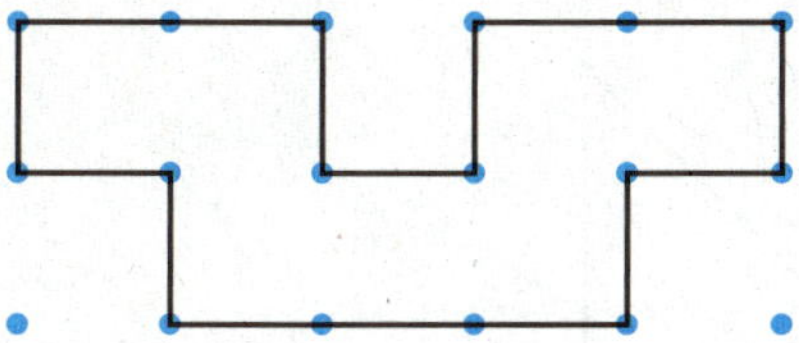

Perimeter = ______________________

Area = ______________________

6.

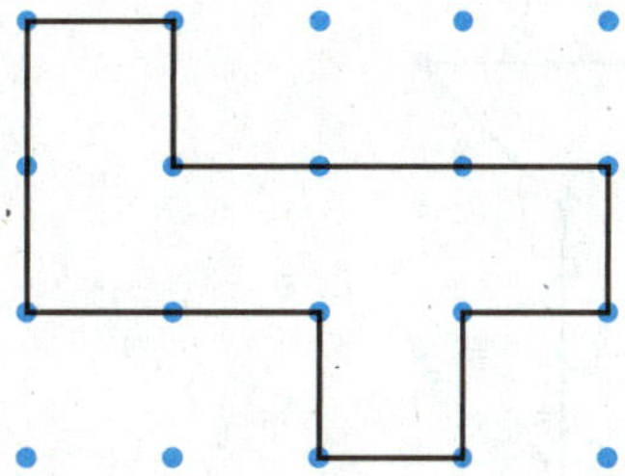

Perimeter = ______________________

Area = ______________________

Name ______________________ Date ____________

►Count Whole- and Half-Square Units to Find Area

7. Find the area of this figure and explain what you did.

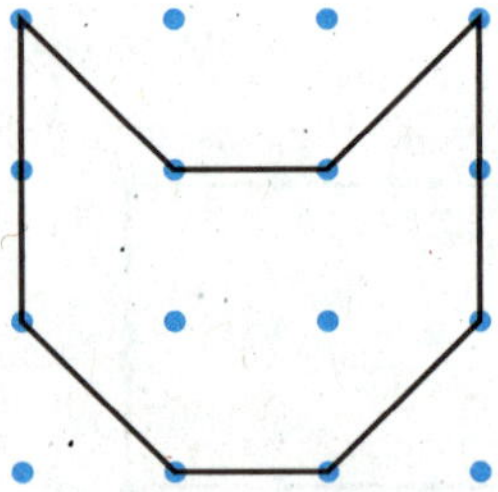

Area = ______________________

____

____

____

____

Find the area of each figure.

8.

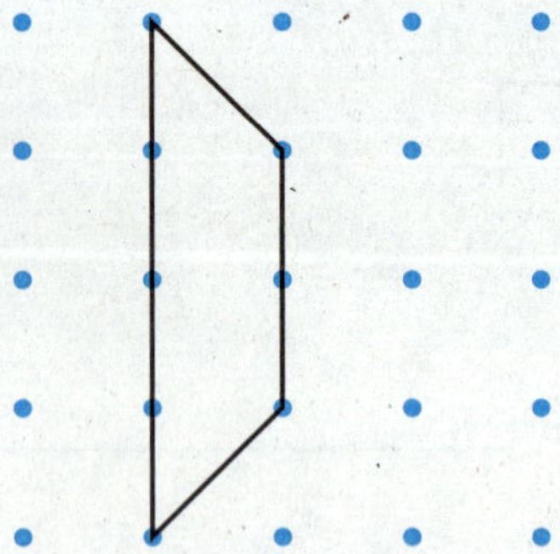

Area = ______________________

9.

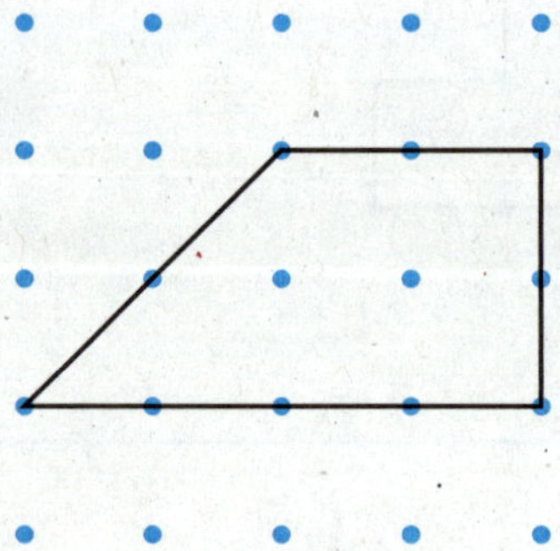

Area = ______________________

10.

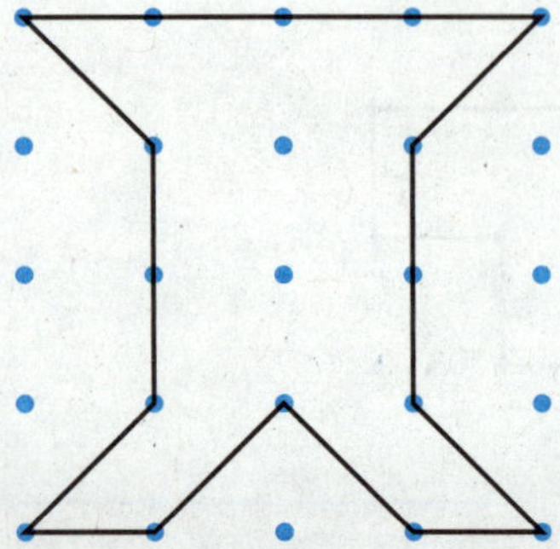

Area = ______________________

11.

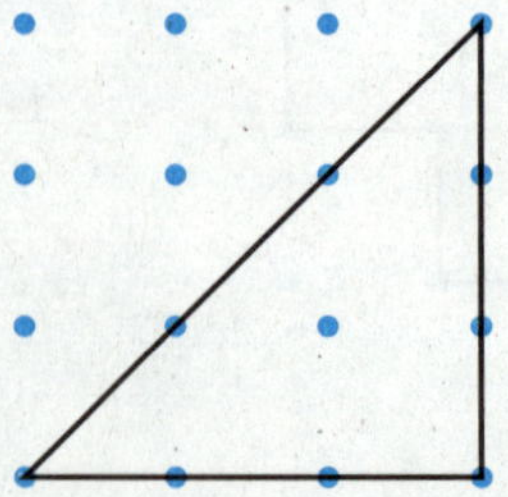

Area = ______________________

8–1 **Class Activity**

Name ______________________ Date ______________

►Solve Area and Perimeter Problems

Read the problem below and complete exercises 12 and 13.

> Debra wants to tile the floor of a rectangular room in her house. The floor is 9 feet long and 8 feet wide. The tiles are squares with sides that are 1 foot long. How many tiles does she need?

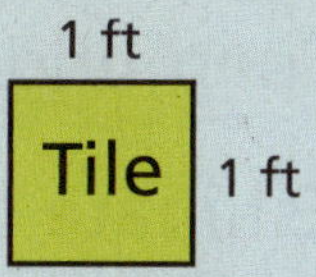

12. To find the total number of tiles, do you need to find the perimeter or area of the room? Explain.

____

____

____

13. How many tiles does Debra need? ______________

Read the problem below and complete exercises 14 and 15.

> Deshawn wants to build a fence around a rectangular space in his backyard. The space is 5 yards long and 3 yards wide. The fence sections are 1 yard long. How many fence sections does Deshawn need?

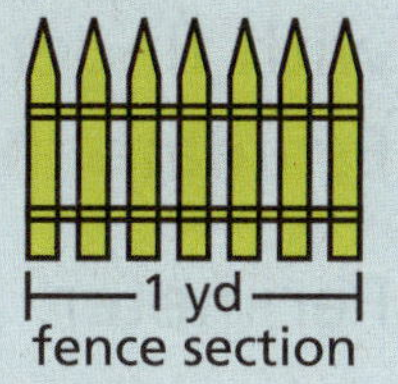

14. To find the number of fence sections, do you need to find the perimeter or area of the rectangle? Explain.

____

____

____

15. How many fence sections does Deshawn need? ______________

16. Math Journal Create and solve a word problem that involves finding the area of a figure. Draw a picture to show your answer is correct.

8–1 Class Activity

Name ______________________ Date ______________

▶ Estimate Perimeter and Area

17. Estimate the perimeter of an index card and CD case in centimeters. Record your estimates in the table. Then find the actual perimeters.

18. Estimate the area of an index card and CD case in centimeters. Record your estimates in the table. Then find the actual areas using a calculator.

	Perimeter		Area	
Object	Estimate (cm)	Actual (cm)	Estimate (cm^2)	Actual (cm^2)
Index card				
CD case				

▶ Estimate the Perimeter and Area of Irregular Figures

19. Use centimeter grid paper (TRB M31). Trace your hand with fingers together and thumb out on the grid. Estimate the perimeter and area.

Perimeter: About ________ cm Area: About ________ cm^2

Family Letter

Dear Family,

Your child is currently participating in Geometry activities involving perimeter and area. In this unit, students find the area of a rectangle by counting the number of square units inside the figure. Students also find the perimeter of a rectangle by counting linear units around the outside of the figure.

Students develop and use formulas to find the perimeter and area of a rectangle, as shown below.

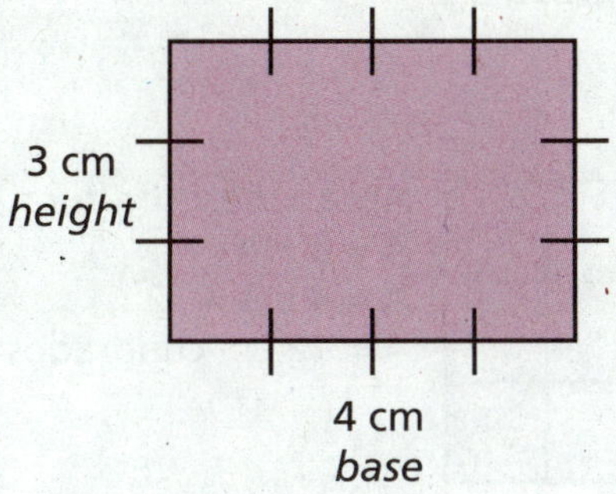

Perimeter = base + height + base + height

$P = b + h + b + h$

$P = 4 + 3 + 4 + 3$

$P = 14$ cm

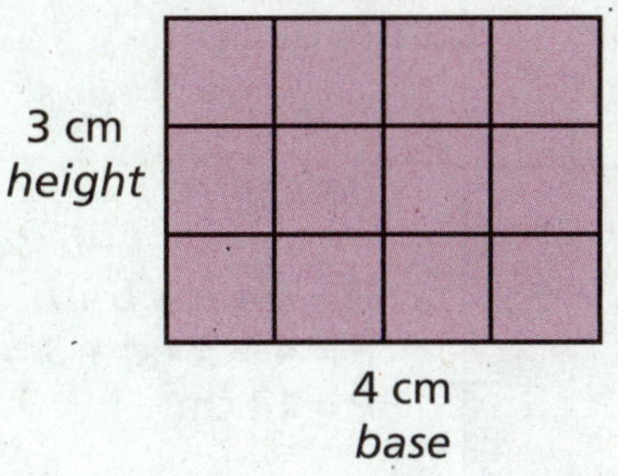

Area = base x height

$A = b \times h$

$A = 4 \times 3 = 12$

$A = 12$ sq cm

Students draw rectangles that have the same perimeter but different areas. They discover that for a given perimeter, the longest, skinniest rectangle has the smallest area and the rectangle with sides closest to the same length or the same length has the greatest area.

Students also draw rectangles that have the same area but different perimeters. They discover that for a given area, the longest, skinniest rectangle has the greatest perimeter and the rectangle with sides closest to the same length or the same length has the least perimeter.

Throughout the unit students apply what they have learned about perimeter and area to real-world problems.

If you have any questions or comments, please call or write to me.

Thank you.

Sincerely,
Your child's teacher

Carta a la familia

Estimada familia:

Su niño está participando en actividades de geometría relacionadas con el perímetro y el área. En esta unidad los estudiantes hallan el área de un rectángulo contando el número de unidades cuadradas que caben en la figura. Los estudiantes también hallan el perímetro de un rectángulo contando el número de unidades lineales que hay alrededor de la figura.

Los estudiantes desarrollan fórmulas y las usan para hallar el perímetro y el área de un rectángulo, como se muestra a continuación.

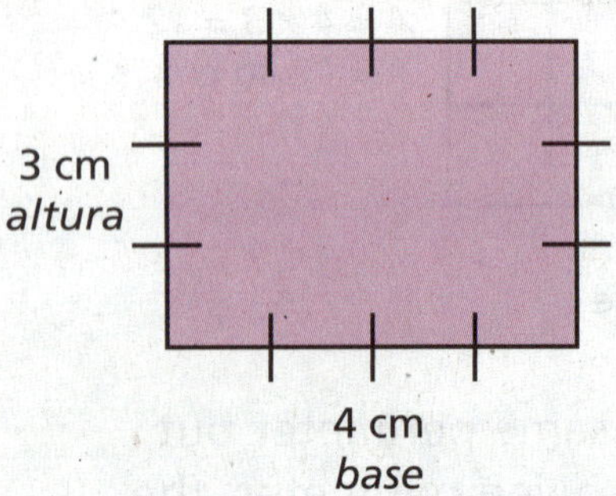

Perímetro = base + altura + base + altura

$P = b + h + b + h$

$P = 4 + 3 + 4 + 3 = 14$

$P = 14$ cm

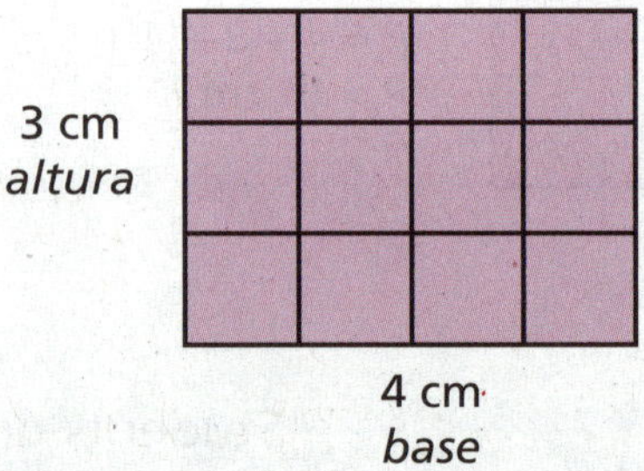

Área = base x altura

$A = b \times h$

$A = 4 \times 3 = 12$

$A = 12$ cm cuadrados

Los estudiantes dibujan rectángulos que tienen el mismo perímetro pero diferentes áreas. Van a notar que, para un determinado perímetro, el rectángulo más largo y delgado tiene el área más pequeña, y el rectángulo con lados que tienen longitudes iguales o casi iguales tiene el área más grande.

Los estudiantes también dibujan rectángulos que tienen la misma área pero diferentes perímetros. Descubren que, para un área determinada, el rectángulo más largo y delgado tiene el perímetro mayor y el rectángulo con lados que tienen longitudes iguales o casi iguales tiene el perímetro menor.

En esta unidad los estudiantes aplican lo que han aprendido acerca del perímetro y el área a problemas de la vida diaria.

Si tiene alguna duda o comentario, por favor comuníquese conmigo.

Atentamente,
El maestro de su niño

8–2 Class Activity

Name _______________ Date _______________

▸ Explore Rectangles with the Same Perimeter

Complete.

1. On a centimeter dot array, draw all possible rectangles with a **perimeter** of 12 cm and sides whose lengths are whole centimeters. Label the lengths of two adjacent sides of each rectangle.

2. Find and label the **area** of each rectangle. In the table, record the lengths of the sides and the area of each rectangle.

3. Compare the shapes of the rectangles with the least and greatest areas.

____

____

Rectangles with Perimeter 12 cm

Lengths of Two Adjacent Sides	Area

4. On a centimeter dot array, draw all possible rectangles with a perimeter of 22 cm and sides whose lengths are whole centimeters. Label the lengths of two adjacent sides of each rectangle.

5. Find and label the area of each rectangle. In the table, record the lengths of the sides and the area of each rectangle.

Rectangles with Perimeter 22 cm

Lengths of Two Adjacent Sides	Area

6. Compare the shapes of the rectangles with the least and greatest areas.

____

____

Name ________________________ Date ________

► Explore Rectangles with the Same Area

Complete.

7. On a centimeter dot array, draw all possible rectangles with an area of 12 sq cm and sides whose lengths are whole centimeters. Label the lengths of two adjacent sides of each rectangle.

8. Find and label the perimeter of each rectangle. In the table, record the lengths of the sides and the perimeter of each rectangle.

Rectangles with Area 12 sq cm

Lengths of Two Adjacent Sides	Perimeter

9. Compare the shapes of the rectangles with the least and greatest perimeter.

____

____

10. On a centimeter dot array, draw all possible rectangles with an area of 18 sq cm and with sides whose lengths are whole centimeters. Label the lengths of two adjacent sides of each rectangle.

11. Find and label the perimeter of each rectangle. In the table, record the lengths of the sides and the perimeter of each rectangle.

Rectangles with Area 18 sq cm

Lengths of Two Adjacent Sides	Perimeter

12. Compare the shapes of the rectangles with the least and greatest perimeter.

____

____

Name ______________________ Date __________

▶ Find the Area of a Rectangle

Find the area of each rectangle. Draw the square units inside rectangles 1 and 2. Label your answer in square units. Write an equation to show how the length of the adjacent sides and area are related.

1.

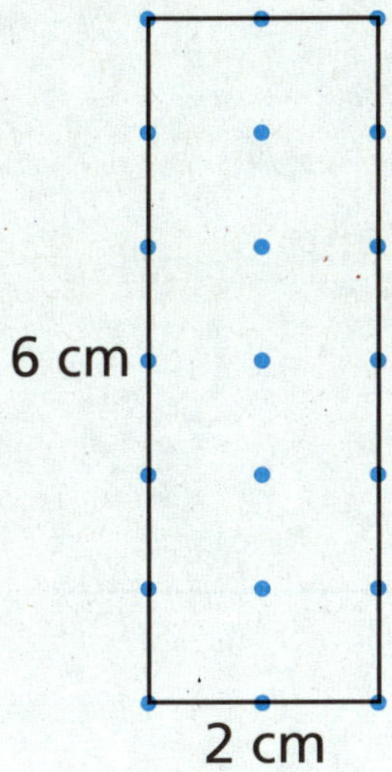

Area = ______________

____

2.

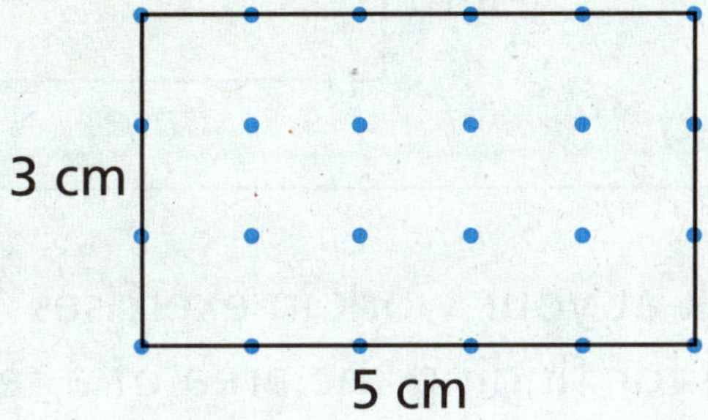

Area = ______________

____

3.

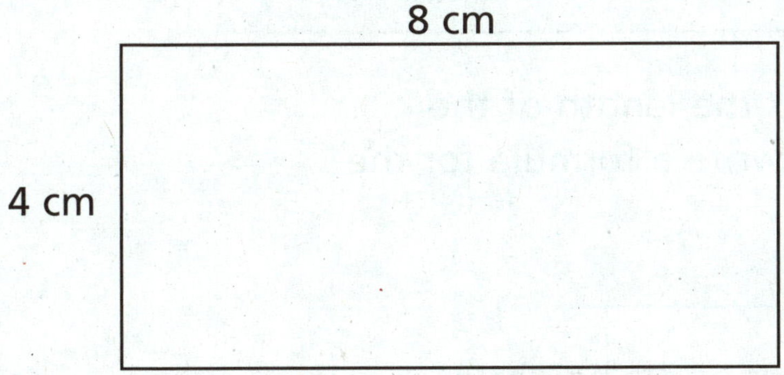

Area = ______________

____

Name ____________________ Date ____________

Vocabulary
base
height
formula

▶ Formula for the Area of a Rectangle

You can call the bottom side of a rectangle the **base**.
You can call one of the adjacent sides the **height**.

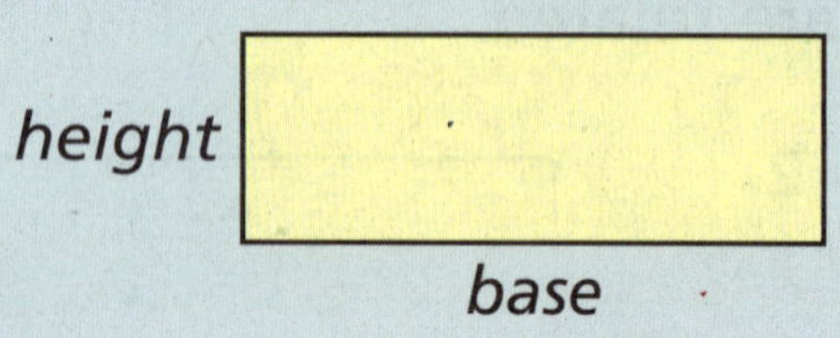

4. Look at your work in exercises 1–3. Complete this rule for finding the area of a rectangle using the words *height* and *base*.

The area of a rectangle is ______________________________

5. Fill in the blanks with words to create a shorter form of the rule for the area of a rectangle.

__________ = __________ × __________

A **formula** is an equation with variables that describes a rule.

6. Use the letter *A* for area, *b* for the length of the base, and *h* for the height to write a formula for the area of a rectangle.

__________ = __________ × __________

7. A rectangle has a base of 7 feet and a height of 3 feet. Use the formula from exercise 6 to find the area of this rectangle. Remember to include the correct unit in your answer.

____

8–3 Class Activity

Name ______________________ Date ______________

Vocabulary
perimeter
formula

► Formula for the Perimeter of a Rectangle

Find the perimeter of each rectangle. Remember to include the correct units in your answers.

8.

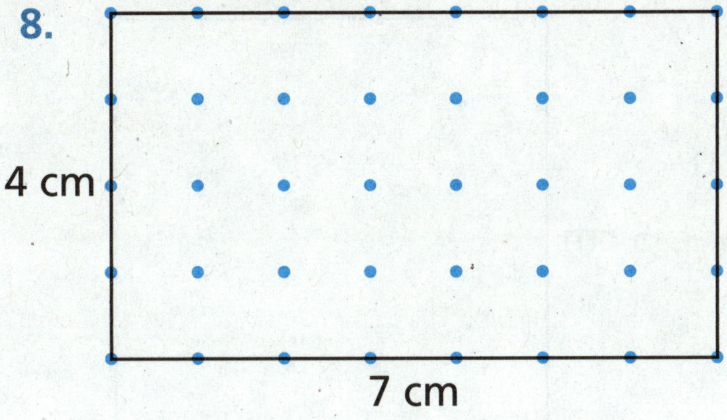

Perimeter = ______________

9.

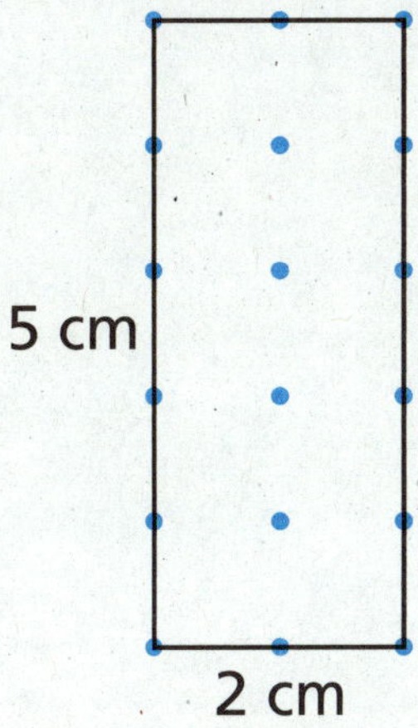

Perimeter = ______________

10.

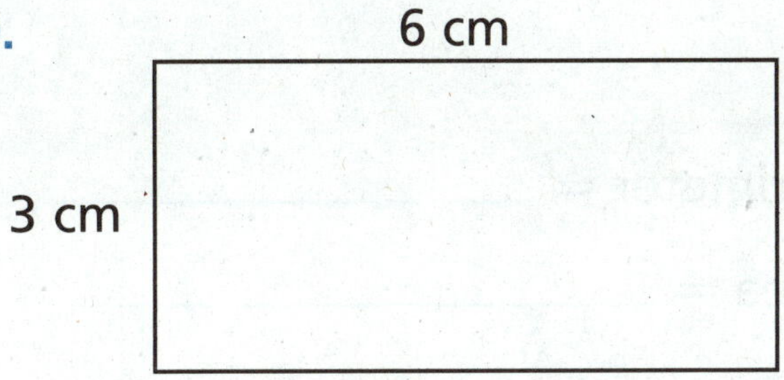

Perimeter = ______________

11. Write a formula for finding the perimeter of a rectangle. Use the letter P to represent the perimeter of a rectangle, b to represent the length of the base, and h to represent the height.

____

12. A football field (including the end zones) is shaped like a rectangle with a base of 360 feet and a height of 160 feet. Use a formula to find the perimeter of the field.

____

8–3 Class Activity

Name ____________________ Date ____________

▶ Formulas for the Perimeter and Area of a Square

Find the perimeter and area of each square. Remember to include the correct units in your answers.

13.

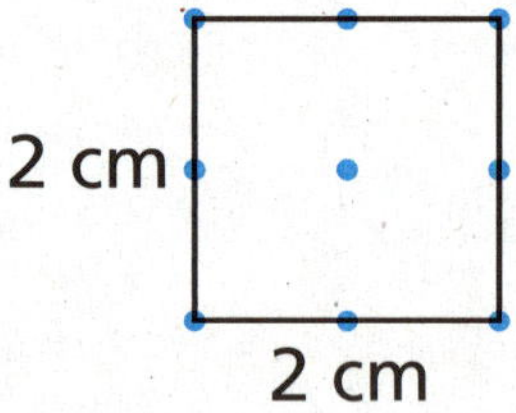

Perimeter = ____________________

Area = ____________________

14.

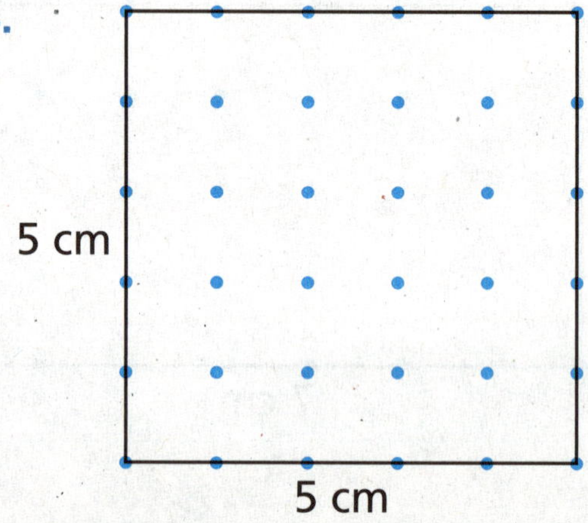

Perimeter = ____________________

Area = ____________________

15.

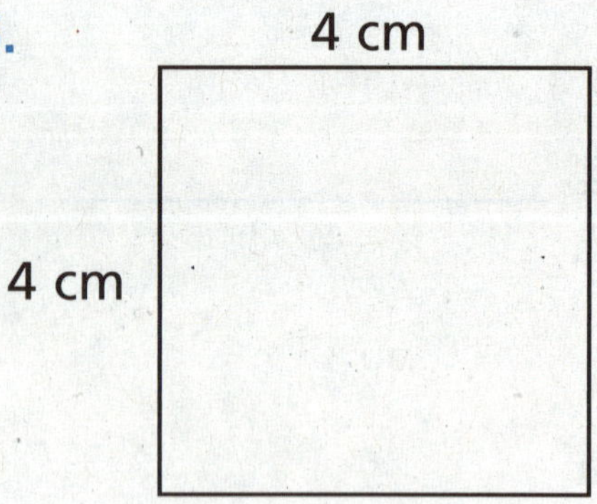

Perimeter = ____________________

Area = ____________________

16. Write a formula for the area of a square and for the perimeter of a square. Let the letter *s* stand for the length of a side of a square.

$A =$ ____________________

$P =$ ____________________

17. Use your formulas to find the area and perimeter of a square with sides that are 8 feet long.

____

Name ______________________ Date ______________

Find the perimeter and area. Include the correct units in your answers.

1.

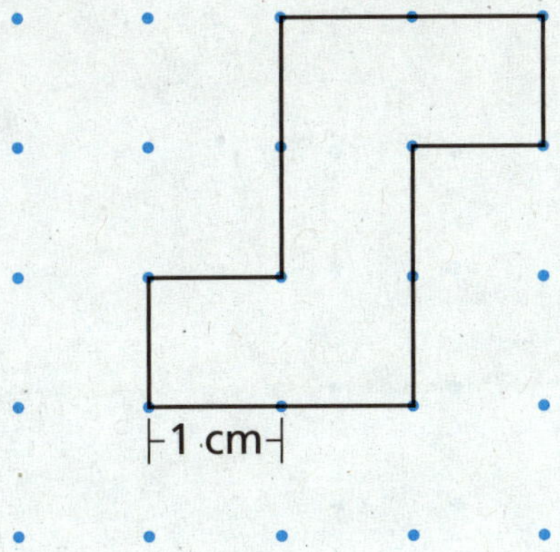

Perimeter = ______________________

Area = ______________________

2.

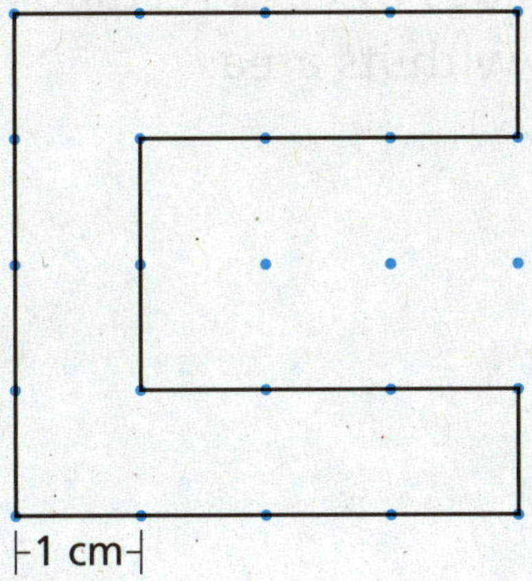

Perimeter = ______________________

Area = ______________________

Find the area.

3.

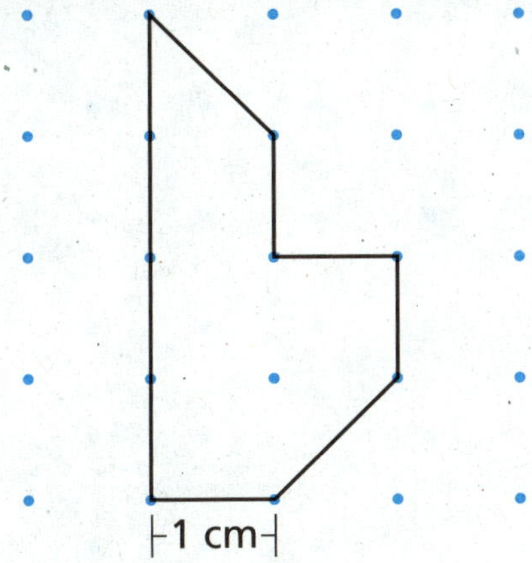

Area = ______________________

Estimate the area.

4.

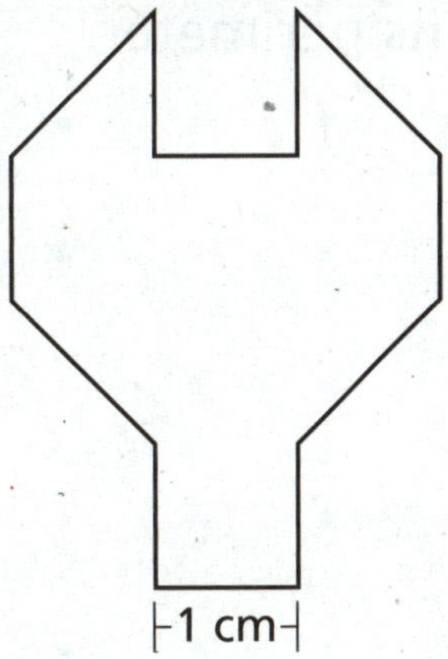

Area: ______________________

Name ____________________ Date ________

5. On the dot array, draw all possible rectangles with a perimeter of 14 cm and sides whose lengths are whole centimeters. Label the lengths of the two adjacent sides of each rectangle. Label each rectangle with its area.

6. On the dot array, draw all possible rectangles with an area of 12 sq cm and sides whose lengths are whole centimeters. Label the lengths of the two adjacent sides of each rectangle. Label each rectangle with its perimeter.

Name ________________________ Date ____________

7. Use the letter A to represent the area of the rectangle, b to represent the length of the base, and h to represent the height.

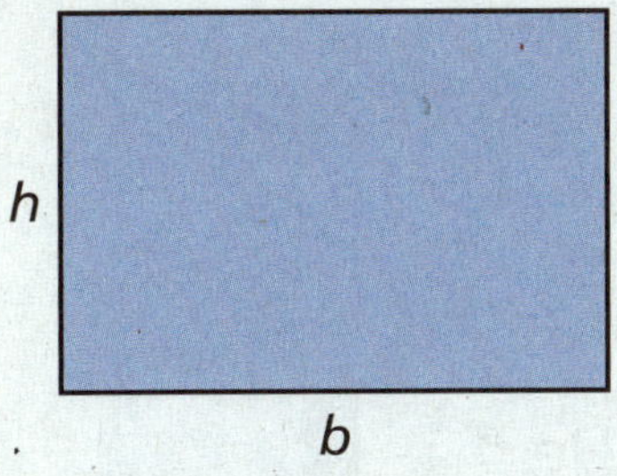

Write a formula for the area of the rectangle.

____

Use your formula to find the area of a rectangle with a height of 3 feet and a base of 5 feet.

____

8. Use the letter P to represent the perimeter of the rectangle, b to represent the length of the base, and h to represent the height.

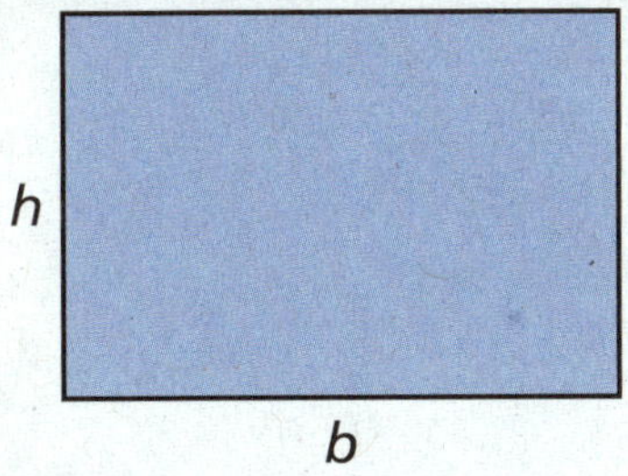

Write a formula for the perimeter of the rectangle.

____

Use your formula to find the perimeter of a rectangle with a width of 3 feet and a length of 5 feet.

____

Name ______________________ Date ______________

9. Liana wants to put a rope around a rectangular space in her yard where she plans to plant a vegetable garden. The garden will be 8 meters long and 6 meters wide. How much rope does Liana need?

____

10. Extended Response David is sewing together a quilt from quilt squares his grandmother made. He wants the quilt to be a rectangle, with sides of length 5 feet and 7 feet. The quilt squares have sides of length 1 foot.

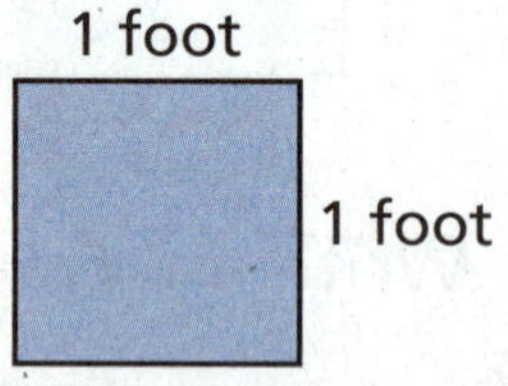

Quilt square

To find the number of quilt squares he needs, do you need to find the perimeter of the quilt or the area? Explain your reasoning.

____

____

____

How many quilt squares does David need? Explain how you found your answer.

____

____

____

Draw a picture of the quilt to show your answer is correct.

Name ________________ Date ________

▶ Explore Patterns with 6s

What patterns do you see below?

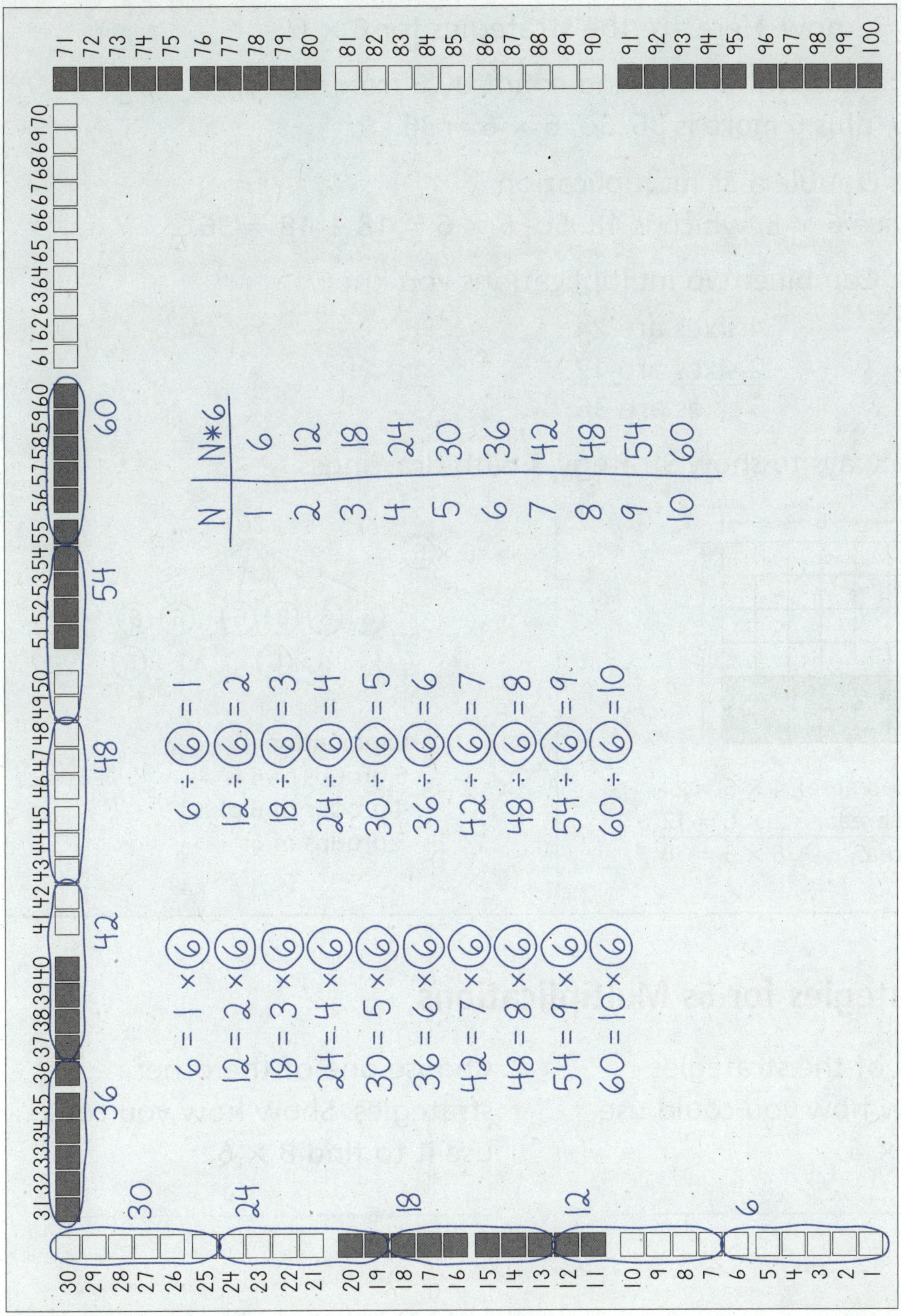

Name ________________________ Date ____________

►Strategies for Multiplying with 6

You can use 6s multiplications that you know to find 6s multiplications that you don't know. Here are the strategies for 6×6.

- **Strategy 1:** Start with 5×6, and count by 6 from there.
  $5 \times 6 = 30$, plus 6 more is 36. So, $6 \times 6 = 36$.
- **Strategy 2:** Double a 3s multiplication.
  6×6 is twice 6×3, which is 18. So, $6 \times 6 = 18 + 18 = 36$.
- **Strategy 3:** Combine two multiplications you know.

$4 \times 6 = 24$	4 sixes are 24.
$2 \times 6 = 12$	2 sixes are 12.
$6 \times 6 = 36$	6 sixes are 36.

Here are two ways to show Strategy 3 with drawings.

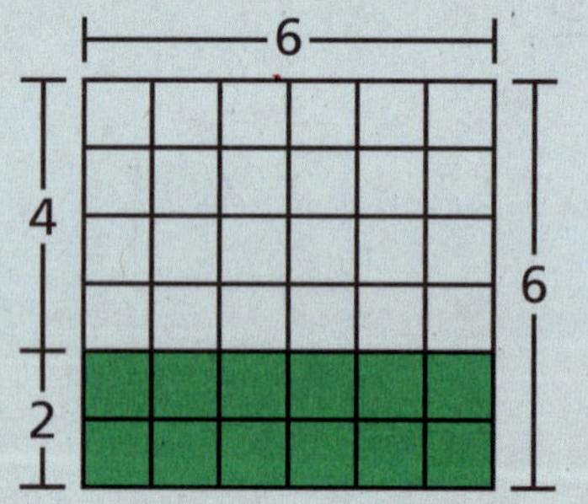

unshaded area: $4 \times 6 = 24$
shaded area: $2 \times 6 = 12$
total area: $6 \times 6 = 36$

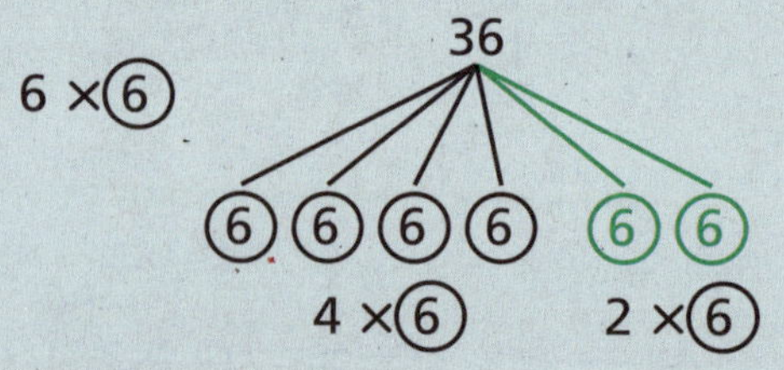

Explanation:
6 groups of 6 is
4 groups of 6 plus
2 groups of 6.

►Apply Strategies for 6s Multiplications

1. Choose one of the strategies above. Show how you could use it to find 7×6.

2. Choose one of the other strategies. Show how you could use it to find 8×6.

Family Letter

Dear Family,

In this unit, students learn multiplications and divisions for 6s, 7s, and 8s, while continuing to practice the rest of the basic multiplications and divisions covered in Unit 4.

Although students practice all the 6s, 7s, and 8s multiplications, they really have only six new multiplications to learn: 6×6, 6×7, 6×8, 7×7, 7×8, and 8×8. The lessons for these multiplications focus on strategies for finding the products using multiplications they know.

Students are also introduced to comparisons involving multiplication and division. Such comparisons involve one quantity that is a number of times *as many as* or *as much as* another. Here are two examples:

- Teresa has 2 gerbils. Owen has 4 times as many gerbils as Teresa has. How many gerbils does Owen have?
- Eduardo has 12 posters in his room. Manuela has $\frac{1}{3}$ as many posters as Eduardo. How many posters does Manuela have?

This unit also focuses on word problems. Students are presented with a variety of one-step word problems. They use the language and context of each problem to determine which operation—multiplication, division, addition, or subtraction—they must use to solve it. Students solve multi-step problems using a variety of methods.

Please continue to help your child get faster on multiplications and divisions. Use all of the practice materials that your child has brought home. Your support is crucial to your child's learning.

Please call if you have any questions or comments.

Thank you.

Sincerely,
Your child's teacher

Carta a la familia

Estimada familia:

En esta unidad los estudiantes aprenden las multiplicaciones y divisiones con el 6, el 7 y el 8, mientras siguen practicando las demás multiplicaciones y divisiones que se presentaron en la Unidad 4.

Aunque los estudiantes practican todas las multiplicaciones con el 6, el 7 y el 8, en realidad sólo tienen que aprender seis multiplicaciones nuevas: 6×6, 6×7, 6×8, 7×7, 7×8 y 8×8. Las lecciones de estas multiplicaciones se centran en estrategias para hallar los productos usando multiplicaciones que ya se conocen.

Los estudiantes también empiezan a hacer comparaciones de cantidades que resultan de la multiplicación y la división. Las comparaciones de este tipo tratan de una cantidad que es *tantas veces*. Aquí hay dos ejemplos:

- Teresa tiene 2 gerbos. Owen tiene 4 veces más gerbos que Teresa. ¿Cuántos gerbos tiene Owen?
- Eduardo tiene 12 carteles en su cuarto. Manuela tiene $\frac{1}{3}$ del número de carteles que tiene Eduardo. ¿Cuántos carteles tiene Manuela?

Esta unidad también se centra en problemas verbales. A los estudiantes se les presenta una varidad de problemas verbales de un paso. Aprovechan el lenguaje y el contexto de cada problema para determinar qué operación deben usar para resolverlo: la multiplicación, la división, la suma o la resta. Los estudiantes también resuelven problemas de varios pasos utilizando una variedad de métodos.

Por favor continúe ayudando a su niño a practicar las multiplicaciones y las divisiones. Use todos los materiales de práctica que su niño ha llevado a casa. Su apoyo es importante para el aprendizaje de su niño.

Si tiene alguna duda o pregunta, por favor comuníquese conmigo.

Atentamente,
El maestro de su niño

Name ____________________ Date ____________________

Study Sheet C

6s

Count-bys	Mixed Up ×	Mixed Up ÷
1 × 6 = 6	10 × 6 = 60	54 ÷ 6 = 9
2 × 6 = 12	8 × 6 = 48	30 ÷ 6 = 5
3 × 6 = 18	2 × 6 = 12	12 ÷ 6 = 2
4 × 6 = 24	6 × 6 = 36	60 ÷ 6 = 10
5 × 6 = 30	4 × 6 = 24	48 ÷ 6 = 8
6 × 6 = 36	1 × 6 = 6	36 ÷ 6 = 6
7 × 6 = 42	9 × 6 = 54	6 ÷ 6 = 1
8 × 6 = 48	3 × 6 = 18	42 ÷ 6 = 7
9 × 6 = 54	7 × 6 = 42	18 ÷ 6 = 3
10 × 6 = 60	5 × 6 = 30	24 ÷ 6 = 4

7s

Count-bys	Mixed Up ×	Mixed Up ÷
1 × 7 = 7	6 × 7 = 42	70 ÷ 7 = 10
2 × 7 = 14	8 × 7 = 56	14 ÷ 7 = 2
3 × 7 = 21	5 × 7 = 35	28 ÷ 7 = 4
4 × 7 = 28	9 × 7 = 63	56 ÷ 7 = 8
5 × 7 = 35	4 × 7 = 28	42 ÷ 7 = 6
6 × 7 = 42	10 × 7 = 70	63 ÷ 7 = 9
7 × 7 = 49	3 × 7 = 21	21 ÷ 7 = 3
8 × 7 = 56	1 × 7 = 7	49 ÷ 7 = 7
9 × 7 = 63	7 × 7 = 49	7 ÷ 7 = 1
10 × 7 = 70	2 × 7 = 14	35 ÷ 7 = 5

8s

Count-bys	Mixed Up ×	Mixed Up ÷
1 × 8 = 8	6 × 8 = 48	16 ÷ 8 = 2
2 × 8 = 16	10 × 8 = 80	40 ÷ 8 = 5
3 × 8 = 24	7 × 8 = 56	72 ÷ 8 = 9
4 × 8 = 32	2 × 8 = 16	32 ÷ 8 = 4
5 × 8 = 40	4 × 8 = 32	8 ÷ 8 = 1
6 × 8 = 48	8 × 8 = 64	80 ÷ 8 = 10
7 × 8 = 56	5 × 8 = 40	64 ÷ 8 = 8
8 × 8 = 64	10 × 8 = 80	24 ÷ 8 = 3
9 × 8 = 72	3 × 8 = 24	56 ÷ 8 = 7
10 × 8 = 80	1 × 8 = 8	48 ÷ 8 = 6

Squares

Count-bys	Mixed Up ×	Mixed Up ÷
1 × 1 = 1	3 × 3 = 9	25 ÷ 5 = 5
2 × 2 = 4	9 × 9 = 81	4 ÷ 2 = 2
3 × 3 = 9	4 × 4 = 16	81 ÷ 9 = 9
4 × 4 = 16	6 × 6 = 36	9 ÷ 3 = 3
5 × 5 = 25	2 × 2 = 4	36 ÷ 6 = 6
6 × 6 = 36	7 × 7 = 49	100 ÷ 10 = 10
7 × 7 = 49	10 × 10 = 100	16 ÷ 4 = 4
8 × 8 = 64	1 × 1 = 1	49 ÷ 7 = 7
9 × 9 = 81	5 × 5 = 25	1 ÷ 1 = 1
10 × 10 = 100	8 × 8 = 64	64 ÷ 8 = 8

Name ____________________ Date __________

► Missing Number Puzzles

Complete each Missing Number puzzle.

1.

×	5	2	
	30		48
4		8	32
	45		72

2.

×		3	
6	30		42
4			28
	40	24	56

3.

×	4		8
9		81	
	12		24
	20	45	40

► Solve and Discuss Area Word Problems

Solve each problem. Label your answers with the correct units.

Show your work.

4. The mattress has a length of 7 feet and a width of 6 feet. What is the area of the mattress?

____

5. The wading pool at Evans Park is shaped like a square with sides 8 feet long. What is the area of the wading pool?

____

6. Milo's rug has a length of 5 feet and an area of 40 square feet. What is the width of his rug?

____

7. Lana wants to enclose a garden plot with a piece of rope that is 36 feet long. Lana wants to have the most space possible for gardening. Draw a picture of what Lana's garden will look like. Label the drawing.

Name ______________________ Date __________

▶Problem-Solving Strategy: Draw a Picture

Draw a picture to help solve each problem.

1. Ana has a ribbon that is 18 inches long. She cut the ribbon into 3 equal pieces. Then she cut each of those pieces in half. How many small pieces of ribbon are there? How long is each piece?

____

2. A sign is shaped like a square. Eva draws lines in the sign to make 3 equal rectangles. Each rectangle is 3 inches wide and 9 inches long. What is the area of the square?

____

3. Ty puts up a 20-foot-long fence to make a rectangular garden. He divides the rectangle into 4 equal squares all in one row. The side of each square is 2 feet long. What is the area of the garden?

____

4. Aaron is stacking cans in a grocery store. The bottom row has 7 cans. Each row above has 1 fewer can. How many cans will be stacked in all?

____

5. There are 4 cars in a row. Each car is 13 feet long. There are 6 feet between each car. What is the length from the front of the first car to the back of the last car in the row?

____

Name Date

►Check Sheet 8: 6s and 8s

6s Multiplications	6s Divisions	8s Multiplications	8s Divisions
10 × 6 = 60	24 / 6 = 4	2 × 8 = 16	72 / 8 = 9
6 • 4 = 24	48 ÷ 6 = 8	8 • 10 = 80	16 ÷ 8 = 2
6 * 7 = 42	60 / 6 = 10	3 * 8 = 24	40 / 8 = 5
2 × 6 = 12	12 ÷ 6 = 2	9 × 8 = 72	8 ÷ 8 = 1
6 • 5 = 30	42 / 6 = 7	8 • 4 = 32	80 / 8 = 10
6 * 8 = 48	30 ÷ 6 = 5	8 * 7 = 56	48 ÷ 8 = 6
9 × 6 = 54	6 / 6 = 1	5 × 8 = 40	56 / 8 = 7
6 • 1 = 6	18 ÷ 6 = 3	8 • 6 = 48	24 ÷ 8 = 3
6 * 6 = 36	54 / 6 = 9	1 * 8 = 8	64 / 8 = 8
6 × 3 = 18	36 / 6 = 6	8 × 8 = 64	32 / 8 = 4
6 • 6 = 36	48 ÷ 6 = 8	4 • 8 = 32	80 ÷ 8 = 10
5 * 6 = 30	12 / 6 = 2	6 * 8 = 48	56 / 8 = 7
6 × 2 = 12	24 ÷ 6 = 4	8 × 3 = 24	8 ÷ 8 = 1
4 • 6 = 24	60 / 6 = 10	7 • 8 = 56	24 / 8 = 3
6 * 9 = 54	6 ÷ 6 = 1	8 * 2 = 16	64 ÷ 8 = 8
8 × 6 = 48	42 / 6 = 7	8 × 9 = 72	16 / 8 = 2
7 • 6 = 42	18 ÷ 6 = 3	8 • 1 = 8	72 ÷ 8 = 9
6 * 10 = 60	36 ÷ 6 = 6	8 * 8 = 64	32 ÷ 8 = 4
1 × 6 = 6	30 / 6 = 5	10 × 8 = 80	40 / 8 = 5
4 • 6 = 24	54 ÷ 6 = 9	5 • 8 = 40	48 ÷ 8 = 6

9–3 Class Activity

Name ____________________ Date ____________________

►Explore Patterns with 8s.

What patterns do you see below?

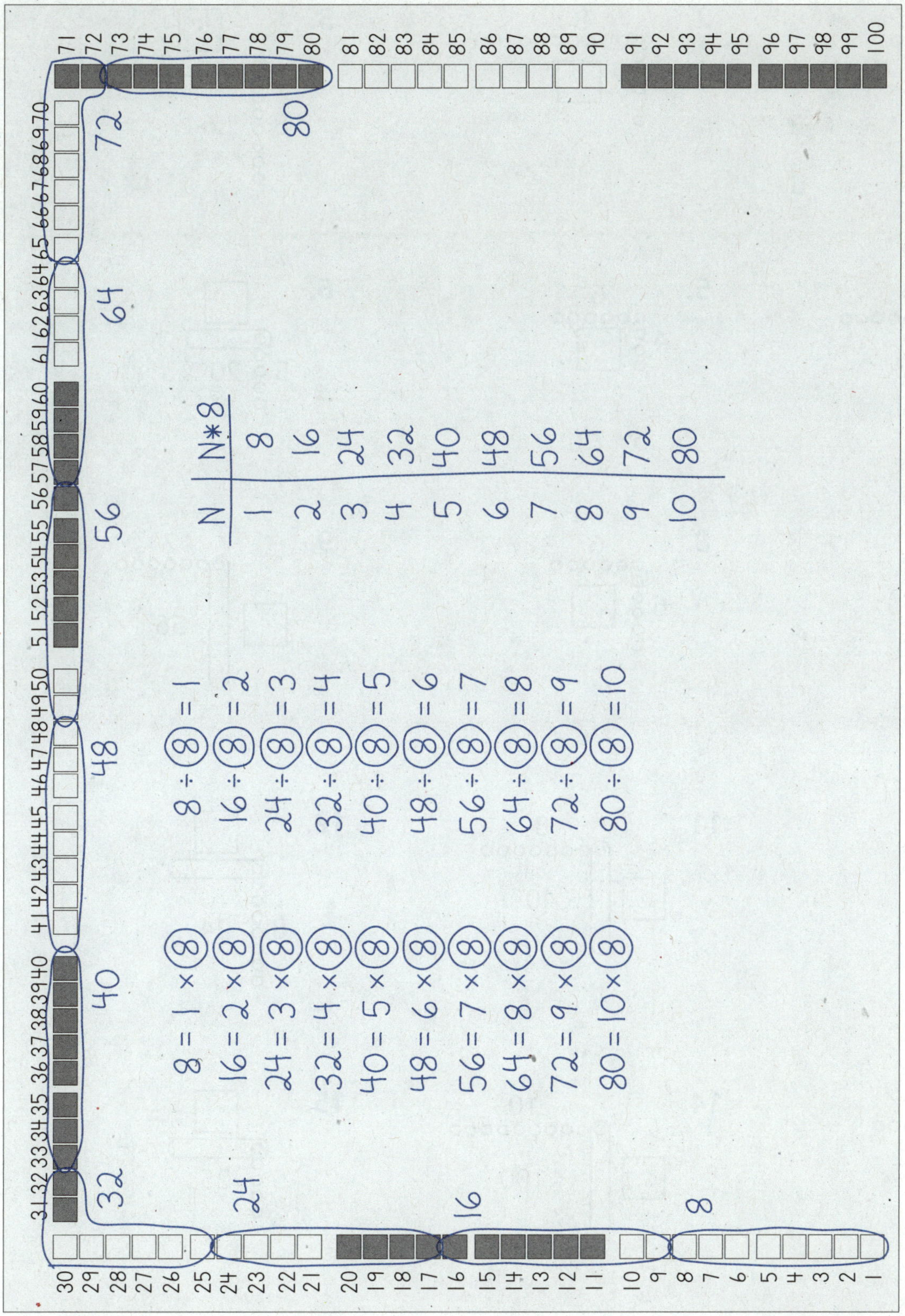

9–3 Class Activity

Name ____________________ Date ____________

▶ Fast-Array Drawings

Find the missing number for each Fast-Array drawing.

1.

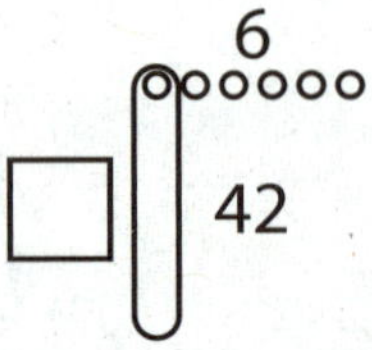

2.

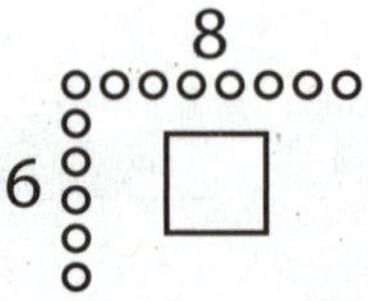

3.

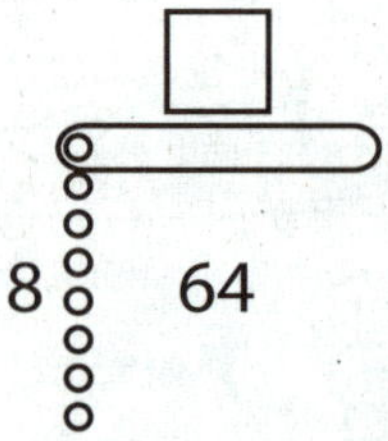

4.

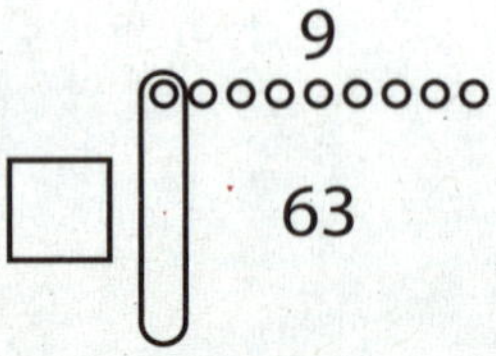

5.

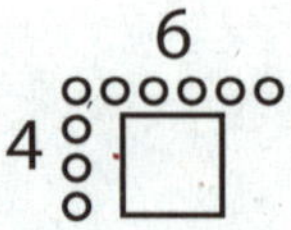

6.

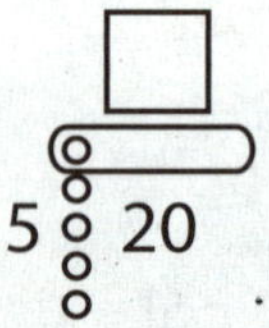

7.

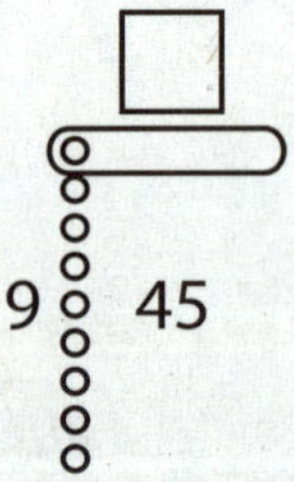

8.

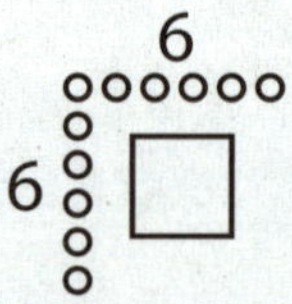

9.

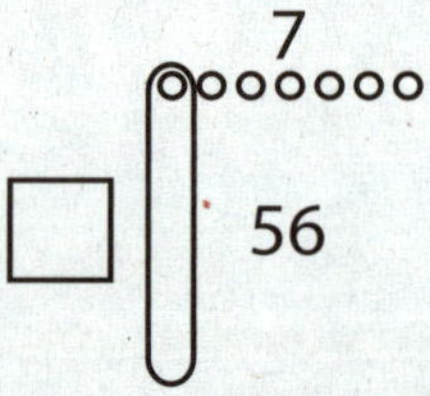

10.

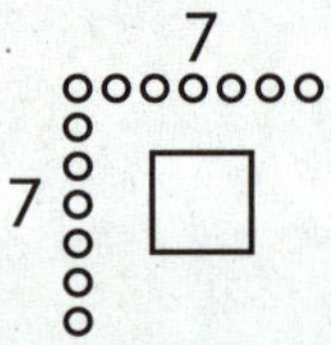

11.

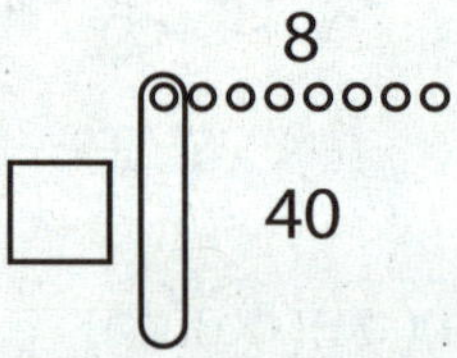

12.

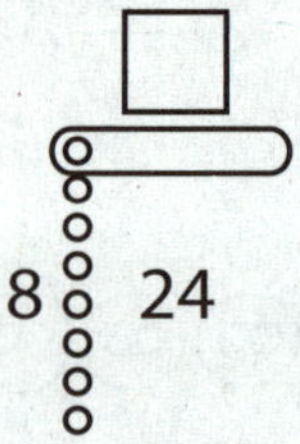

13.

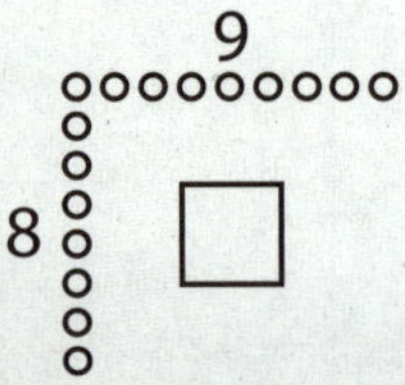

14.

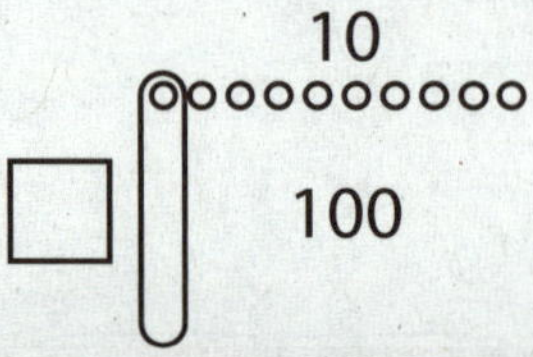

15.

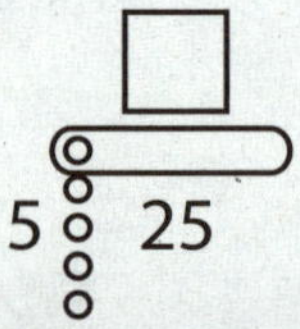

Name ______________________ Date ______________

►Sprints for 6s

As your teacher reads each multiplication or division, write your answer in the space provided.

× 6	÷ 6
a. ________	a. ________
b. ________	b. ________
c. ________	c. ________
d. ________	d. ________
e. ________	e. ________
f. ________	f. ________
g. ________	g. ________
h. ________	h. ________
i. ________	i. ________
j. ________	j. ________

9–4 Class Activity

Name ______ Date ______

▶ Identify the Type and Choose the Operation

Solve. Then circle what type it is and what operation you use.

1. Students in Mr. Till's class hung their paintings on the wall. They made 6 rows, with 5 paintings in each row. How many paintings did the students hang?

   ______

   Circle one: array repeated groups area
   Circle one: multiplication division

2. Write your own problem that is the same type as problem 1. ______

   ______

   ______

3. There are 8 goldfish in each tank at the pet store. If there are 56 goldfish in all, how many tanks are there?

   ______

   Circle one: array repeated groups area
   Circle one: multiplication division

4. Write your own problem that is the same type as problem 3. ______

   ______

   ______

5. Pierre built a rectangular pen for his rabbits. The pen is 4 feet wide and 6 feet long. What is the area of the pen? ______

   Circle one: array repeated groups area
   Circle one: multiplication division

Name ______ Date ______

6. Write your own problem that is the same type as problem 5. ______

______

______

______

Solve the word problem. Then circle what type it is and circle the operation you would use.

7. Paulo arranged 72 baseball cards in 9 rows and a certain number of columns. How many columns did he arrange the cards into? ______

Circle one: array repeated groups area
Circle one: multiplication division

8. Write your own problem that is the same type as Problem 7. ______

______

______

______

9. The store sells bottles of juice in six-packs. Mr. Lee bought 9 six-packs for a picnic. How many bottles did he buy? ______

Circle one: array repeated groups area
Circle one: multiplication division

10. Write your own problem that is the same type as Problem 9. ______

______

______

______

11. **Math Journal** Write an area multiplication problem. Draw a Fast Array to solve it.

9–4 Class Activity

Name ____________________ Date ____________

Vocabulary
equation
variable

▶ Use Variables in Equations

When you write **equations** you can use a letter to represent an unknown number. This letter is called a **variable**.

These equations have variables.

$a + 4 = 6$	$7 = c + 3$	$w = 8 - 3$	$9 = 18 - c$
$6 \times y = 18$	$p = 6 \times 3$	$f = 18 \div 3$	$18 \div n = 3$

Solve each equation.

13. $21 = 7 \times a$

$a =$ ______

14. $63 \div g = 9$

$g =$ ______

15. $10 - n = 6$

$n =$ ______

16. $8 + f = 13$

$f =$ ______

▶ Write and Solve Equations with Variables

Write an equation for each word problem. Then solve the equation.

17. A large box of crayons holds 60 crayons. There are 10 crayons in each row. How many rows are there?

____

18. A poster covers 12 square feet. The poster is 4 feet long. How wide is the poster?

____

19. There are 7 groups of students with an equal number of students in each group working on a social studies project. There are 28 students working on the project. How many students are there in each group?

____

20. Amanda has 15 bracelets. She gave a number of bracelets to friends. She has 10 bracelets left. How many bracelets did she give to friends?

____

Name ______________________ Date ____________

►Explore Patterns with 7s

What patterns do you see below?

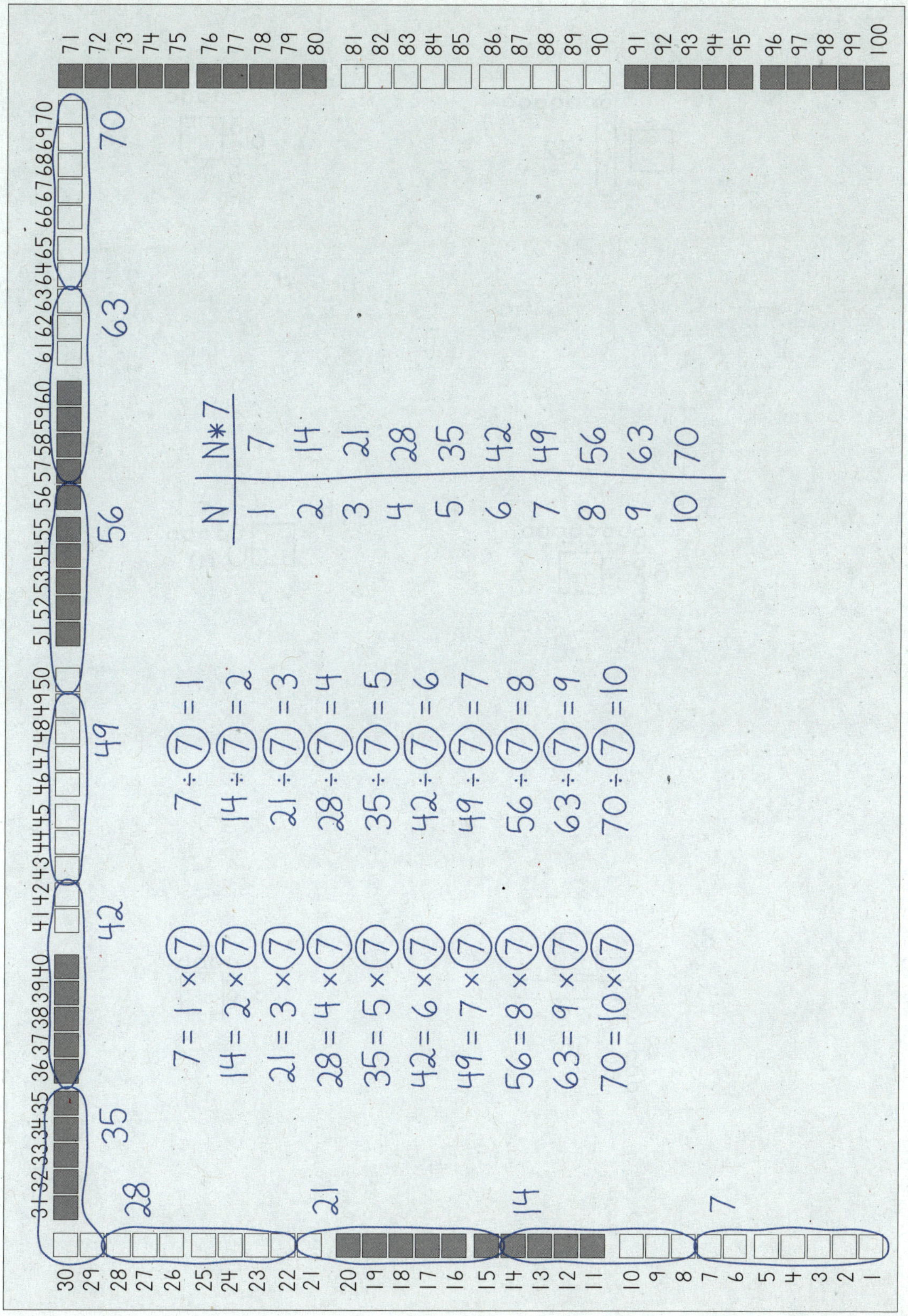

9–5
Class Activity

Name ______________________ Date ____________

► More Fast-Array Drawings

Fill in the missing number in each Fast-Array Drawing.

1.
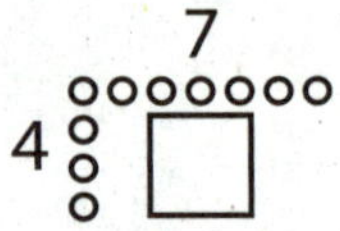

2.
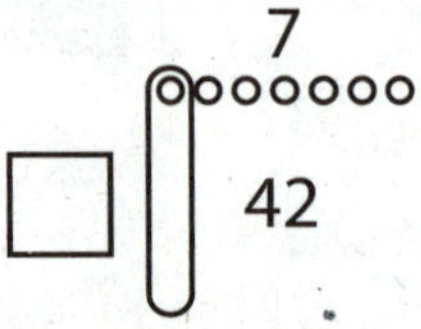

3.
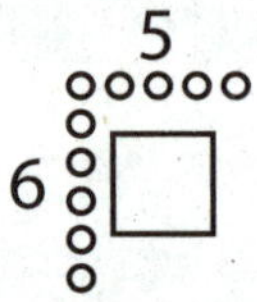

4.
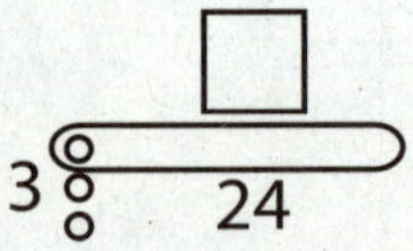

5.
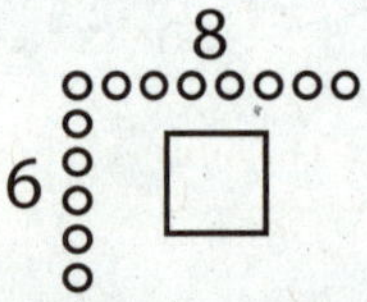

6.
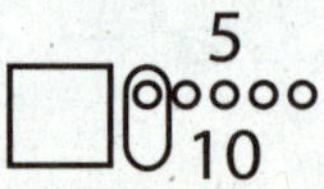

7.
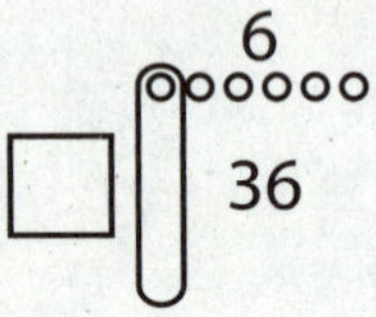

8.
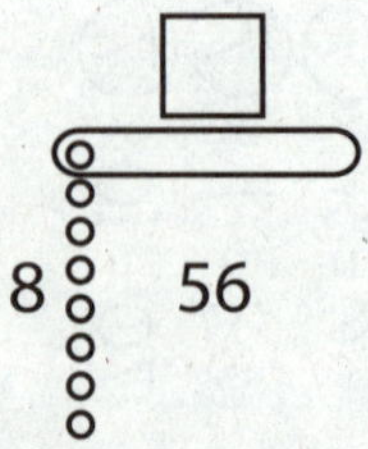

9.
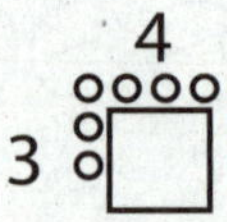

Name ______________________ Date ______________

▶Dashes 5–8

Complete each multiplication and division Dash.
Check your answers on page 321.

Dash 5
2s, 5s, 9s, 10s Multiplications

a. 6 × 2 = ___
b. 9 • 4 = ___
c. 8 * 5 = ___
d. 1 × 10 = ___
e. 2 • 7 = ___
f. 9 * 9 = ___
g. 5 × 6 = ___
h. 10 • 4 = ___
i. 7 * 5 = ___
j. 8 × 2 = ___
k. 10 • 10 = ___
l. 5 * 3 = ___
m. 9 × 7 = ___
n. 9 • 2 = ___
o. 5 * 5 = ___
p. 6 × 9 = ___
q. 5 • 2 = ___
r. 9 * 5 = ___
s. 8 × 10 = ___
t. 5 • 10 = ___

Dash 6
2s, 5s, 9s, 10s Divisions

a. 18 / 2 = ___
b. 25 ÷ 5 = ___
c. 70 / 10 = ___
d. 54 ÷ 9 = ___
e. 50 / 5 = ___
f. 81 ÷ 9 = ___
g. 8 / 2 = ___
h. 90 ÷ 10 = ___
i. 35 / 5 = ___
j. 27 / 9 = ___
k. 2 ÷ 2 = ___
l. 36 / 9 = ___
m. 45 ÷ 5 = ___
n. 14 / 2 = ___
o. 20 ÷ 10 = ___
p. 9 / 9 = ___
q. 20 ÷ 5 = ___
r. 45 ÷ 9 = ___
s. 5 / 5 = ___
t. 4 ÷ 2 = ___

Dash 7
0s, 1s, 3s, 4s Multiplications

a. 7 × 1 = ___
b. 0 • 6 = ___
c. 4 * 4 = ___
d. 7 × 3 = ___
e. 3 • 1 = ___
f. 4 * 7 = ___
g. 9 × 0 = ___
h. 1 • 1 = ___
i. 3 * 4 = ___
j. 4 × 9 = ___
k. 8 • 1 = ___
l. 3 * 3 = ___
m. 0 × 4 = ___
n. 10 • 3 = ___
o. 6 * 4 = ___
p. 1 × 4 = ___
q. 3 • 6 = ___
r. 4 * 8 = ___
s. 7 × 0 = ___
t. 5 • 3 = ___

Dash 8
1s, 3s, 4s Divisions

a. 2 / 1 = ___
b. 28 ÷ 4 = ___
c. 3 / 3 = ___
d. 1 ÷ 1 = ___
e. 40 / 4 = ___
f. 21 ÷ 3 = ___
g. 5 / 1 = ___
h. 16 ÷ 4 = ___
i. 15 / 3 = ___
j. 6 / 1 = ___
k. 12 ÷ 4 = ___
l. 27 / 3 = ___
m. 9 ÷ 1 = ___
n. 8 / 4 = ___
o. 12 ÷ 3 = ___
p. 3 / 1 = ___
q. 36 ÷ 4 = ___
r. 6 ÷ 3 = ___
s. 4 / 1 = ___
t. 4 ÷ 4 = ___

Name ______________________ Date ______________________

▶Dashes 5–8

Complete each multiplication and division Dash. Check your answers on page 321.

Dash 5 2s, 5s, 9s, 10s Multiplications	Dash 6 2s, 5s, 9s, 10s Divisions	Dash 7 0s, 1s, 3s, 4s Multiplications	Dash 8 1s, 3s, 4s Divisions
a. 6 × 2 = ___	a. 18 / 2 = ___	a. 7 × 1 = ___	a. 2 / 1 = ___
b. 9 • 4 = ___	b. 25 ÷ 5 = ___	b. 0 • 6 = ___	b. 28 ÷ 4 = ___
c. 8 * 5 = ___	c. 70 / 10 = ___	c. 4 * 4 = ___	c. 3 / 3 = ___
d. 1 × 10 = ___	d. 54 ÷ 9 = ___	d. 7 × 3 = ___	d. 1 ÷ 1 = ___
e. 2 • 7 = ___	e. 50 / 5 = ___	e. 3 • 1 = ___	e. 40 / 4 = ___
f. 9 * 9 = ___	f. 81 ÷ 9 = ___	f. 4 * 7 = ___	f. 21 ÷ 3 = ___
g. 5 × 6 = ___	g. 8 / 2 = ___	g. 9 × 0 = ___	g. 5 / 1 = ___
h. 10 • 4 = ___	h. 90 ÷ 10 = ___	h. 1 • 1 = ___	h. 16 ÷ 4 = ___
i. 7 * 5 = ___	i. 35 / 5 = ___	i. 3 * 4 = ___	i. 15 / 3 = ___
j. 8 × 2 = ___	j. 27 / 9 = ___	j. 4 × 9 = ___	j. 6 / 1 = ___
k. 10 • 10 = ___	k. 2 ÷ 2 = ___	k. 8 • 1 = ___	k. 12 ÷ 4 = ___
l. 5 * 3 = ___	l. 36 / 9 = ___	l. 3 * 3 = ___	l. 27 / 3 = ___
m. 9 × 7 = ___	m. 45 ÷ 5 = ___	m. 0 × 4 = ___	m. 9 ÷ 1 = ___
n. 9 • 2 = ___	n. 14 / 2 = ___	n. 10 • 3 = ___	n. 8 / 4 = ___
o. 5 * 5 = ___	o. 20 ÷ 10 = ___	o. 6 * 4 = ___	o. 12 ÷ 3 = ___
p. 6 × 9 = ___	p. 9 / 9 = ___	p. 1 × 4 = ___	p. 3 / 1 = ___
q. 5 • 2 = ___	q. 20 ÷ 5 = ___	q. 3 • 6 = ___	q. 36 ÷ 4 = ___
r. 9 * 5 = ___	r. 45 ÷ 9 = ___	r. 4 * 8 = ___	r. 6 ÷ 3 = ___
s. 8 × 10 = ___	s. 5 / 5 = ___	s. 7 × 0 = ___	s. 4 / 1 = ___
t. 5 • 10 = ___	t. 4 ÷ 2 = ___	t. 5 • 3 = ___	t. 4 ÷ 4 = ___

Name ____________________ Date ____________________

▶ Answers to Dashes 5–8

Use this sheet to check your answers to the Dashes on page 319.

Dash 5 2s, 5s, 9s, 10s Multiplications	Dash 6 2s, 5s, 9s, 10s Divisions	Dash 7 0s, 1s, 3s, 4s Multiplications	Dash 8 1s, 3s, 4s Divisions
a. 6 × 2 = 12	a. 18 / 2 = 9	a. 7 × 1 = 7	a. 2 / 1 = 2
b. 9 • 4 = 36	b. 25 ÷ 5 = 5	b. 0 • 6 = 0	b. 28 ÷ 4 = 7
c. 8 * 5 = 40	c. 70 / 10 = 7	c. 4 * 4 = 16	c. 3 / 3 = 1
d. 1 × 10 = 10	d. 54 ÷ 9 = 6	d. 7 × 3 = 21	d. 1 ÷ 1 = 1
e. 2 • 7 = 14	e. 50 / 5 = 10	e. 3 • 1 = 3	e. 40 / 4 = 10
f. 9 * 9 = 81	f. 81 ÷ 9 = 9	f. 4 * 7 = 28	f. 21 ÷ 3 = 7
g. 5 × 6 = 30	g. 8 / 2 = 4	g. 9 × 0 = 0	g. 5 / 1 = 5
h. 10 • 4 = 40	h. 90 ÷ 10 = 9	h. 1 • 1 = 1	h. 16 ÷ 4 = 4
i. 7 * 5 = 35	i. 35 / 5 = 7	i. 3 * 4 = 12	i. 15 / 3 = 5
j. 8 × 2 = 16	j. 27 / 9 = 3	j. 4 × 9 = 36	j. 6 / 1 = 6
k. 10 • 10 = 100	k. 2 ÷ 2 = 1	k. 8 • 1 = 8	k. 12 ÷ 4 = 3
l. 5 * 3 = 15	l. 36 / 9 = 4	l. 3 * 3 = 9	l. 27 / 3 = 9
m. 9 × 7 = 63	m. 45 ÷ 5 = 9	m. 0 × 4 = 0	m. 9 ÷ 1 = 9
n. 9 • 2 = 18	n. 14 / 2 = 7	n. 10 • 3 = 30	n. 8 / 4 = 2
o. 5 * 5 = 25	o. 20 ÷ 10 = 2	o. 6 * 4 = 24	o. 12 ÷ 3 = 4
p. 6 × 9 = 54	p. 9 / 9 = 1	p. 1 × 4 = 4	p. 3 / 1 = 3
q. 5 • 2 = 10	q. 20 ÷ 5 = 4	q. 3 • 6 = 18	q. 36 ÷ 4 = 9
r. 9 * 5 = 45	r. 45 ÷ 9 = 5	r. 4 * 8 = 32	r. 6 ÷ 3 = 2
s. 8 × 10 = 80	s. 5 / 5 = 1	s. 7 × 0 = 0	s. 4 / 1 = 4
t. 5 • 10 = 50	t. 4 ÷ 2 = 2	t. 5 • 3 = 15	t. 4 ÷ 4 = 1

9–6 Class Activity

Name ______________________ Date ______________

▶ Comparison Statements

Use the sentences and pictures below to complete the comparison statements.

Martina has 6 tennis balls. Chris has 2 tennis balls.

Martina

Chris

1. Martina has __________ more tennis balls than Chris.
2. Chris has __________ fewer tennis balls than Martina.
3. Martina has __________ times as many tennis balls as Chris.
4. Chris has __________ as many tennis balls as Martina.

Use the sentences and pictures below to complete the comparison statements.

Bobby has 3 hockey pucks. Wayne has 15 hockey pucks.

Bobby

Wayne

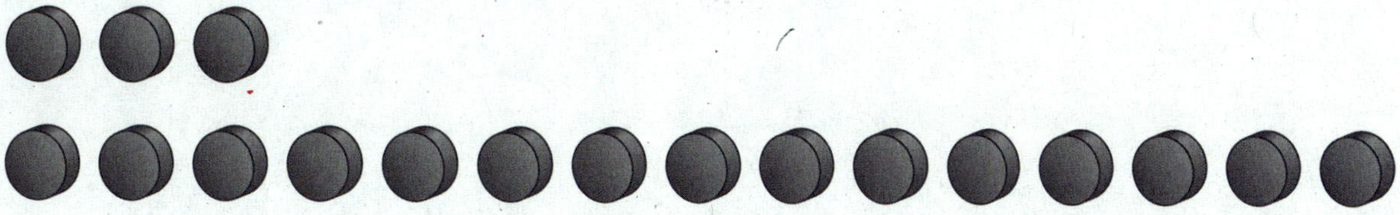

5. Write a comparison statement about the hockey pucks using the word *more.*

   ____

6. Write a comparison statement about the hockey pucks using the word *fewer.*

   ____

7. Wayne has __________ times as many hockey pucks as Bobby.
8. Bobby has __________ as many hockey pucks as Wayne.

Name ______________________ Date ______________

Make a math drawing to show the situation. Then use the sentences to write and complete the comparison statements.

Abby has 8 comic books. Pascal has 2 comic books.

9. Write a comparison statement about the comic books using the word *more*.

____

10. Write a comparison statement about the comic books using the word *fewer*.

____

11. Abby has __________ as many comic books as Pascal.

12. Pascal has __________ as many comic books as Abby.

Kai has 3 paintbrushes. Neeta has 18 paintbrushes.

13. Write a comparison statement about the paintbrushes using the word *more*.

____

14. Write a comparison statement about the paintbrushes using the word *fewer*.

____

15. Kai has __________ as many paint brushes as Neeta.

16. Neeta has __________ as many paint brushes as Kai.

9–6

Class Activity

Name ____________ Date ____________

▶ Solve Comparison Word Problems

Solve each problem.

17. Teresa has 2 gerbils. Owen has 4 times as many gerbils as Teresa has. How many gerbils does Owen have? ____________

18. Eduardo has 12 posters in his room. Manuela has $\frac{1}{3}$ as many posters as Eduardo. How many posters does Manuela have? ____________

19. Bart rides his bike 8 blocks to school. Melinda rides 5 times as far as Bart does. How many blocks does Melinda ride? ____________

20. Jay ate 14 grapes. Ti ate $\frac{1}{7}$ as many grapes as Jay. How many grapes did Ti eat? ____________

21. Lucille has 7 books. Javier has 3 times as many books as Lucille. How many books does Javier have? ____________

22. Cho's father is 48 years old. Cho is $\frac{1}{6}$ as old as her father. How old is Cho? ____________

9–6 Going Further

Name ________________________ Date ____________

Vocabulary
multiple

▶ Use a Venn Diagram to Show Relationships

A **multiple** is the product of a number and any other number.

For example, 6, 12, 18, and 24 are multiples of 6.

Find the rule that was used for sorting the data. Then label the Venn diagram.

1.

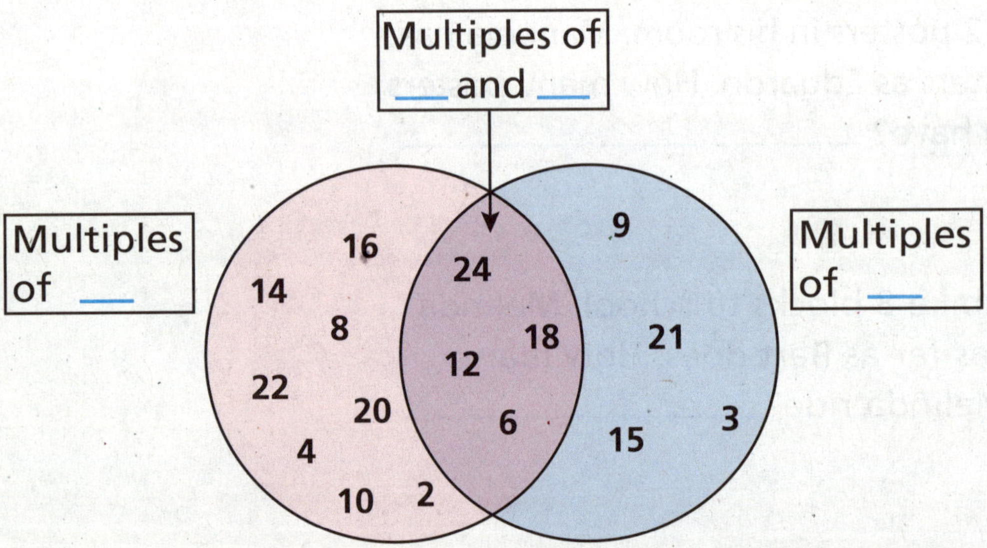

2.

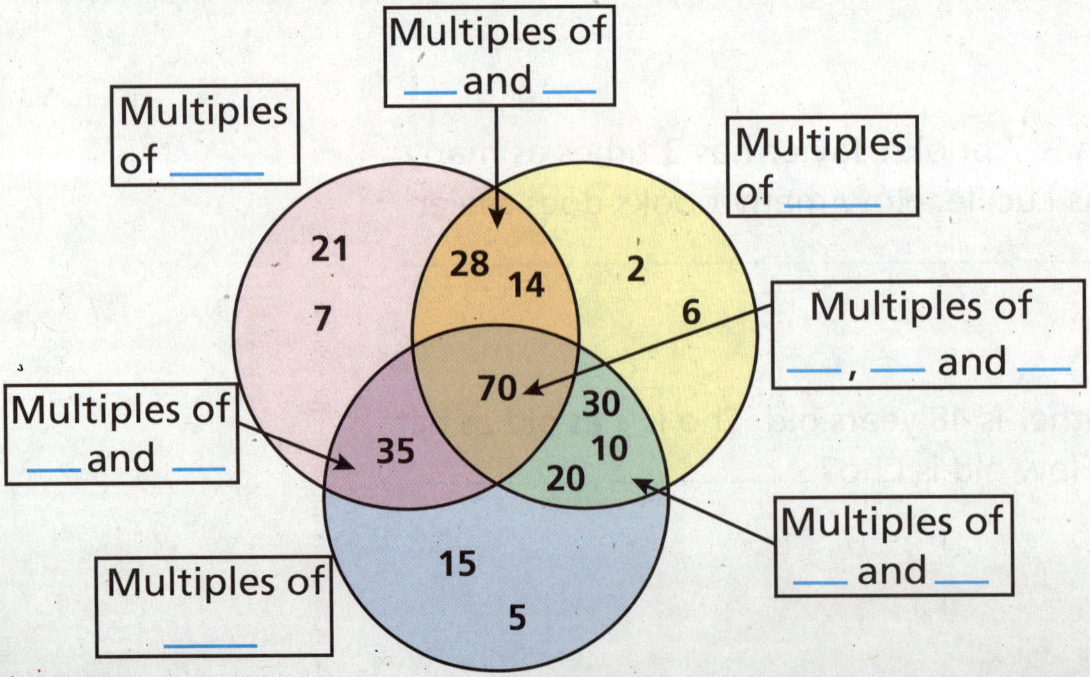

Name ______________________ Date ______________

▶ Use Comparison Bars

Draw comparison bars to help you solve each problem.

Jadzia's dog Roscoe competes in dog shows. He has won 42 blue ribbons and 6 red ribbons.

1. Roscoe has won ____________ as many blue ribbons as red ribbons.

2. Roscoe has won ____________ as many red ribbons as blue ribbons.

Daphne is 7 years old. Her grandfather is 56 years old.

3. Daphne is ____________ as old as her grandfather.

4. Daphne's grandfather is ____________ as old as Daphne.

Beatrice has 48 dolls. Cathy has 8 dolls.

5. Beatrice has ____________ as many dolls as Cathy.

6. Cathy has ____________ as many dolls as Beatrice.

Name _______________ Date _______________

Make a drawing to help you solve each problem. *Show your work.*

7. Last month Elle earned \$8 helping her aunt with chores. This month she earned 4 times as much by doing yard work for her neighbor. How much did Elle earn this month?

____

8. Minh picked 48 peaches. His little brother Bao picked $\frac{1}{8}$ as many peaches as Minh. How many peaches did Bao pick?

____

9. Carlos has 49 music CDs. His cousin Luisa has $\frac{1}{7}$ as many music CDs as Carlos. How many CDs does Luisa have?

____

10. Rose rode the roller coaster 6 times. Leila rode the roller coaster 3 times as many times as Rose. How many times did Leila ride the roller coaster?

____

Name ______________________ Date ______________

► Use a Bar Graph to Compare

Shannon collects souvenir T-shirts from the places she visits. She made this bar graph to show the colors of the shirts in her collection.

11. Shannon has ____________ as many red shirts as green shirts.

Shannon has ____________ as many green shirts as red shirts.

12. Shannon has ____________ as many red shirts as orange shirts.

Shannon has ____________ as many orange shirts as red shirts.

13. Shannon has ____________ as many blue shirts as orange shirts.

Shannon has ____________ as many orange shirts as blue shirts.

14. Shannon has ____________ as many orange shirts as green shirts.

Shannon has ____________ as many green shirts as orange shirts.

Name Date

▶ Solve Comparison Problems

Solve.

15. Maddie took 21 photographs on her vacation. Jack took $\frac{1}{3}$ as many photos as Maddie. How many photos did Jack take?

____

16. Franco has 18 toy cars. Roberto has 6 more toy cars than Franco. How many toy cars does Roberto have?

____

17. Arvin delivered 42 newspapers. Kelly delivered 7 fewer papers than Arvin. How many papers did Kelly deliver?

____

18. Jasmine's dog weighs 8 pounds. Shaunda's dog weighs 5 times as much as Jasmine's dog. How much does Shaunda's dog weigh?

____

19. Charles is $\frac{1}{4}$ as old as his father. His father is 36 years old. How old is Charles?

____

9–8 Class Activity

Name ______ Date ______

▶ Sprints for 8s

As your teacher reads each multiplication or division, write your answer in the space provided.

× 8	÷ 8
a. ______	a. ______
b. ______	b. ______
c. ______	c. ______
d. ______	d. ______
e. ______	e. ______
f. ______	f. ______
g. ______	g. ______
h. ______	h. ______
i. ______	i. ______
j. ______	j. ______

Name ______________________________ Date ______________________________

► Check Sheet 9: 7s and Squares

7s Multiplications	7s Divisions	Squares Multiplications	Squares Divisions
4 × 7 = 28	14 / 7 = 2	8 × 8 = 64	81 / 9 = 9
7 • 2 = 14	28 ÷ 7 = 4	10 • 10 = 100	4 ÷ 2 = 2
7 * 8 = 56	70 / 7 = 10	3 * 3 = 9	25 / 5 = 5
7 × 7 = 49	56 ÷ 7 = 8	9 × 9 = 81	1 ÷ 1 = 1
7 • 1 = 7	42 / 7 = 6	4 • 4 = 16	100 / 10 = 10
7 * 10 = 70	63 ÷ 7 = 9	7 * 7 = 49	36 ÷ 6 = 6
3 × 7 = 21	7 / 7 = 1	5 × 5 = 25	49 / 7 = 7
7 • 6 = 42	49 ÷ 7 = 7	6 • 6 = 36	9 ÷ 3 = 3
5 * 7 = 35	21 / 7 = 3	1 * 1 = 1	64 / 8 = 8
7 × 9 = 63	35 / 7 = 5	5 * 5 = 25	16 / 4 = 4
7 • 4 = 28	7 ÷ 7 = 1	1 • 1 = 1	100 ÷ 10 = 10
9 * 7 = 63	63 / 7 = 9	3 • 3 = 9	49 / 7 = 7
2 × 7 = 14	14 ÷ 7 = 2	10 × 10 = 100	1 ÷ 1 = 1
7 • 5 = 35	70 / 7 = 10	4 × 4 = 16	9 / 3 = 3
8 * 7 = 56	21 ÷ 7 = 3	9 * 9 = 81	64 ÷ 8 = 8
7 × 3 = 21	49 / 7 = 7	2 × 2 = 4	4 / 2 = 2
6 • 7 = 42	28 ÷ 7 = 4	6 * 6 = 36	81 ÷ 9 = 9
10 * 7 = 70	56 ÷ 7 = 8	7 × 7 = 49	16 ÷ 4 = 4
1 × 7 = 7	35 / 7 = 5	5 • 5 = 25	25 / 5 = 5
7 • 7 = 49	42 ÷ 7 = 6	8 • 8 = 64	36 ÷ 6 = 6

9–8 **Class Activity**

Name ______________________ Date ______________

►Explore Square Numbers

Write an equation to show the area of each large square.

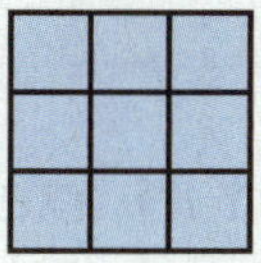

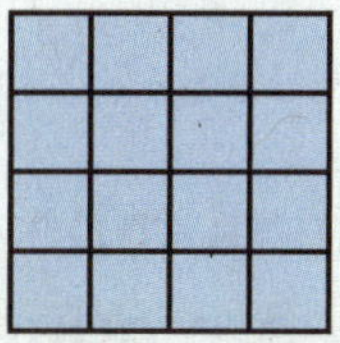

1. 1 × 1 = 1
2. ______________
3. ______________
4. ______________

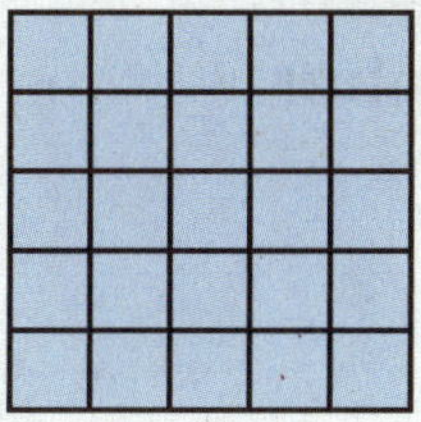

5. ______________
6. ______________

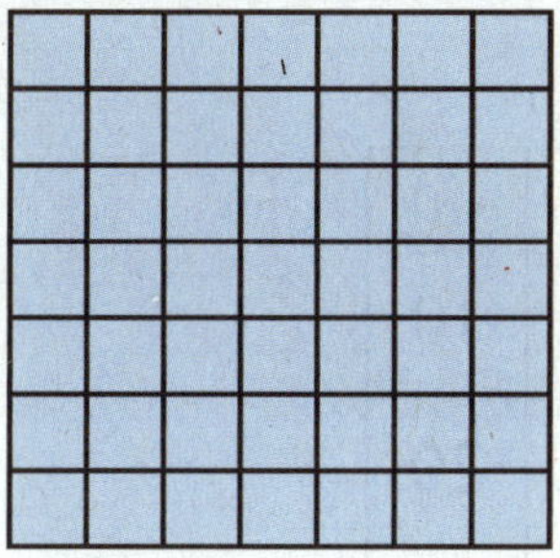

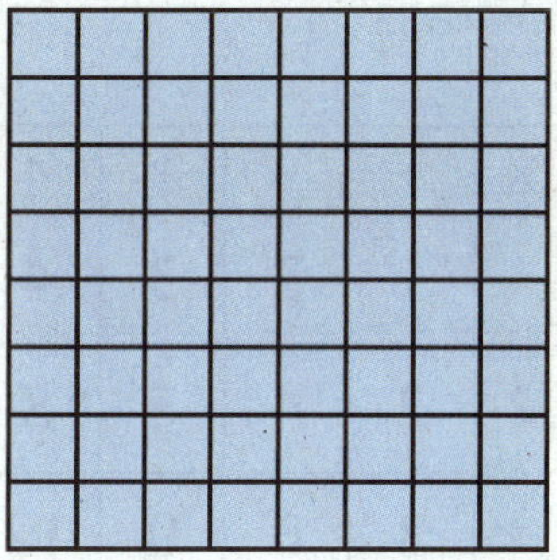

7. ______________
8. ______________

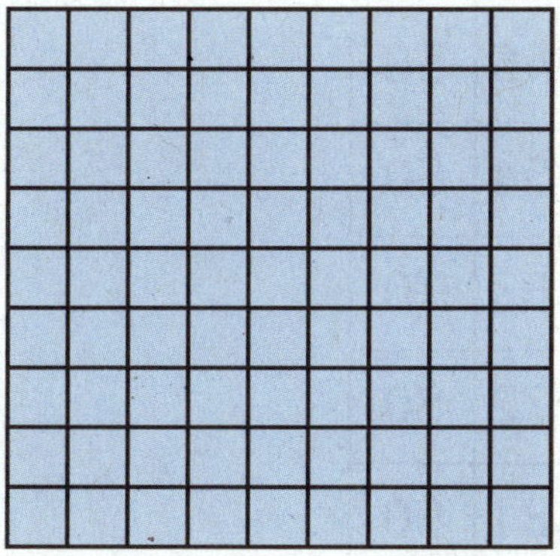

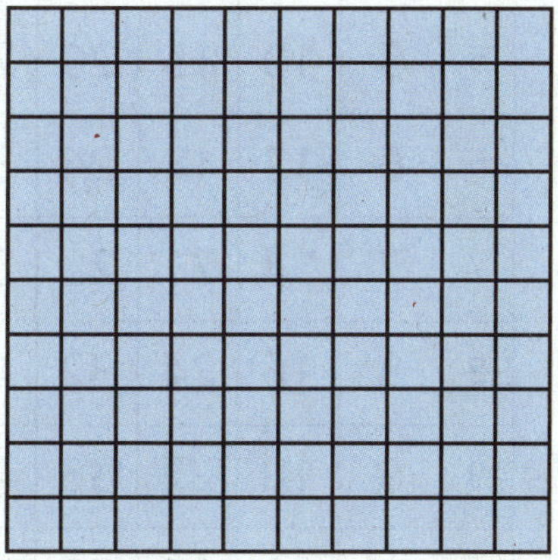

9. ______________
10. ______________

Name ______________________ Date ______________

Vocabulary
square numbers

▶ Look for Patterns

11. List the products in exercises 1–10 in order. Discuss the patterns you see with your class.

____

The numbers you listed in exercise 11 are called **square numbers** because they are the areas of squares with whole-number lengths of sides. A square number is the product of a whole number and itself. So, if n is a whole number, $n \times n$ is a square number.

▶ Patterns on the Multiplication Table

12. In the table below, circle the products that are square numbers. Discuss the patterns you see with your class.

X	1	2	3	4	5	6	7	8	9	10
1	1	2	3	4	5	6	7	8	9	10
2	2	4	6	8	10	12	14	16	18	20
3	3	6	9	12	15	18	21	24	27	30
4	4	8	12	16	20	24	28	32	36	40
5	5	10	15	20	25	30	35	40	45	50
6	6	12	18	24	30	36	42	48	54	60
7	7	14	21	28	35	42	49	56	63	70
8	8	16	24	32	40	48	56	64	72	80
9	9	18	27	36	45	54	63	72	81	90
10	10	20	30	40	50	60	70	80	90	100

Name _______________ Date _______________

►Check Sheet 10: 6s, 7s, and 8s

6s, 7s, and 8s Multiplications	6s, 7s, and 8s Multiplications	6s, 7s, and 8s Divisions	6s, 7s, and 8s Divisions
1 × 6 = 6	0 × 8 = 0	24 / 6 = 4	54 / 6 = 9
6 • 7 = 42	6 • 2 = 12	21 ÷ 7 = 3	24 ÷ 8 = 3
3 * 8 = 24	4 * 7 = 28	16 / 8 = 2	14 / 7 = 2
6 × 2 = 12	8 × 3 = 24	24 ÷ 8 = 3	32 ÷ 8 = 4
7 • 5 = 35	5 • 6 = 30	14 / 7 = 2	18 / 6 = 3
8 * 4 = 32	7 * 2 = 14	30 ÷ 6 = 5	56 ÷ 7 = 8
6 × 6 = 36	3 × 8 = 24	35 / 7 = 5	40 / 8 = 5
8 • 7 = 56	6 • 4 = 24	24 ÷ 8 = 3	35 ÷ 7 = 5
9 * 8 = 72	0 * 7 = 0	18 / 6 = 3	12 / 6 = 2
6 × 10 = 60	8 × 1 = 8	12 / 6 = 2	21 / 7 = 3
7 • 1 = 7	8 • 6 = 48	42 ÷ 7 = 6	16 ÷ 8 = 2
8 * 3 = 24	7 * 9 = 63	56 / 8 = 7	42 / 6 = 7
5 × 6 = 30	10 × 8 = 80	49 ÷ 7 = 7	80 ÷ 8 = 10
4 • 7 = 28	6 • 10 = 60	16 / 8 = 2	36 / 6 = 6
2 * 8 = 16	3 * 7 = 21	60 ÷ 6 = 10	7 ÷ 7 = 1
7 × 7 = 49	8 × 4 = 32	54 / 6 = 9	64 / 8 = 8
7 • 6 = 42	6 • 5 = 30	8 ÷ 8 = 1	24 ÷ 6 = 4
8 * 8 = 64	7 * 4 = 28	28 ÷ 7 = 4	21 ÷ 7 = 3
9 × 6 = 54	8 × 8 = 64	72 / 8 = 9	49 / 7 = 7
10 • 7 = 70	6 • 9 = 54	56 ÷ 7 = 8	24 ÷ 8 = 3

Name ______________________ Date ______________________

►Check Sheet 11: 0s–10s

0s–10s Multiplications	0s–10s Multiplications	0s–10s Divisions	0s–10s Divisions
9 × 0 = 0	9 × 4 = 36	9 / 1 = 9	90 / 10 = 9
1 • 1 = 1	5 • 9 = 45	12 ÷ 3 = 4	64 ÷ 8 = 8
2 * 3 = 6	6 * 10 = 60	14 / 2 = 7	15 / 5 = 3
1 × 3 = 3	7 × 3 = 21	20 ÷ 4 = 5	12 ÷ 6 = 2
5 • 4 = 20	5 • 3 = 15	10 / 5 = 2	14 / 7 = 2
7 * 5 = 35	4 * 1 = 4	48 ÷ 8 = 6	45 ÷ 9 = 5
6 × 9 = 54	7 × 5 = 35	35 / 7 = 5	8 / 1 = 8
0 • 7 = 0	6 • 3 = 18	60 ÷ 6 = 10	30 ÷ 3 = 10
1 * 8 = 8	8 * 7 = 56	81 / 9 = 9	16 / 4 = 4
9 × 8 = 72	5 × 8 = 40	20 / 10 = 2	8 / 2 = 4
2 • 10 = 20	9 • 9 = 81	16 ÷ 2 = 8	80 ÷ 10 = 8
0 * 7 = 0	9 * 10 = 90	30 / 5 = 6	36 / 4 = 9
4 × 1 = 4	0 × 0 = 0	49 ÷ 7 = 7	25 ÷ 5 = 5
2 • 4 = 8	1 • 0 = 0	60 / 6 = 10	42 / 7 = 6
10 * 3 = 30	1 * 6 = 6	30 ÷ 3 = 10	36 ÷ 6 = 6
8 × 4 = 32	7 × 2 = 14	8 / 1 = 8	90 / 9 = 10
5 • 8 = 40	6 • 3 = 18	16 ÷ 4 = 4	24 ÷ 8 = 3
4 * 6 = 24	4 * 5 = 20	16 ÷ 8 = 2	6 ÷ 2 = 3
7 × 0 = 0	6 × 6 = 36	40 / 10 = 4	9 / 3 = 3
1 • 8 = 8	10 • 7 = 70	36 ÷ 9 = 4	1 ÷ 1 = 1

Name ____________________ Date ____________________

▶Dashes 9–12

Complete each Dash. Check your answers on page 339.

Dash 9 2s, 3s, 4s, 5s, 9s Multiplications	Dash 10 2s, 3s, 4s, 5s, 9s Divisions	Dash 11 6s, 7s, 8s Multiplications	Dash 12 6s, 7s, 8s Divisions
a. 6 × 3 = ___	a. 16 / 4 = ___	a. 7 × 7 = ___	a. 21 / 7 = ___
b. 4 • 7 = ___	b. 54 ÷ 9 = ___	b. 6 • 3 = ___	b. 16 ÷ 8 = ___
c. 8 * 2 = ___	c. 4 / 2 = ___	c. 8 * 6 = ___	c. 54 / 6 = ___
d. 5 × 3 = ___	d. 28 ÷ 4 = ___	d. 6 × 6 = ___	d. 48 ÷ 8 = ___
e. 4 • 4 = ___	e. 25 / 5 = ___	e. 7 • 6 = ___	e. 64 / 8 = ___
f. 3 * 9 = ___	f. 21 ÷ 3 = ___	f. 4 * 7 = ___	f. 42 ÷ 6 = ___
g. 9 × 9 = ___	g. 40 / 4 = ___	g. 9 × 7 = ___	g. 56 / 7 = ___
h. 8 • 9 = ___	h. 81 ÷ 9 = ___	h. 6 • 9 = ___	h. 72 ÷ 8 = ___
i. 6 * 4 = ___	i. 35 / 5 = ___	i. 6 * 4 = ___	i. 18 / 6 = ___
j. 3 × 3 = ___	j. 12 / 3 = ___	j. 8 × 8 = ___	j. 28 / 7 = ___
k. 2 • 7 = ___	k. 2 ÷ 2 = ___	k. 7 • 3 = ___	k. 56 ÷ 8 = ___
l. 8 * 5 = ___	l. 63 / 9 = ___	l. 8 * 7 = ___	l. 30 / 6 = ___
m. 4 × 9 = ___	m. 36 ÷ 4 = ___	m. 6 × 7 = ___	m. 63 ÷ 7 = ___
n. 9 • 5 = ___	n. 18 / 2 = ___	n. 3 • 6 = ___	n. 32 / 8 = ___
o. 7 * 3 = ___	o. 9 ÷ 3 = ___	o. 2 * 7 = ___	o. 48 ÷ 6 = ___
p. 2 × 2 = ___	p. 36 / 9 = ___	p. 9 × 8 = ___	p. 49 / 7 = ___
q. 8 • 4 = ___	q. 40 ÷ 5 = ___	q. 5 • 6 = ___	q. 36 ÷ 6 = ___
r. 5 * 1 = ___	r. 12 ÷ 4 = ___	r. 7 * 8 = ___	r. 24 ÷ 8 = ___
s. 5 × 5 = ___	s. 9 / 9 = ___	s. 3 × 7 = ___	s. 42 / 7 = ___
t. 6 • 9 = ___	t. 14 ÷ 2 = ___	t. 9 • 6 = ___	t. 24 ÷ 6 = ___

Name ______________________ Date ______________________

▶Dashes 9–12

Complete each Dash. Check your answers on page 339.

Dash 9 2s, 3s, 4s, 5s, 9s Multiplications	Dash 10 2s, 3s, 4s, 5s, 9s Divisions	Dash 11 6s, 7s, 8s Multiplications	Dash 12 6s, 7s, 8s Divisions
a. 6 × 3 = ___	a. 16 / 4 = ___	a. 7 × 7 = ___	a. 21 / 7 = ___
b. 4 • 7 = ___	b. 54 ÷ 9 = ___	b. 6 • 3 = ___	b. 16 ÷ 8 = ___
c. 8 * 2 = ___	c. 4 / 2 = ___	c. 8 * 6 = ___	c. 54 / 6 = ___
d. 5 × 3 = ___	d. 28 ÷ 4 = ___	d. 6 × 6 = ___	d. 48 ÷ 8 = ___
e. 4 • 4 = ___	e. 25 / 5 = ___	e. 7 • 6 = ___	e. 64 / 8 = ___
f. 3 * 9 = ___	f. 21 ÷ 3 = ___	f. 4 * 7 = ___	f. 42 ÷ 6 = ___
g. 9 × 9 = ___	g. 40 / 4 = ___	g. 9 × 7 = ___	g. 56 / 7 = ___
h. 8 • 9 = ___	h. 81 ÷ 9 = ___	h. 6 • 9 = ___	h. 72 ÷ 8 = ___
i. 6 * 4 = ___	i. 35 / 5 = ___	i. 6 * 4 = ___	i. 18 / 6 = ___
j. 3 × 3 = ___	j. 12 / 3 = ___	j. 8 × 8 = ___	j. 28 / 7 = ___
k. 2 • 7 = ___	k. 2 ÷ 2 = ___	k. 7 • 3 = ___	k. 56 ÷ 8 = ___
l. 8 * 5 = ___	l. 63 / 9 = ___	l. 8 * 7 = ___	l. 30 / 6 = ___
m. 4 × 9 = ___	m. 36 ÷ 4 = ___	m. 6 × 7 = ___	m. 63 ÷ 7 = ___
n. 9 • 5 = ___	n. 18 / 2 = ___	n. 3 • 6 = ___	n. 32 / 8 = ___
o. 7 * 3 = ___	o. 9 ÷ 3 = ___	o. 2 * 7 = ___	o. 48 ÷ 6 = ___
p. 2 × 2 = ___	p. 36 / 9 = ___	p. 9 × 8 = ___	p. 49 / 7 = ___
q. 8 • 4 = ___	q. 40 ÷ 5 = ___	q. 5 • 6 = ___	q. 36 ÷ 6 = ___
r. 5 * 1 = ___	r. 12 ÷ 4 = ___	r. 7 * 8 = ___	r. 24 ÷ 8 = ___
s. 5 × 5 = ___	s. 9 / 9 = ___	s. 3 × 7 = ___	s. 42 / 7 = ___
t. 6 • 9 = ___	t. 14 ÷ 2 = ___	t. 9 • 6 = ___	t. 24 ÷ 6 = ___

Name Date

►Answers to Dashes 9–12

Use this sheet to check your answers to the dashes on page 337.

Dash 9 2s, 3s, 4s, 5s, 9s Multiplications	Dash 10 2s, 3s, 4s, 5s, 9s Divisions	Dash 11 6s, 7s, 8s Multiplications	Dash 12 6s, 7s, 8s Divisions
a. $6 \times 3 = 18$	a. $16 / 4 = 4$	a. $7 \times 7 = 49$	a. $21 / 7 = 3$
b. $4 \bullet 7 = 28$	b. $54 \div 9 = 6$	b. $6 \bullet 3 = 18$	b. $16 \div 8 = 2$
c. $8 * 2 = 16$	c. $4 / 2 = 2$	c. $8 * 6 = 48$	c. $54 / 6 = 9$
d. $5 \times 3 = 15$	d. $28 \div 4 = 7$	d. $6 \times 6 = 36$	d. $48 \div 8 = 6$
e. $4 \bullet 4 = 16$	e. $25 / 5 = 5$	e. $7 \bullet 6 = 42$	e. $64 / 8 = 8$
f. $3 * 9 = 27$	f. $21 \div 3 = 7$	f. $4 * 7 = 28$	f. $42 \div 6 = 7$
g. $9 \times 9 = 81$	g. $40 / 4 = 10$	g. $9 \times 7 = 63$	g. $56 / 7 = 8$
h. $8 \bullet 9 = 72$	h. $81 \div 9 = 9$	h. $6 \bullet 9 = 54$	h. $72 \div 8 = 9$
i. $6 * 4 = 24$	i. $35 / 5 = 7$	i. $6 * 4 = 24$	i. $18 / 6 = 3$
j. $3 \times 3 = 9$	j. $12 / 3 = 4$	j. $8 \times 8 = 64$	j. $28 / 7 = 4$
k. $2 \bullet 7 = 14$	k. $2 \div 2 = 1$	k. $7 \bullet 3 = 21$	k. $56 \div 8 = 7$
l. $8 * 5 = 40$	l. $63 / 9 = 7$	l. $8 * 7 = 56$	l. $30 / 6 = 5$
m. $4 \times 9 = 36$	m. $36 \div 4 = 9$	m. $6 \times 7 = 42$	m. $63 \div 7 = 9$
n. $9 \bullet 5 = 45$	n. $18 / 2 = 9$	n. $3 \bullet 6 = 18$	n. $32 / 8 = 4$
o. $7 * 3 = 21$	o. $9 \div 3 = 3$	o. $2 * 7 = 14$	o. $48 \div 6 = 8$
p. $2 \times 2 = 4$	p. $36 / 9 = 4$	p. $9 \times 8 = 72$	p. $49 / 7 = 7$
q. $8 \bullet 4 = 32$	q. $40 \div 5 = 8$	q. $5 \bullet 6 = 30$	q. $36 \div 6 = 6$
r. $5 * 1 = 5$	r. $12 \div 4 = 3$	r. $7 * 8 = 56$	r. $24 \div 8 = 3$
s. $5 \times 5 = 25$	s. $9 / 9 = 1$	s. $3 \times 7 = 21$	s. $42 / 7 = 6$
t. $6 \bullet 9 = 54$	t. $14 \div 2 = 7$	t. $9 \bullet 6 = 54$	t. $24 \div 6 = 4$

Name ____________________ Date ____________

►Play *High Card Wins*

Read the rules for playing *High Card Wins.* Then play the game with your partner.

Rules for *High Card Wins*

Number of players: 2
What you will need: 1 set of multiplication Strategy Cards *or* 1 set of division Strategy Cards

1. Shuffle the cards. Then deal all the cards evenly between the two players.
2. Players put their stacks in front of them, problem side up.
3. Each player takes the top card from his or her stack and puts it problem side up in the center of the table.
4. Each player says the answer (product or quotient) and then turns the card over to check. Then do one of the following:
   - If one player says the wrong answer, the other player takes both cards and puts them at the bottom of his or her pile.
   - If both players say the wrong answer, both players take back their cards and put them at the bottom of their piles.
   - If both players say the correct answer, the player with the higher product takes both cards and puts them at the bottom of his or her pile. If the answers are the same, the players set the cards aside and play another round. The winner of the next round takes all the cards.
5. When time is up, the player with the most cards wins.

9–9 Going Further

Name ______________________ Date ______________

► Multiply and Divide with 11 and 12

What patterns do you see?

× 11	÷ 11
1 × 11 = 11	11 ÷ 11 = 1
2 × 11 = 22	22 ÷ 11 = 2
3 × 11 = 33	33 ÷ 11 = 3
4 × 11 = 44	44 ÷ 11 = 4
5 × 11 = 55	55 ÷ 11 = 5
6 × 11 = 66	66 ÷ 11 = 6
7 × 11 = 77	77 ÷ 11 = 7
8 × 11 = 88	88 ÷ 11 = 8
9 × 11 = 99	99 ÷ 11 = 9
10 × 11 = 110	110 ÷ 11 = 10

× 12	÷ 12
1 × 12 = 12	12 ÷ 12 = 1
2 × 12 = 24	24 ÷ 12 = 2
3 × 12 = 36	36 ÷ 12 = 3
4 × 12 = 48	48 ÷ 12 = 4
5 × 12 = 60	60 ÷ 12 = 5
6 × 12 = 72	72 ÷ 12 = 6
7 × 12 = 84	84 ÷ 12 = 7
8 × 12 = 96	96 ÷ 12 = 8
9 × 12 = 108	108 ÷ 12 = 9
10 × 12 = 120	120 ÷ 12 = 10

► 11s and 12s Multiplication Table

Complete the multiplication table.

You can use multiplications you know to help.

$8 \times 12 = 8 \times (5 + 7)$
$= (8 \times 5) + (8 \times 7)$
$= 40 + 56$
$= 96$

or

$8 \times 12 = 8 \times (10 + 2)$
$= (8 \times 10) + (8 \times 2)$
$= 80 + 16$
$= 96$

X	1	2	3	4	5	6	7	8	9	10	11	12
1	1	2	3	4	5	6	7	8	9	10		
2	2	4	6	8	10	12	14	16	18	20		
3	3	6	9	12	15	18	21	24	27	30		
4	4	8	12	16	20	24	28	32	36	40		
5	5	10	15	20	25	30	35	40	45	50		
6	6	12	18	24	30	36	42	48	54	60		
7	7	14	21	28	35	42	49	56	63	70		
8	8	16	24	32	40	48	56	64	72	80		
9	9	18	27	36	45	54	63	72	81	90		
10	10	20	30	40	50	60	70	80	90	100		
11												
12												

Name ____________________ Date ____________

▶ Sprints for 7s

As your teacher reads each multiplication or division, write your answer in the space provided.

× 7	÷ 7
a. ______	a. ______
b. ______	b. ______
c. ______	c. ______
d. ______	d. ______
e. ______	e. ______
f. ______	f. ______
g. ______	g. ______
h. ______	h. ______
i. ______	i. ______
j. ______	j. ______

Name ______________________ Date ______________

▶Choose the Operation

Solve.

1. Ernie helped his mother work in the yard for 3 days. He earned $6 each day. How much did he earn in all?

____

2. Ernie helped his mother work in the yard for 3 days. He earned $6 the first day, $5 the second day, and $7 the third day. How much did he earn in all?

____

3. Troy had $18. He gave $6 to each of his brothers and had no money left. How many brothers does Troy have?

____

4. Troy gave $18 to his brothers. He gave $4 to Raj, $7 to Darnell, and the rest to Jai. How much money did Jai get?

____

5. Jinja has 4 cousins. Grant has 7 more cousins than Jinja. How many cousins does Grant have?

____

6. Jinja has 4 cousins. Grant has 7 times as many cousins as Jinja. How many cousins does Grant have?

____

7. Camille has 15 fewer books than Jane has. Camille has 12 books. How many does Jane have?

____

8. Camille has half as many books as Jane has. Camille has 15 books. How many books does Jane have?

____

Name Date

▶Write an Equation

Write an equation to solve each problem. *Show your work.*

9. Luke had a $5 bill. He spent $3.73 on a sandwich. How much change did he get?

____

10. Ramona is putting tiles on the kitchen floor. She will lay 8 rows of tiles, with 7 tiles in each row. How many tiles will Ramona use?

____

11. Josh earned As on 6 tests last year. Jenna earned As on 6 times as many tests. How many As did Jenna earn?

____

12. Sophie bought a stuffed animal for $2.76 and a board game for $6.99. How much money did Sophie spend?

____

13. The Duarte family has 15 pets. Each of the 3 Duarte children care for the same number of pets. How many pets does each child care for?

____

14. Ahmed spent $9 on CD. Zal paid $6 more for the same CD at a different store. How much did Zal spend on the CD?

____

Name ________________________ Date ________

►Write the Question

Write a question for the given information and solve.

15. Anna read 383 pages this month. Chris read 416 pages.

Question: ____________________

Solution: ____________________

16. Marisol had 128 beads in her jewelry box. She gave away 56 of them.

Question: ____________________

Solution: ____________________

17. Louis put 72 marbles in 8 bags. He put the same number of marbles in each bag.

Question: ____________________

Solution: ____________________

18. Geoff planted 4 pots of seeds. He planted 6 seeds in each pot.

Question: ____________________

Solution: ____________________

19. Last week, Marly read for 2 hours. Jamal read for 7 times as many hours as Marly did.

Question: ____________________

Solution: ____________________

Name ______________________ Date ______________

▶Write the Problem

Write a problem that can be solved using the given equation. Then solve.

20. $9 \times 6 = \square$ **Solution:** ______________

21. $324 - 176 = \square$ **Solution:** ______________

22. $56 \div 7 = \square$ **Solution:** ______________

23. $459 + 635 = \square$ **Solution:** ______________

24. Math Journal Choose an operation. Write a word problem that involves that operation. Write an equation to solve your word problem.

Name ______ Date ______

►Solve Open-Ended Problems

1. Hilda has $20.00 to buy her school supplies. She needs 12 pencils, 2 pens, a box of crayons, and a backpack. She also needs either a box of markers or a calculator, but not both. How should Hilda spend her $20.00 to get everything she needs and still have money left over? Explain your thinking.

2. Ivan and his dad are planning to make 12 identical party bags with 3 different items in each bag for a total cost under $25.00. List the 3 items they should buy. Explain your thinking.

3. **Math Journal** Find another combination of toys that Ivan and his dad could buy.

9–11 Class Activity

Name ____________________ Date ____________

► Use Order of Operations

This exercise involves subtraction and multiplication:

$$10 - 3 \times 2$$

1. What do you get if you subtract first and then multiply? ________

2. What do you get if you multiply first and then subtract? ________

To make sure everyone has the same answer to problems like this one, people have decided that multiplication and division will be done *before* addition and subtraction. The answer you found in question 2 is correct.

If you want to tell people to add or subtract first, you must use parentheses. Parentheses mean "Do this first." For example, if you want people to subtract first in the exercise above, write it like this:

$$(10 - 3) \times 2$$

Find the answer.

3. $5 + 4 \times 2 =$ ________

4. $(9 - 3) \times 6 =$ ________

5. $8 \div 2 + 2 =$ ________

6. $6 \times (8 - 1) =$ ________

Rewrite each statement, using symbols and numbers instead of words.

7. Add 4 and 3, and multiply the total by 8. ________

8. Multiply 3 by 8, and add 4 to the total. ________

Name Date

▶ Multi-Step Problems

Solve each problem.

Show your work.

9. A roller coaster has 7 cars. Each car has 4 seats. If there were 3 empty seats, how many people were on the roller coaster?

______

10. Each week, Marta earns $10 babysitting. She always spends $3 and saves the rest. How much does she save in 8 weeks?

______

11. Abu bought 6 packs of stickers. Each pack had 8 stickers. Then Abu's friend gave him 10 more stickers. How many stickers does Abu have now?

______

12. Zoe made some snacks. She put 4 apple slices and 2 melon slices on each plate. She prepared 5 plates. How many slices of fruit did Zoe use in all?

______

13. Kyle ordered 8 pizzas for his party. Each pizza was cut into 8 slices. 48 of the slices were plain cheese, and the rest had mushrooms. How many slices of pizza had mushrooms?

______

14. Nadia counted 77 birds on the pond. 53 were ducks, and the rest were geese. Then the geese flew away in 4 equal flocks. How many geese were in each flock?

______

Name ______ Date ______

▶ More Multi-Step Problems

Solve each problem. Draw a picture if you need to. *Show your work.*

15. Lakesha has filled two pages of her stamp book. Both pages have 5 rows of stamps. On one page, there are 5 stamps in each row. On the opposite page, there are 3 stamps in each row. How many stamps are on the two pages?

______

16. Kagami baked 86 blueberry muffins. Her sisters ate 5 of them. Kagami divided the remaining muffins equally among 9 plates. How many muffins did she put on each plate?

______

17. Lucia had 42 plums. Jorge had 12 more plums than Lucia. Jorge divided his plums equally among 6 people. How many plums did each person get?

______

18. Dana arranged her books on 5 shelves, with 8 books on each shelf. Hassan arranged his books on 4 shelves, with 9 books on each shelf. Who has more books? How many more?

______

19. Juana has 21 shirts. Leslie had one third as many shirts as Juana, but then she bought 4 more. How many shirts does Leslie have now?

______

9–11 **Going Further**

Name ____________________ Date ____________________

▶ Multiply 2- and 3-Digit Numbers by 1-Digit Numbers

There are 26 cars in the water ride at Smiley Park. Each car can fit 7 people. How many people in all can fit in the cars of the water ride?

$26 \times 7 = \square$

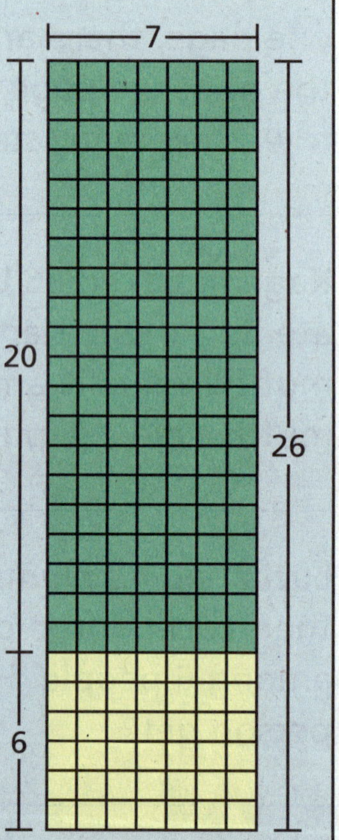

The Expanded Notation Method

$$\begin{array}{rr} 26 = & 20 + 6 \\ \times\ 7 = & \times\ 7 \\ \hline 6 \times 7 = & 42 \\ 20 \times 7 = & +140 \\ \hline & 182 \end{array}$$

The Rectangle Sections Method

$$\begin{array}{c|c|} & 7 \\ \hline 20 & \begin{array}{r} 7 \\ \times\ 20 \\ \hline 140 \end{array} \\ \hline + \\ 6 & \begin{array}{r} 7 \\ \times\ 6 \\ \hline 42 \end{array} \\ \hline \end{array}$$

$$\begin{array}{r} 140 \\ +\ 42 \\ \hline 182 \end{array}$$

You can multiply by the ones first.

$$\begin{array}{rr} 346 = & 300 + 40 + 6 \\ \times\ 2 = & 2 \\ \hline 2 \times 300 = & 600 \\ 2 \times 40 = & 80 \\ 2 \times 6 = & +\ 12 \\ \hline & 692 \end{array}$$

$$\begin{array}{c|c|c|c|} & 300\ + & 40\ + & 6 \\ \hline 2 & \begin{array}{r} 300 \\ \times\ 2 \\ \hline 600 \end{array} & \begin{array}{r} 40 \\ \times\ 2 \\ \hline 80 \end{array} & \begin{array}{r} 6 \\ \times\ 2 \\ \hline 12 \end{array} \\ \hline \end{array}$$

$$\begin{array}{r} 600 \\ 80 \\ +\ 12 \\ \hline 692 \end{array}$$

Multiply.

1. $\begin{array}{r} 14 \\ \times\ 4 \\ \hline \end{array}$

2. $\begin{array}{r} 78 \\ \times\ 8 \\ \hline \end{array}$

3. $\begin{array}{r} 86 \\ \times\ 6 \\ \hline \end{array}$

4. $\begin{array}{r} 325 \\ \times\ 3 \\ \hline \end{array}$

5. $\begin{array}{r} 497 \\ \times\ 2 \\ \hline \end{array}$

6. $\begin{array}{r} 637 \\ \times\ 5 \\ \hline \end{array}$

Name ______________________ Date ______________

►Dashes 13–16

Complete each Dash. Check your answers on page 357.

Dash 13 2s, 3s, 4s, 5s, 9s Multiplications	Dash 14 2s, 3s, 4s, 5s, 9s Divisions	Dash 15 6s, 7s, 8s Multiplications	Dash 16 6s, 7s, 8s Divisions
a. 7 × 4 = ___	a. 9 / 3 = ___	a. 8 × 8 = ___	a. 72 / 8 = ___
b. 5 • 5 = ___	b. 45 ÷ 9 = ___	b. 9 • 6 = ___	b. 49 ÷ 7 = ___
c. 2 * 9 = ___	c. 81 / 9 = ___	c. 7 * 6 = ___	c. 35 / 7 = ___
d. 3 × 8 = ___	d. 36 ÷ 4 = ___	d. 5 × 7 = ___	d. 64 ÷ 8 = ___
e. 4 • 4 = ___	e. 20 / 5 = ___	e. 3 • 8 = ___	e. 14 / 7 = ___
f. 5 * 9 = ___	f. 16 ÷ 4 = ___	f. 8 * 6 = ___	f. 18 ÷ 6 = ___
g. 6 × 3 = ___	g. 12 / 2 = ___	g. 6 × 3 = ___	g. 64 / 8 = ___
h. 7 • 2 = ___	h. 54 ÷ 9 = ___	h. 7 • 7 = ___	h. 48 ÷ 6 = ___
i. 9 * 9 = ___	i. 15 / 3 = ___	i. 4 * 8 = ___	i. 8 / 8 = ___
j. 6 × 4 = ___	j. 27 / 3 = ___	j. 6 × 6 = ___	j. 56 / 7 = ___
k. 2 • 2 = ___	k. 18 ÷ 2 = ___	k. 4 • 6 = ___	k. 32 ÷ 8 = ___
l. 5 * 3 = ___	l. 28 / 4 = ___	l. 7 * 9 = ___	l. 63 / 7 = ___
m. 4 × 8 = ___	m. 40 ÷ 5 = ___	m. 5 × 6 = ___	m. 30 ÷ 6 = ___
n. 3 • 3 = ___	n. 45 / 5 = ___	n. 4 • 7 = ___	n. 56 / 8 = ___
o. 7 * 5 = ___	o. 4 ÷ 2 = ___	o. 8 * 2 = ___	o. 72 ÷ 8 = ___
p. 8 × 5 = ___	p. 9 / 3 = ___	p. 1 × 6 = ___	p. 36 / 6 = ___
q. 4 • 3 = ___	q. 32 ÷ 4 = ___	q. 2 • 7 = ___	q. 40 ÷ 8 = ___
r. 2 * 8 = ___	r. 63 ÷ 9 = ___	r. 8 * 5 = ___	r. 21 ÷ 7 = ___
s. 9 × 4 = ___	s. 15 / 3 = ___	s. 8 × 1 = ___	s. 42 / 6 = ___
t. 6 • 9 = ___	t. 24 ÷ 4 = ___	t. 9 • 8 = ___	t. 7 ÷ 7 = ___

Name ____________________ Date ____________________

►Dashes 13–16

Complete each Dash. Check your answers on page 357.

Dash 13 2s, 3s, 4s, 5s, 9s Multiplications	Dash 14 2s, 3s, 4s, 5s, 9s Divisions	Dash 15 6s, 7s, 8s Multiplications	Dash 16 6s, 7s, 8s Divisions
a. 7 × 4 = ___	a. 9 / 3 = ___	a. 8 × 8 = ___	a. 72 / 8 = ___
b. 5 • 5 = ___	b. 45 ÷ 9 = ___	b. 9 • 6 = ___	b. 49 ÷ 7 = ___
c. 2 * 9 = ___	c. 81 / 9 = ___	c. 7 * 6 = ___	c. 35 / 7 = ___
d. 3 × 8 = ___	d. 36 ÷ 4 = ___	d. 5 × 7 = ___	d. 64 ÷ 8 = ___
e. 4 • 4 = ___	e. 20 / 5 = ___	e. 3 • 8 = ___	e. 14 / 7 = ___
f. 5 * 9 = ___	f. 16 ÷ 4 = ___	f. 8 * 6 = ___	f. 18 ÷ 6 = ___
g. 6 × 3 = ___	g. 12 / 2 = ___	g. 6 × 3 = ___	g. 64 / 8 = ___
h. 7 • 2 = ___	h. 54 ÷ 9 = ___	h. 7 • 7 = ___	h. 48 ÷ 6 = ___
i. 9 * 9 = ___	i. 15 / 3 = ___	i. 4 * 8 = ___	i. 8 / 8 = ___
j. 6 × 4 = ___	j. 27 / 3 = ___	j. 6 × 6 = ___	j. 56 / 7 = ___
k. 2 • 2 = ___	k. 18 ÷ 2 = ___	k. 4 • 6 = ___	k. 32 ÷ 8 = ___
l. 5 * 3 = ___	l. 28 / 4 = ___	l. 7 * 9 = ___	l. 63 / 7 = ___
m. 4 × 8 = ___	m. 40 ÷ 5 = ___	m. 5 × 6 = ___	m. 30 ÷ 6 = ___
n. 3 • 3 = ___	n. 45 / 5 = ___	n. 4 • 7 = ___	n. 56 / 8 = ___
o. 7 * 5 = ___	o. 4 ÷ 2 = ___	o. 8 * 2 = ___	o. 72 ÷ 8 = ___
p. 8 × 5 = ___	p. 9 / 3 = ___	p. 1 × 6 = ___	p. 36 / 6 = ___
q. 4 • 3 = ___	q. 32 ÷ 4 = ___	q. 2 • 7 = ___	q. 40 ÷ 8 = ___
r. 2 * 8 = ___	r. 63 ÷ 9 = ___	r. 8 * 5 = ___	r. 21 ÷ 7 = ___
s. 9 × 4 = ___	s. 15 / 3 = ___	s. 8 × 1 = ___	s. 42 / 6 = ___
t. 6 • 9 = ___	t. 24 ÷ 4 = ___	t. 9 • 8 = ___	t. 7 ÷ 7 = ___

Name ____________________ Date ____________________

►Answers to Dashes 13–16

Use this sheet to check your answers to the dashes on page 355.

Dash 13 2s, 3s, 4s, 5s, 9s Multiplications	Dash 14 2s, 3s, 4s, 5s, 9s Divisions	Dash 15 6s, 7s, 8s Multiplications	Dash 16 6s, 7s, 8s Divisions
a. 7 × 4 = 28	a. 9 / 3 = 3	a. 8 × 8 = 64	a. 72 / 8 = 9
b. 5 • 5 = 25	b. 45 ÷ 9 = 5	b. 9 • 6 = 54	b. 49 ÷ 7 = 7
c. 2 * 9 = 18	c. 81 / 9 = 9	c. 7 * 6 = 42	c. 35 / 7 = 5
d. 3 × 8 = 24	d. 36 ÷ 4 = 9	d. 5 × 7 = 35	d. 64 ÷ 8 = 8
e. 4 • 4 = 16	e. 20 / 5 = 4	e. 3 • 8 = 24	e. 14 / 7 = 2
f. 5 * 9 = 45	f. 16 ÷ 4 = 4	f. 8 * 6 = 48	f. 18 ÷ 6 = 3
g. 6 × 3 = 18	g. 12 / 2 = 6	g. 6 × 3 = 18	g. 64 / 8 = 8
h. 7 • 2 = 14	h. 54 ÷ 9 = 6	h. 7 • 7 = 49	h. 48 ÷ 6 = 8
i. 9 * 9 = 81	i. 15 / 3 = 5	i. 4 * 8 = 32	i. 8 / 8 = 1
j. 6 × 4 = 24	j. 27 / 3 = 9	j. 6 × 6 = 36	j. 56 / 7 = 8
k. 2 • 2 = 4	k. 18 ÷ 2 = 9	k. 4 • 6 = 24	k. 32 ÷ 8 = 4
l. 5 * 3 = 15	l. 28 / 4 = 7	l. 7 * 9 = 63	l. 63 / 7 = 9
m. 4 × 8 = 32	m. 40 ÷ 5 = 8	m. 5 × 6 = 30	m. 30 ÷ 6 = 5
n. 3 • 3 = 9	n. 45 / 5 = 9	n. 4 • 7 = 28	n. 56 / 8 = 7
o. 7 * 5 = 35	o. 4 ÷ 2 = 2	o. 8 * 2 = 16	o. 72 ÷ 8 = 9
p. 8 × 5 = 40	p. 9 / 3 = 3	p. 1 × 6 = 6	p. 36 / 6 = 6
q. 4 • 3 = 12	q. 32 ÷ 4 = 8	q. 2 • 7 = 14	q. 40 ÷ 8 = 5
r. 2 * 8 = 16	r. 63 ÷ 9 = 7	r. 8 * 5 = 40	r. 21 ÷ 7 = 3
s. 9 × 4 = 36	s. 15 / 3 = 5	s. 8 × 1 = 8	s. 42 / 6 = 7
t. 6 • 9 = 54	t. 24 ÷ 4 = 6	t. 9 • 8 = 72	t. 7 ÷ 7 = 1

9–12

Class Activity

Name ______________________ Date ______________

►Complex Multi-Step Word Problems

Solve.

1. A farm had 413 chickens. Then 9 of the hens laid 6 eggs each. All of the eggs have hatched except 3. How many chickens does the farm have now?

   ____

2. There are 8 houses on Jeremiah's street. Each house has 1 willow tree, 6 apple trees, and 2 olive trees. How many trees are on Jeremiah's street in all?

   ____

3. Tim has 6 marbles. Adrian has twice as many marbles as Tim. Ryan has 3 fewer marbles than Adrian. Leslie has 5 times as many marbles as Ryan. How many marbles does Leslie have?

   ____

4. Allen has 548 baseball cards. Drew has 362 more cards than Allen. Lacy has 76 fewer baseball cards than Drew. How many more baseball cards does Lacy have than Allen?

   ____

5. Angela had $4.00. She bought 3 gumballs for 9¢ each and 2 apples for 63¢ each. How much money does Angela have now?

   ____

6. Jasmine has $40. Ahmad has half as much money. Ahmad wants to buy an action figure for $5.76 and a backpack for $14.89. Does Ahmad have enough money?

   ____

9–12 Class Activity

Name ______________________ Date ______________

▶ More Complex Word Problems

Solve. Show your work on another sheet of paper.

7. Mr. Marconi made 9 pizzas. He divided the pizzas into 3 equal groups. One group was pizzas with mushrooms, one group had peppers, and one group was plain cheese. He cut each pizza into 8 slices. How many slices had either mushrooms or peppers?

____

8. Kelsey wants to see all 700 paintings in the art museum. Last week she saw 473 of them. Today she visited 9 more rooms in the museum. There are 8 paintings in each room. How many paintings does Kelsey still have to see?

____

9. The Nelson Notebook Company makes 3 kinds of wire spirals for their notebooks.

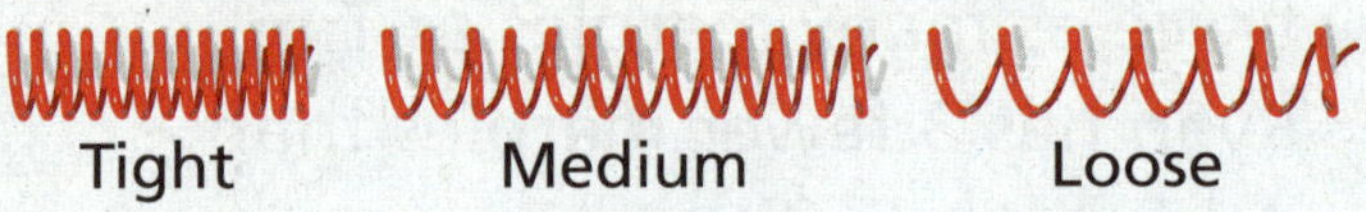

Color	Length of Wire Before Spiral	Length of Spiral
Blue	18 in.	9 in.
Red	20 in.	10 in.
Black	21 in.	7 in.
Green	24 in.	6 in.
White	26 in.	13 in.
Orange	27 in.	9 in.
Silver	28 in.	7 in.
Purple	33 in.	11 in.
Gold	40 in.	10 in.

Each type of spiral comes in 3 colors. The table gives information about all 9 spirals the company makes.

Which spiral colors are tight, which are medium, and which are loose? How do you know?

____

____

____

____

____

Name ____________________ Date ____________________

▶Dashes 17–20

Complete each Dash. Check your answers on page 363.

Dash 17 All Factors Multiplications	Dash 18 All Factors Divisions	Dash 19 All Factors Multiplications	Dash 20 All Factors Divisions
a. 5 × 4 = ___	a. 100 / 10 = ___	a. 4 × 5 = ___	a. 81 / 9 = ___
b. 8 • 10 = ___	b. 36 ÷ 4 = ___	b. 8 • 8 = ___	b. 21 ÷ 7 = ___
c. 6 * 6 = ___	c. 56 / 7 = ___	c. 6 * 1 = ___	c. 30 / 6 = ___
d. 9 × 2 = ___	d. 14 ÷ 2 = ___	d. 6 × 7 = ___	d. 42 ÷ 6 = ___
e. 7 • 7 = ___	e. 32 / 8 = ___	e. 9 • 3 = ___	e. 15 / 3 = ___
f. 3 * 8 = ___	f. 36 ÷ 6 = ___	f. 7 * 8 = ___	f. 72 ÷ 8 = ___
g. 8 × 9 = ___	g. 40 / 5 = ___	g. 10 × 7 = ___	g. 28 / 4 = ___
h. 4 • 1 = ___	h. 64 ÷ 8 = ___	h. 6 • 0 = ___	h. 48 ÷ 8 = ___
i. 2 * 2 = ___	i. 5 / 1 = ___	i. 4 * 4 = ___	i. 49 / 7 = ___
j. 8 × 7 = ___	j. 21 / 3 = ___	j. 7 × 5 = ___	j. 18 / 2 = ___
k. 5 • 5 = ___	k. 48 ÷ 6 = ___	k. 6 • 4 = ___	k. 63 ÷ 9 = ___
l. 7 * 6 = ___	l. 42 / 7 = ___	l. 9 * 7 = ___	l. 54 / 9 = ___
m. 4 × 8 = ___	m. 5 ÷ 5 = ___	m. 2 × 6 = ___	m. 20 ÷ 10 = ___
n. 9 • 4 = ___	n. 72 / 9 = ___	n. 4 • 7 = ___	n. 24 / 4 = ___
o. 9 * 9 = ___	o. 54 ÷ 6 = ___	o. 9 * 6 = ___	o. 56 ÷ 8 = ___
p. 10 × 3 = ___	p. 18 / 6 = ___	p. 6 × 3 = ___	p. 60 / 6 = ___
q. 6 • 8 = ___	q. 60 ÷ 6 = ___	q. 3 • 3 = ___	q. 36 ÷ 9 = ___
r. 5 * 9 = ___	r. 63 ÷ 7 = ___	r. 10 * 10 = ___	r. 20 ÷ 4 = ___
s. 6 × 9 = ___	s. 16 / 4 = ___	s. 8 × 2 = ___	s. 45 / 5 = ___
t. 0 • 1 = ___	t. 24 ÷ 6 = ___	t. 5 • 9 = ___	t. 28 ÷ 7 = ___

Name ______________________ Date ______________________

▶ Dashes 17–20

Complete each Dash. Check your answers on page 363.

Dash 17 All Factors Multiplications	Dash 18 All Factors Divisions	Dash 19 All Factors Multiplications	Dash 20 All Factors Divisions
a. 5 × 4 = ___	a. 100 / 10 = ___	a. 4 × 5 = ___	a. 81 / 9 = ___
b. 8 • 10 = ___	b. 36 ÷ 4 = ___	b. 8 • 8 = ___	b. 21 ÷ 7 = ___
c. 6 * 6 = ___	c. 56 / 7 = ___	c. 6 * 1 = ___	c. 30 / 6 = ___
d. 9 × 2 = ___	d. 14 ÷ 2 = ___	d. 6 × 7 = ___	d. 42 ÷ 6 = ___
e. 7 • 7 = ___	e. 32 / 8 = ___	e. 9 • 3 = ___	e. 15 / 3 = ___
f. 3 * 8 = ___	f. 36 ÷ 6 = ___	f. 7 * 8 = ___	f. 72 ÷ 8 = ___
g. 8 × 9 = ___	g. 40 / 5 = ___	g. 10 × 7 = ___	g. 28 / 4 = ___
h. 4 • 1 = ___	h. 64 ÷ 8 = ___	h. 6 • 0 = ___	h. 48 ÷ 8 = ___
i. 2 * 2 = ___	i. 5 / 1 = ___	i. 4 * 4 = ___	i. 49 / 7 = ___
j. 8 × 7 = ___	j. 21 / 3 = ___	j. 7 × 5 = ___	j. 18 / 2 = ___
k. 5 • 5 = ___	k. 48 ÷ 6 = ___	k. 6 • 4 = ___	k. 63 ÷ 9 = ___
l. 7 * 6 = ___	l. 42 / 7 = ___	l. 9 * 7 = ___	l. 54 / 9 = ___
m. 4 × 8 = ___	m. 5 ÷ 5 = ___	m. 2 × 6 = ___	m. 20 ÷ 10 = ___
n. 9 • 4 = ___	n. 72 / 9 = ___	n. 4 • 7 = ___	n. 24 / 4 = ___
o. 9 * 9 = ___	o. 54 ÷ 6 = ___	o. 9 * 6 = ___	o. 56 ÷ 8 = ___
p. 10 × 3 = ___	p. 18 / 6 = ___	p. 6 × 3 = ___	p. 60 / 6 = ___
q. 6 • 8 = ___	q. 60 ÷ 6 = ___	q. 3 • 3 = ___	q. 36 ÷ 9 = ___
r. 5 * 9 = ___	r. 63 ÷ 7 = ___	r. 10 * 10 = ___	r. 20 ÷ 4 = ___
s. 6 × 9 = ___	s. 16 / 4 = ___	s. 8 × 2 = ___	s. 45 / 5 = ___
t. 0 • 1 = ___	t. 24 ÷ 6 = ___	t. 5 • 9 = ___	t. 28 ÷ 7 = ___

Name Date

►Answers to Dashes 17–20

Use this sheet to check your answers to the dashes on page 361.

Dash 17 All Factors Multiplications	Dash 18 All Factors Divisions	Dash 19 All Factors Multiplications	Dash 20 All Factors Divisions
a. 5 × 4 = 20	a. 100 / 10 = 10	a. 4 × 5 = 20	a. 81 / 9 = 9
b. 8 • 10 = 80	b. 36 ÷ 4 = 9	b. 8 • 8 = 64	b. 21 ÷ 7 = 3
c. 6 * 6 = 36	c. 56 / 7 = 8	c. 6 * 1 = 6	c. 30 / 6 = 5
d. 9 × 2 = 18	d. 14 ÷ 2 = 7	d. 6 × 7 = 42	d. 42 ÷ 6 = 7
e. 7 • 7 = 49	e. 32 / 8 = 4	e. 9 • 3 = 27	e. 15 / 3 = 5
f. 3 * 8 = 24	f. 36 ÷ 6 = 6	f. 7 * 8 = 56	f. 72 ÷ 8 = 9
g. 8 × 9 = 72	g. 40 / 5 = 8	g. 10 × 7 = 70	g. 28 / 4 = 7
h. 4 • 1 = 4	h. 64 ÷ 8 = 8	h. 6 • 0 = 0	h. 48 ÷ 8 = 6
i. 2 * 2 = 4	i. 5 / 1 = 5	i. 4 * 4 = 16	i. 49 / 7 = 7
j. 8 × 7 = 56	j. 21 / 3 = 7	j. 7 × 5 = 35	j. 18 / 2 = 9
k. 5 • 5 = 25	k. 48 ÷ 6 = 8	k. 6 • 4 = 24	k. 63 ÷ 9 = 7
l. 7 * 6 = 42	l. 42 / 7 = 6	l. 9 * 7 = 63	l. 54 / 9 = 6
m. 4 × 8 = 32	m. 5 ÷ 5 = 1	m. 2 × 6 = 12	m. 20 ÷ 10 = 2
n. 9 • 4 = 36	n. 72 / 9 = 8	n. 4 • 7 = 28	n. 24 / 4 = 6
o. 9 * 9 = 81	o. 54 ÷ 6 = 9	o. 9 * 6 = 54	o. 56 ÷ 8 = 7
p. 10 × 3 = 30	p. 18 / 6 = 3	p. 6 × 3 = 18	p. 60 / 6 = 10
q. 6 • 8 = 48	q. 60 ÷ 6 = 10	q. 3 • 3 = 9	q. 36 ÷ 9 = 4
r. 5 * 9 = 45	r. 63 ÷ 7 = 9	r. 10 * 10 = 100	r. 20 ÷ 4 = 5
s. 6 × 9 = 54	s. 16 / 4 = 4	s. 8 × 2 = 16	s. 45 / 5 = 9
t. 0 • 1 = 0	t. 24 ÷ 6 = 4	t. 5 • 9 = 45	t. 28 ÷ 7 = 4

9–13

Class Activity

Name ____________________ Date ____________

▶ Solve Multi-Step Word Problems

Solve.

Show your work.

1. Raul spent 8 minutes doing his homework. His older sister spent 5 minutes less than 7 times as many minutes doing her homework. How many minutes did Raul's sister spend on her homework?

____

2. At Sonya's cello recital, there were 8 rows of chairs, with 6 chairs in each row. There was a person in each chair, and there were 17 more people standing. How many people were in the audience altogether?

____

3. Tova's art teacher asked her to cut out construction paper squares with an area of 36 square centimeters each. What should the side lengths of the squares be?

____

4. Mukesh was making 7 salads. He opened a can of olives and put 6 olives on each salad. Then he ate the rest of the olives in the can. If there were 51 olives to start with, how many olives did Mukesh eat?

____

5. Peter wallpapered a wall that was 8 feet wide and 9 feet high. He had 28 square feet of wallpaper left over. How many square feet of wallpaper did he start with?

____

9–13 Class Activity

Name ________________ Date ________

Vocabulary
function table

▶ What's My Rule?

A **function table** is a table of ordered pairs. For every input number, there is only one output number. The rule describes what to do to the input number to get the output number.

Write the rule and then complete the function table.

6. Rule: ________

Input	Output
7	42
8	____
____	54
6	36

7. Rule: ________

Input	Output
81	9
45	5
72	____
____	7

8. Rule: ________

Input	Output
4	28
8	56
6	____
7	____

9. Rule: ________

Input	Output
32	8
8	2
____	3
24	____

10. Rule: ________

Input	Output
21	7
27	9
____	6
15	____

11. Rule: ________

Input	Output
5	25
____	40
9	____
3	15

9–13

Class Activity

Name _______________ Date _______________

► Play *Division Three-in-a-Row*

Rules for *Division Three-in-a-Row*

Number of players: 2

What You Will Need: Division Strategy Cards, one *Three-in-a-Row* Game Grid for each player

1. Each player writes any nine quotients in the squares of a game grid. A player may write the same quotient more than once.
2. Shuffle the cards. Place them division side up in the center of the table.
3. Players take turns. On each turn, a player completes the division on the top card and then turns the card over to check the answer.
4. For a correct answer, if the quotient is on the game grid, the player puts an X through that grid square. If the answer is wrong, or if the quotient is not on the grid, the player doesn't mark anything. The player puts the card division side up on the bottom of the stack.
5. The first player to mark three squares in a row (horizontally, vertically, or diagonally) wins.

Name ____________________ Date ____________

▶ Math and Social Studies

Every state has a state bird.

- The meadowlark is the state bird of 6 states.
- The robin is the state bird of half of the number of states that have the meadowlark as a state bird.
- The wren is the state bird of 1 fewer states than the states with the robin as state bird.
- The bluebird is the state bird of twice the number of states with the wren as state bird.

1. On a piece of grid paper, make a graph that shows the data about state birds above.

2. Put the birds in order from most often used as a state bird to least often used as a state bird.

   ____

3. The number of states with a cardinal as state bird is one more than the number of states with the meadowlark as the state bird. How many states have the cardinal as state bird?

   ____

4. Write a word problem about the data in the graph and give the answer. Trade problems with a partner and solve.

   ____

Name Date

▶Street Chalk Art Fair

Around the country cities block off streets and hold Chalk Art Fairs. Each person or group is given a rectangle outlined on the street for their chalk painting.

5. One of the rectangles on the street has a perimeter of 12 feet. Each side of the rectangle is a whole number of feet. What is the greatest area it could have? Explain.

6. One of the rectangles has a perimeter of 16 feet. Each side of the rectangle is a whole number of feet. What is the smallest area it could have? Explain.

7. Lupe and her friends have their choice of a rectangle that is 9 feet by 2 feet or a rectangle that is 4 feet by 5 feet. They want to choose the rectangle with the greatest area. Which rectangle should they choose? Explain.

8. Which of the rectangles described in Problem 7 should Lupe and her friends choose if they want the rectangle with the greatest perimeter? Explain.

Name ____________________ Date ____________________

Basic Multiplications

1. 8 × 9 = ___	2. 1 * 10 = ___	3. 3 • 5 = ___	4. 2 * 8 = ___
5. 5 * 3 = ___	6. 0 × 7 = ___	7. 8 × 8 = ___	8. 2 * 7 = ___
9. 4 • 10 = ___	10. 7 • 2 = ___	11. 3 • 8 = ___	12. 7 * 10 = ___
13. 4 • 4 = ___	14. 1 * 3 = ___	15. 0 × 0 = ___	16. 4 * 9 = ___
17. 10 • 6 = ___	18. 1 × 5 = ___	19. 7 • 5 = ___	20. 2 • 6 = ___
21. 5 × 8 = ___	22. 4 * 5 = ___	23. 6 • 8 = ___	24. 0 × 3 = ___
25. 9 * 9 = ___	26. 9 * 2 = ___	27. 0 × 10 = ___	28. 0 × 2 = ___
29. 7 * 8 = ___	30. 8 • 7 = ___	31. 1 • 7 = ___	32. 1 × 9 = ___
33. 2 * 9 = ___	34. 6 • 10 = ___	35. 5 × 9 = ___	36. 5 × 5 = ___
37. 2 * 3 = ___	38. 3 • 2 = ___	39. 3 × 4 = ___	40. 0 * 4 = ___
41. 9 × 10 = ___	42. 3 × 6 = ___	43. 0 × 6 = ___	44. 9 × 6 = ___
45. 6 × 7 = ___	46. 10 × 10 = ___	47. 8 × 3 = ___	48. 6 × 2 = ___
49. 10 × 5 = ___	50. 6 × 4 = ___		

Name ______________________ Date ______________________

Basic Multiplications

51. 1 * 0 = ___	52. 8 • 2 = ___	53. 10 * 7 = ___	54. 1 * 2 = ___
55. 5 * 2 = ___	56. 9 • 7 = ___	57. 8 × 5 = ___	58. 6 • 6 = ___
59. 7 • 9 = ___	60. 1 * 1 = ___	61. 7 * 3 = ___	62. 0 * 9 = ___
63. 4 * 2 = ___	64. 10 × 8 = ___	65. 2 • 4 = ___	66. 4 • 8 = ___
67. 2 * 2 = ___	68. 1 * 4 = ___	69. 1 × 6 = ___	70. 0 • 1 = ___
71. 5 • 10 = ___	72. 3 • 10 = ___	73. 0 • 8 = ___	74. 7 * 4 = ___
75. 9 * 3 = ___	76. 4 × 3 = ___	77. 6 × 9 = ___	78. 7 * 6 = ___
79. 3 • 7 = ___	80. 2 • 10 = ___	81. 8 * 4 = ___	82. 9 * 8 = ___
83. 6 • 3 = ___	84. 5 × 6 = ___	85. 3 * 9 = ___	86. 9 • 5 = ___
87. 1 × 8 = ___	88. 8 × 10 = ___	89. 2 × 5 = ___	90. 5 × 4 = ___
91. 0 × 5 = ___	92. 10 × 9 = ___	93. 4 × 7 = ___	94. 7 × 7 = ___
95. 6 × 5 = ___	96. 9 × 4 = ___	97. 4 × 6 = ___	98. 5 × 7 = ___
99. 8 × 6 = ___	100. 3 × 3 = ___		

Name ____________________ Date ____________________

Basic Divisions

1. 6 / 3 = ___	**2.** 40 / 8 = ___	**3.** 10 ÷ 1 = ___	**4.** 40 ÷ 10 = ___
5. 32 / 8 = ___	**6.** 2 ÷ 2 = ___	**7.** 80 ÷ 10 = ___	**8.** 4 ÷ 1 = ___
9. 16 ÷ 2 = ___	**10.** 30 / 6 = ___	**11.** 90 / 10 = ___	**12.** 24 ÷ 6 = ___
13. 4 / 2 = ___	**14.** 8 / 4 = ___	**15.** 9 / 9 = ___	**16.** 6 ÷ 1 = ___
17. 24 ÷ 3 = ___	**18.** 81 / 9 = ___	**19.** 15 ÷ 5 = ___	**20.** 7 ÷ 7 = ___
21. 12 ÷ 6 = ___	**22.** 20 / 10 = ___	**23.** 35 ÷ 7 = ___	**24.** 72 / 9 = ___
25. $7\overline{)28}$	**26.** $9\overline{)27}$	**27.** $3\overline{)3}$	**28.** $7\overline{)49}$
29. $3\overline{)27}$	**30.** $3\overline{)15}$	**31.** $4\overline{)28}$	**32.** $8\overline{)16}$
33. $1\overline{)2}$	**34.** $5\overline{)45}$	**35.** $5\overline{)10}$	**36.** $8\overline{)72}$
37. $10\overline{)70}$	**38.** $5\overline{)5}$	**39.** $7\overline{)70}$	**40.** $6\overline{)18}$
41. $\frac{56}{7}$ = ___	**42.** $\frac{48}{8}$ = ___	**43.** $\frac{21}{7}$ = ___	**44.** $\frac{36}{4}$ = ___
45. $\frac{3}{1}$ = ___	**46.** $\frac{42}{6}$ = ___	**47.** $\frac{18}{3}$ = ___	**48.** $\frac{30}{3}$ = ___
49. $\frac{45}{9}$ = ___	**50.** $\frac{16}{4}$ = ___		

Name ____________ Date ____________

Basic Divisions

51. $6 \div 6 =$ ___
52. $42 / 7 =$ ___
53. $20 \div 5 =$ ___
54. $90 / 9 =$ ___
55. $36 / 9 =$ ___
56. $35 \div 5 =$ ___
57. $1 / 1 =$ ___
58. $50 \div 10 =$ ___
59. $54 / 9 =$ ___
60. $12 \div 2 =$ ___
61. $10 \div 2 =$ ___
62. $24 / 8 =$ ___
63. $14 \div 7 =$ ___
64. $12 \div 3 =$ ___
65. $63 / 7 =$ ___
66. $4 \div 4 =$ ___
67. $6 / 2 =$ ___
68. $25 \div 5 =$ ___
69. $5 \div 1 =$ ___
70. $7 \div 1 =$ ___
71. $60 / 10 =$ ___
72. $18 \div 2 =$ ___
73. $60 / 6 =$ ___
74. $9 / 3 =$ ___
75. $5\overline{)50}$
76. $10\overline{)10}$
77. $4\overline{)12}$
78. $8\overline{)80}$
79. $5\overline{)30}$
80. $8\overline{)56}$
81. $6\overline{)54}$
82. $9\overline{)63}$
83. $4\overline{)24}$
84. $8\overline{)8}$
85. $8\overline{)64}$
86. $1\overline{)7}$
87. $2\overline{)8}$
88. $10\overline{)30}$
89. $4\overline{)40}$
90. $6\overline{)48}$
91. $\frac{32}{4} =$ ___
92. $\frac{9}{1} =$ ___
93. $\frac{36}{6} =$ ___
94. $\frac{100}{10} =$ ___
95. $\frac{14}{2} =$ ___
96. $\frac{21}{3} =$ ___
97. $\frac{40}{5} =$ ___
98. $\frac{20}{4} =$ ___
99. $\frac{20}{2} =$ ___
100. $\frac{18}{9} =$ ___

9 Unit Test

Name ______________________ Date ____________

Multiply or divide.

1. $7 \times 8 = \square$
2. $6 \bullet 9 = \square$
3. $55 \div 1 = \square$
4. $72 \div 9 = \square$
5. $30 \times 0 = \square$
6. $49 / 7 = \square$
7. $4 \bullet 3 = \square$
8. $2 * 10 = \square$
9. $3 \times 9 = \square$
10. $6\overline{)24}$
11. $7\overline{)28}$
12. $9\overline{)45}$

Solve.

Show your work.

13. Lucinda collected 4 eggs from the chicken house. Mark collected 32 eggs. How many times as many eggs did Mark collect than Lucinda?

____

14. Carrie found 7 seashells at the beach. Her brother found 4 times as many. How many seashells did her brother find?

____

15. The supermarket sells small boxes of cereal in packages of 8. Mrs. Smith bought 6 packages. How many boxes of cereal did she buy?

____

16. The area of Keshawn's garden is 36 square feet. Its width is 4 feet. What is the length of his garden?

____

Name ______________________ Date ______________

Write an equation to solve the problem.

17. A class has 35 goldfish and 5 fish bowls. How many fish will be in each bowl if the same number of fish are in each bowl?

____

Solve.

18. Mr. Howell arranged 56 books on 8 shelves with the same number on each shelf. How many books were on each shelf?

____

19. Mr. Alberto has 48 students to divide into teams of 8. Mr. Yates has 81 students to divide into teams of 9. How many more teams does Mr. Yates have than Mr. Alberto?

____

20. **Extended Response** Marcie has 7 bean bag dolls. Lucy has 3 times as many dolls as Marcie. Janice has twice as many dolls as Marcie and Lucy combined. How many more dolls does Janice have than Marcie? Explain the steps you used to solve the problem.

____

____

____

____

____

____

____

Name Date

► Make an Analog Clock

Attach the clock hands to the clock face using a prong fastener.

10–1 Class Activity

Name ________________________ Date ____________

► Time to 15 Minutes

Write the time on the digital clock. Then write how to say the time.

1. 

____

2. 

____

3. 

____

4. 

____

Write the time on the digital clock. Write two ways to say the time.

5. 

____

____

6. 

____

____

7. 

____

____

8. 

____

____

9. 

____

____

10. 

____

____

11. 

____

____

12. 

____

____

10–1 Class Activity

Name ____________________ Date ____________

▶Show Time to 15 Minutes

Draw the hands on the analog clock. Write the time on the digital clock.

13. nine fifteen

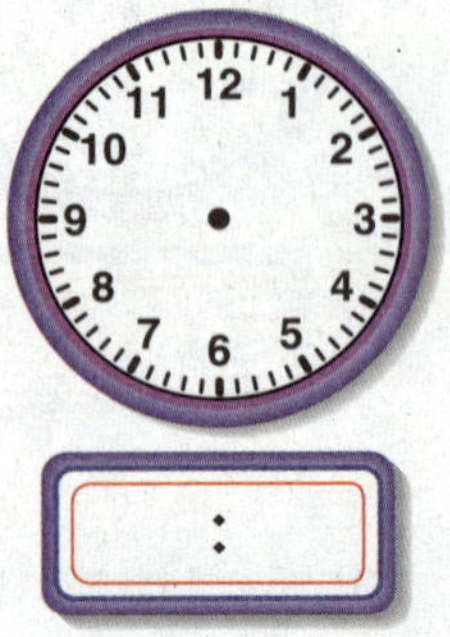

14. half past seven

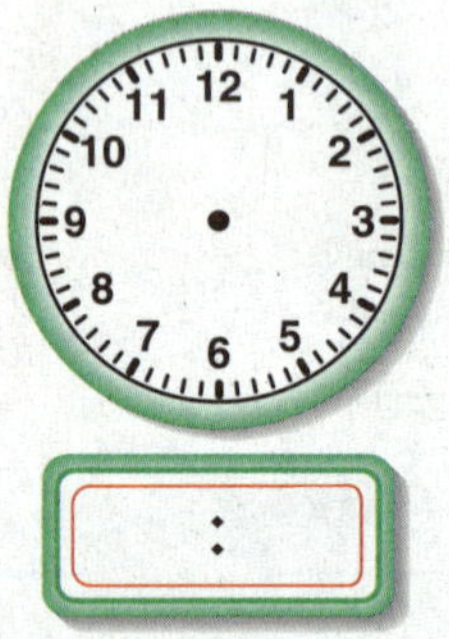

15. three o'clock

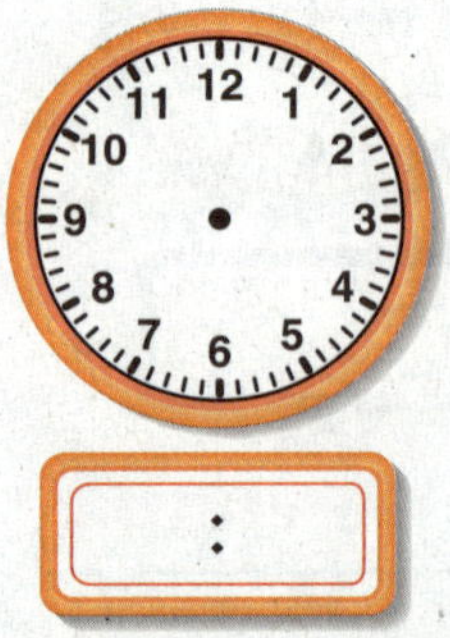

16. seven thirty

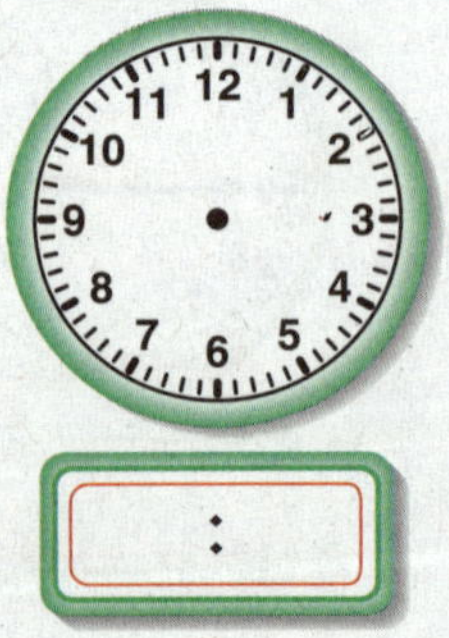

17. one forty-five

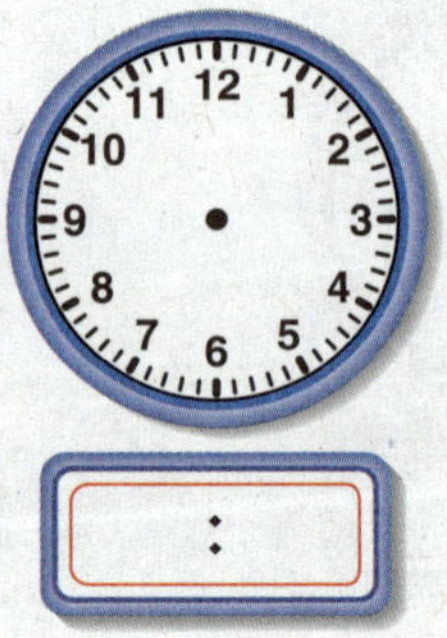

18. fifteen minutes after two

▶Times of Daily Activities

19. Complete the table.

Time	Light or Dark	Part of the Day	Activity
3:15 A.M.			
8:00 A.M.			
2:30 P.M.			
6:15 P.M.			
8:45 P.M.			

10–1 **Class Activity**

Name ______________________ Date ____________

► Time to 5 Minutes

Write the time on the digital clock. Then write how to say the time.

20.

[:]

____

21.

[:]

____

22.

[:]

____

23.

[:]

____

Write the time on the digital clock.

24. ten minutes after eight

[:]

25. seven twenty-five

[:]

26. eleven fifty

[:]

► Time to 1 Minute

Write the time on the digital clock. Then write how to say the time.

27.

[:]

____

28.

[:]

____

29.

[:]

____

30.

[:]

____

Write the time on the digital clock.

31. ten fourteen

[:]

32. fifty-two minutes after eight

[:]

33. seven twenty-eight

[:]

10–1 Class Activity

Name ______________________________ Date ____________

▶ Times Before and After the Hour

Write the time as minutes *after* an hour and minutes *before* an hour.

34.

35.

36.

37.

38.

39.

40.

41.

42.

Family Letter

Dear Family,

In math class, your child is beginning a unit about time. This topic is directly connected to home and community and involves skills your child will use often in everyday situations.

Students are reading time to the hour, half-hour, quarter-hour, five minutes, and minute, as well as describing the time before the hour and after the hour.

For example, you can read 3:49 both as after and before the hour.

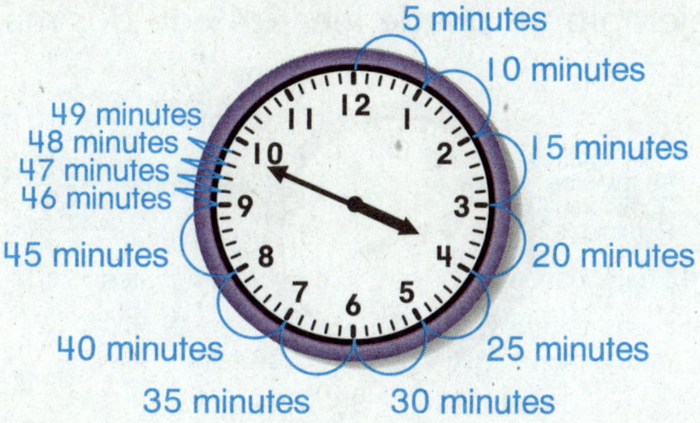

Forty-nine minutes after three

Eleven minutes before four

Students use calendars and clocks to find elapsed time and to solve problems involving elapsed time in days, weeks, months, hours, and minutes.

At the end of the unit, students will link the movement of the minute hand around a clock to angle measures in degrees. They will divide the 360° rotation of a circle by 60 minutes to find that each minute on a clock represents a 6° rotation. They will use this fact to solve word problems involving elapsed time, problems which give them practice multiplying and dividing by 6.

Help your child read time and find elapsed time. Ask your child to estimate how long it takes to do activities such as eating a meal, traveling to the store, or doing homework. Have your child look at the clock when starting an activity and then again at the end of the activity. Ask how long the activity took.

Talk to your child about events that will be happening over the next year and ask how many days or months there are until those events. Talk about past events in the year and ask your child how many days or months it has been since those events happened.

If you have any questions or comments, please call or write to me.

Sincerely,
Your child's teacher

Carta a la familia

Estimada familia:

En la clase de matemáticas su niño empieza una unidad sobre la hora. Este tema se relaciona directamente con la casa y la comunidad, y trata de destrezas que su niño usará a menudo en situaciones de la vida diaria.

Los estudiantes leen la hora, la media hora, el cuarto de hora, cinco minutos y un minuto; también describen la hora antes y después de la hora en punto.

Por ejemplo, se puede leer 3:49 de dos maneras:

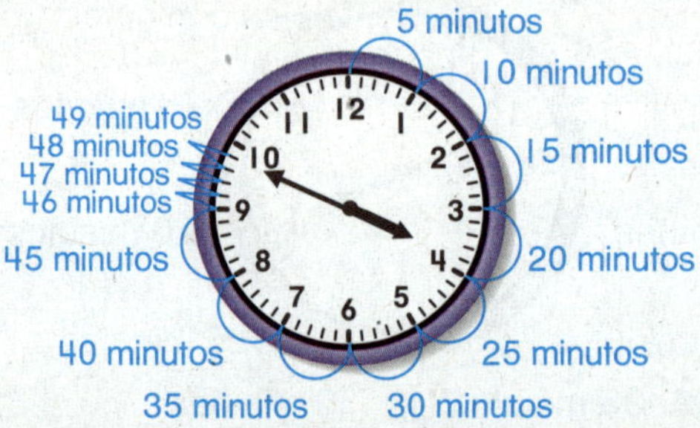

Las tres y cuarenta y nueve

Las cuatro menos once

Los estudiantes usan calendarios y relojes para hallar el tiempo transcurrido y para resolver problemas de tiempo transcurrido en días, semanas, meses, horas y minutos.

Al final de la unidad, los estudiantes harán la conexión entre el movimiento del minutero del reloj y las medidas de ángulos en grados. Dividirán la rotación de 360° de un círculo entre 60 minutos para hallar que cada minuto del reloj representa una rotación de 6°. Luego usarán este dato para resolver problemas verbales que tratan de tiempo transcurrido, lo que a su vez les deja practicar la multiplicación y la división por 6.

Ayude a su niño a leer la hora y hallar el tiempo transcurrido. Pídale que estime cuánto le lleva hacer actividades como comer, una comida, ir a la tienda o hacer la tarea. Pídale que se fije en la hora antes de empezar una actividad y luego otra vez al completar la actividad. Pídale que le diga cuánto tiempo le llevó hacer la actividad.

Háblele a su niño acerca de sucesos que ocurrirán durante el año que viene y pregúntele cuántos días o meses faltan para que sucedan. Háblele de sucesos pasados del año y pregúntele cuántos días o meses hace que pasaron estos sucesos.

Si tiene alguna pregunta o comentario, por favor comuníquese conmigo.

Atentamente,
El maestro de su niño

10–2 Class Activity

Name ____________________ Date ____________________

▶ Features of Calendars

January						
Sun	Mon	Tues	Wed	Thurs	Fri	Sat
	1	2	3	4	5	6
7	8	9	10	11	12	13
14	15	16	17	18	19	20
21	22	23	24	25	26	27
28	29	30	31			

February						
Sun	Mon	Tues	Wed	Thurs	Fri	Sat
				1	2	3
4	5	6	7	8	9	10
11	12	13	14	15	16	17
18	19	20	21	22	23	24
25	26	27	28			

March						
Sun	Mon	Tues	Wed	Thurs	Fri	Sat
				1	2	3
4	5	6	7	8	9	10
11	12	13	14	15	16	17
18	19	20	21	22	23	24
25	26	27	28	29	30	31

April						
Sun	Mon	Tues	Wed	Thurs	Fri	Sat
1	2	3	4	5	6	7
8	9	10	11	12	13	14
15	16	17	18	19	20	21
22	23	24	25	26	27	28
29	30					

May						
Sun	Mon	Tues	Wed	Thurs	Fri	Sat
		1	2	3	4	5
6	7	8	9	10	11	12
13	14	15	16	17	18	19
20	21	22	23	24	25	26
27	28	29	30	31		

June						
Sun	Mon	Tues	Wed	Thurs	Fri	Sat
					1	2
3	4	5	6	7	8	9
10	11	12	13	14	15	16
17	18	19	20	21	22	23
24	25	26	27	28	29	30

Name Date

July

Sun	Mon	Tues	Wed	Thurs	Fri	Sat
1	2	3	4	5	6	7
8	9	10	11	12	13	14
15	16	17	18	19	20	21
22	23	24	25	26	27	28
29	30	31				

August

Sun	Mon	Tues	Wed	Thurs	Fri	Sat
			1	2	3	4
5	6	7	8	9	10	11
12	13	14	15	16	17	18
19	20	21	22	23	24	25
26	27	28	29	30	31	

September

Sun	Mon	Tues	Wed	Thurs	Fri	Sat
						1
2	3	4	5	6	7	8
9	10	11	12	13	14	15
16	17	18	19	20	21	22
23	24	25	26	27	28	29
30						

October

Sun	Mon	Tues	Wed	Thurs	Fri	Sat
	1	2	3	4	5	6
7	8	9	10	11	12	13
14	15	16	17	18	19	20
21	22	23	24	25	26	27
28	29	30	31			

November

Sun	Mon	Tues	Wed	Thurs	Fri	Sat
				1	2	3
4	5	6	7	8	9	10
11	12	13	14	15	16	17
18	19	20	21	22	23	24
25	26	27	28	29	30	

December

Sun	Mon	Tues	Wed	Thurs	Fri	Sat
						1
2	3	4	5	6	7	8
9	10	11	12	13	14	15
16	17	18	19	20	21	22
23	24	25	26	27	28	29
30	31					

10–2 Class Activity

Name _______________ Date _______________

Vocabulary	
month	day
week	elapsed time

▶ Use a Calendar

Use the calendars on pages 383–384 to complete exercises 1–3.

1. What is the fourth **month** of the year?

____

2. What is the date of the twenty-second **day** of the third month?

____

3. What day of the **week** is the third day of the seventh month?

____

▶ Elapsed Time on a Calendar

Write the elapsed time.

4. August 1 to November 1 is _____ months.
5. 7:00 A.M. May 2 to 7:00 A.M. May 19 is _____ days.

Write the month.

6. Eight months after March _______________
7. Six months before December _______________

Write the date.

8. Seven days after the third of July _______________
9. Two weeks after November 2 _______________
10. Four days before June 10 _______________
11. One week before August 23 _______________

10–2 Class Activity

Name ____________________ Date ____________

▶ Solve Problems About Elapsed Time on a Calendar

Solve.

Show your work.

12. Garnetta worked on her project from October 4 to October 11. She then had 4 more days to complete it. How many days did she work on her project?

____

13. David's family left for their vacation on June 3. After 2 weeks, they returned home. What date did they arrive home?

____

14. Randi planted flower seeds in the house on January 15. On May 15, she planted the small plants outside. Three months later, they bloomed. How long did it take the seeds to grow into blooming plants?

____

15. Irene went to the aquarium on July 16. Bruce went to the aquarium 1 week later. Chantal went to the aquarium 4 days after Bruce. On what date did Chantal go to the aquarium?

____

16. Marilyn went to the History Museum on August 5. Alison went 1 week later. If Charlie went to the History Museum 3 days before Alison, what date did he go?

____

10–2 Class Activity

Name _______________ Date _______________

► Elapsed Time in Minutes and Hours

17. Find the elapsed time.

Start Time	End Time	Elapsed Time
4:00 P.M.	7:00 P.M.	
7:45 A.M.	8:15 A.M.	
2:17 P.M.	7:17 P.M.	
11:00 A.M.	2:00 P.M.	
11:55 A.M.	4:25 P.M.	

18. Find the end time.

Start Time	Elapsed Time	End Time
1:00 P.M.	2 hours	
4:15 A.M.	4 hours	
4:55 P.M.	18 minutes	
2:15 A.M.	1 hour and 15 minutes	
11:55 A.M.	2 hours and 5 minutes	

19. Find the start time.

Start Time	Elapsed Time	End Time
	3 hours	4:15 P.M.
	15 minutes	2:45 P.M.
	2 hours and 35 minutes	11:55 A.M.
	1 hour and 20 minutes	3:42 A.M.

Name ____________________ Date ____________

▶ Solve Problems About Elapsed Time on a Clock

Solve. Use your clock if you need to.

Show your work.

20. Loretta left her friend's house at 3:45. She had been there for 2 hours and 20 minutes. What time did she get there?

____

21. Berto spent from 3:45 P.M. to 4:15 P.M. doing math homework and from 4:30 P.M. to 5:10 P.M. doing social studies homework. How much time did he spend on his math and social studies homework?

____

22. Ed arrived at a biking trail at 9:00 A.M. He biked for 1 hour and 45 minutes. He spent 20 minutes riding home. What time did he get home?

____

23. Mario finished swimming at 10:45. He swam for 1 hour and 15 minutes. What time did he start?

____

24. Vasco finished cleaning his room at 4:30. It took him 25 minutes. What time did he start?

____

25. Eric has basketball practice from 3:30 P.M. to 4:15 P.M. He has violin practice at 5:30. Today basketball practice ended 30 minutes late and it takes Eric 15 minutes to walk to violin practice. Will he be on time? Explain.

____

____

10–3 Class Activity

Name ____________________ Date ____________________

► Rotations of the Minute Hand

The clocks on this page show the movement of the minute hand.

1. The minute hand has traveled one quarter of the way around the clock.

_______ minutes have passed.
The minute hand has rotated _______ degrees.

2. The minute hand has traveled halfway around the clock.

_______ minutes have passed.
The minute hand has rotated _______ degrees.

3. The minute hand has traveled three quarters of the way around the clock.

_______ minutes have passed.
The minute hand has rotated _______ degrees.

4. The minute hand has traveled all the way around the clock.

_______ minutes have passed.
The minute hand has rotated _______ degrees.

Find how many minutes have passed and how many degrees the minute hand has rotated.

5.

minutes: _______
degrees: _______

6.

minutes: _______
degrees: _______

7.

minutes: _______
degrees: _______

8.

minutes: _______
degrees: _______

10–3 Class Activity

Name ________ Date ________

Vocabulary
degrees

► Degrees of Rotation in 1 Minute

The minute hand rotates 6 degrees (°) in 1 minute.
Complete the sentence.

9. Between 12:00 and 12:08, the minute hand rotates ________ degrees.

10. Between 12:00 and 12:07, the minute hand rotates ________ degrees.

11. Between 12:00 and 12:10, the minute hand rotates ________ degrees.

► Elapsed Time

Complete the sentence.

12. From 4:16 to 4:25, ________ minutes pass. The minute hand rotates ________ degrees.

13. From 2:43 to 2:48, ________ minutes pass. The minute hand rotates ________ degrees.

14. From 8:55 to 9:01, ________ minutes pass. The minute hand rotates ________ degrees.

15. From 12:59 to 1:01, ________ minutes pass. The minute hand rotates ________ degrees.

► Find End Times Using Clock Angles

Solve.

16. A clock starts at 4:15. What time is it after the minute hand rotates 18 degrees? ________

17. A clock starts at 7:57. What time is it after the minute hand rotates 24 degrees? ________

18. A clock starts at 10:59. What time is it after the minute hand rotates 42 degrees? ________

10

Unit Test

Name ______________________ Date ____________

Write each time on the digital clock. Then write how to say the time.

1.

____

2.

____

3.

____

4.

____

Write the time as minutes after an hour and minutes before an hour.

5.

____

____

6.

____

____

Name ____________ Date ____________

Solve.

Show your work.

7. Diego went to his grandparents' house on August 3. He stayed there until August 21. How many days did he stay at his grandparents' house?

____

8. At 8:45 Tamara went to basketball practice. Her practice lasted 1 hour and 15 minutes. What time did she finish her practice?

____

9. A clock shows 7:00. What time is it after the minute hand rotates 90°? Use the clock in exercise 1 if you need to.

____

10. **Extended Response** Carla finished her homework at 8:30. She had spent 30 minutes on math and 45 minutes on a science report. Show what time she started her homework on the clock below.

Explain how you found your answer.

____

____

____

____

11–1 Class Activity

Name ______________________ Date ______________

Vocabulary

fraction | denominator
numerator | unit fraction

▶ The Meaning of Fractions

A **fraction** can be used to represent a part of a whole. The bottom number of a fraction is called the **denominator**. It tells how many equal parts the whole is divided into. The top number is the **numerator**. It tells how many of the equal parts you are talking about.

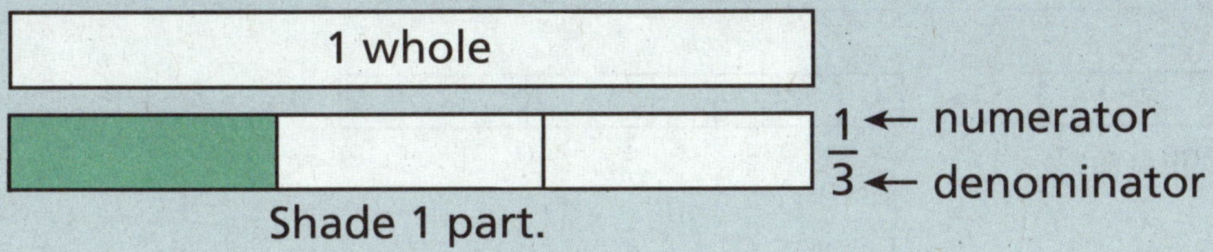

▶ Unit Fractions

A **unit fraction** is a fraction with a numerator of 1. The fraction strips at the right below all represent unit fractions. What patterns do you see?

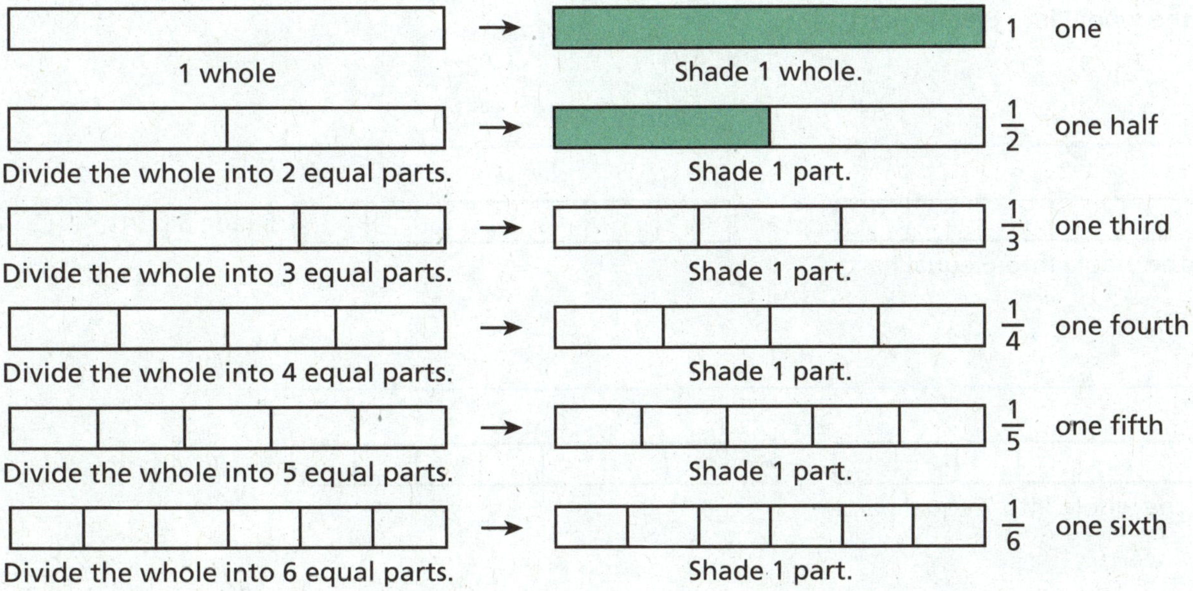

Name _______________ Date _______________

▶ Build Fractions from Unit Fractions

Write the unit fractions. Show your shaded unit fractions as a whole number times a unit fraction and as a total of unit fractions.

1. Divide the whole into 5 equal parts. → Shade 2 parts.

$\frac{1}{5} + \frac{1}{5} + \frac{1}{5} + \frac{1}{5} + \frac{1}{5}$ $\frac{1}{5} + \frac{1}{5} = 2 \times \frac{1}{5} = \frac{2}{5}$

2. Divide the whole into 9 equal parts. → Shade 4 parts.

3. Divide the whole into 7 equal parts. → Shade 5 parts.

4. Divide the whole into 8 equal parts. → Shade 7 parts.

5. Divide the whole into 6 equal parts. → Shade 3 parts.

6. Divide the whole into 7 equal parts. → Shade 7 parts.

11–1 Class Activity

Name ______________________ Date ____________

▶Fractions as Parts of a Whole

Write a fraction to represent the divided 1 whole and then the shaded part.

7.

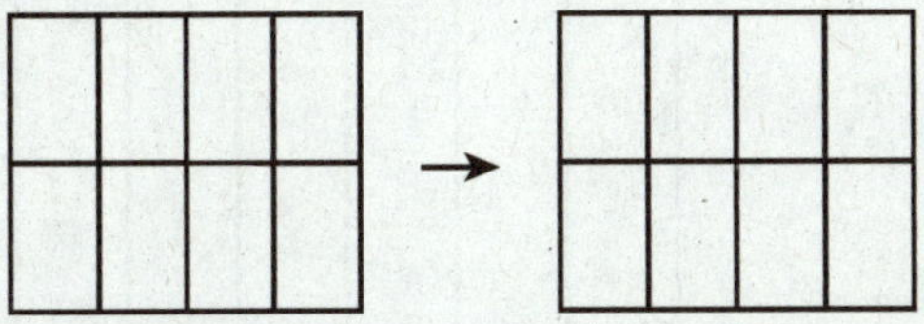

Divide a rectangle into 8 equal parts. → Shade 3 of the parts.

$1 = \frac{8}{8}$ ______ $\frac{3}{8}$ ______

8.

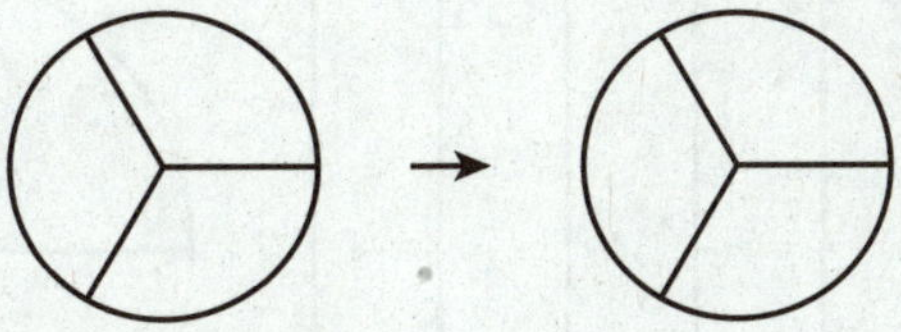

Divide a circle into 3 equal parts. → Shade 1 of the parts.

1 = ______ ______

9.

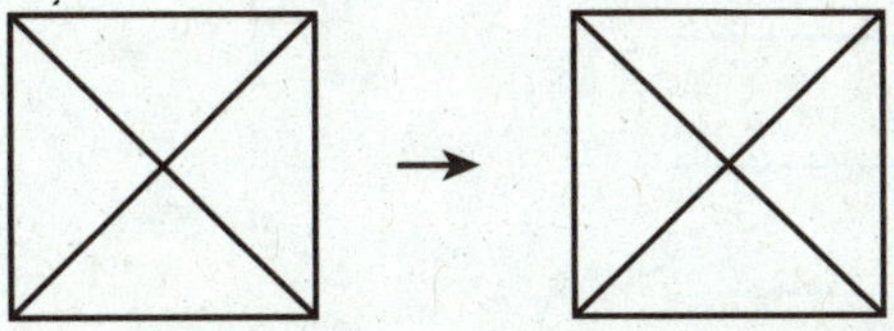

Divide a square into 4 equal parts. → Shade 3 of the parts.

1 = ______ ______

10.

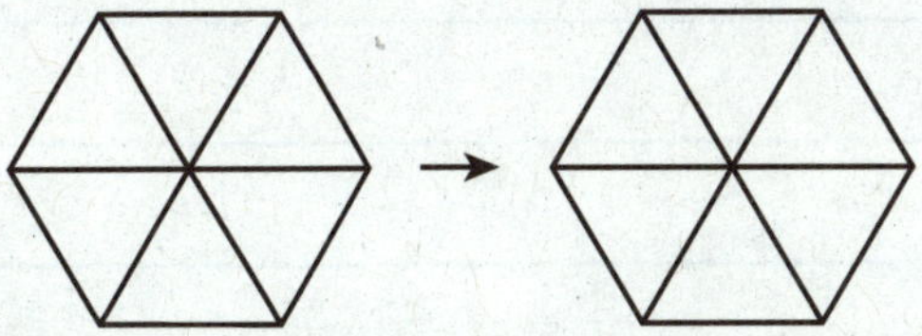

Divide a hexagon into 6 equal parts. → Shade 2 of the parts.

1 = ______ ______

11.

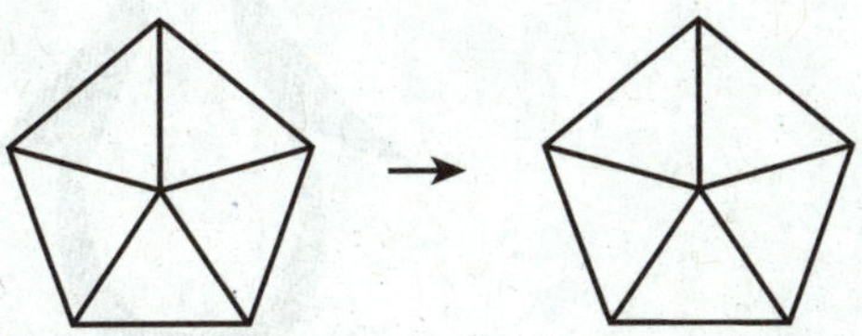

Divide a pentagon into 5 equal parts. → Shade 4 of the parts.

1 = ______ ______

12.

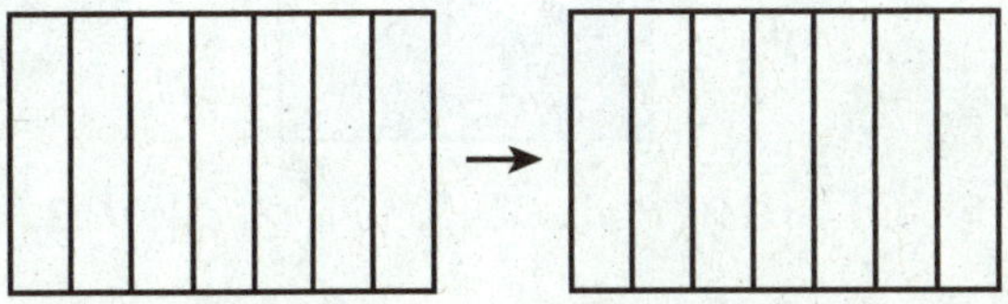

Divide a rectangle into 7 equal parts. → Shade 5 of the parts.

1 = ______ ______

11–1 Class Activity

Name ____________________ Date __________

Shade the given fraction of the whole.

13. $\frac{5}{6}$

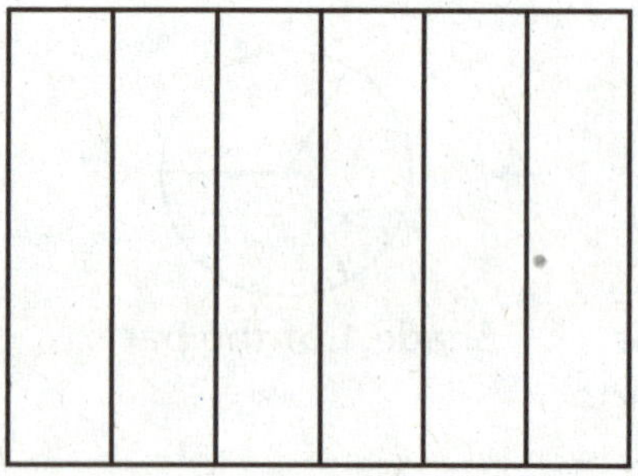

14. $\frac{2}{4}$

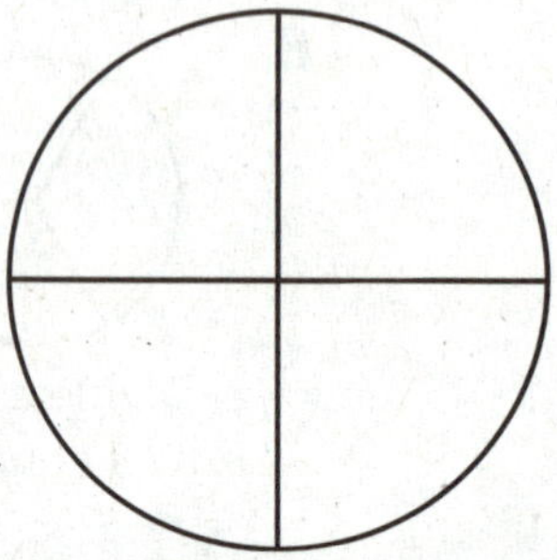

15. $\frac{3}{7}$

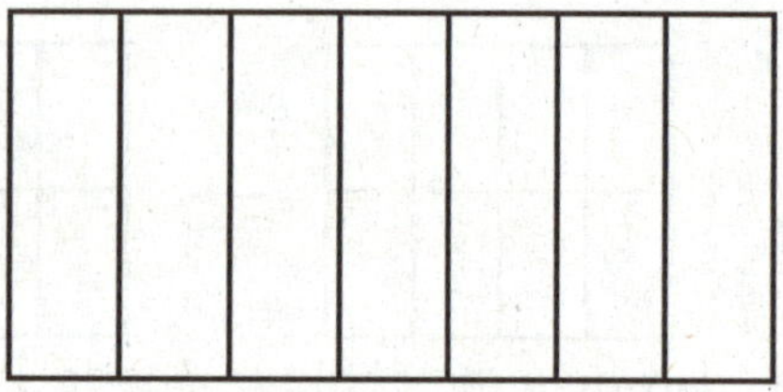

16. Suppose you shade one fourth of two different-size squares. Is one fourth of one square the same size as one fourth of the other square? Explain.

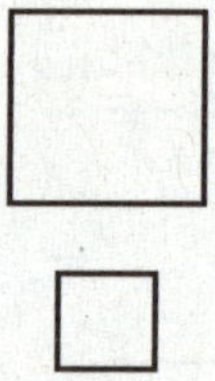

____

____

____

Dear Math Students:

Today my teacher asked us to shade a square to show $\frac{1}{3}$. Here is my drawing. Is my drawing right?

If not, make a correct drawing. Explain below.

Thank you,

The Puzzled Penguin

____

____

Family Letter

Dear Family,

In this unit, your child will be introduced to fractions. Students will build fractions from unit fractions and explore fractions as parts of a whole and parts of a set.

Unit Fraction

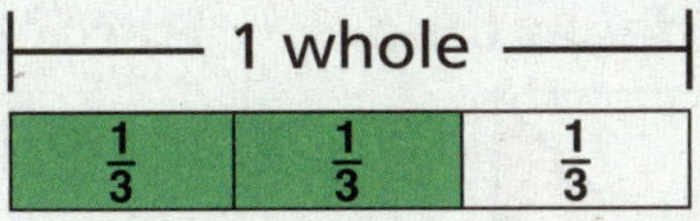

$$\frac{1}{3} + \frac{1}{3} = \frac{2}{3}$$

Fraction of a Whole

$3 \leftarrow$ numerator
$4 \leftarrow$ denominator

Fraction of a Set

$$\frac{1}{5}$$

Students will find a fraction of a number.

$\frac{2}{3}$ of 12 is 8

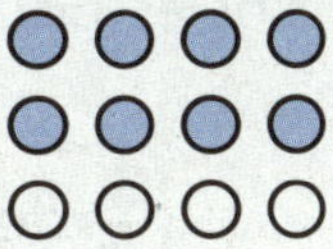

Students will also find equivalent fractions, and compare, add, and subtract fractions.

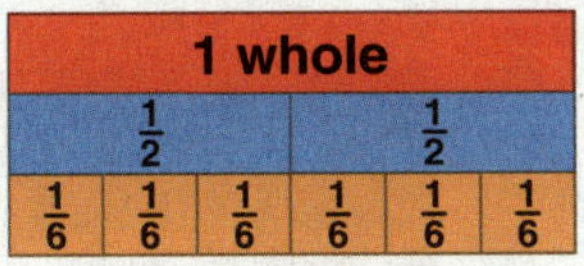

$$\frac{1}{2} = \frac{3}{6}$$

$$\frac{1}{2} > \frac{1}{6}$$

$$\frac{2}{8} + \frac{3}{8} = \frac{5}{8}$$

$$\frac{7}{8} - \frac{4}{8} = \frac{3}{8}$$

In this unit, your child will also be introduced to division with remainders.

$$8\overline{)75} \quad 9 \text{ R3}$$

Please call if you have any questions or comments.

Sincerely,
Your child's teacher

Carta a la familia

Estimada familia:

En esta unidad su niño conocerá las fracciones pro primera vez. Los estudiantes formarán fracciones a partir de fracciones cuyo numerador es uno y explorarán las fracciones como partes de un todo y partes de un conjunto.

Fracción cuyo numerador es uno

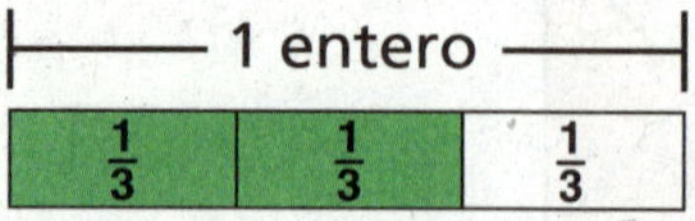

$\frac{1}{3} + \frac{1}{3} = \frac{2}{3}$

Fracción de un todo

$\frac{3}{4}$ ← numerador, ← denominador

Fracción de un conjunto

$\frac{1}{5}$

Los estudiantes hallarán una fracción de un número.

$\frac{2}{3}$ de 12 son 8

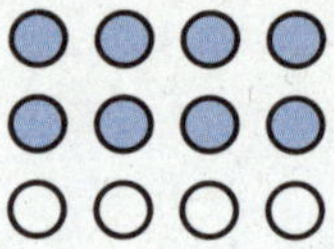

Los estudiantes también hallarán fracciones equivalentes y compararán, sumarán y restarán fracciones.

$\frac{1}{2} = \frac{3}{6}$

$\frac{1}{2} > \frac{1}{6}$

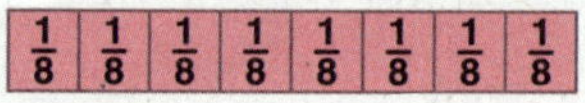

$\frac{2}{8} + \frac{3}{8} = \frac{5}{8}$

$\frac{7}{8} - \frac{4}{8} = \frac{3}{8}$

En esta unidad su niño también conocerá por primera vez la división con residuos.

$8\overline{)75}$ = 9 R3

Si tiene alguna duda o comentario, por favor comuníquese conmigo.

Atentamente,
El maestro de su niño

Name ______________________ Date ______________

▶ Review Building Fractions from Unit Fractions

Write an addition equation to represent the part of the whole that is shaded. Then show it as the product of a whole number and a unit fraction.

1. 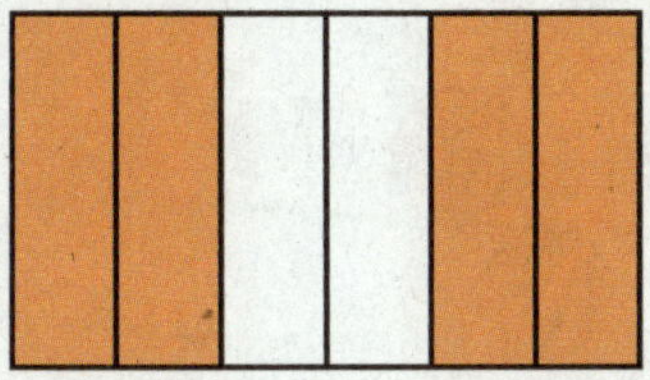

$\frac{1}{6} + \frac{1}{6} + \frac{1}{6} + \frac{1}{6} = \frac{4}{6}$

$4 \times \frac{1}{6} = \frac{4}{6}$

2. 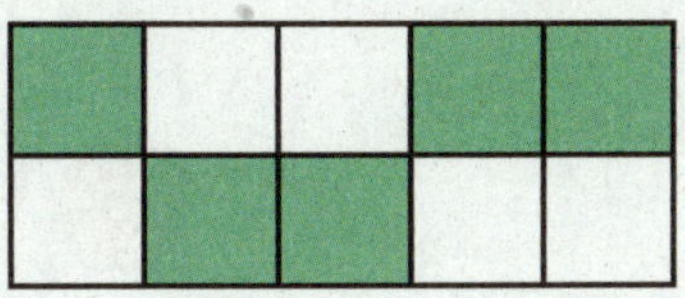

____

____

3. 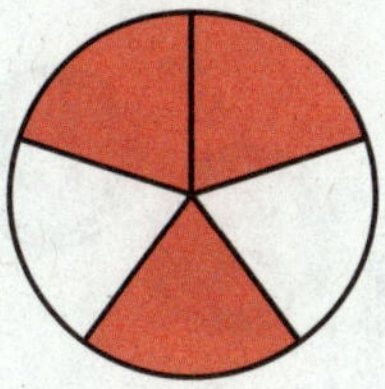

____

____

Shade the given fraction of the whole.

4. $\frac{4}{6}$ 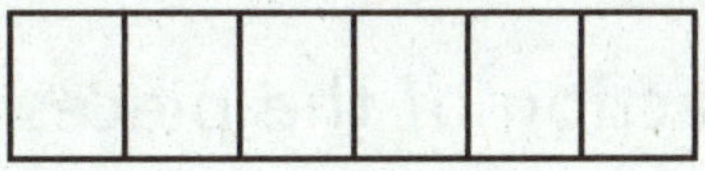

5. $\frac{1}{2}$ 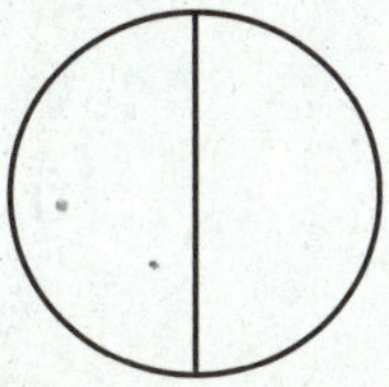

6. $\frac{6}{8}$ 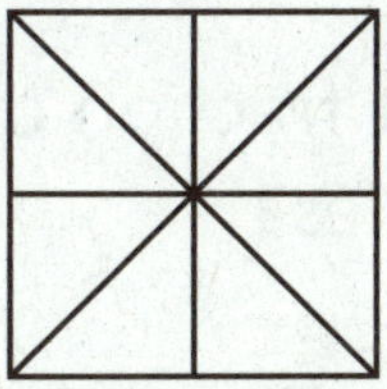

7. Complete the table.

In Words	$\frac{N}{D}$	Total and Product of Unit Fractions	Description	Drawing
two thirds			_____ parts out of _____ equal parts in a whole.	
			2 parts out of 10 equal parts in a whole.	
		$\frac{1}{8} + \frac{1}{8} + \frac{1}{8} + \frac{1}{8} + \frac{1}{8} = \frac{\square}{8}$, $5 \times \frac{1}{8} = \frac{\square}{8}$	_____ parts out of _____ equal parts in a whole.	
	$\frac{3}{7}$		_____ parts out of _____ equal parts in a whole.	
two sixths			_____ parts out of _____ equal parts in a whole.	

11–2 Class Activity

Name ______________________ Date ______________

▶ Fraction of a Set

Answer each question.

8. What fraction of the buttons are square?

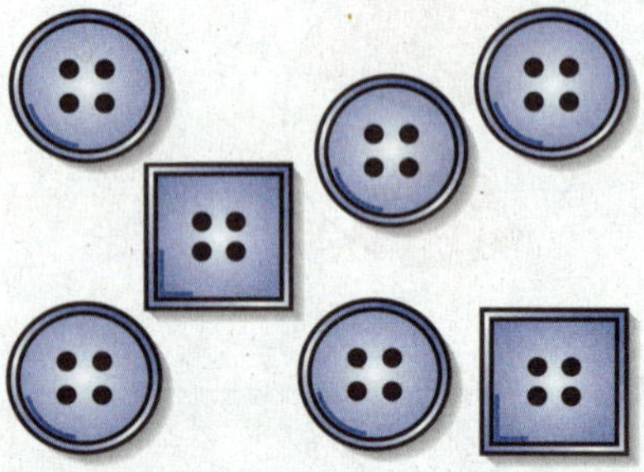

______

9. What fraction of the balls are soccer balls?

______

Give two answers to each question.

10. What fraction of the coins are pennies?

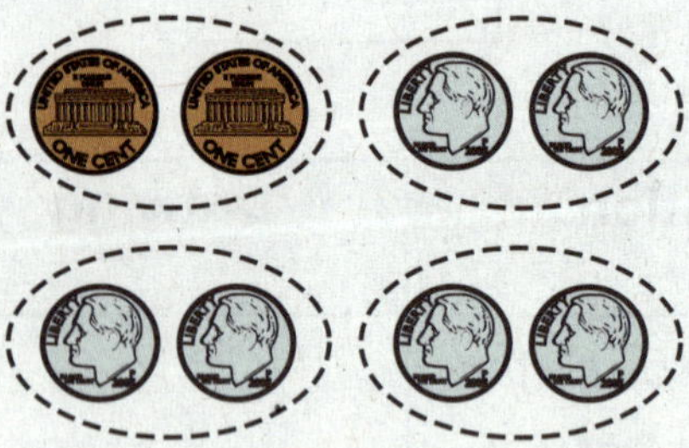

______ ______

11. What fraction of the pieces of fruit are pears?

______ ______

Shade the given fraction of each set.

12. $\frac{7}{11}$

13. $\frac{2}{9}$

14. $\frac{1}{5}$

11–3 Class Activity

Name ____________ Date ____________

► Solve Word Problems Involving Unit Fractions of Sets

Solve each problem.

Show your work.

1. One sixth of Kiera's cousins have red hair. Kiera has 12 cousins. How many cousins have red hair?

   ____

2. One third of the students on the bus are in the third grade. There are 15 students on the bus. How many students are in the third grade?

   ____

3. One half of Angel's crayons are sharp. Angel has 14 crayons. How many crayons are sharp?

   ____

4. One fourth of the roses in a bouquet are pink. There are 24 roses in the bouquet. How many roses are pink?

   ____

5. One tenth of the trees in the forest are oak trees. There are 90 trees in the forest. How many trees are oak trees?

   ____

6. There are 56 seals at the seashore. One eighth of the seals are swimming. How many seals are swimming?

   ____

Name ______________________ Date ____________

▶ Find a Unit Fraction of a Number

Use mental math to find the answer.

7. $\frac{1}{4} \times 8 =$ ________ **8.** $\frac{1}{2} \times 10 =$ ________ **9.** $\frac{1}{3}$ of $12 =$ ________

10. $\frac{1}{6} \times 18 =$ ________ **11.** $\frac{1}{5} \times 15 =$ ________ **12.** $\frac{1}{10}$ of $20 =$ ________

▶ Equivalent Equations

The three equations below all mean the same thing.

$\frac{1}{4}$ of $12 = 3$

$\frac{1}{4} \times 12 = 3$

$12 \div 4 = 3$

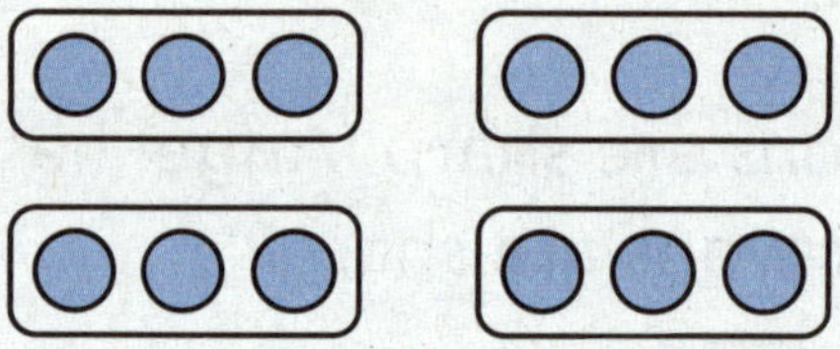

Write each equation in two other ways.

13. $\frac{1}{6}$ of $12 = 2$

____

____

14. $\frac{1}{4} \times 24 = 6$

____

____

15. $21 \div 7 = 3$

____

____

16. $\frac{1}{5}$ of $20 = 4$

____

____

17. $\frac{1}{2} \times 16 = 8$

____

____

18. $9 \div 3 = 3$

____

____

11–4 Class Activity

Name ____________________ Date ____________

▶ Use a Bar Graph to Compare

Use the bar graph below to complete exercises 1–4.

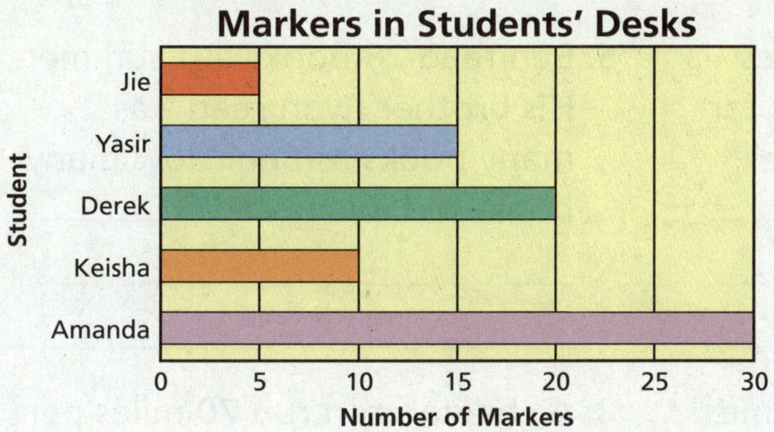

Fill in the blanks.

1. Jie has ____________________ as many markers as Yasir has.

Yasir has ____________________ as many markers as Jie has.

2. Derek has ____________________ as many markers as Jie has.

Jie has ____________________ as many markers as Derek has.

3. Derek has ____________________ as many markers as Keisha has.

Keisha has ____________________ as many markers as Derek has.

4. Amanda has ____________________ as many markers as Yasir has.

Yasir has ____________________ as many markers as Amanda has.

11–4 Class Activity

Name ____________________ Date ____________

▶Solve Comparison Word Problems

Solve each problem. Then write the other comparing sentence. The first one is done for you.

5. Carmen rides the train 7 miles to work. Joe rides 6 times as far as Carmen. How far does Joe ride the train? 42 miles

   Carmen rides $\frac{1}{6}$ as far as Joe.

6. Ben read 28 books last summer. His brother Ryan read $\frac{1}{7}$ as many books as Ben. How many books did Ryan read? ________

7. Kurt has 8 CDs. Julie has 4 times as many CDs as Kurt. How many CDs does Julie have? ________

8. A cheetah can run 70 miles per hour. A rabbit runs about $\frac{1}{2}$ as fast as a cheetah. How fast can a rabbit run? ________

9. The Knights won 36 basketball games last season. The Spartans won $\frac{1}{9}$ as many games. How many games did the Spartans win? ________

10. Raul's father weighs 180 pounds. Raul weighs $\frac{1}{3}$ as much as his father. How much does Raul weigh? ________

11. Lon has 9 books. Jerome has 6 times as many books as Lon has. How many books does Jerome have? ________

12. Barry's father is 48 years old. Barry is $\frac{1}{6}$ as old as his father. How old is Barry? ________

Name Date

▶ More Comparison Statements

Use the bar graph below for Exercises 1–5.

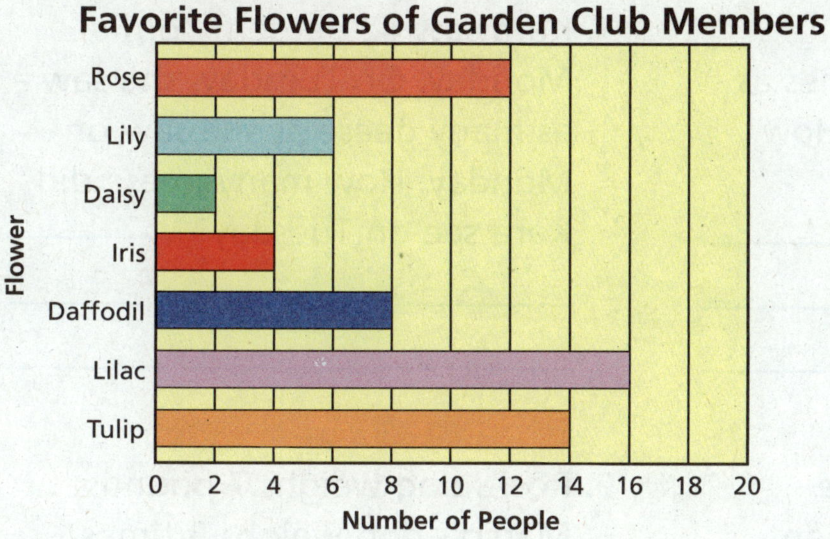

Fill in the blanks.

1. ____________ as many people like daffodils as like daisies.

   ____________ as many people like daisies as like daffodils.

2. ____________ as many people like lilacs as like daffodils.

   ____________ as many people like daffodils as like lilacs.

3. ____________ as many people like irises as like lilacs.

   ____________ as many people like lilacs as like irises.

4. ____________ as many people like lilies as like roses.

   ____________ as many people like roses as like lilies.

5. **Write Your Own** Write two comparison statements involving the number of people who like daisies.

   ____

   ____

11–5 Class Activity

Name ____________________ Date ____________

▶More Comparison Word Problems

Solve each problem. Then write the other comparing sentence.

6. Reyna caught 6 fish. Her grandfather caught 4 times as many fish as Reyna did. How many fish did Reyna's grandfather catch? ____________

____

____

7. Kara saw 42 geese fly on Monday. On Tuesday, she saw $\frac{1}{7}$ as many geese as she saw on Monday. How many geese did Kara see on Tuesday? ____________

____

____

8. There are 72 chairs in the lunchroom. In the basement, there are $\frac{1}{9}$ as many chairs as there are in the lunchroom. How many chairs are in the basement? ____________

____

____

9. Rosi's dog weighs 7 pounds. Marco's dog weighs 8 times as much as Rosi's dog. What is the weight of Marco's dog? ____________

____

____

____

10. Scott and his grandmother made a quilt. Scott's grandmother sewed 36 of the quilt squares. Scott sewed $\frac{1}{6}$ as many quilt squares as his grandmother. How many quilt squares did Scott sew? ____________

____

____

11. Juanita delivered 35 newspapers. Her younger brother delivered $\frac{1}{7}$ as many newspapers as Juanita did. How many newspapers did her brother deliver? ____________

____

____

____

11–6 Class Activity

Name ____________________ Date ____________

►Explore Fractional Parts of a Set

1. The Promo Company prints T-shirts for the rock band MathGrlzz. Complete the table to show how many shirts of each size and color they printed on Monday.

MathGrlzz Shirts Printed on Monday

	$\frac{1}{6}$ Yellow	$\frac{2}{6}$ Red	$\frac{3}{6}$ Blue
18 small shirts			
36 medium shirts			
54 large shirts			
48 extra large shirts			

2. The Promo Company also prints caps and hats for MathGrlzz. Complete the table to show how many caps or hats of each type and color they printed on Monday.

MathGrlzz Caps and Hats Printed on Monday

	$\frac{1}{7}$ Yellow	$\frac{4}{7}$ Red	$\frac{2}{7}$ Blue
49 baseball caps			
21 knit caps			
35 floppy hats			
14 straw hats			

11–6

Class Activity

Name ______ Date ______

► Solve Problems Involving a Fraction of a Set

Harry made 27 birds out of clay. He painted $\frac{4}{9}$ of the birds blue and the rest white.

Show your work.

3. How many birds did he paint blue? ______

4. How many birds did he paint white? ______

5. What fraction of the birds did he paint white?

______

6. Tameka wrote 24 word problems. Three eighths of the problems were subtraction problems. How many subtraction problems did Tameka write?

______

7. Marcel had 15 carrot sticks in his lunch. He gave $\frac{2}{5}$ of the carrot sticks to Joni. How many carrot sticks did Marcel give to Joni?

______

8. Karen baked 48 muffins. She gave $\frac{5}{8}$ of the muffins to her cousin. How many muffins did Karen give to her cousin?

______

9. There are 36 trees in a section of woods. Four ninths of the trees are oak trees. How many oak trees are there?

______

Name ____________________ Date ____________

▶ Write a Rule

10. Write a rule for finding a fraction of a set or a number.

____

____

____

____

____

____

▶ Use a Rule

Use your rule to find each amount.

11. $\frac{2}{4}$ of 12 ________

12. $\frac{2}{6}$ of 30 ________

13. $\frac{5}{7}$ of 35 ________

14. $\frac{2}{2} \times 16$ ________

15. $\frac{4}{6} \times 36$ ________

16. $\frac{5}{9}$ of 81 ________

17. $\frac{7}{8} \times 56$ ________

18. $\frac{2}{3} \times 30$ ________

19. $\frac{5}{6}$ of 18 ________

20. $\frac{3}{8}$ of 32 ________

21. $\frac{7}{10} \times 40$ ________

22. $\frac{3}{4}$ of 24 ________

Name ____________________ Date ____________________

Going Further

▶ Solve a Problem by Acting It Out

1. Olivia picked 28 daisies. She gave $\frac{5}{7}$ of the daisies to her aunt. Olivia kept the rest of the daisies. How many daisies did Olivia keep?

   ____

2. Cesar bought 16 baseball cards. He kept $\frac{5}{8}$ of the cards. He gave the rest of the cards to his friend. How many cards did Cesar give to his friend?

   ____

3. Pavel's father bought a box of 18 pencils. He gave $\frac{2}{9}$ of the pencils to Pavel and $\frac{2}{9}$ of the pencils to Pavel's sister Helena. How many pencils were left?

   ____

4. Akio had 21 stickers. He gave $\frac{3}{7}$ of the stickers to Rich and $\frac{1}{7}$ of the stickers to Imani. Akio kept the rest of the stickers. How many stickers did Akio keep?

   ____

5. Gianna had 25 postcards. She gave $\frac{1}{5}$ of the postcards to her sister. She gave $\frac{1}{4}$ of the remaining postcards to her brother. Gianna kept the rest of the postcards. How many postcards did she keep?

   ____

6. Mr. Redbird caught 32 fish. He gave $\frac{1}{4}$ of the fish to his brother. He kept $\frac{3}{4}$ of the remaining fish for his family. He gave the rest of the fish to his neighbor. How many fish did Mr. Redbird give to his neighbor?

   ____

Name Date

Vocabulary
circle graph

▶ Read a Circle Graph

Kari has 36 animals in her beanbag collection. This **circle graph** shows the fraction of the whole collection for each type of animal. For example, $\frac{1}{6}$ of the animals in her collection are rabbits.

Kari's Beanbag Animal Collection

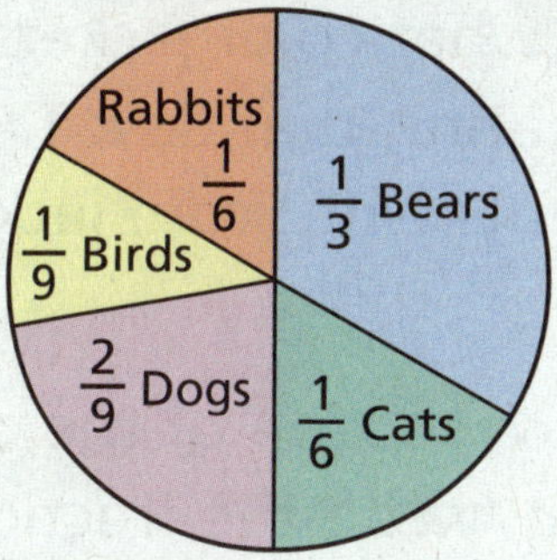

1. Complete the table.

Type of Animal	Fraction of Whole Collection	Number of Animals
Birds		
Rabbits		
Bears		
Cats		
Dogs		

Complete.

2. What type of beanbag animal does Kari have the most of?

____

3. What type of beanbag animal does Kari have the least of?

____

4. What fraction of the collection are the birds and dogs combined?

____

5. What fraction of the collection are the bears and cats combined?

____

11–7 Class Activity

Name ______ Date ______

▶Label and Use a Circle Graph

Ms. Timmer's class made a graph to show what color jackets students were wearing that day. There are 24 students who wore jackets.

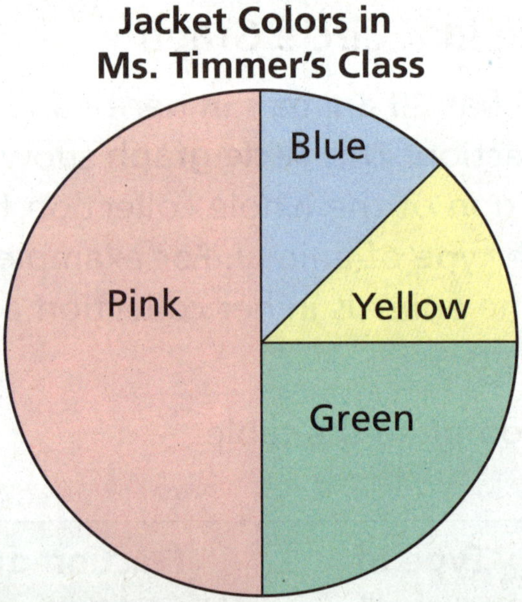

6. In each section of the circle graph, write the fraction for the color.

7. Complete the table.

Jacket Color	Fraction of All Students	Number of Students
Pink		
Blue		
Yellow		
Green		

Complete.

8. Which color jacket did most of the students wear?

______

9. What fraction of the class wore yellow or blue jackets?

______

10. How many more students wore green jackets than yellow jackets?

______

11. What fraction of the class wore blue, yellow, or green jackets?

______

11–8 Class Activity

Name ____ Date ____

Vocabulary
probability
likely
unlikely
certain
impossible
equally likely
event

▶ Use the Language of Probability

Probability describes how likely it is that something will happen. You can use words or a number from 0 to 1 to describe it.

Use the spinner at the right. Write the words *likely, unlikely, equally likely, impossible,* or *certain* to describe the likelihood of the event.

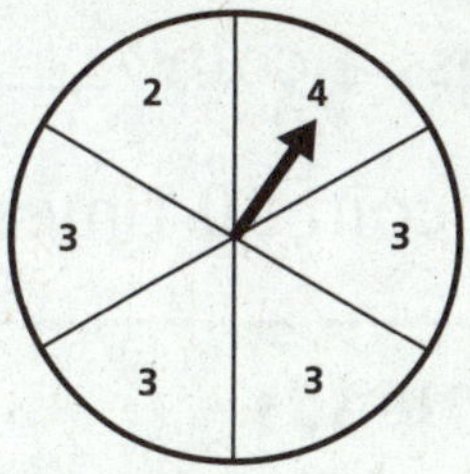

1. Spinning a 2 ____
2. Spinning a 3 ____
3. Spinning either a 2 or a 4 ____
4. Spinning a 5 ____
5. Spinning a number less than 5 ____

▶ Record Probability in Two Ways

Use the spinner above to write the probability of the event.

6. What is the probability of spinning a 3?

   ____ out of ____ or □/□

7. What is the probability of spinning a 2?

   ____ out of ____ or □/□

8. What is the probability of spinning a 4?

   ____ out of ____ or □/□

9. What is the probability of spinning a 1?

   ____

10. What is the probability of spinning a number less than 5?

    ____

11–8
Class Activity

Name ______________________ Date ______________________

▶ Conduct a Coin Toss Experiment

When you toss a coin, heads or tails are equally likely to land up. This means they have the same chance of occurring. Heads has a 1 out of 2 chance of happening. You can expect to get heads about half the time, or about 1 out of every 2 tosses.

11. What is the probability written as a fraction of heads landing up when you toss a coin? ______

12. Toss a coin 20 times and keep a tally.

Heads	Tails

13. How many tosses did you make? ______

14. I tossed heads ________ out of ________ tosses.

15. I tossed tails ________ out of ________ tosses.

16. Did you get heads for about $\frac{1}{2}$ of your tosses? ____________

17. **Explain** If the probability of getting heads is $\frac{1}{2}$, why do you think you and your partner may not have tossed heads half of the time?

____

____

18. Work with your teacher to combine the results for your class.
Class results: Heads: ________ Tails: ________
Did your class get heads closer to one half than you did in exercise 14?
____

11–8 Class Activity

Name ______________________ Date ______________

▶ Make and Test Predictions

Use the rectangles at the right to make predictions about a probability experiment.

19. Suppose you cut out the 10 rectangles, place them in a bag and pull a rectangle out of the bag without looking. Write the probability of pulling each color rectangle.

Blue Rectangle ______ out of ______ or ______

Yellow Rectangle ______ out of ______ or ______

20. Suppose you pull a rectangle out of the bag without looking 20 times. After each pull, you return the rectangle back into the bag. Predict which color rectangle you think you will pull out more times. Explain.

____

____

____

21. Cut out the 10 rectangles on page 416A or Activity Workbook page 189 and place them in a bag. Conduct the experiment described in exercise 20. Record the results in a tally chart.

22. Was your prediction correct? ____________________

23. If you conducted the experiment again, predict if the results will be exactly the same.

____

____

____

____

11–8 Class Activity

Name ______________________ Date ______________

▶ What's in the Bag?

Use the paper bag with the 10 coins (dimes and pennies) that another Student Pair prepared for you to conduct this experiment. Predict how many of each type of coin is in the bag.

Here's what to do:

Step 1: Without looking into the bag, pull a coin out and record the type of coin in the tally chart below.

Dimes	Pennies
Total:	Total:

Step 2: Return the coin to the bag.

Step 3: Take turns doing this until each of you has done this 20 times.

Step 4: Use the results to make a prediction of how many dimes and how many pennies are in your bag.

Dimes ________ Pennies ________

Step 5: Look into the bag and check your prediction.

Explain how you made your prediction.

____

____

____

____

Name _______________________ Date _____________

▶ Probability Experiments

Carefully cut out each rectangle along the dashed lines. Use the cut outs for probability experiments on Student Book pages 415 and 418.

NAVY

TAN

RED

BLACK

YELLOW

BLUE

11–8 Class Activity

Name ______________________ Date ______________

Vocabulary
outcome

▶ List Outcomes

An **outcome** is the result of an experiment.

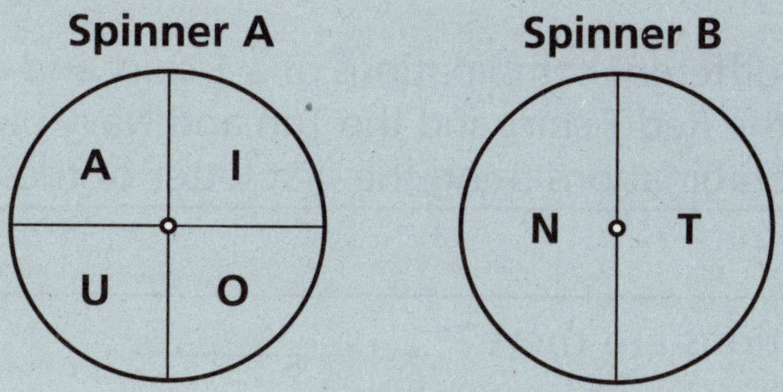

Complete.

1. Look at both spinners. Make an organized list of all the possible pairs of letters you could get if you spin Spinner A and then Spinner B.

2. How many pairs can you make? ______________

3. Cross off any pairs that don't make a two-letter word.

   How many two-letter words can you make? ______________

4. Is the probability of spinning a word more or less than half?

____

▶ Conduct a Spinner Experiment

5. Make the spinners from Spin a Word (TRB M161). Spin both spinners 10 times and record the pairs you spin.

6. How many words did you spin? ______________

7. Was this more or less than half of your spins? ______________________

____

11–8 Class Activity

Name ______________________ Date ______________

▶ Combinations

Use the T-shirts and shorts cutouts to complete this activity. Here's what to do:

Step 1: Make all the different combinations of a T-shirt and a pair of shorts using the Red T-shirt and the Tan and Navy pairs of shorts. Record the combinations using the first letter of the color of the item.

How many combinations are there? ______________

Step 2: Make all the different combinations of a T-shirt and a pair of shorts using the Red and Yellow T-shirts and the Tan and Navy pairs of shorts. Record the combinations using the first letter of the color of the item.

How many combinations are there? ______________

Step 3: Make all the different combinations of a T-shirt and a pair of shorts using the three T-shirts and the Tan and Navy pairs of shorts. Record the combinations using the first letter of the color of the item.

How many combinations are there? ______________

Step 4: Make all the different combinations of a T-Shirt and a pair of shorts using the three T-shirts and all three pairs of shorts. Record the combinations using the first letter of the color of the item.

How many combinations are there? ______________

What pattern do you see?

____

____

►Make Fraction Strips

11–9 Class Activity

Name ____________________ Date ________

Vocabulary
equivalent fractions

▶Halves, Fourths, Eighths, and Sixteenths

Two fractions are **equivalent fractions** if they name the same portion of a whole.

Use your halves, fourths, eighths, and sixteenths strips to answer questions 1–5.

1. If you put your halves strip over your fourths strip, you can see that 2 fourths are the same as 1 half.

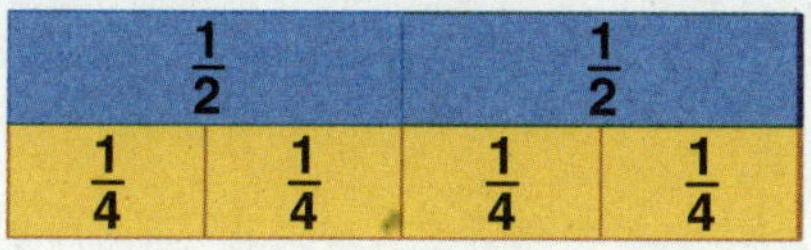

Complete these two equations:

__________ fourths = 1 half $\qquad \frac{\square}{4} = \frac{1}{2}$

2. How many eighths are in a half? __________

Complete these two equations:

__________ eighths = 1 half $\qquad \frac{\square}{8} = \frac{1}{2}$

3. How many sixteenths are in a half? __________

Complete these two equations:

__________ sixteenths = 1 half $\qquad \frac{\square}{16} = \frac{1}{2}$

4. How many eighths are in one fourth? __________

Complete these two equations:

__________ eighths = 1 fourth $\qquad \frac{\square}{8} = \frac{1}{4}$

5. How many sixteenths are in one fourth? __________

Complete these two equations:

__________ sixteenths = 1 fourth $\qquad \frac{\square}{16} = \frac{1}{4}$

Name ______________________ Date ______________

▶Thirds, Sixths, and Twelfths

Use your thirds, sixths, and twelfths strips to answer questions 6–9.

6. How many sixths are in one third? ______

Complete these two equations:

______ sixths = 1 third $\frac{\square}{6} = \frac{1}{3}$

7. How many twelfths are in one third? ______

Complete these two equations:

______ twelfths = 1 third $\frac{\square}{12} = \frac{1}{3}$

8. How many sixths are in two thirds? ______

Complete these two equations:

______ sixths = 2 thirds $\frac{\square}{6} = \frac{2}{3}$

9. How many twelfths are in two thirds? ______

Complete these two equations:

______ twelfths = 2 thirds $\frac{\square}{12} = \frac{2}{3}$

10. Use all your fraction strips to find 4 more pairs of equivalent fractions. Write an equation for each pair of equivalent fractions you find.

____

____

Name Date

►Play *Spinning a Whole*

Play *Spinning a Whole* with your partner. Write down anything interesting you discover while playing the game.

Rules for *Spinning a Whole*

Number of players: 2 or 3
What You Will Need: a Gameboard for Halves or Thirds and matching pair of spinners for each player, paper clip, ruler

1. On each turn, a player chooses and spins one of the two spinners.
2. Using the labeled fraction bars as a guide, the player marks and shades a section of the whole to represent the fraction the spinner landed on.
   - On a player's first turn, the player starts at the left end of the whole.
   - On other turns, the player starts at the right end of the last section shaded.
3. If a player spins a fraction greater than the unshaded portion of the whole, the player does not shade anything on his or her turn.
4. The first player to fill his or her whole bar completely and exactly wins.

Name ____________________ Date ____________________

Game Board for Halves

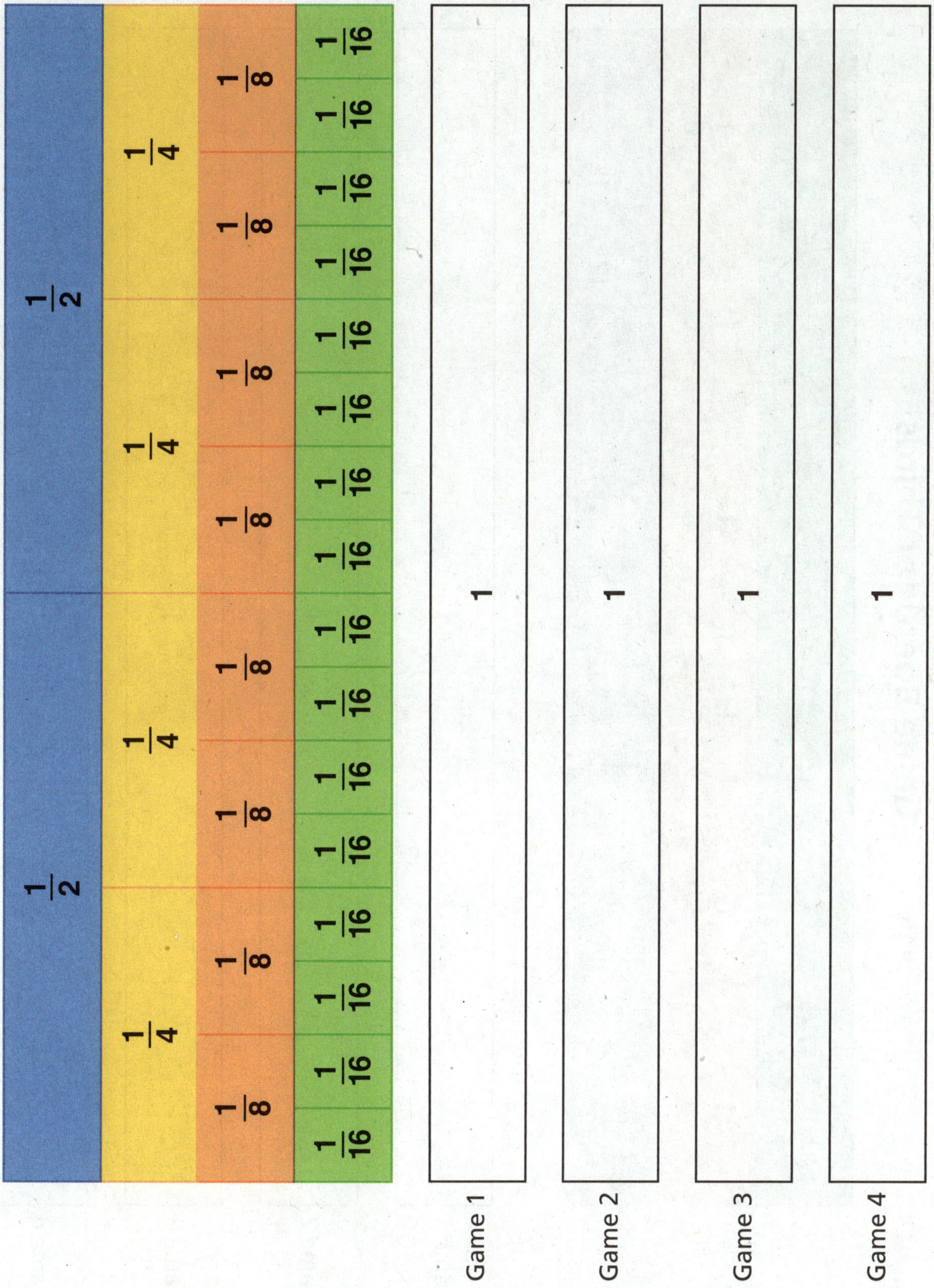

Name _______________________________ Date ______________________

Game Board for Thirds

$\frac{1}{3}$				$\frac{1}{3}$				$\frac{1}{3}$			
$\frac{1}{6}$		$\frac{1}{6}$		$\frac{1}{6}$		$\frac{1}{6}$		$\frac{1}{6}$		$\frac{1}{6}$	
$\frac{1}{12}$	$\frac{1}{12}$	$\frac{1}{12}$	$\frac{1}{12}$	$\frac{1}{12}$	$\frac{1}{12}$	$\frac{1}{12}$	$\frac{1}{12}$	$\frac{1}{12}$	$\frac{1}{12}$	$\frac{1}{12}$	$\frac{1}{12}$

Game 1	1
Game 2	1
Game 3	1
Game 4	1

Spinners for Halves

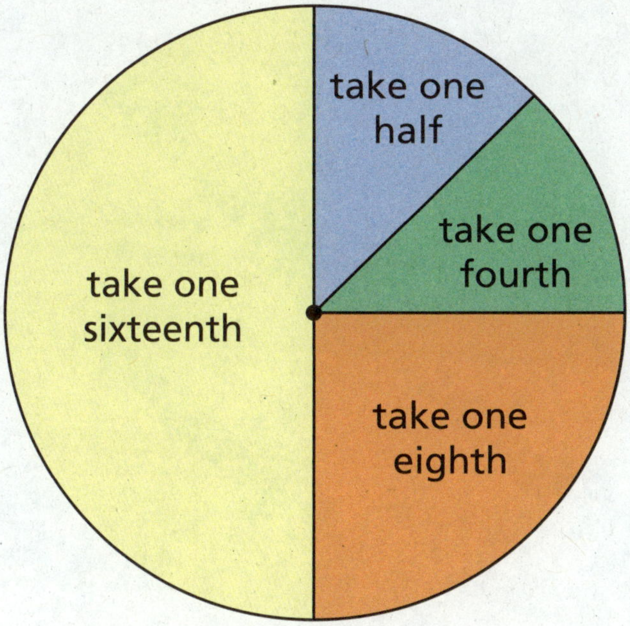

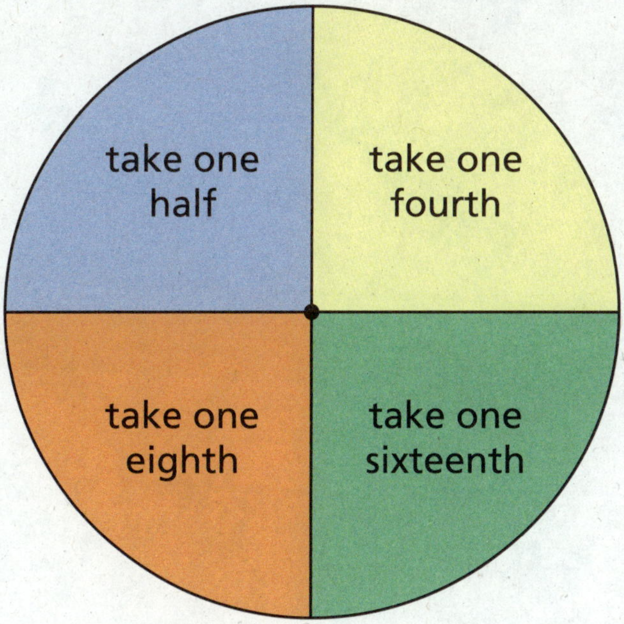

Spinners for Thirds

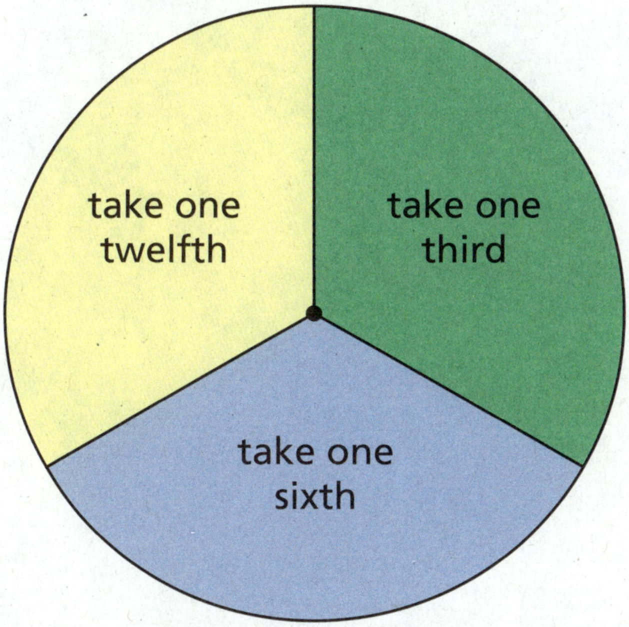

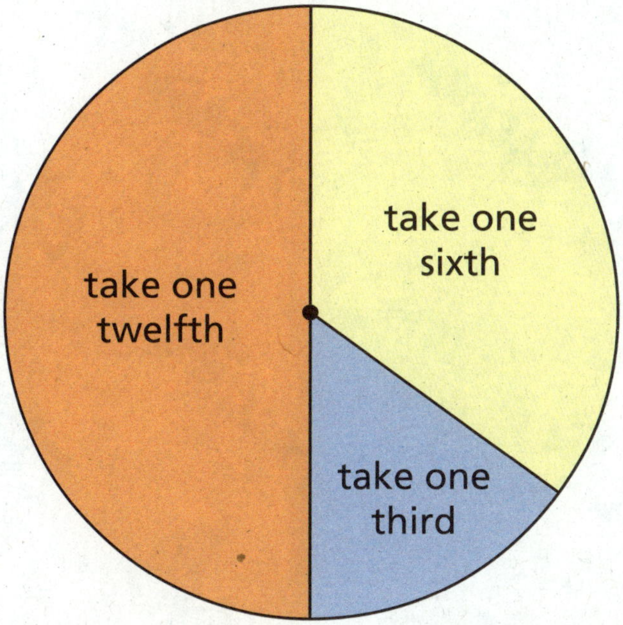

Multiplication Table Rows

1	2	3	4	5	6	7	8	9	10
2	4	6	8	10	12	14	16	18	20
3	6	9	12	15	18	21	24	27	30
4	8	12	16	20	24	28	32	36	40
5	10	15	20	25	30	35	40	45	50
6	12	18	24	30	36	42	48	54	60
7	14	21	28	35	42	49	56	63	70
8	16	24	32	40	48	56	64	72	80
9	18	27	36	45	54	63	72	81	90
10	20	30	40	50	60	70	80	90	100

Equivalent Fraction Box

× 1	× 2	× 3	× 4	× 5	× 6	× 7	× 8	× 9	× 10
___ =	___ =	___ =	___ =	___ =	___ =	___ =	___ =	___ =	___
× 1	× 2	× 3	× 4	× 5	× 6	× 7	× 8	× 9	× 10

Name ____________________ Date ____________

Vocabulary
equivalent

► Model Equivalence Chains

1. Show that $\frac{2}{7} = \frac{6}{21}$ by 3-fracturing each part of the second model.

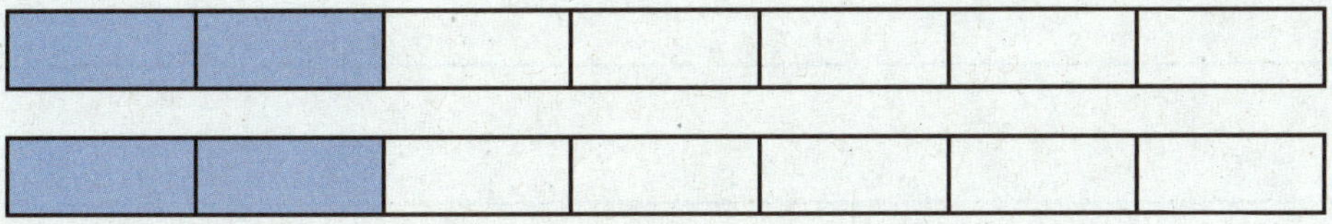

► Identify Equivalent Fractions

Write the multiplier in the box. Are the fractions equivalent? Write yes or no. If the fractions are equivalent, write the common multiplier.

2. $\frac{2}{7}$ $\times\square$ $\frac{6}{21}$ $\times\square$ ______

3. $\frac{1}{5}$ $\times\square$ $\frac{4}{25}$ $\times\square$ ______

4. $\frac{3}{4}$ $\times\square$ $\frac{6}{8}$ $\times\square$ ______

5. $\frac{5}{8}$ $\times\square$ $\frac{15}{24}$ $\times\square$ ______

6. $\frac{4}{9}$ $\times\square$ $\frac{40}{90}$ $\times\square$ ______

7. $\frac{7}{8}$ $\times\square$ $\frac{42}{56}$ $\times\square$ ______

► Make Equivalence Chains

Make an equivalence chain starting with the fraction given.

8. $\frac{1}{2} =$

9. $\frac{2}{3} =$

10. **On the Back** Explain the meaning of equivalent fractions. Draw a picture to help explain.

11–12 Class Activity

Name ______________________________ Date ____________

▶ Fracturing a Fraction

Equivalent fractions show the same amount, but they are divided into a different unit fraction. Fracturing a fraction gives us an equivalent fraction with more unit fractions, but the unit fractions are smaller.

Complete to write the equivalent fractions shown on the fraction strips.

Fewer but larger unit fractions — More but smaller unit fractions

5-fracture each third

1. 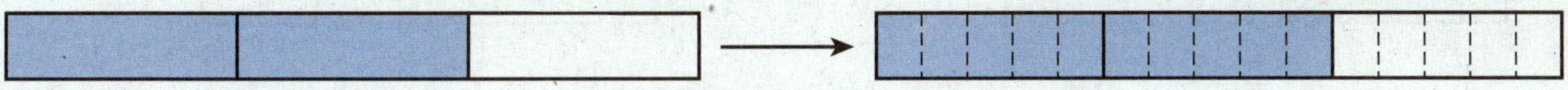

$$\frac{2}{3} = \frac{2 \times 5}{3 \times 5} = \frac{\square}{\square}$$

3-fracture each fourth

2. 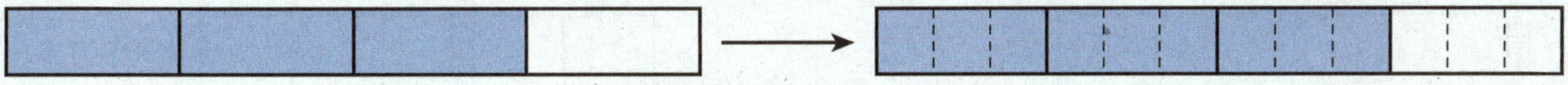

$$\frac{\square}{\square} = \frac{\square \times 3}{\square \times 3} = \frac{\square}{\square}$$

7-fracture each half

3. 

$$\frac{\square}{\square} = \frac{\square \times 7}{\square \times 7} = \frac{\square}{\square}$$

2-fracture each sixth

4. 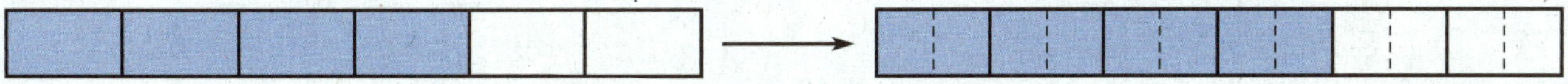

$$\frac{\square}{\square} = \frac{\square \times 2}{\square \times 2} = \frac{\square}{\square}$$

3-fracture each eighth

5. 

$$\frac{\square}{\square} = \frac{\square \times 3}{\square \times 3} = \frac{\square}{\square}$$

Name ____________________ Date ____________

▶Show that Fractions are Equivalent

Shade the fraction strips to show that each pair of fractions is equivalent. Then fill in the missing multipliers in the answer boxes.

6. $\frac{1}{2}$ and $\frac{5}{10}$

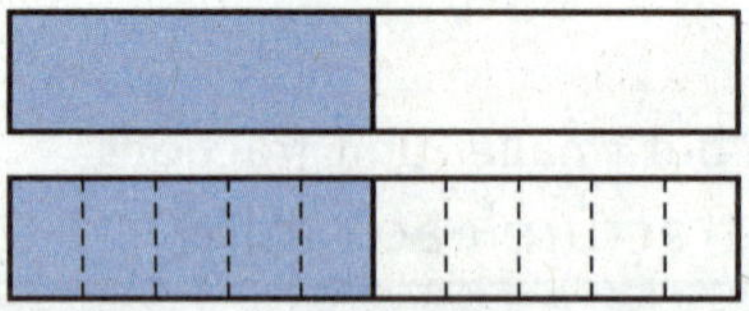

$$\frac{1}{2} = \frac{1 \times \boxed{5}}{2 \times \boxed{5}} = \frac{5}{10}$$

7. $\frac{1}{4}$ and $\frac{2}{8}$

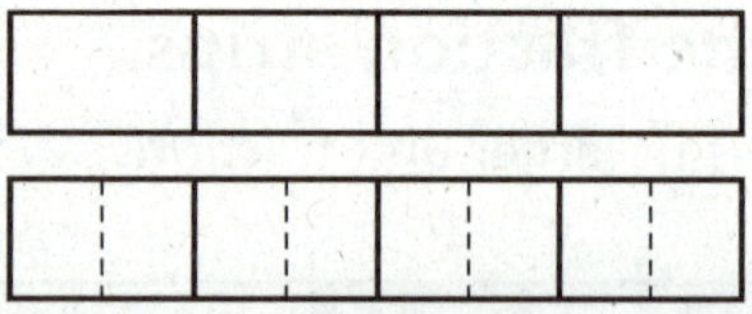

$$\frac{1}{4} = \frac{1 \times \square}{4 \times \square} = \frac{2}{8}$$

8. $\frac{2}{3}$ and $\frac{6}{9}$

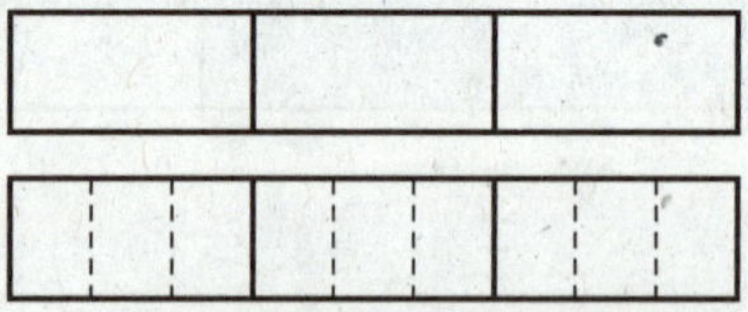

$$\frac{2}{3} = \frac{2 \times \square}{3 \times \square} = \frac{6}{9}$$

9. $\frac{3}{5}$ and $\frac{6}{10}$

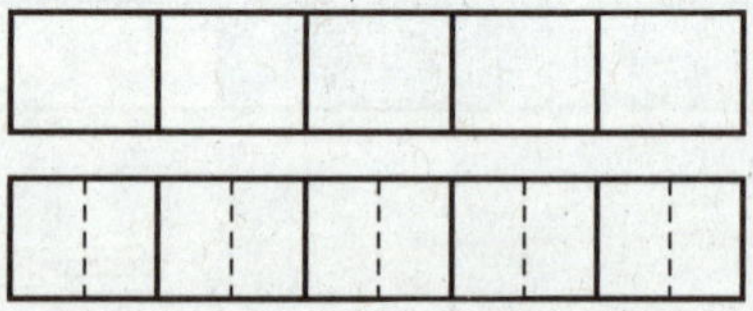

$$\frac{3}{5} = \frac{3 \times \square}{5 \times \square} = \frac{6}{10}$$

Complete to show that the fractions are equivalent.

10. $\frac{5}{8}$ and $\frac{15}{24}$

$$\frac{5}{8} = \frac{5 \times \square}{8 \times \square} = \frac{15}{24}$$

11. $\frac{4}{9}$ and $\frac{28}{63}$

$$\frac{4}{9} = \frac{4 \times \square}{9 \times \square} = \frac{28}{63}$$

Find the missing numbers.

12. $\frac{3}{8} = \frac{3 \times \square}{8 \times \square} = \frac{9}{\square}$

13. $\frac{2}{5} = \frac{2 \times \square}{5 \times \square} = \frac{\square}{40}$

14. $\frac{5}{9} = \frac{5 \times \square}{9 \times \square} = \frac{35}{\square}$

15. $\frac{4}{7} = \frac{4 \times \square}{7 \times \square} = \frac{\square}{35}$

16. $\frac{5}{6} = \frac{5 \times \square}{6 \times \square} = \frac{25}{\square}$

17. $\frac{3}{4} = \frac{3 \times \square}{4 \times \square} = \frac{24}{\square}$

11–13 **Class Activity**

Name ____________________ Date ____________

Vocabulary
simplify

► Simplify Fractions with Fraction Strips

Fracturing a fraction gives us an equivalent fraction with more unit fractions. **Simplifying** a fraction is just the opposite. It gives us an equivalent fraction with fewer unit fractions.

Write the simplified fraction shown on the second fraction strip.

4-group the twelfths to make thirds

1.

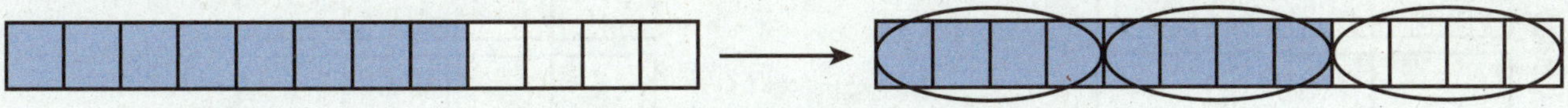

$$\frac{8}{12} = \frac{8 \div 4}{12 \div 4} = \frac{\square}{\square}$$

2-group the tenths to make fifths

2.

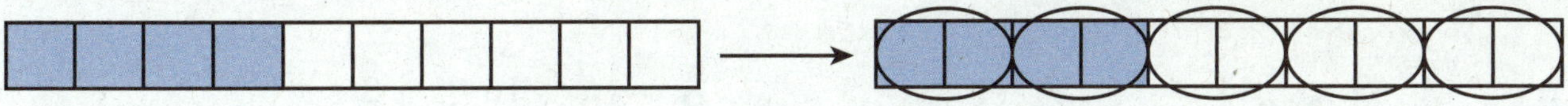

$$\frac{4}{10} = \frac{4 \div 2}{10 \div 2} = \frac{\square}{\square}$$

8-group the sixteenths to make halves

3.

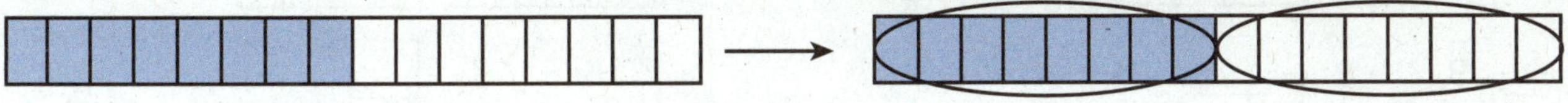

$$\frac{8}{16} = \frac{8 \div 8}{16 \div 8} = \frac{\square}{\square}$$

6-group the eighteenths to make thirds

4.

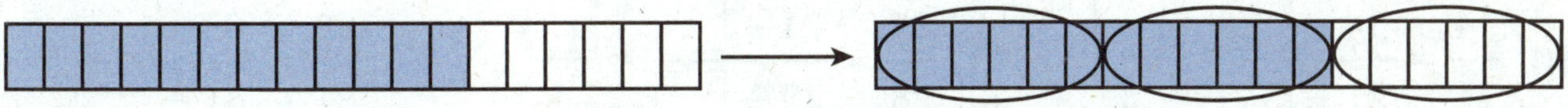

$$\frac{12}{18} = \frac{12 \div 6}{18 \div 6} = \frac{\square}{\square}$$

5-group the twenty-fifths to make fifths

5.

$$\frac{15}{25} = \frac{15 \div 5}{25 \div 5} = \frac{\square}{\square}$$

11–13 Class Activity

Name ____________________ Date ____________

▶ Simplify Fractions

Shade the fraction strips to show that the fractions are equivalent. Group the top unit fractions to make the bottom unit fractions. Then fill in the missing divisors.

6. $\frac{14}{21}$ and $\frac{2}{3}$

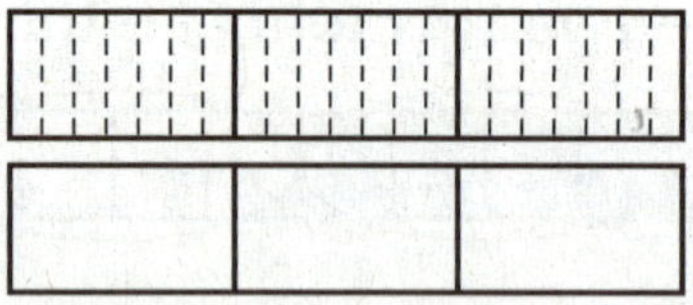

$$\frac{14}{21} = \frac{14 \div \boxed{7}}{21 \div \boxed{7}} = \frac{2}{3}$$

7. $\frac{12}{16}$ and $\frac{3}{4}$

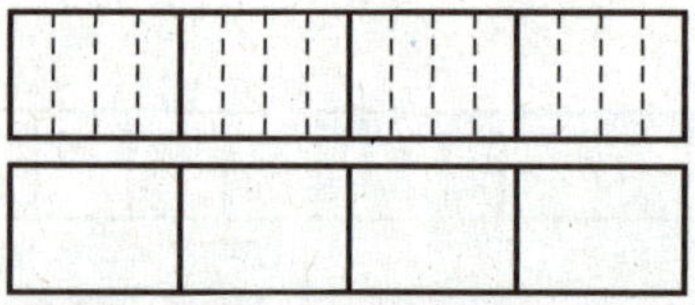

$$\frac{12}{16} = \frac{12 \div \square}{16 \div \square} = \frac{3}{4}$$

8. $\frac{9}{15}$ and $\frac{3}{5}$

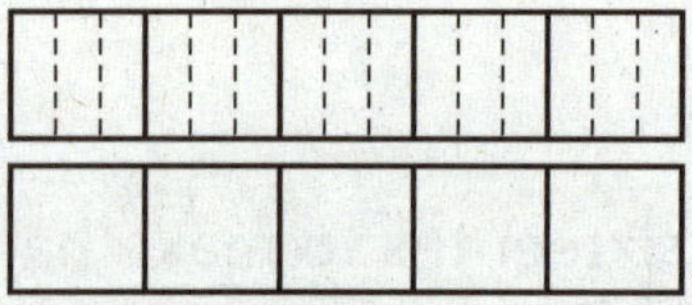

$$\frac{9}{15} = \frac{9 \div \square}{15 \div \square} = \frac{3}{5}$$

9. $\frac{16}{18}$ and $\frac{8}{9}$

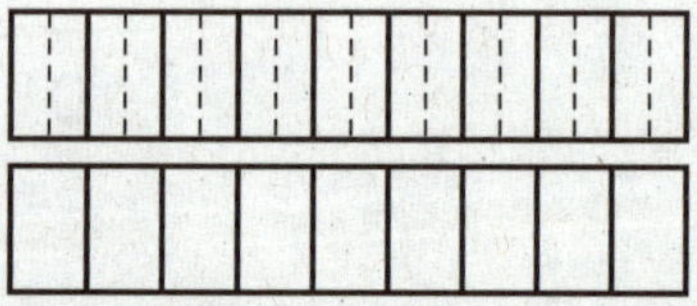

$$\frac{16}{18} = \frac{16 \div \square}{18 \div \square} = \frac{8}{9}$$

Simplify the fraction.

10. $\frac{14}{21} = \frac{14 \div \square}{21 \div \square} = \frac{\square}{3}$

11. $\frac{21}{28} = \frac{21 \div \square}{28 \div \square} = \frac{\square}{4}$

12. $\frac{63}{81} = \frac{63 \div \square}{81 \div \square} = \frac{7}{\square}$

13. $\frac{16}{18} = \frac{16 \div \square}{18 \div \square} = \frac{8}{\square}$

14. $\frac{30}{42} = \frac{30 \div \square}{42 \div \square} = \frac{\square}{7}$

15. $\frac{20}{24} = \frac{20 \div \square}{24 \div \square} = \frac{5}{\square}$

16. $\frac{10}{20} = \frac{10 \div \square}{20 \div \square} = \frac{1}{\square}$

17. $\frac{20}{25} = \frac{20 \div \square}{25 \div \square} = \frac{\square}{5}$

18. $\frac{27}{36} = \frac{27 \div \square}{36 \div \square} = \frac{3}{\square}$

Name Date

▶ Use Fraction Strips to Add

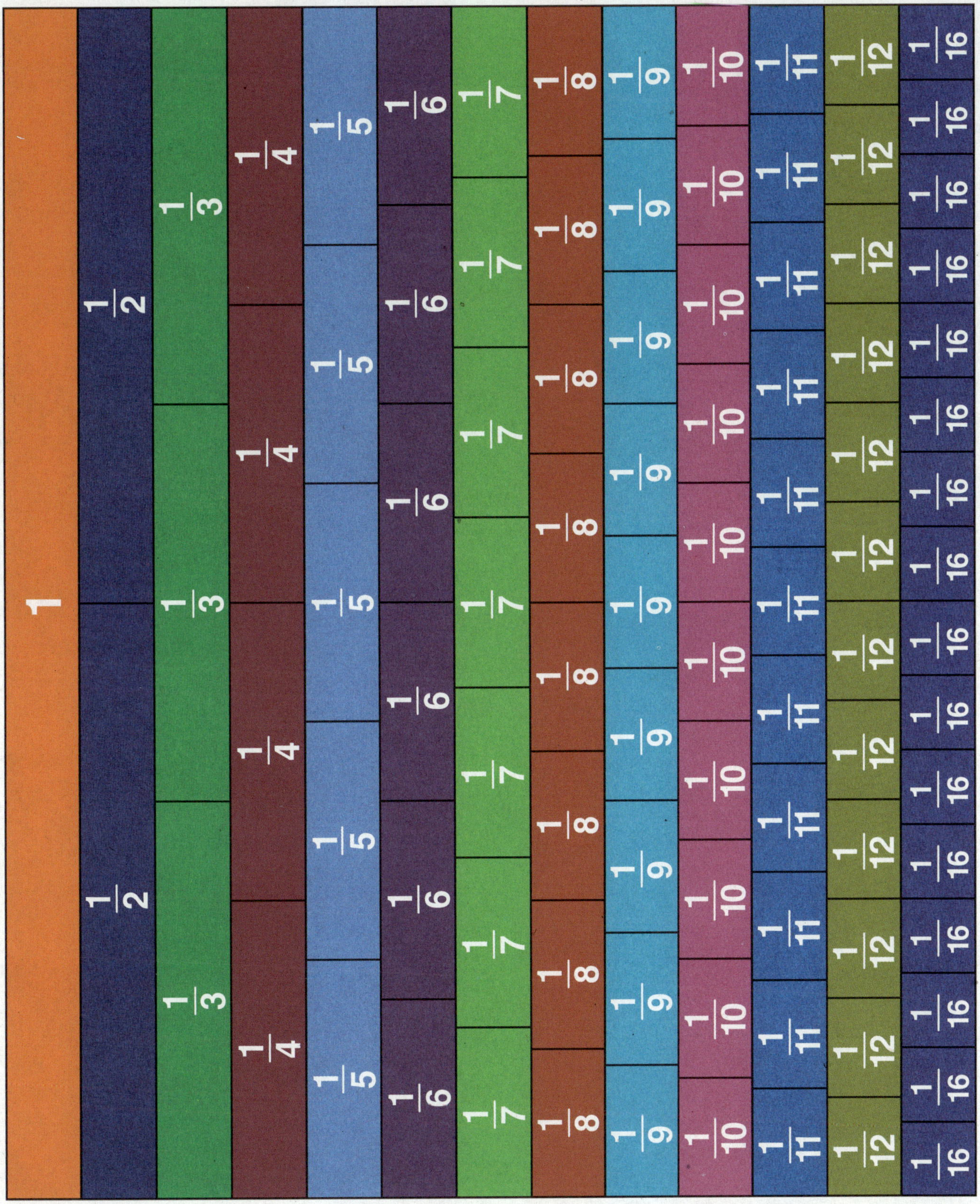

11–14 Class Activity

Name ____________________ Date ____________

▶ Add Fractions Using Fraction Strips

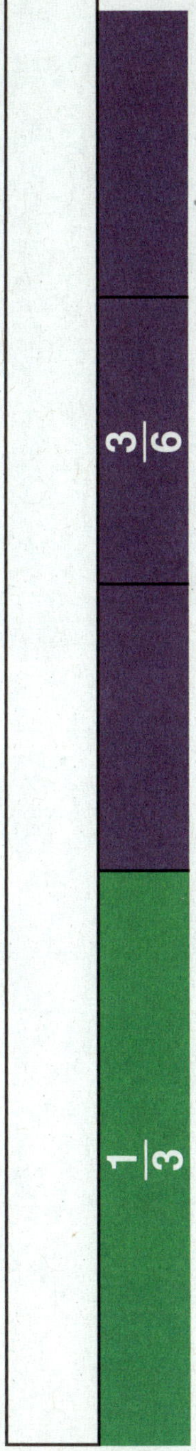

$\frac{1}{3} + \frac{3}{6} = \frac{2}{6} + \frac{3}{6} = \frac{5}{6}$

2 sixths + 3 sixths = 5 sixths

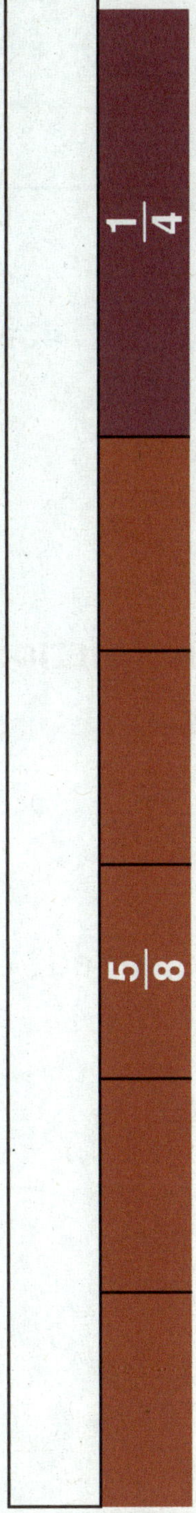

$\frac{5}{8} + \frac{1}{4} = \frac{5}{8} + \frac{2}{8} = \frac{7}{8}$

5 eighths + 2 eighths = 7 eighths

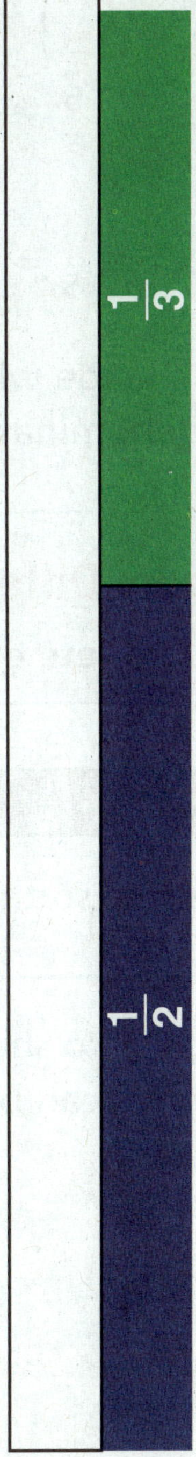

$\frac{1}{2} + \frac{1}{3} = \frac{3}{6} + \frac{2}{6} = \frac{5}{6}$

3 sixths + 2 sixths = 5 sixths

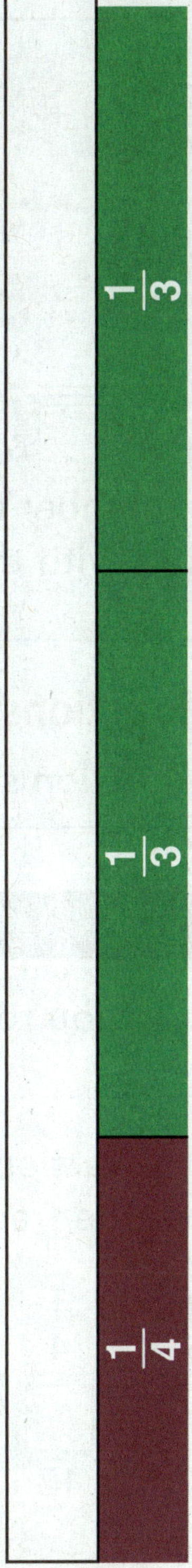

$\frac{1}{4} + \frac{2}{3} = \frac{3}{12} + \frac{8}{12} = \frac{11}{12}$

3 twelfths + 8 twelfths = 11 twelfths

Name ______________________ Date ______________

► Add Fractions Made from the Same Unit Fraction

Circle the fractions on the strip. Then add.

1. 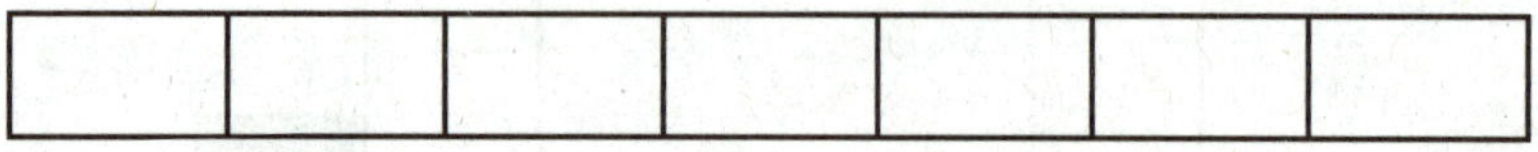

$\frac{2}{7} + \frac{4}{7} = \frac{\square}{\square}$

2 sevenths + 4 sevenths = 6 ______________

Complete.

2. $\frac{3}{6} + \frac{2}{6} = \frac{\square}{\square}$

3. $\frac{1}{5} + \frac{3}{5} = \frac{\square}{\square}$

4. $\frac{3}{8} + \frac{2}{8} = \frac{\square}{\square}$

5. Which number does not change when you add fractions with the same denominator? Why?

____

► Add Fractions Made from Different Unit Fractions

Use the fraction strips to complete exercises 6–8.

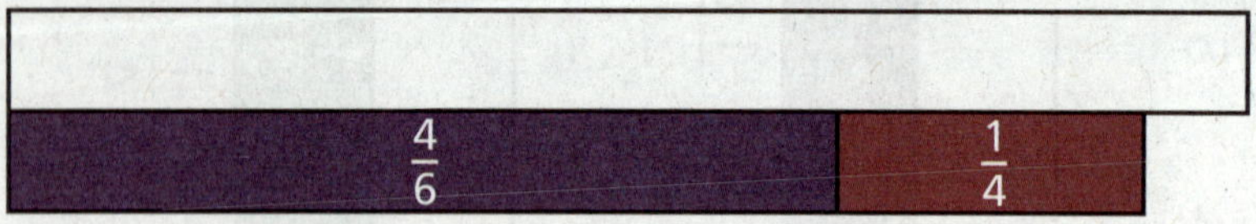

6. How can you rename $\frac{4}{6}$ and $\frac{1}{4}$ so they can be added?

____

7. Use the fraction strips above to show how to rename the fractions so they can be added.

8. $\frac{4}{6} + \frac{1}{4}$

$\frac{\square}{12} + \frac{\square}{12} = \frac{\square}{12}$

8 twelfths + 3 twelfths = $\square$ ______________

11–14 **Class Activity**

Name ______________________ Date ____________

Add. Use the fraction strips to help you.

9. $\frac{3}{7} + \frac{2}{7} =$ ______

10. $\frac{3}{9} + \frac{5}{9} =$ ______

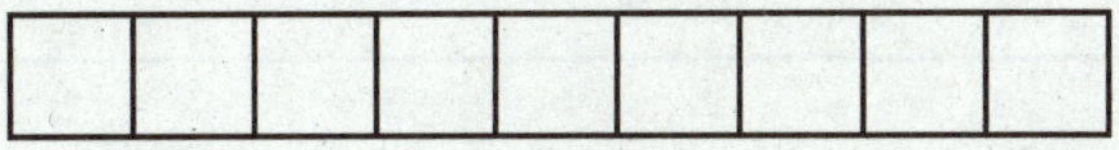

11. $\frac{6}{11} + \frac{2}{11} =$ ______

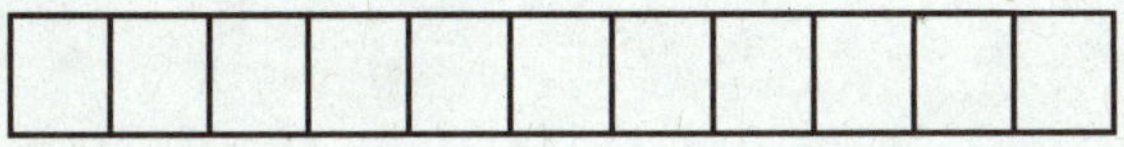

12. $\frac{4}{12} + \frac{7}{12} =$ ______

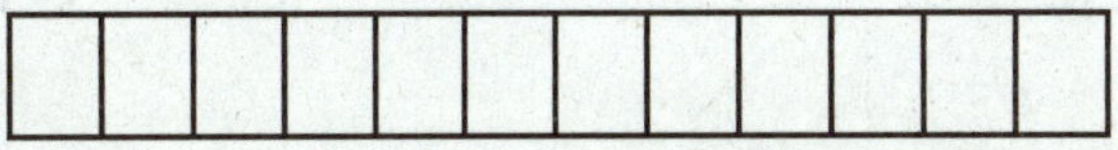

13. $\frac{2}{3} + \frac{2}{9} =$ ______

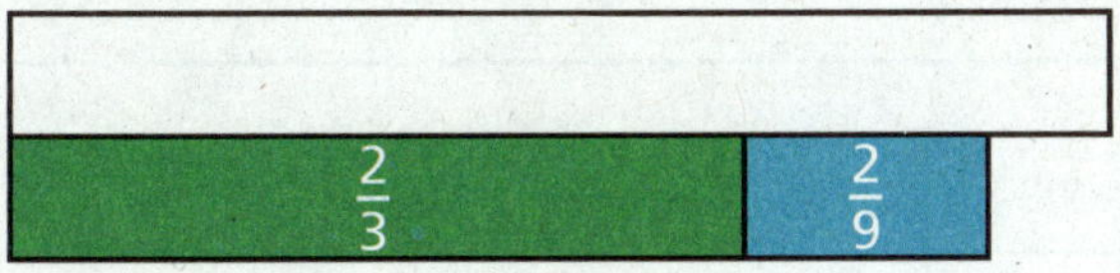

14. $\frac{5}{8} + \frac{3}{16} =$ ______

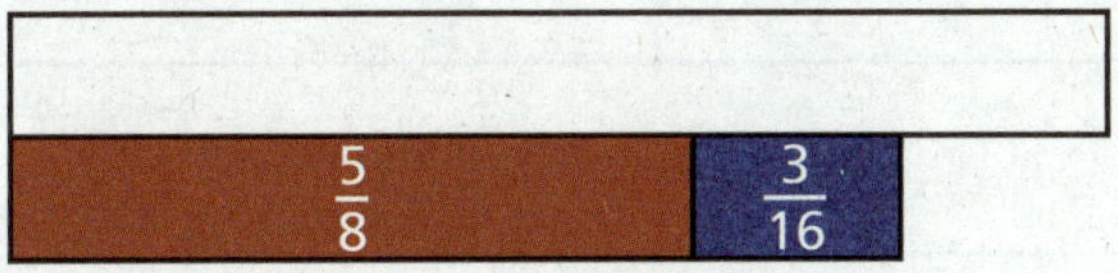

15. $\frac{3}{4} + \frac{3}{12} =$ ______

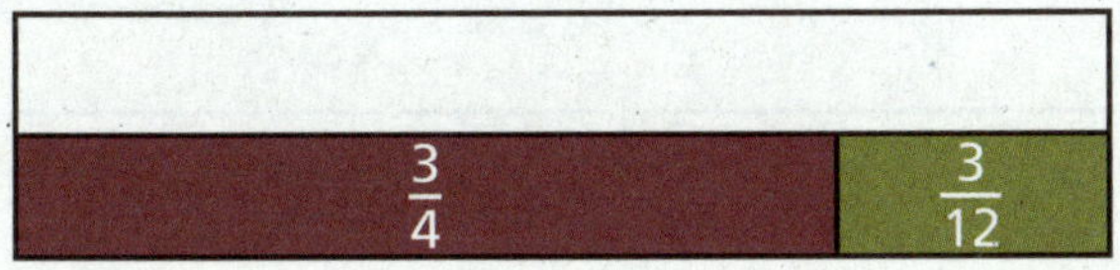

16. $\frac{2}{3} + \frac{1}{5} =$ ______

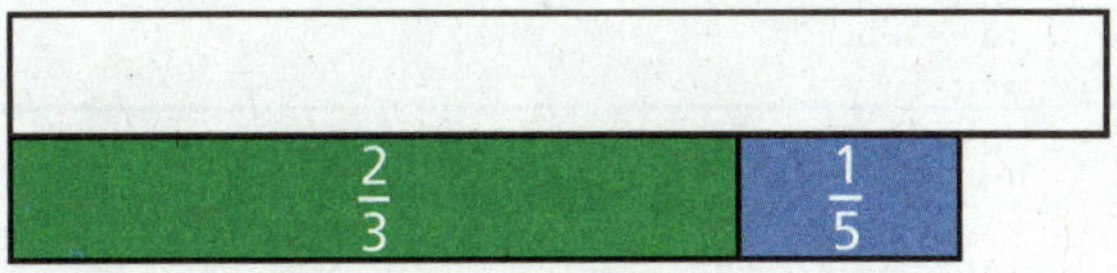

17. $\frac{1}{4} + \frac{1}{6} =$ ______

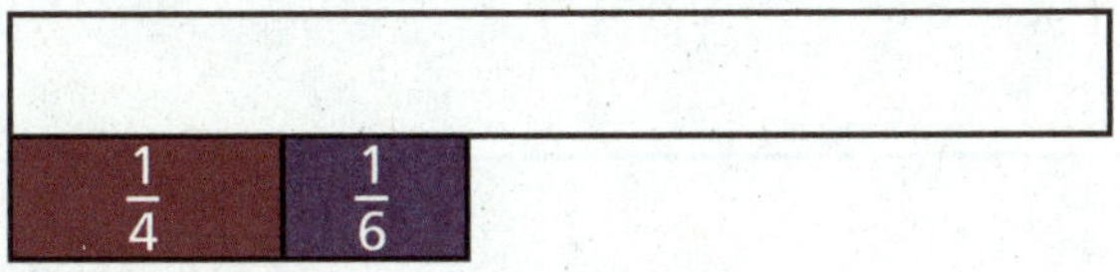

18. $\frac{3}{6} + \frac{1}{4} =$ ______

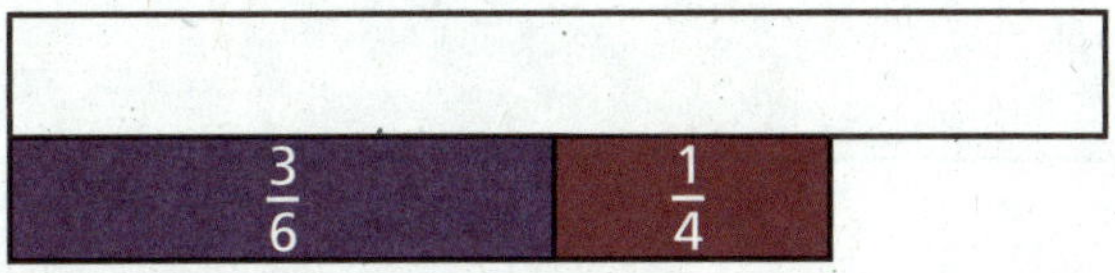

19. $\frac{1}{2} + \frac{2}{5} =$ ______

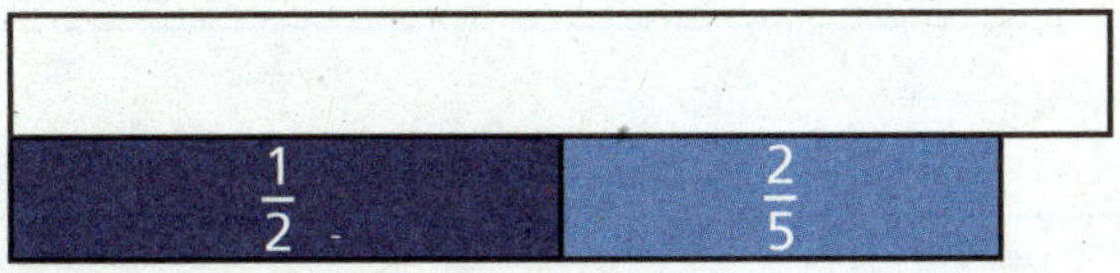

20. $\frac{1}{3} + \frac{2}{4} =$ ______

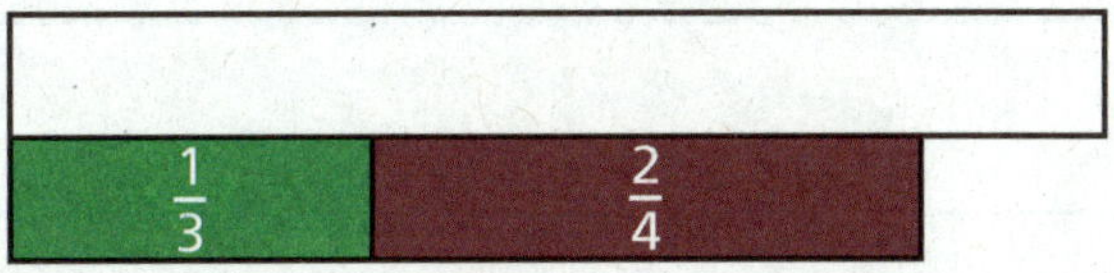

21. On the Back Explain how you found the answer to exercise 18.

Name Date

11–15 Class Activity

Name ____________________ Date ____________

▶ Subtract Fractions Made from the Same Unit Fraction

Circle $\frac{6}{7}$ of the fraction strip. Then subtract $\frac{4}{7}$.

1. 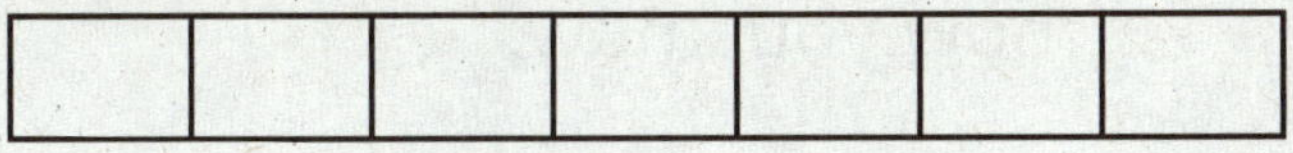

$\frac{6}{7} - \frac{4}{7} = \frac{\square}{\square}$

6 sevenths − 4 sevenths = ____________

Complete.

2. $\frac{5}{8} - \frac{2}{8} =$ ______

3. $\frac{9}{10} - \frac{5}{10} =$ ______

4. $\frac{11}{12} - \frac{7}{12} =$ ______

5. Which number does not change when you subtract fractions with the same denominator?

____

▶ Subtract Fractions Made from Different Unit Fractions

Use the fraction strip to complete exercises 6–8.

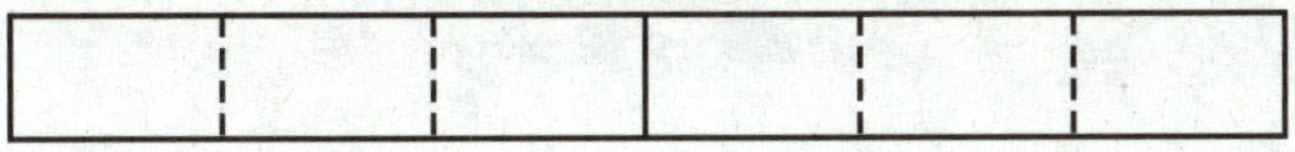

Find $\frac{1}{2} - \frac{1}{6}$.

6. How can you rename $\frac{1}{2}$ so $\frac{1}{6}$ can be subtracted?

____

7. Use the fraction strip above to show how to rename $\frac{1}{2}$ so that $\frac{1}{6}$ can be subtracted.

8. $\frac{1}{2} - \frac{1}{6}$

$\frac{\square}{6} - \frac{1}{6} = \frac{\square}{\square}$

☐ sixths − one sixth = ____________

9. Show $\frac{3}{4} - \frac{3}{8}$ on the fraction strip to the right.

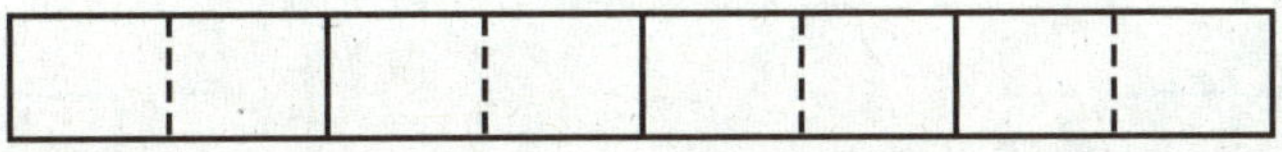

Name ______________________ Date ______________

▶ Compare Fractions

10. Which is greater, $\frac{3}{6}$ or $\frac{2}{6}$? Explain how you know.

11. Which is greater, $\frac{1}{3}$ or $\frac{1}{4}$? Explain how you know.

12. Which is greater, $\frac{2}{3}$ or $\frac{2}{4}$? Explain how you know.

Compare these fractions. Write >, <, or = in the ◯.

13. $\frac{1}{5}$ ◯ $\frac{1}{4}$

14. $\frac{1}{2}$ ◯ $\frac{1}{4}$

15. $\frac{4}{8}$ ◯ $\frac{2}{8}$

16. $\frac{4}{7}$ ◯ $\frac{4}{9}$

17. $\frac{3}{12}$ ◯ $\frac{3}{11}$

18. $\frac{4}{10}$ ◯ $\frac{4}{5}$

19. $\frac{6}{8}$ ◯ $\frac{7}{8}$

20. $\frac{5}{5}$ ◯ $\frac{6}{6}$

21. $\frac{7}{8}$ ◯ $\frac{7}{9}$

Use fraction strips to compare these fractions. Write >, <, or = in the ◯.

22. $\frac{4}{6}$ ◯ $\frac{1}{3}$

23. $\frac{2}{7}$ ◯ $\frac{1}{6}$

24. $\frac{9}{10}$ ◯ $\frac{4}{5}$

25. $\frac{1}{2}$ ◯ $\frac{5}{8}$

26. $\frac{5}{6}$ ◯ $\frac{9}{12}$

27. $\frac{5}{9}$ ◯ $\frac{2}{3}$

Write the fractions in order from least to greatest.

28. $\frac{1}{2}$, $\frac{1}{4}$, $\frac{1}{3}$

29. $\frac{3}{5}$, $\frac{2}{5}$, $\frac{4}{5}$

11–15 Class Activity

Name ____________________ Date ____________

►Add, Compare, and Subtract Fractions

Add, compare, and subtract each pair of fractions.

Add	Compare	Subtract
30. $\frac{3}{8} + \frac{5}{8} =$ ____	$\frac{3}{8}$ ◯ $\frac{5}{8}$	
31. $\frac{1}{4} + \frac{1}{3} =$ ____	$\frac{1}{4}$ ◯ $\frac{1}{3}$	
32. $\frac{1}{3} + \frac{1}{2} =$ ____	$\frac{1}{3}$ ◯ $\frac{1}{2}$	
33. $\frac{5}{6} + \frac{1}{3}$ ____	$\frac{5}{6}$ ◯ $\frac{1}{3}$	
34. $\frac{1}{2} + \frac{2}{4} =$ ____	$\frac{1}{2}$ ◯ $\frac{2}{4}$	

Name ______ Date ______

▶ Fractions in Word Problems

Solve.

Show your work.

35. Layton ate $\frac{1}{6}$ of the cake. Kyra ate $\frac{3}{6}$ of the cake. Who ate more cake? How much more?

______

36. Jorie ate $\frac{5}{6}$ of her popsicle. Nat ate $\frac{3}{4}$ of his popsicle. Who ate more? How much more?

______

37. One fourth of the cars in the parking lot are red. Three eighths of the cars are blue. Are there more red cars or more blue cars?

______

38. The red squirrel ate $\frac{2}{3}$ of the acorns. The gray squirrel ate $\frac{1}{4}$ of the acorns. What fraction of the acorns did they eat altogether?

______

39. Camille has two cats, Cole and Nicky. Every day, Cole eats $\frac{1}{3}$ of a can of food. Nicky eats $\frac{4}{6}$ of a can of food. How much of the can do the two cats eat together?

______

40. Oakton School and Pine School use the same amount of paper. Oakton recycles $\frac{3}{4}$ of its paper. Pine recycles $\frac{2}{4}$ of its paper. How much more of its paper does Oakton recycle than Pine recycles?

______

11–16 Class Activity

Name ______________________ Date ______________

▶ Identify and Locate Whole Numbers on a Number Line

You can use points already on a number line to locate and label other points. Locate the points for the numbers 150 and 375 on the number line and label them.

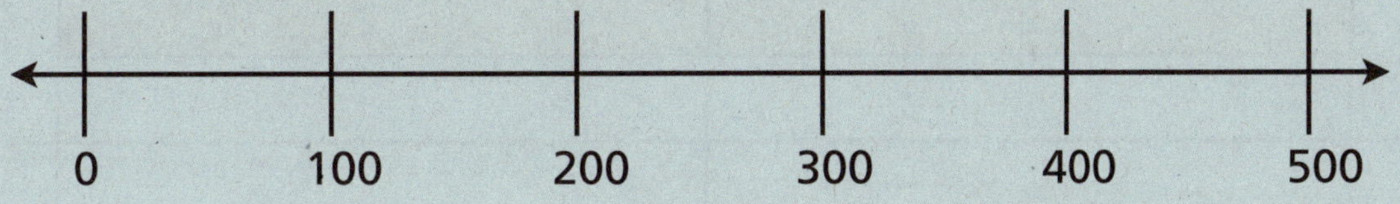

Locate the points for the numbers and label them.

1. 35, 18, 45, 90, 75

2. 90, 225, 425, 275, 380

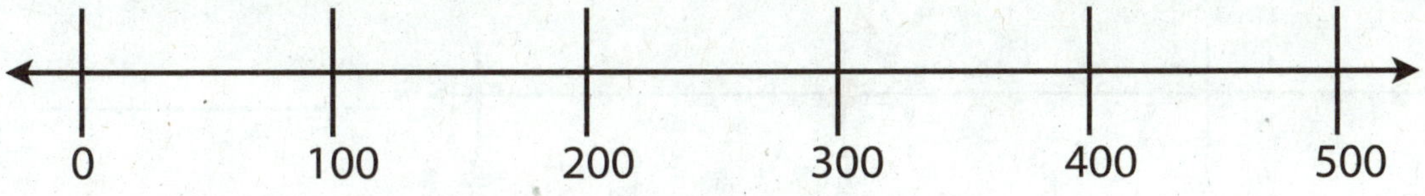

▶ Find the Distance Between Two Points

Locate the points for the numbers on the number line and label them. Then use the number line to find the distance between the two points.

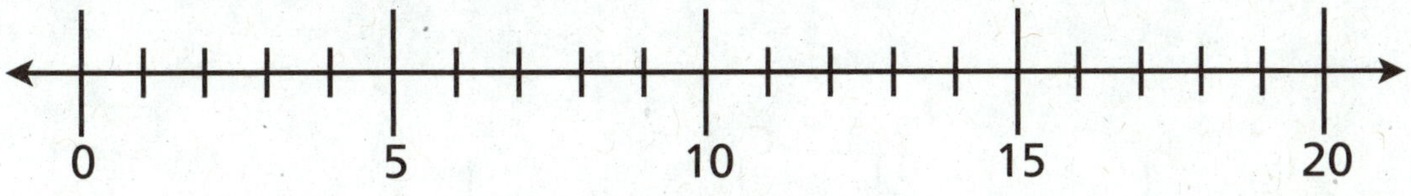

3. 17 and 8 __________
4. 15 and 7 __________
5. 12 and 8 __________
6. 11 and 4 __________
7. 14 and 9 __________
8. 20 and 10 __________

Name ______________________ Date ______________

▶Identify and Locate Fractions on a Number Line

The number lines and fraction bars below show the halves and fourths between 0 and 1.

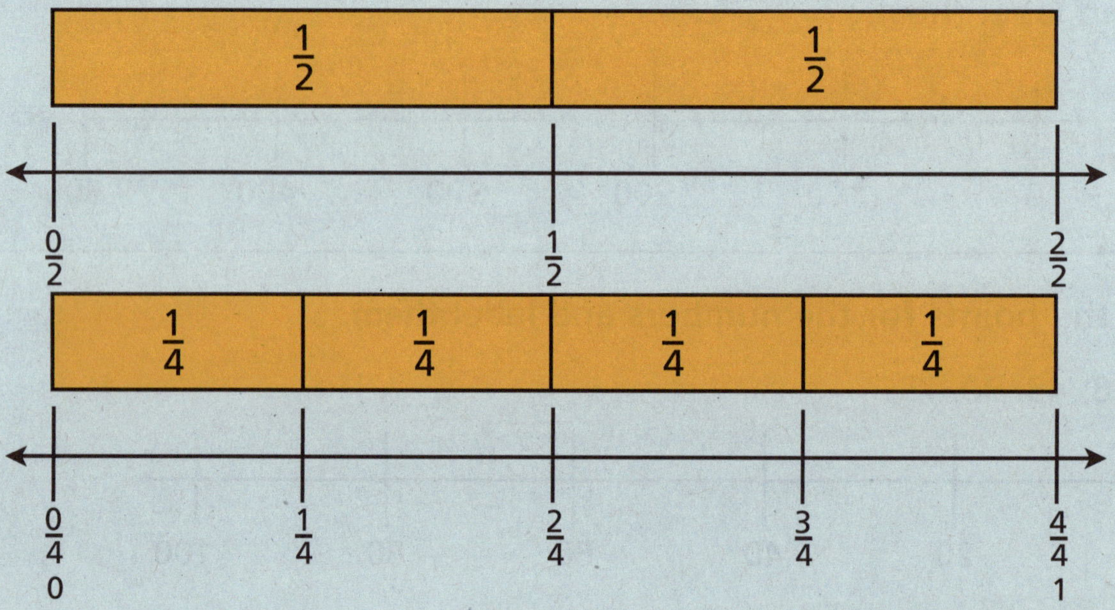

Write the fraction or whole number and fraction for each lettered point.

9. 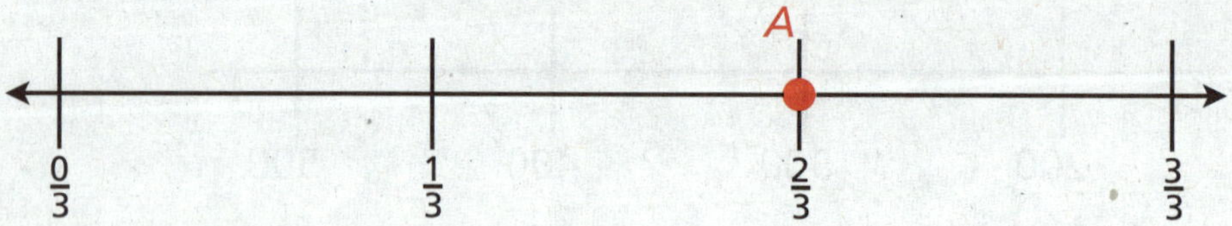

____

10. 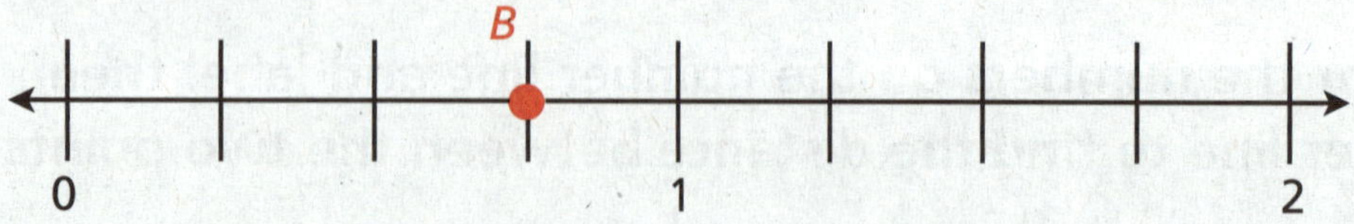

____

11. 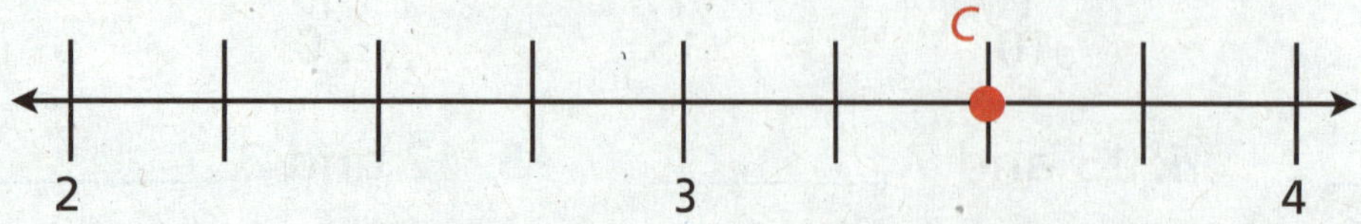

____

11–16 Class Activity

Name ____________________ Date ____________

► Compare Fractions on a Number Line

Circle the lengths to show each fraction. Then compare them. Write <, >, or = in the ◯.

1. $\frac{3}{6}$ ◯ $\frac{5}{6}$

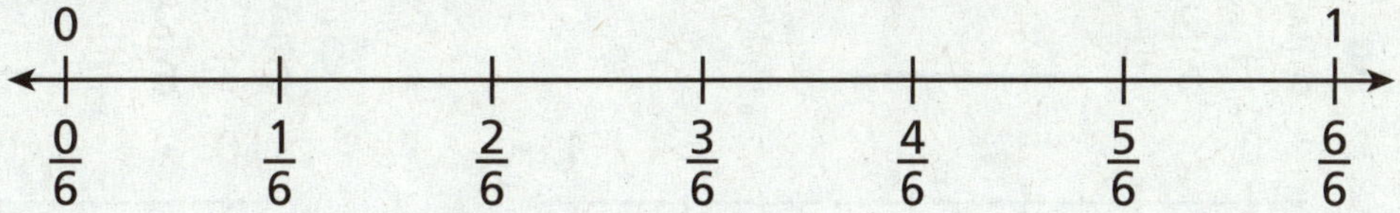

2. $\frac{3}{8}$ ◯ $\frac{2}{8}$

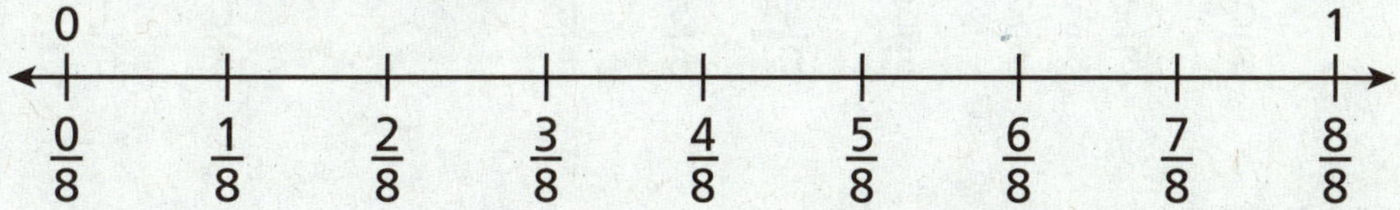

3. $\frac{2}{5}$ ◯ $\frac{1}{3}$

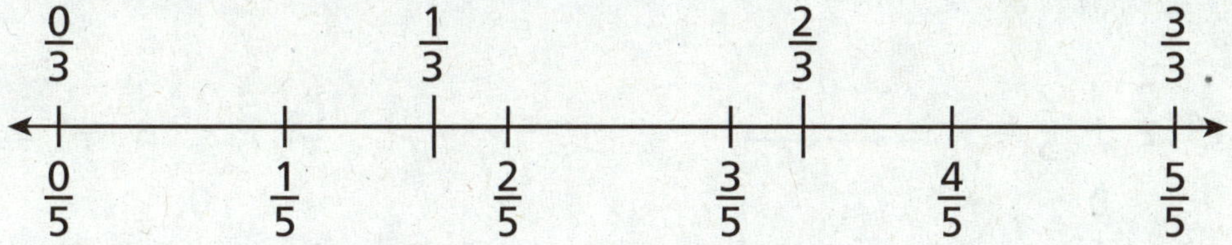

4. $\frac{2}{3}$ ◯ $\frac{1}{2}$

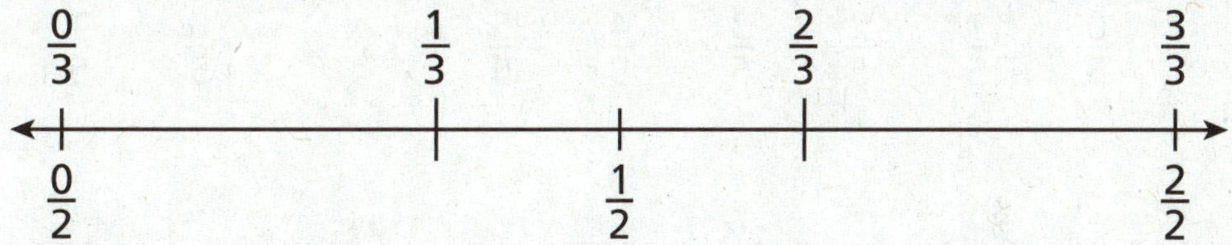

5. $\frac{1}{4}$ ◯ $\frac{2}{8}$

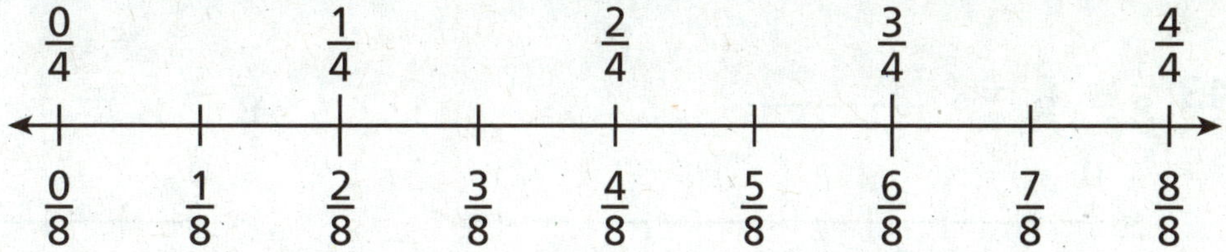

6. $\frac{2}{3}$ ◯ $\frac{5}{6}$

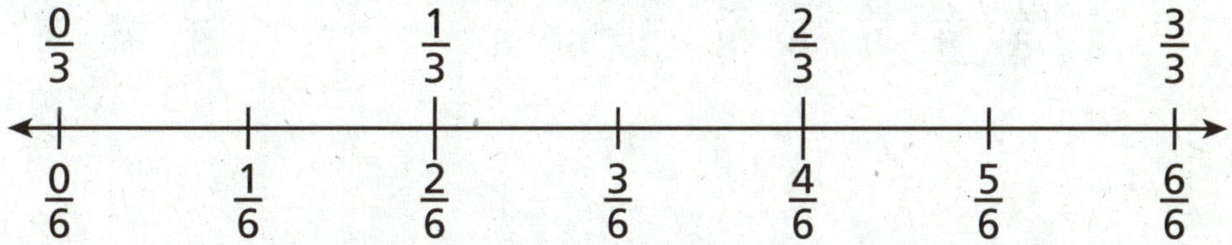

7. $\frac{1}{4}$ ◯ $\frac{3}{6}$

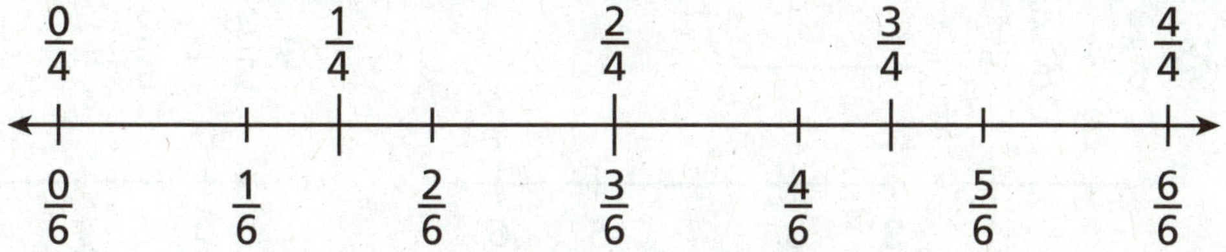

8. $\frac{1}{3}$ ◯ $\frac{2}{4}$

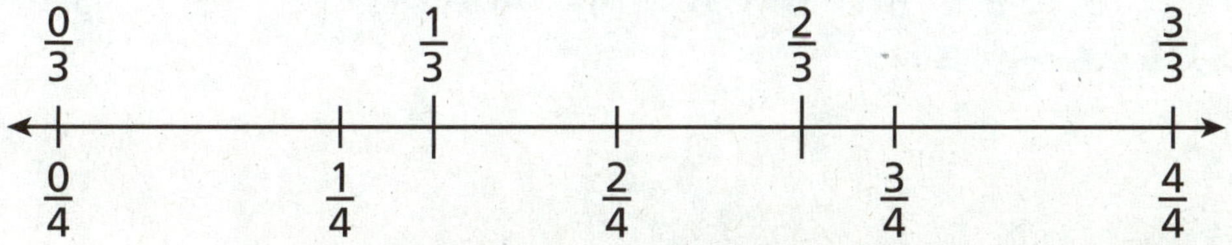

11–16 Class Activity

Name ______________________ Date ______________

► Add and Subtract Fractions on a Number Line

Circle the lengths on the number lines to add or subtract.

9. $\frac{3}{6} + \frac{2}{6} =$ ______

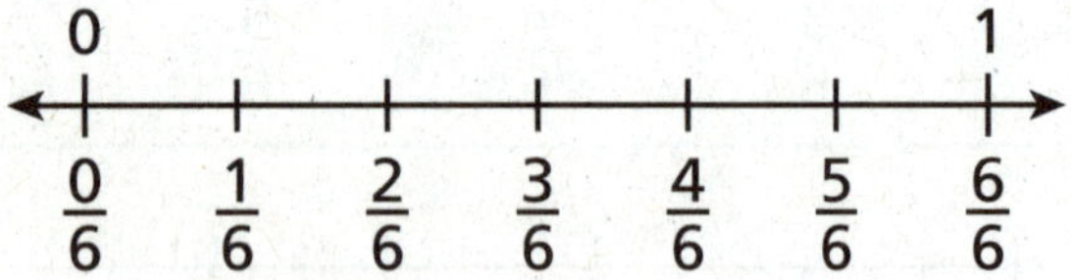

10. $\frac{3}{6} - \frac{2}{6} =$ ______

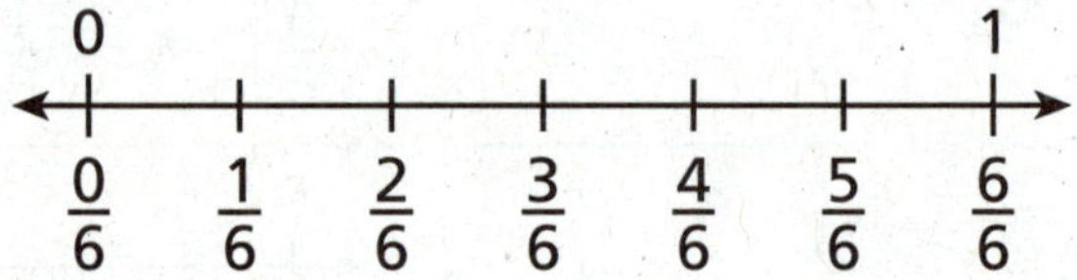

11. $\frac{2}{5} + \frac{2}{5} =$ ______

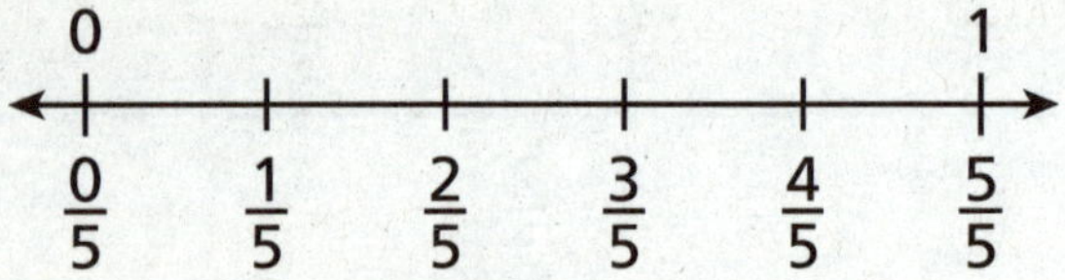

12. $\frac{4}{5} - \frac{3}{5} =$ ______

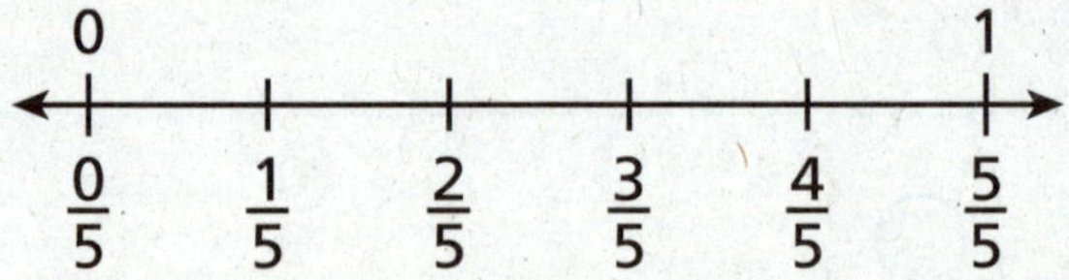

13. $\frac{1}{8} + \frac{3}{8} =$ ______

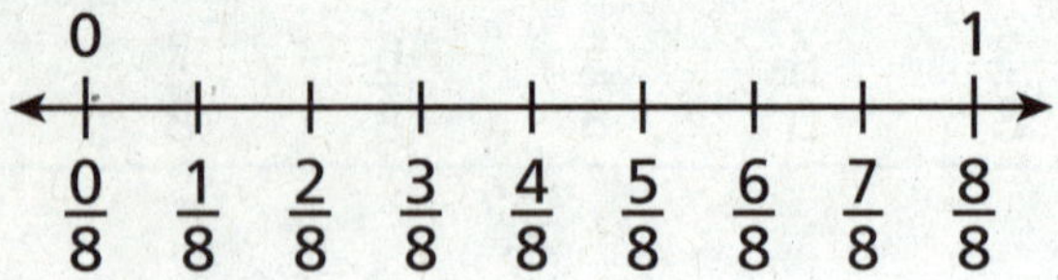

14. $\frac{7}{8} - \frac{5}{8} =$ ______

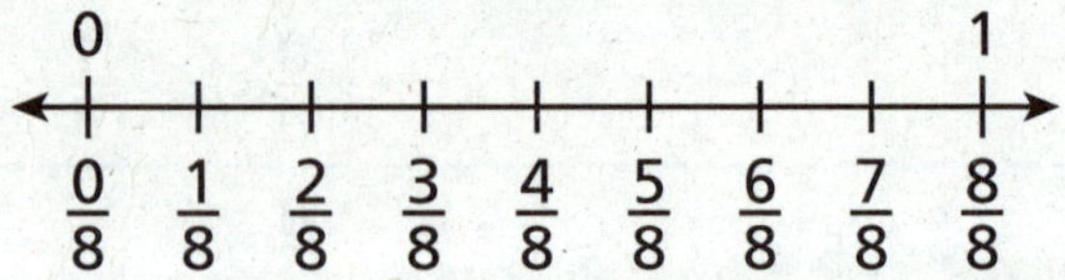

15. $\frac{2}{6} + \frac{3}{6} =$ ______

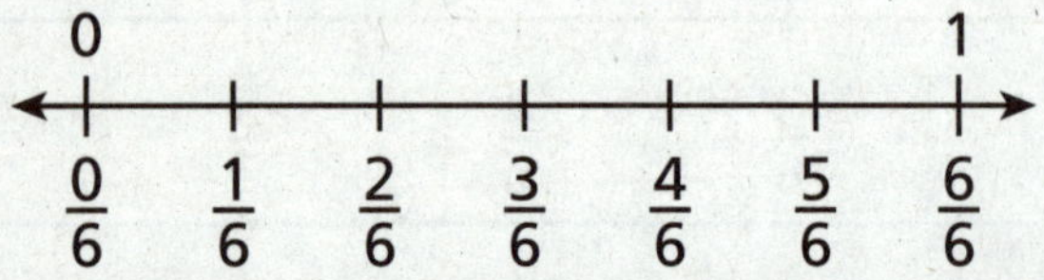

16. $\frac{4}{5} - \frac{2}{5} =$ ______

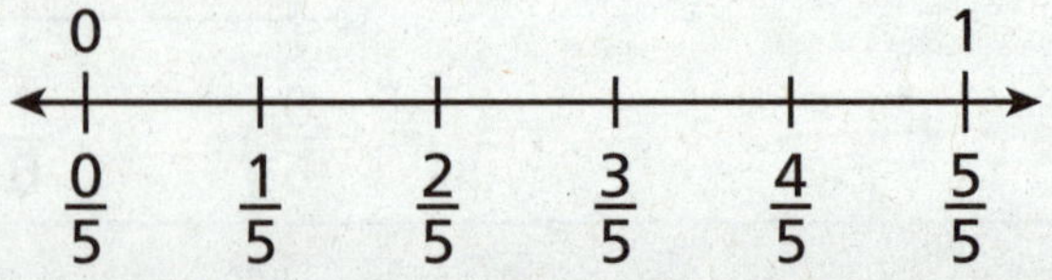

Name ____________________ Date ____________

► Fraction, Decimals, and Money

Equal shares of 1 whole can be written as a fraction or as a decimal. Each whole dollar below is equal to 100 pennies. Discuss the patterns you see.

$\frac{1}{2}$ — 1 of 2 equal parts

2 equal parts

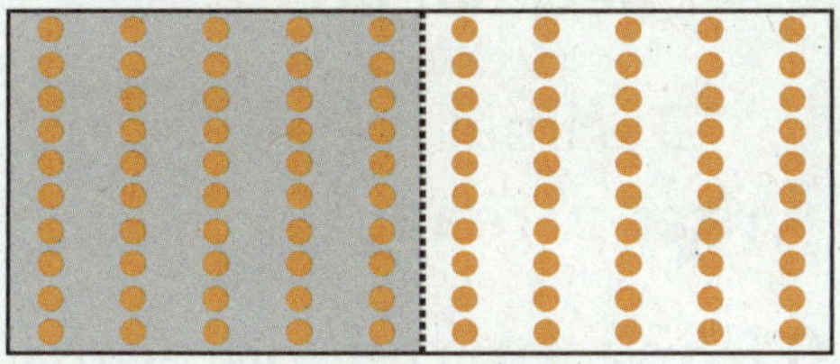

0.5 0.50 \$0.50

$\frac{5}{10}$ $\frac{50}{100}$ 50 pennies

$\frac{1}{2} + \frac{1}{2} = \frac{2}{2}$ — 2 of 2 equal parts = 1 whole

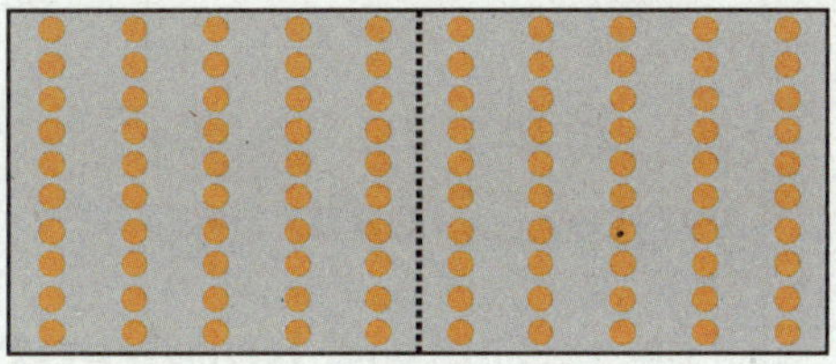

$0.5 + 0.5 = 1.00 = \frac{5}{10} + \frac{5}{10} = \frac{10}{10}$

$0.50 + 0.50 = 1.00 = \frac{50}{100} + \frac{50}{100} = \frac{100}{100}$

\$0.50 + \$0.50 = \$1.00

$\frac{1}{4}$ — 1 of 4 equal parts

4 equal parts

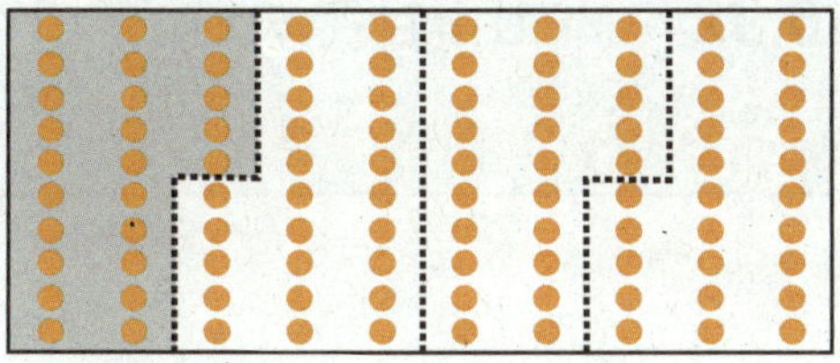

0.25 \$0.25

$\frac{25}{100}$ 25 pennies

0.25 \$0.25

$\frac{25}{100}$ 1 quarter

$\frac{1}{4}$ — 1 of 4 equal parts

4 equal parts

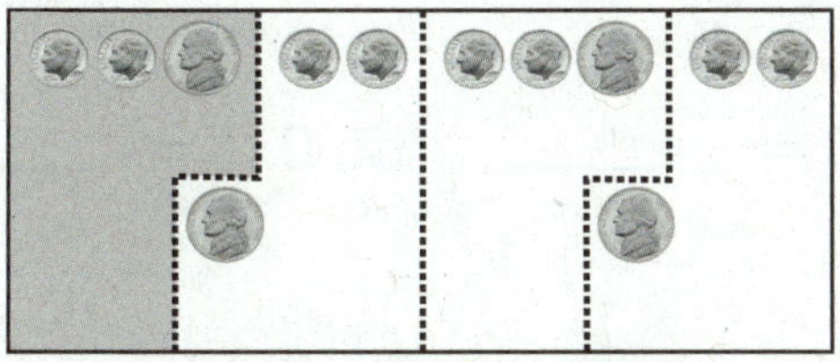

0.10 + 0.10 + 0.05 = 0.25

\$0.10 + \$0.10 + \$0.05 = \$0.25

2 dimes + 1 nickel

$\frac{1}{4}$ — 1 of 4 equal parts

4 equal parts

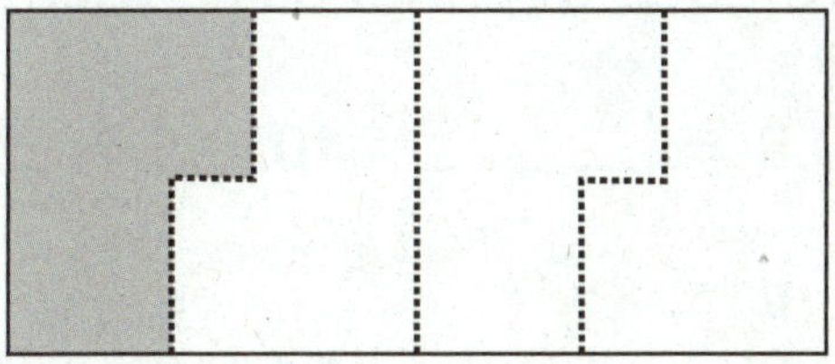

0.25

$\frac{25}{100}$

11–17 Class Activity

Name ______________________ Date ______________

Vocabulary
decimal
decimal point
tenths
hundredths

▶ Tenths and Hundredths

Fractions can be written as **decimals**.

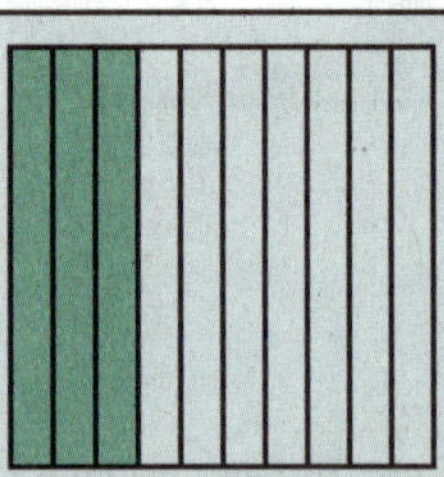

Fraction		Decimal	
write:	**read:**	**write:**	**read:**
$\frac{3}{10}$	three **tenths**	**0.3**	three tenths

↑ **decimal point**

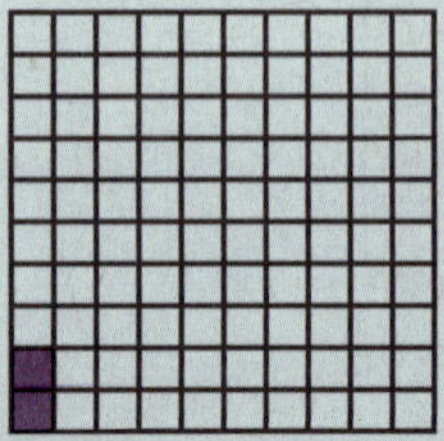

Fraction		Decimal	
write:	**read:**	**write:**	**read:**
$\frac{2}{100}$	two **hundredths**	**0.02**	two hundredths

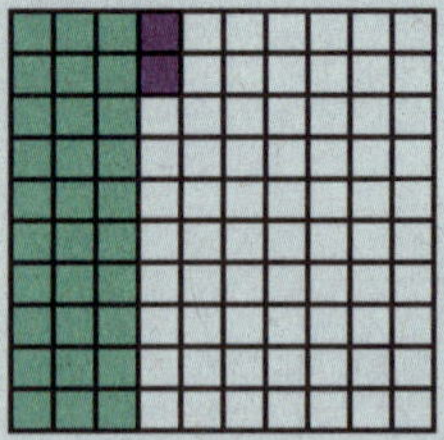

Fraction		Decimal	
write:	**read:**	**write:**	**read:**
$\frac{32}{100}$	thirty-two hundredths	**0.32**	thirty-two hundredths

Write each fraction as a decimal.

1. $\frac{1}{10}$ = ______ 2. $\frac{5}{10}$ = ______ 3. $\frac{9}{10}$ = ______ 4. $\frac{6}{10}$ = ______

5. $\frac{34}{100}$ = ______ 6. $\frac{50}{100}$ = ______ 7. $\frac{6}{100}$ = ______ 8. $\frac{85}{100}$ = ______

Write each decimal as a fraction.

9. 0.8 = ______ 10. 0.5 = ______ 11. 0.7 = ______ 12. 0.2 = ______

13. 0.09 = ______ 14. 0.65 = ______ 15. 0.40 = ______ 16. 0.72 = ______

17. Jeb has 72 red marbles in a bag of 100 marbles. Write a decimal that represents the red marbles as a part of all the marbles in the bag.

______

11–17 Class Activity

Name ______________________ Date ____________

▶ Decimals Greater than 1

These models show decimals greater than 1.

Write: 2.3 **Read:** two and three tenths

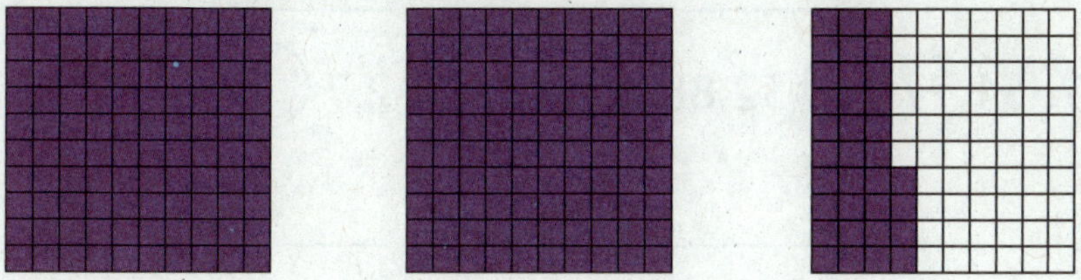

Write: 2.34 **Read:** two and thirty-four hundredths

Write a decimal for the shaded part.

18. 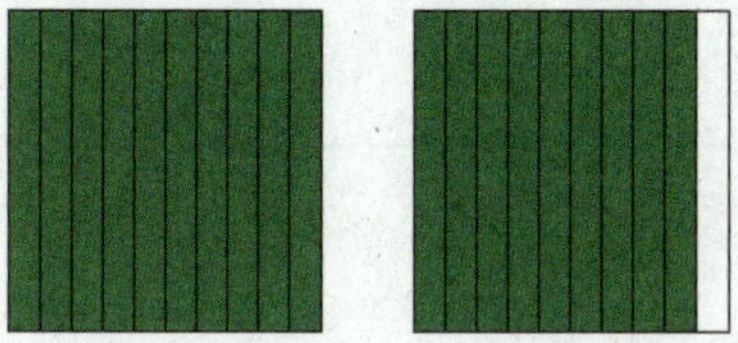

____

19. 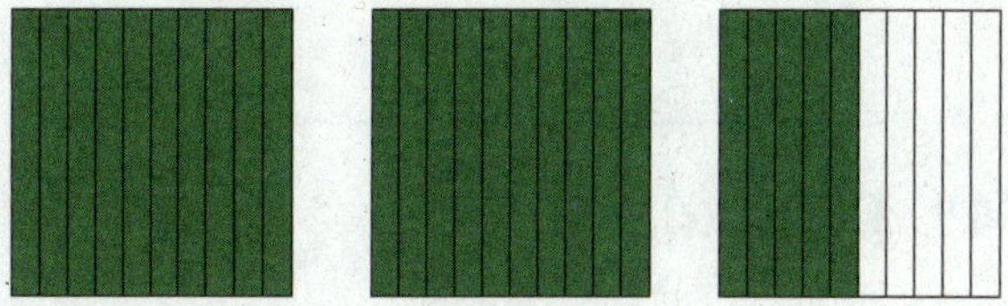

____

20. 

____

21. 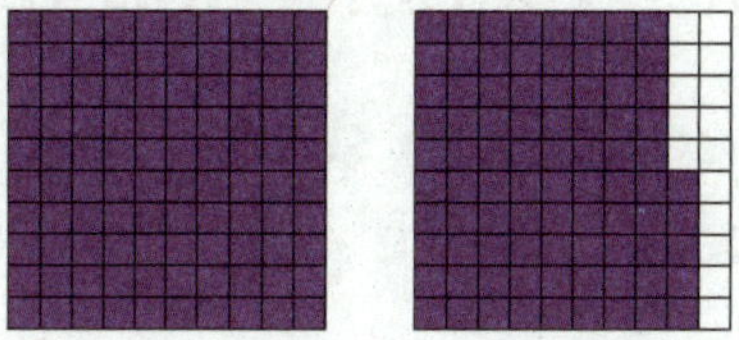

____

▶ Equivalent Decimals

Write an equivalent decimal.

22. 0.4 = _______ 23. 0.90 = _______ 24. 0.60 = _______ 25. 0.7 = _______

26. 0.50 = _______ 27. 0.20 = _______ 28. 2.8 = _______ 29. 1.90 = _______

11–17 Class Activity

Name ________________ Date ________________

►Compare and Order Decimals

Write >, < or = in the ◯.

30. $0.25 ◯ $0.35 ____________

31. 0.5 ◯ 0.15 ____________

32. $0.50 ◯ $0.45 ____________

33. 0.6 ◯ 0.60 ____________

34. $0.77 ◯ $0.88 ____________

35. 0.85 ◯ 0.7 ____________

36. $0.95 ◯ $1.00 ____________

37. $1.77 ◯ $2.88 ____________

38. 2.7 ◯ 1.75 ____________

Write these amounts in order from least to greatest.

39. $\frac{1}{2}$ dollar, $0.45, $0.75 ____________________

40. $\frac{1}{4}$ of a dollar, $0.55, $0.15 ____________________

41. 0.7, 0.42, 0.84 ____________________

►Compare Fractions and Decimals on a Number Line

Circle the lengths to show each fraction and decimal. Then compare. Write <, >, or = in the ◯.

42. $\frac{1}{2}$ ◯ 0.6

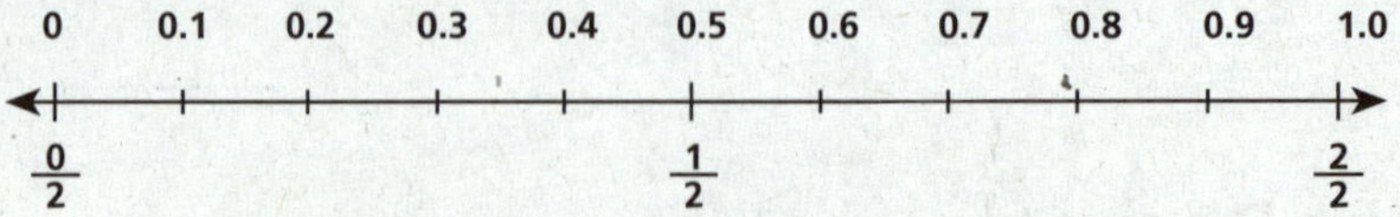

43. $\frac{1}{4}$ ◯ 0.3

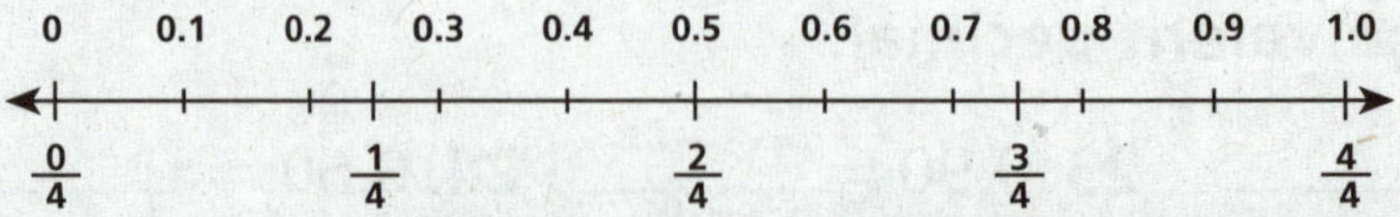

44. $\frac{3}{4}$ ◯ 0.7

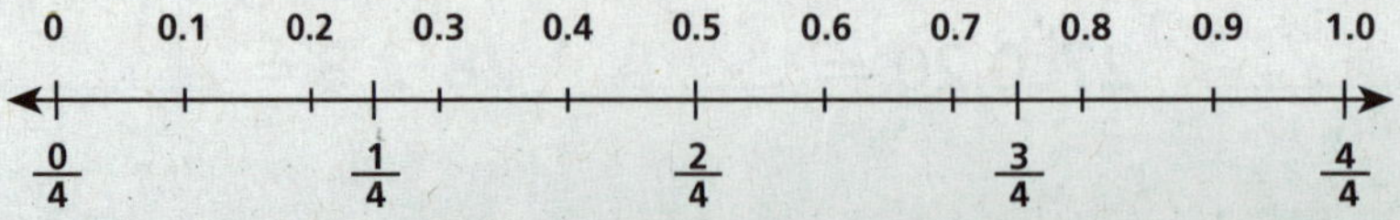

11–18 **Class Activity**

Name ______________________ Date ______________

► Use Models to Visualize Mixed Numbers and Improper Fractions

Write the mixed number and improper fraction that the drawing shows.

1.

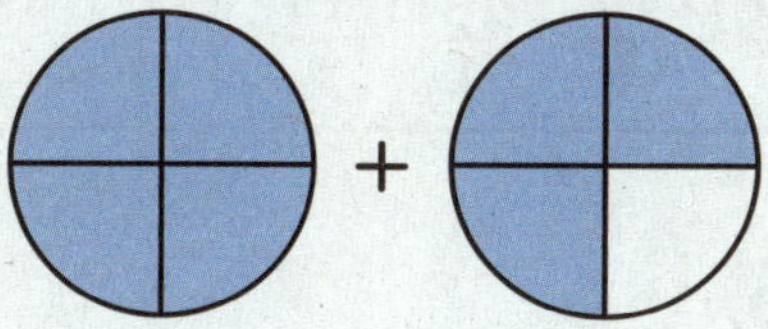

$1 + \underline{\tfrac{3}{4}} = \underline{1\tfrac{3}{4}}$

$\tfrac{4}{4} + \underline{\tfrac{3}{4}} = \underline{\tfrac{7}{4}}$

2.

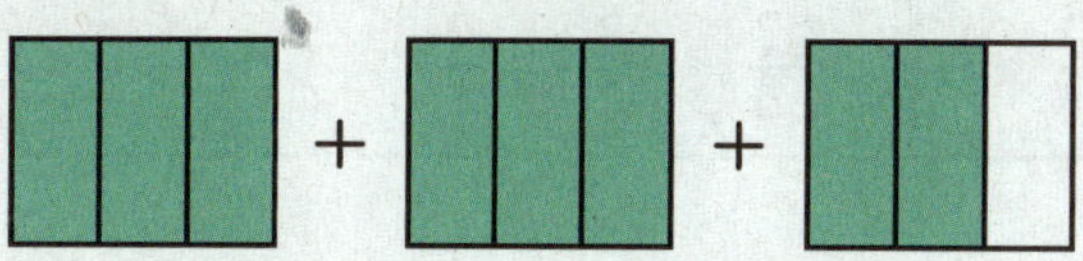

$1 + \_\_\_ + \_\_\_ = \_\_\_$

$\tfrac{3}{3} + \_\_\_ + \_\_\_ = \_\_\_$

3.

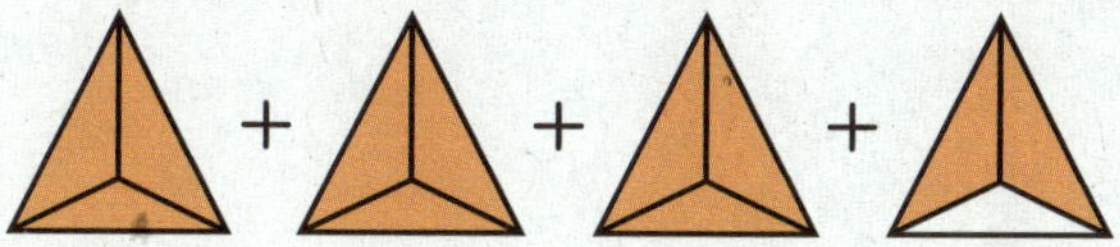

$1 + \_\_\_ + \_\_\_ + \_\_\_ = \_\_\_$

$\tfrac{3}{3} + \_\_\_ + \_\_\_ + \_\_\_ = \_\_\_$

4.

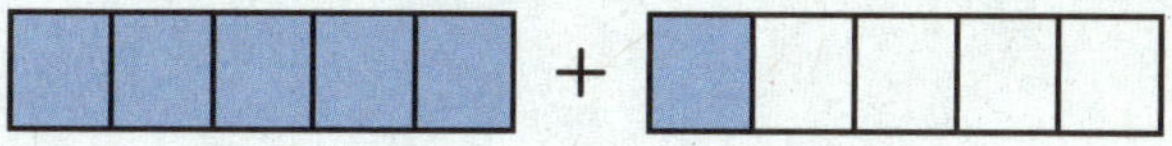

$1 + \_\_\_ = \_\_\_$

$\_\_\_ + \_\_\_ = \_\_\_$

5.

$1 + \_\_\_ = \_\_\_$

$\_\_\_ + \_\_\_ = \_\_\_$

6.

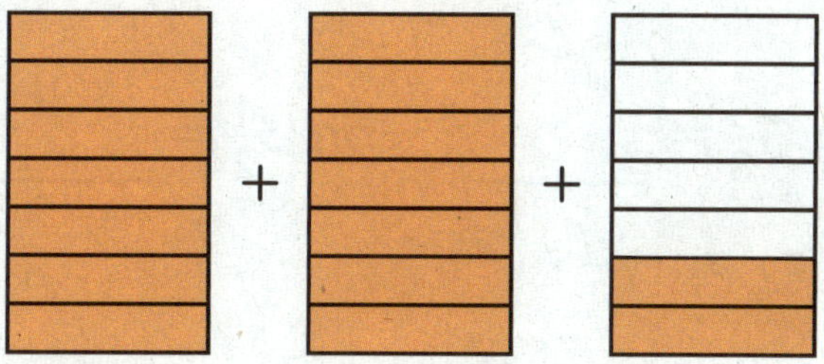

$1 + \_\_\_ + \_\_\_ = \_\_\_$

$\tfrac{7}{7} + \_\_\_ + \_\_\_ = \_\_\_$

Name ____________________ Date ____________

▶ Mixed Numbers and Improper Fractions on a Number Line

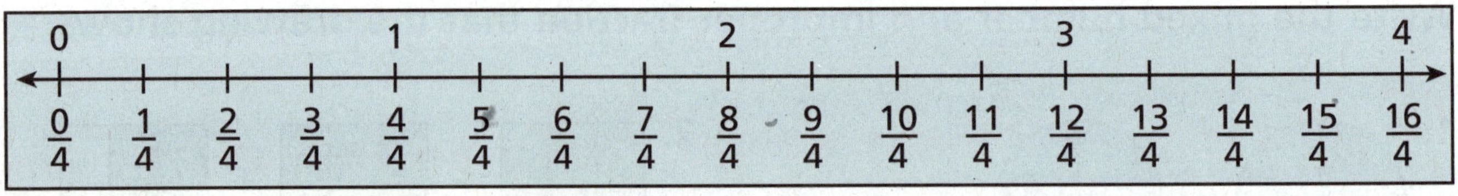

Use the number line to write the improper fraction, mixed number, or whole number.

7. $\frac{13}{4}$ = ______
8. $\frac{7}{4}$ = ______
9. $\frac{10}{4}$ = ______
10. $\frac{16}{4}$ = ______
11. $1\frac{1}{4}$ = ______
12. $2\frac{1}{4}$ = ______
13. $3\frac{1}{4}$ = ______
14. $2\frac{3}{4}$ = ______

▶ Practice with Mixed Numbers and Improper Fractions

Write the improper fraction or mixed number.

15. $2\frac{3}{5}$ = ______

$\frac{5}{5} + \frac{5}{5} + \frac{3}{5} = \frac{13}{5}$

16. $\frac{8}{6}$ = ______
17. $1\frac{2}{7}$ = ______
18. $\frac{11}{9}$ = ______
19. $1\frac{5}{8}$ = ______
20. $3\frac{1}{2}$ = ______
21. $\frac{19}{4}$ = ______
22. $\frac{7}{5}$ = ______
23. $\frac{10}{3}$ = ______
24. $2\frac{1}{6}$ = ______
25. $1\frac{3}{9}$ = ______
26. $\frac{11}{7}$ = ______

Name Date

►Explore Division with Remainders

Solve.

1. Hassan is making party decorations for the classroom. He needs 5 inches of string for each one. He has 15 inches of string. How many decorations can Hassan make?

2. Ana is also making decorations. She needs 5 inches of string per decoration. She has 16 inches of string. How many decorations can she make? How many inches of string will be left over?

3. Glenna is making copies of a story she wrote. She needs 4 pieces of paper per copy. She has 34 pieces of paper. How many copies can Glenna make?

4. Owen needs to pack 44 snacks into boxes. He can fit 8 snacks in each box. How many boxes does Owen need to pack all of the snacks?

5. Ty plans to write 60 math problems. He can fit 8 problems on a page. How many pages will Ty need for all 60 math problems?

6. The Science Club is renting vans for 37 people to take a field trip. Each van holds 8 people. How many vans are needed?

7. A truck company will carry 65 tons of gravel today. Each truck can hold 9 tons. How many trucks will be needed to carry the gravel?

8. Hector needs to put 9 flowers in each vase. He has 59 flowers in all. How many vases can Hector fill? How many flowers will be left over?

11–19 Class Activity

Name ______________________ Date ______________

▶Practice Dividing with Remainders

Write the answer.

9. $3\overline{)17}$ 10. $6\overline{)26}$ 11. $8\overline{)27}$ 12. $7\overline{)39}$

13. $6\overline{)40}$ 14. $9\overline{)56}$ 15. $5\overline{)48}$ 16. $2\overline{)15}$

17. $5\overline{)33}$ 18. $8\overline{)45}$ 19. $7\overline{)44}$ 20. $3\overline{)29}$

21. $4\overline{)30}$ 22. $9\overline{)71}$ 23. $3\overline{)31}$ 24. $8\overline{)63}$

25. $2\overline{)17}$ 26. $4\overline{)27}$ 27. $5\overline{)37}$ 28. $6\overline{)56}$

29. $7\overline{)54}$ 30. $8\overline{)54}$ 31. $9\overline{)73}$ 32. $10\overline{)55}$

11–20 Class Activity

Name ____________________ Date ____________

►Express the Remainder as a Fraction

Write the answer with a remainder and then as a mixed number.

1. $6\overline{)56}$

2. $8\overline{)49}$

3. $3\overline{)17}$

4. $7\overline{)68}$

5. $9\overline{)42}$

6. $5\overline{)48}$

7. $8\overline{)30}$

8. $7\overline{)18}$

9. $4\overline{)22}$

10. $7\overline{)36}$

11. $6\overline{)28}$

12. $9\overline{)88}$

13. $8\overline{)75}$

14. $5\overline{)49}$

15. $9\overline{)38}$

16. $7\overline{)58}$

17. $2\overline{)19}$

18. $3\overline{)26}$

19. $6\overline{)53}$

20. $8\overline{)54}$

11–20 Class Activity

Name ____________________ Date ____________

▶ Interpret Remainders

Solve.

21. At the end of each day, the 3 bakers at Ben's Bakery each take home an equal amount of leftover cake. On Tuesday, 7 cakes were left over. How much cake will each baker take home?

____

22. A delivery man has 78 jugs of water in his truck. He will leave 9 jugs of water at each delivery stop. How many stops will he make? How many jugs will be left in his truck?

____

23. Today 6 people went on a picnic in the park. They agreed to share 14 cups of lemonade equally. How much lemonade will each person get to drink?

____

24. Ben's Bakery has 54 cupcakes. The bakery packs cupcakes in boxes of 8 each. How many boxes will be filled? How many cupcakes will be left over?

____

25. Mr. Calvert has 7 cats. Each week, he divides 38 cans of cat food equally among his cats. How many cans of cat food does each cat eat per week?

____

26. There are 89 goldfish in the fishpond. They will be put in fish tanks for the winter. If each fish tank holds 9 fish, how many tanks are needed?

____

27. Thirty-nine people are traveling to the basketball game. If each van holds 9 people, how many vans will be needed?

____

28. Jamal has 41 CDs. Each shelf in his CD rack holds 6 CDs. How many shelves does he need to hold all his CDs?

____

Name ______________________ Date __________

►More Division Word Problems with Remainders

Solve.

1. Eileen is putting popcorn balls into bags for a party. She has 51 popcorn balls. Each bag holds 6. How many bags can Eileen fill completely? How many popcorn balls will be left over?

   ____

2. Luis is making hot chocolate for 8 friends. The friends would like to share it equally. If Luis makes 25 cups of hot chocolate, how much hot chocolate can each friend have?

   ____

3. Rey is filling the fish tanks at the zoo. He has 63 gallons of water. Each tank holds 10 gallons. How many tanks can Rey fill? How much water will be left over?

   ____

4. Lisa is putting cans on shelves in the grocery store. There are 37 cans. Each shelf holds 8 cans. How many shelves can Lisa fill? How many cans will be left over?

   ____

5. Mrs. Lin ordered 34 mini-pizzas for her niece's party. Nine girls are coming to the party. How many mini-pizzas can each girl have if the pizzas are shared equally?

   ____

6. Crystal needs to pack 40 pieces of clothing into her dresser drawers. If each drawer holds 7 pieces of clothing, how many dresser drawers does she need to fit all her clothing?

   ____

7. Sunny has 43 rings. She can put 8 rings in a jewelry box. How many jewelry boxes does Sunny need to store all the rings?

   ____

8. Emilio is arranging daisies in vases. He has 54 daisies. Each vase will hold 7 daisies. How many vases can Emilio fill?

   ____

11–21 Class Activity

Name ______ Date ______

▶ Practice Dividing with Remainders

Write the answer with a remainder and as a mixed number.

9. 23 ÷ 7 ______ ______

10. 31 ÷ 6 ______ ______

11. 75 ÷ 9 ______ ______

12. 63 ÷ 8 ______ ______

13. 44 ÷ 9 ______ ______

14. 52 ÷ 7 ______ ______

15. 85 ÷ 9 ______ ______

16. 17 ÷ 5 ______ ______

17. 38 ÷ 7 ______ ______

18. 46 ÷ 6 ______ ______

19. 67 ÷ 8 ______ ______

20. 57 ÷ 7 ______ ______

21. 43 ÷ 5 ______ ______

22. 37 ÷ 4 ______ ______

23. 79 ÷ 8 ______ ______

Name Date

▶ Math and Art

The Ndebele people in Africa paint their houses with geometric figures.

On a separate piece of paper, draw a picture of a house. Color the house with geometric figures.

1. What figures did you use?

____

2. How many of each figure did you use?

____

3. Did you use parallel or perpendicular lines?

____

4. What kind of angles did you use?

____

5. Are any of the shapes in your design congruent?

____

6. Is your design symmetrical?

____

Name ______________________ Date ______________

▶The Great Game Company

The Great Game Company has asked you to help them with the spinners they make for games.

7. The company wants a fair spinner where it will be equally likely to get red, blue, or green. Which of the spinners below are fair? Which are unfair? Explain.

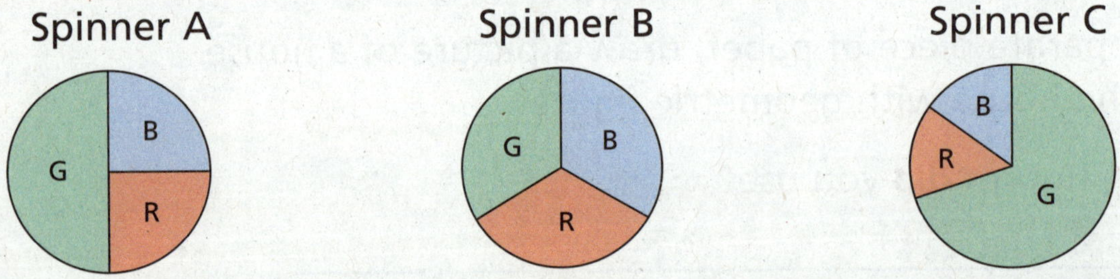

____

____

____

8. The company wants a spinner where it is impossible to get blue and where it is more likely for a player to get red than green. Design a spinner for them.

Name ______________________ Date ____________

1. Write a fraction to represent the part of the whole that is shaded.

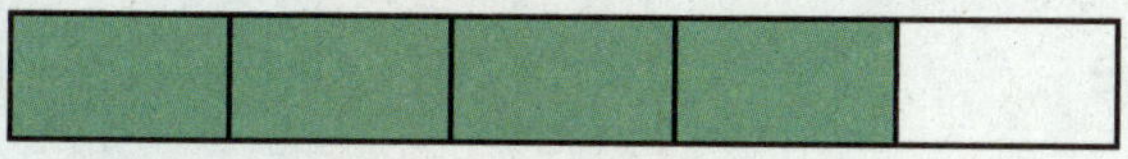

____

2. What fraction of the circles are shaded?

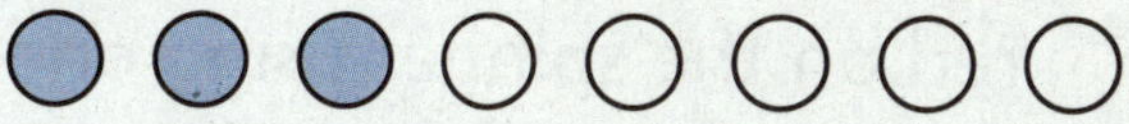

____

Use mental math to find the answer.

3. $\frac{1}{5} \times 40 =$ ________

4. $\frac{3}{4}$ of $24 =$ ________

Use the fraction strips to show the fractions are equivalent. Then fill the missing numbers in the boxes.

5. $\frac{4}{5}$ and $\frac{8}{10}$

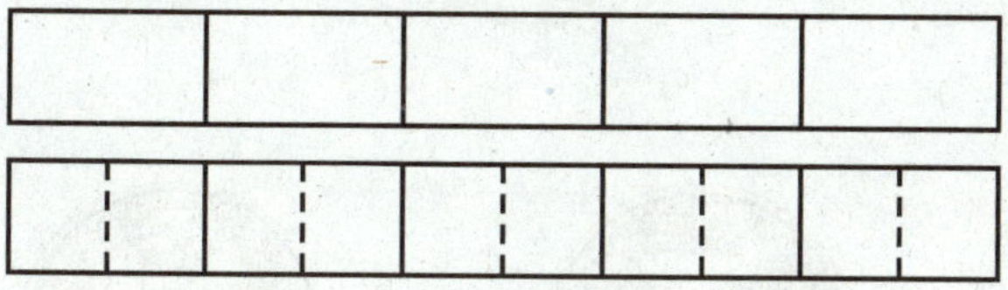

$$\frac{4}{5} = \frac{4 \times \square}{5 \times \square} = \frac{8}{10}$$

6. $\frac{9}{12}$ and $\frac{3}{4}$

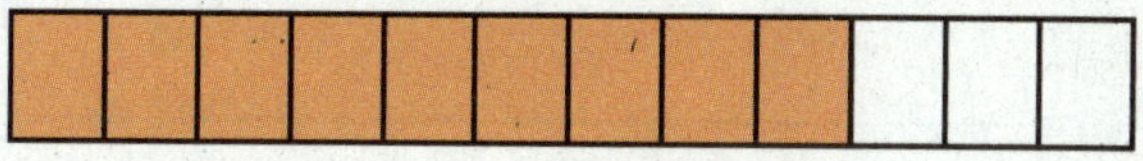

$$\frac{9}{12} = \frac{9 \div \square}{12 \div \square} = \frac{3}{4}$$

Complete.

7. $$\frac{3}{8} = \frac{3 \times \square}{8 \times \square} = \frac{15}{\square}$$

8. $$\frac{8}{12} = \frac{8 \div \square}{12 \div \square} = \frac{2}{\square}$$

9. **Compare. Write >, <, or = in the ◯.**

$\frac{1}{5}$ ◯ $\frac{1}{4}$

Name ______________________________ Date ______________

Use the spinner to answer exercises 10a. and 10b.

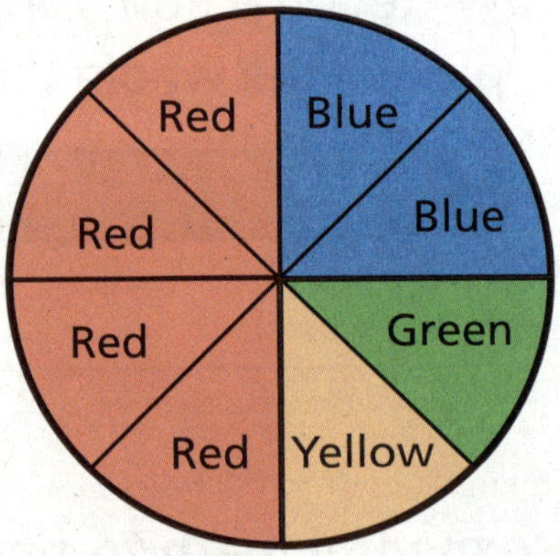

10. a. Describe the probability of spinning red on the spinner using one of these words: likely, unlikely, equally likely, certain, or impossible.

____

b. Write the probability of spinning blue.

__________ out of __________ or ____

Complete.

11. a. Suppose you pull a marble out of the bag 20 times and return it to the bag each time. Which color marble do you predict will be pulled out most often?

____

b. What are all the possible outcomes when you toss 2 coins? Use H for heads and T for tails to make an organized list.

Name ____________________ Date ____________

Write each fraction as a decimal or vice versa.

12. a. $\frac{3}{10}$ = ______ **b.** $\frac{42}{100}$ = ______ **c.** 0.65 = ______ **d.** 0.5 = ______

Write an equivalent decimal.

13. a. 0.7 = __________ **b.** 0.1 = __________

Compare. Write >, <, or =.

14. a. \$0.75 ◯ \$0.95 **b.** 0.6 ◯ 0.25

15. Write the answer with a remainder and as a mixed number.

$6\overline{)38}$

Write the mixed number or improper fraction.

16. $\frac{15}{4}$ = __________ **17.** $2\frac{7}{8}$ = __________

Add or subtract.

18. $\frac{2}{7} + \frac{3}{7}$ = __________ **19.** $\frac{6}{9} - \frac{3}{9}$ = __________

Add or subtract. Use the fraction strips to help you.

20. $\frac{1}{6} + \frac{3}{12}$ = __________ **21.** $\frac{2}{3} - \frac{4}{9}$ = __________

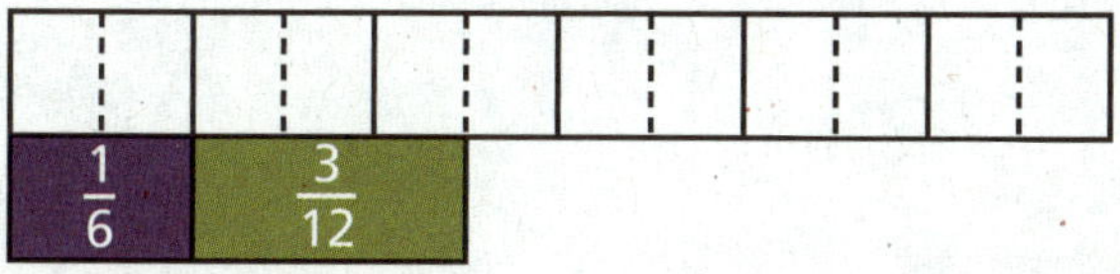

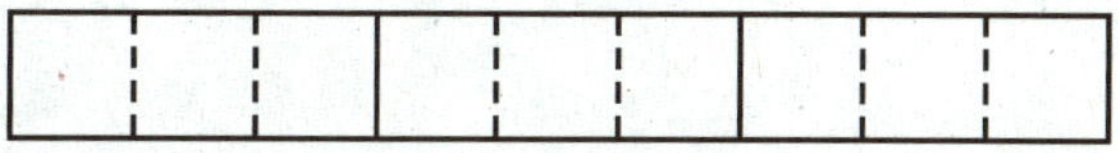

Name ______________________ Date __________

22. Use the bar graph to fill in the blanks.

Vanessa has ____________ as many cousins as Andrew.

Andrew has ____________ as many cousins as Vanessa.

Number of Cousins

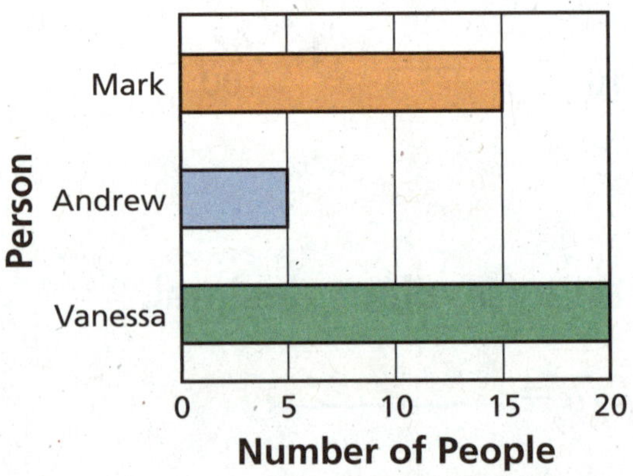

Solve.

23. Harris has 41 books. Each shelf in his bookshelf holds 6 books. How many shelves does he need to hold all his books?

____

24. A store has 63 caps. $\frac{2}{9}$ of the caps are blue. How many blue caps does the store have?

____

25. **Extended Response** Use the circle graph to answer the question.

A bakery made 36 batches of cookies in all. How many batches of coconut cookies were made?

____

Batches of Cookies Baked

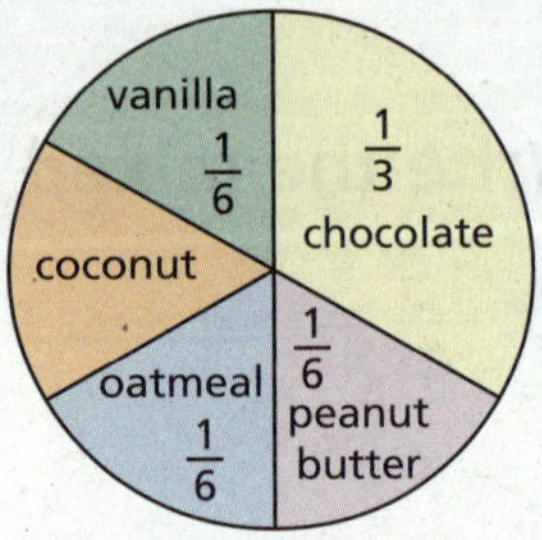

Explain how you found your answer.

____

____

____

12–1 Class Activity

Name ______________________ Date ______________

Vocabulary
net
cube

► Make a Cube

Cut around the outside of the first net. Fold to make a cube. Which of the other two nets will make a cube? Cut out the nets to test your prediction.

1.

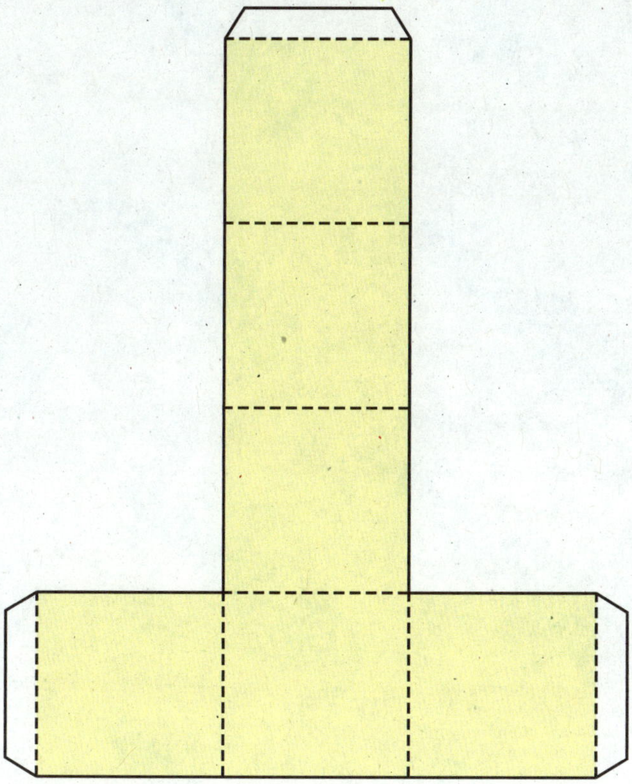

2.

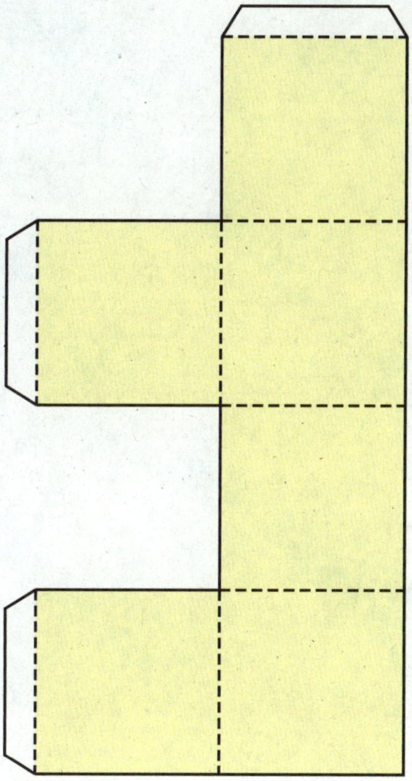

3.

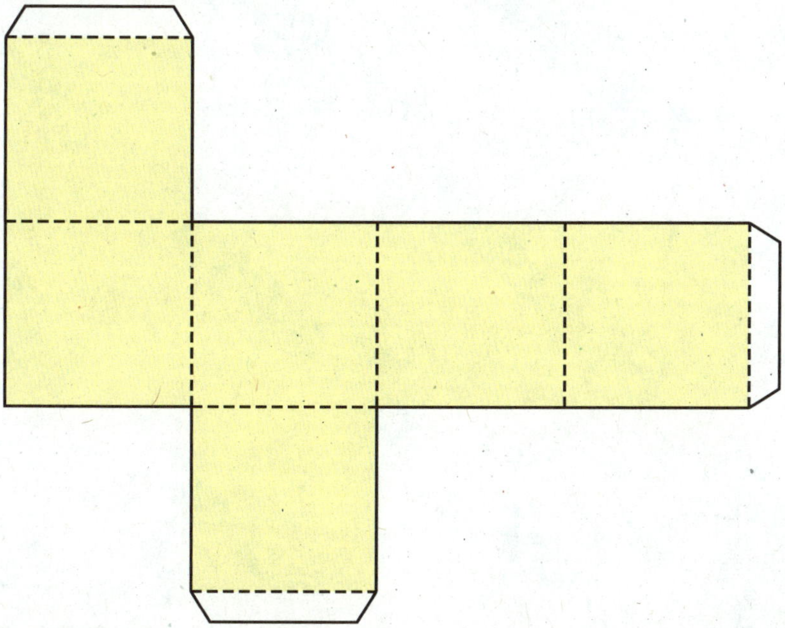

12–1 Class Activity

Name ______________________________ Date ____________

▶Identify Cube Nets

Circle the nets that you think will form a cube. Cut out the ones you circled and test your predictions.

4.

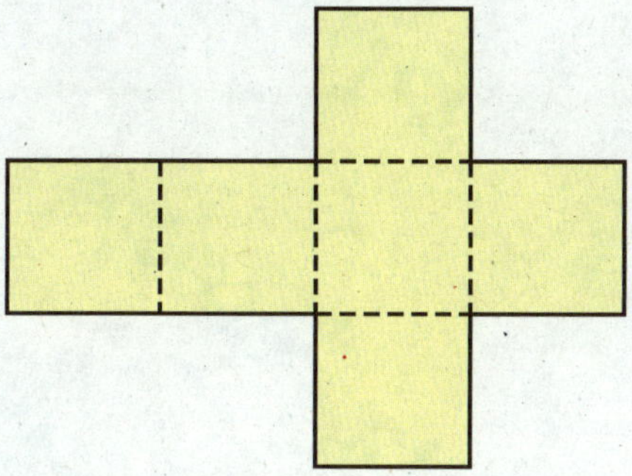

5.

6.

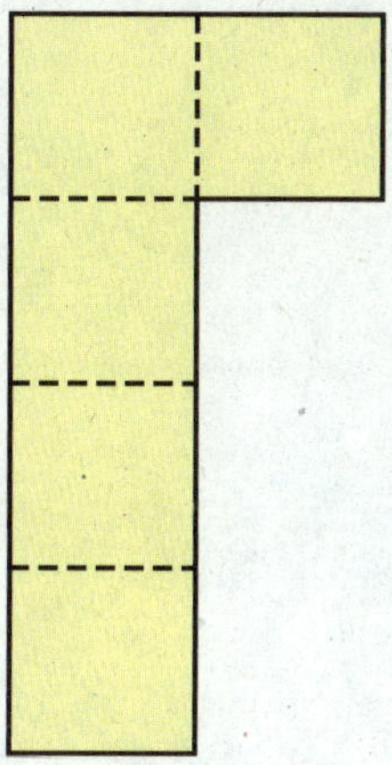

7.

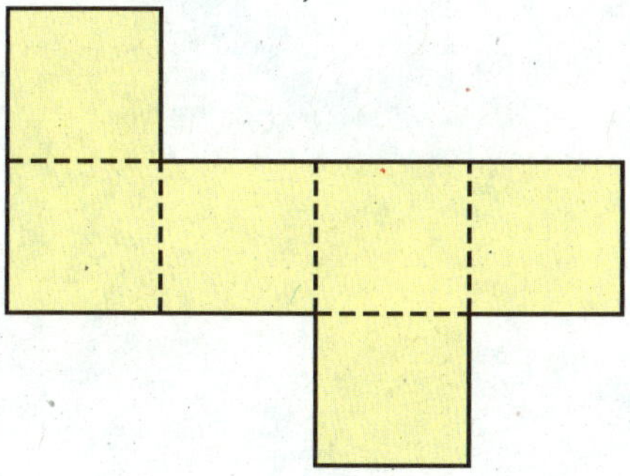

8.

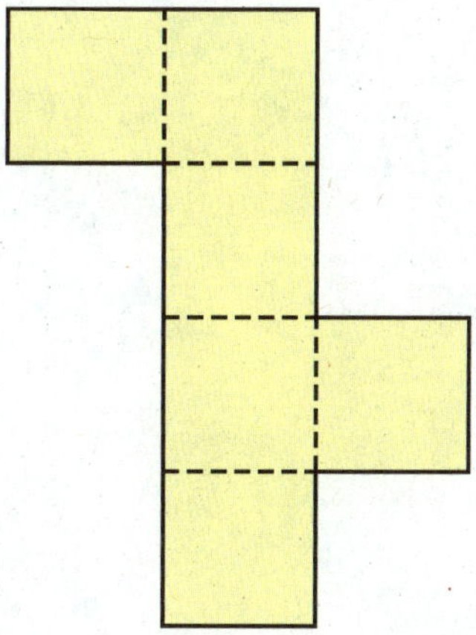

9.

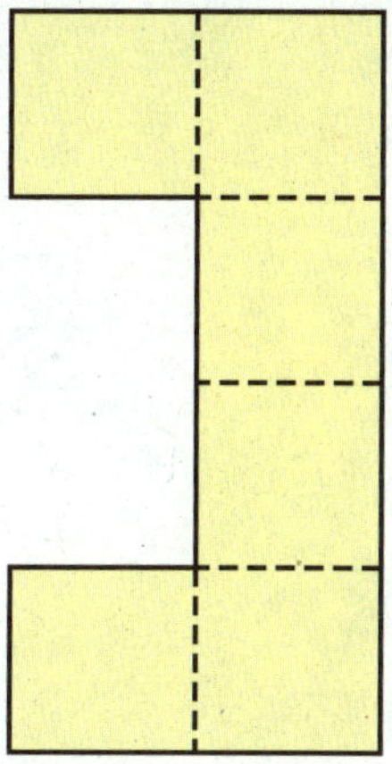

12–1 Class Activity

Name ____________________ Date ____________

► Create a Cube Net

10. Draw a net that will form a cube when it is folded. Then, cut it out and form the cube.

Family Letter

Dear Family,

Your child is exploring three-dimensional or solid figures.

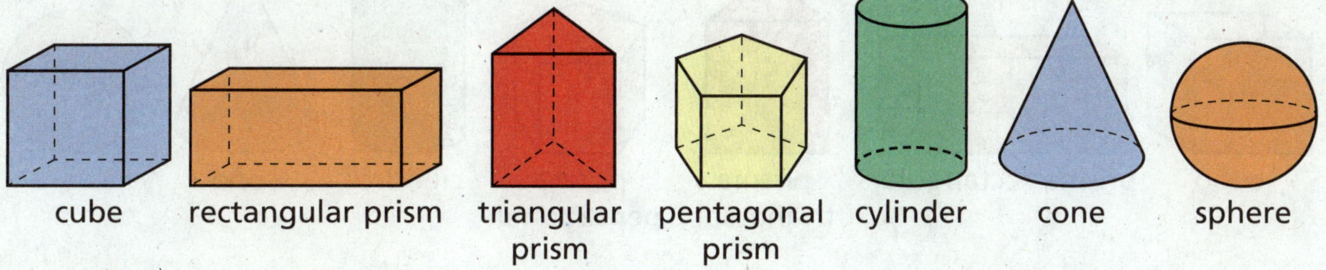

Your child will be making most of these solid figures by cutting out, folding, and taping a two-dimensional net of the object. This is a net for a triangular prism.

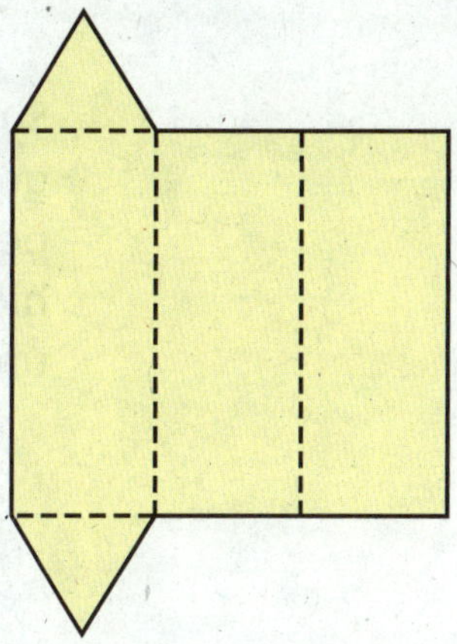

At home, point out different solid figures and discuss them with your child. Ask questions, such as: What is the name of that solid figure? What do you think it would look like from the side, top, back, or front? How is it different from another solid figure?

Encourage your child to build solid figures from cubes, clay, or folded paper.

When you are shopping with your child, discuss the different solid figures used for packaging. Ask your child to consider why particular solid figures are used for certain products.

If you have any questions or comments, please call or write to me.

Sincerely,
Your child's teacher

Estimada familia:

Su niño está explorando figuras tridimensionales o cuerpos geométricos.

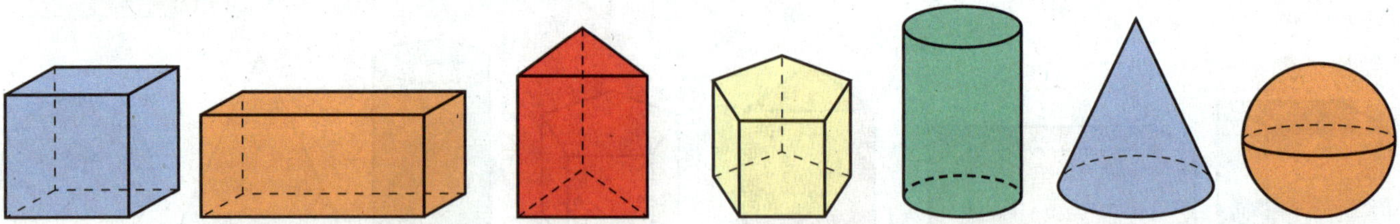

Su niño va a construir estos cuerpos geométricos cortando, doblando y pegando con cinta adhesiva una red bidimensional del objeto. Ésta es una red para un prisma triangular.

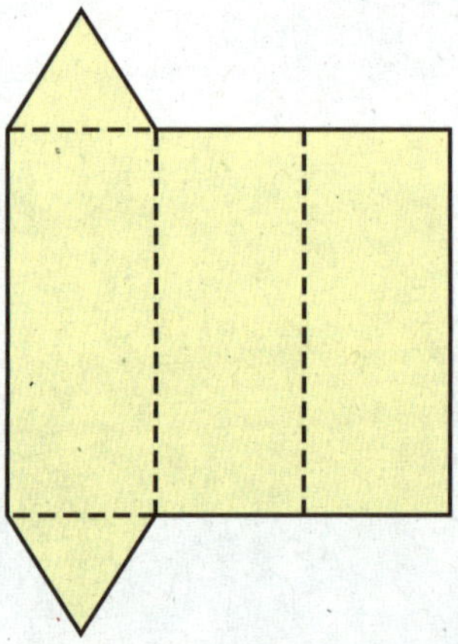

En casa señale diferentes cuerpos geométricos y coméntelos con su niño. Hágale preguntas como: ¿Cómo se llama este cuerpo geométrico? ¿Cómo crees que se vería desde el lado, desde arriba, desde atrás o desde adelante? ¿Cómo se diferencia de otro cuerpo geométrico?

Anime a su niño a que construya cuerpos geométricos usando cubos, arcilla o papel doblando.

Cuando uaya de compras con su niño, comente con él o con ella los distintos cuerpos geométricos que se usan para los envases. Pídale que piense por qué se usan determinados cuerpos geométricos para ciertos productos.

Si tiene alguna duda o comentario, por favor comuníquese conmigo.

Atentamente,
El maestro de su niño

12–2 Class Activity

Name _______________ Date _______________

▶ Cube Models From Drawings

Use cubes to build a model from each drawing.

1.

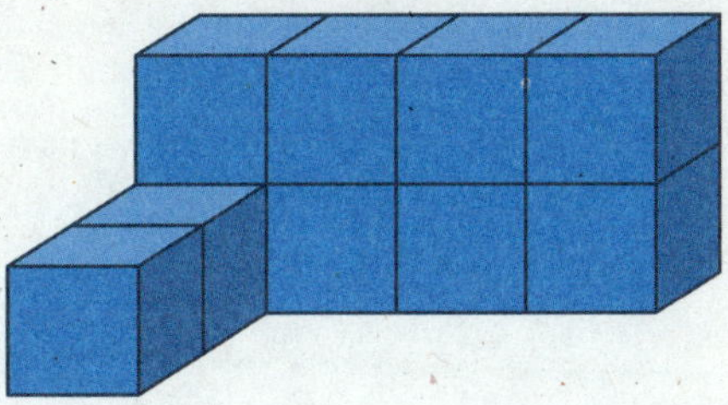

2.

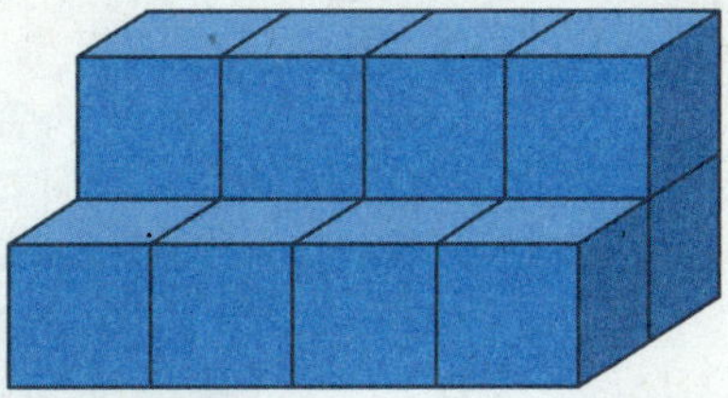

3.

4.

5.

6.

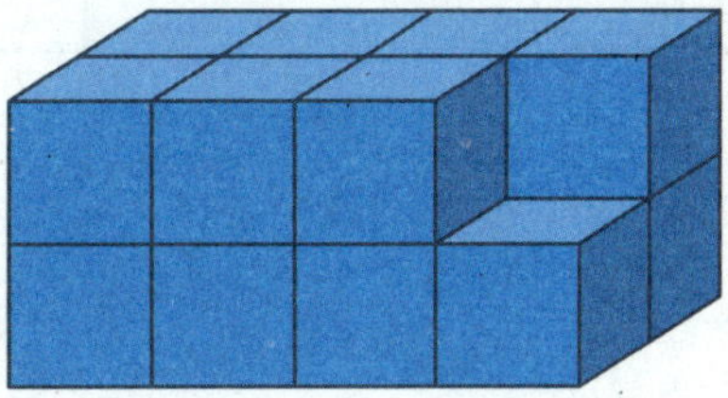

12–2 Class Activity

Name ______________________ Date ______________

▶ Views of Three-Dimensional Objects

7. Label the front, back, left, and right edges of a sheet of paper. Build a model to match the picture.

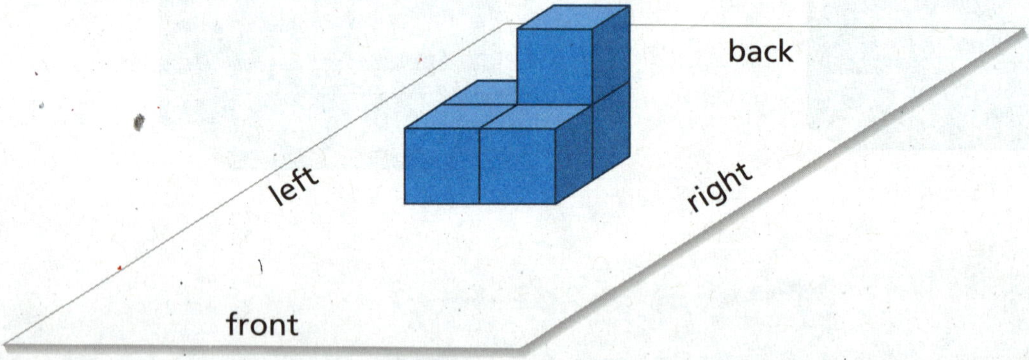

8. Using your model, label the drawings below as the *front, back, right,* or *left* views of the building. Each drawing will have two labels.

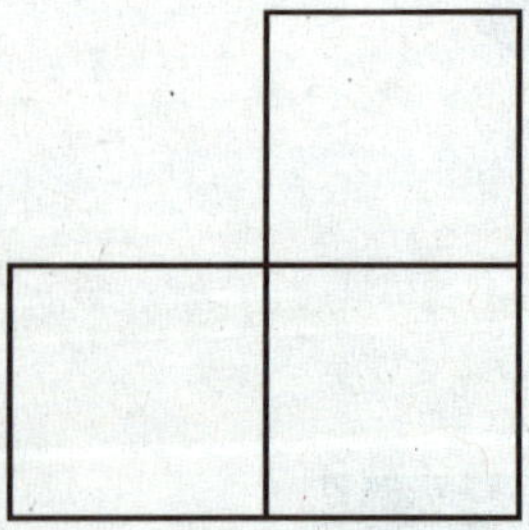

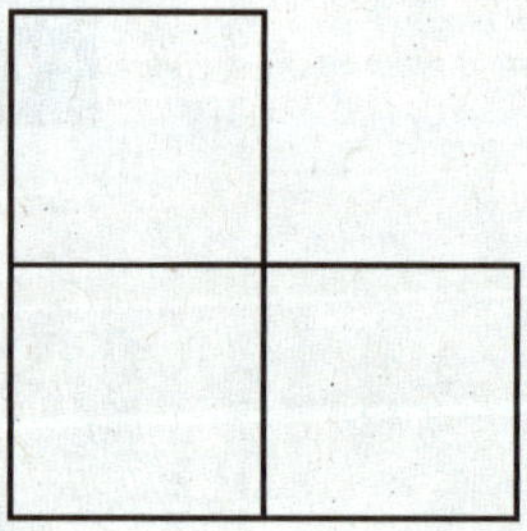

______________________ ______________________

______________________ ______________________

9. Draw the top view of the model from exercise 7.

Name ______________________________ Date ______________

10. Build a model to match the drawing below. Place it on a sheet of paper with edges labeled *front, back, right,* and *left.*

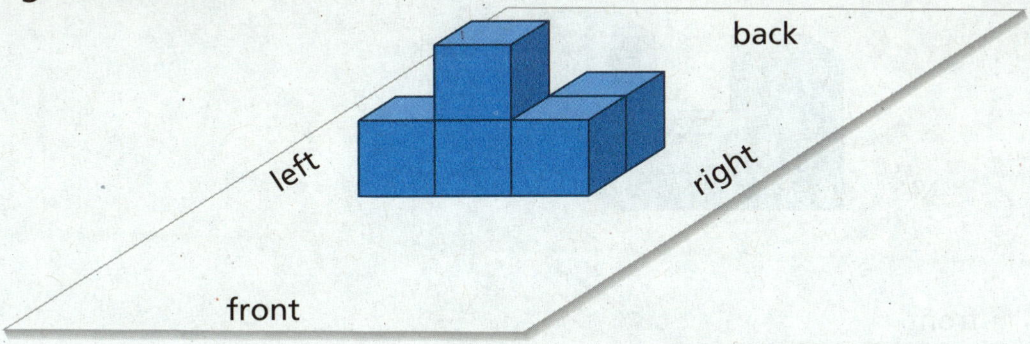

11. Using your model, label the views below as *front, back, right,* or *left.* One drawing will have two labels.

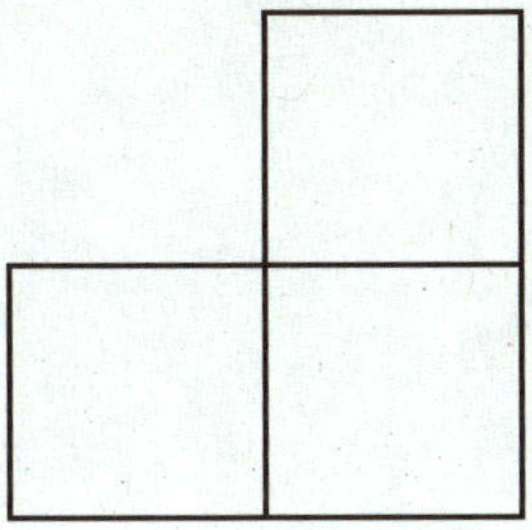

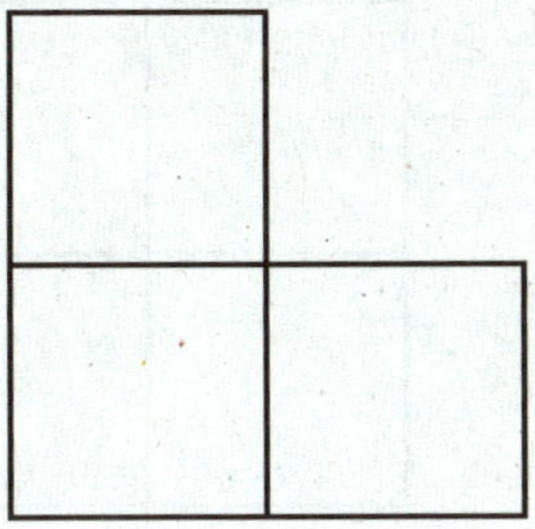

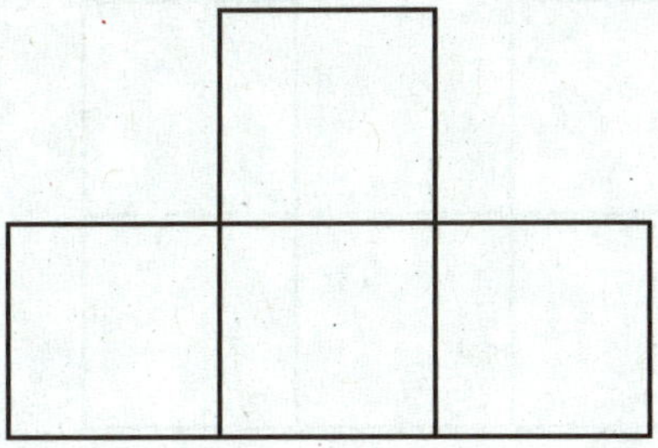

______________________ ______________________ ______________________

______________________ ______________________ ______________________

12. Draw the top view of the model from exercise 10.

12–2 **Class Activity**

Name ______________________ Date ______________

13. Build a model from the drawing below and place it on a sheet of paper with edges labeled *front, back, right,* and *left.*

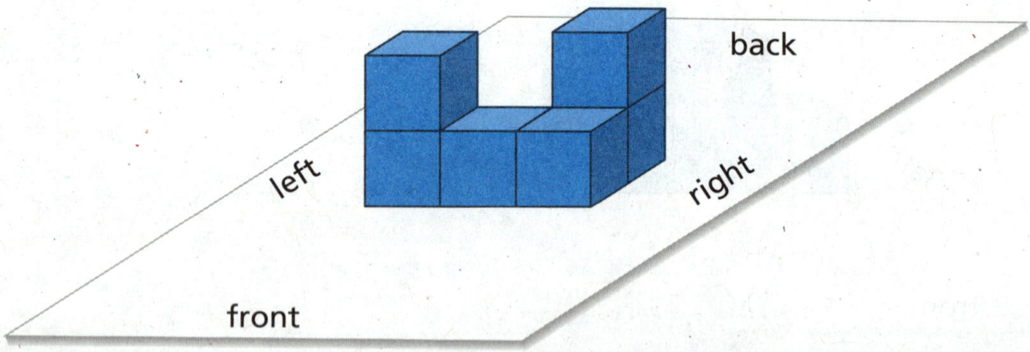

14. Using your model, label the views below as *front, back, left,* or *right.* Each drawing will have two labels.

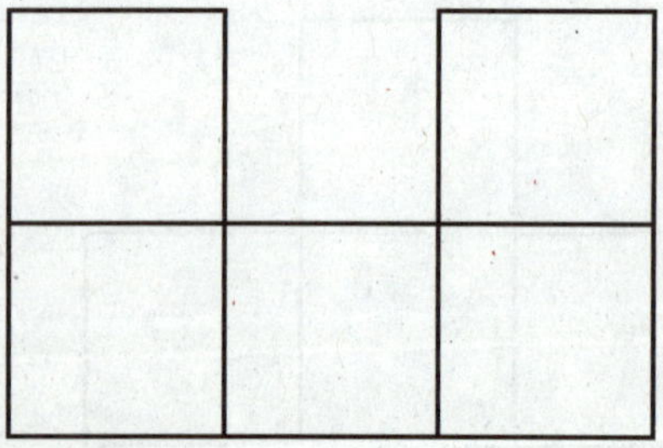

____

____

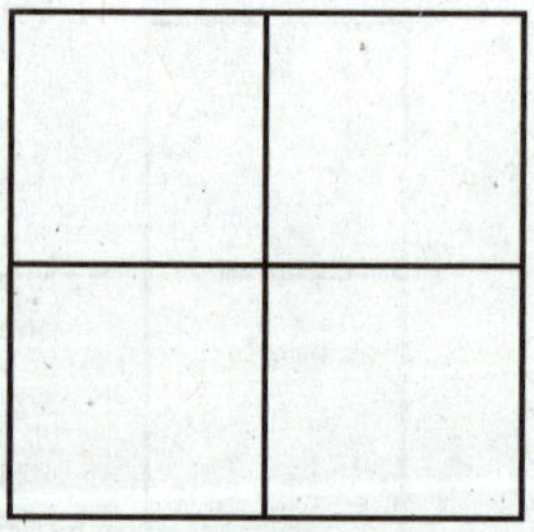

____

____

15. Draw the top view of the model from exercise 13.

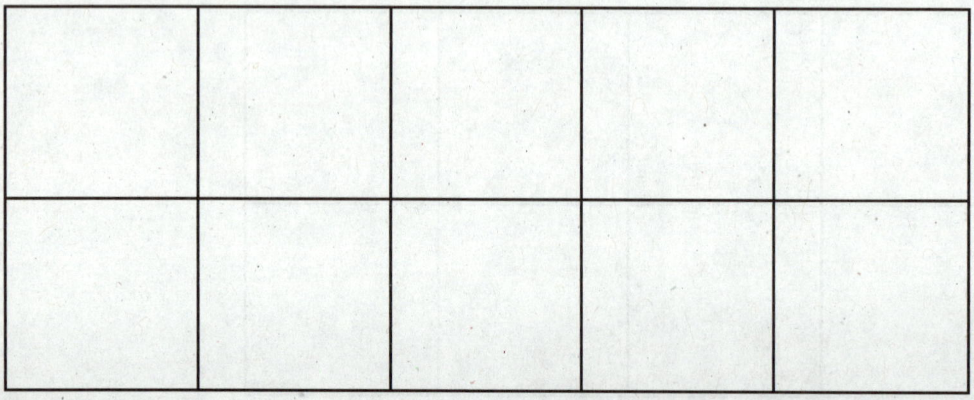

12–2 Class Activity

Name ______________________________ Date ______________

▶ Make Models From Views

Each exercise shows three views of the same model.

Use the views to build a model on a sheet of paper with edges labeled *front, back, right,* and *left.* Compare your model with your partner's.

16.

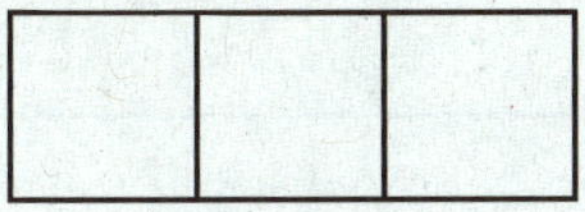
Top

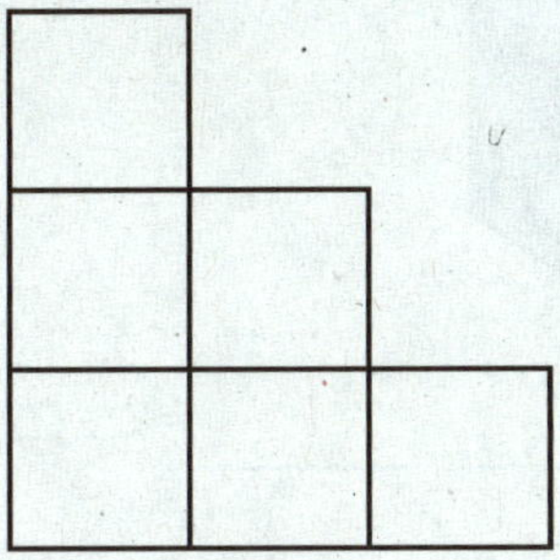
Front

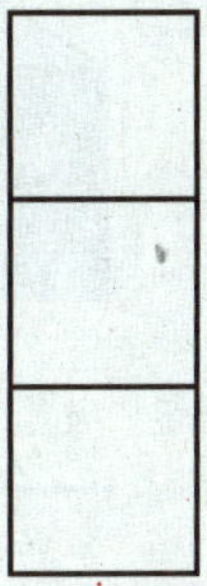
Left/Right

17.

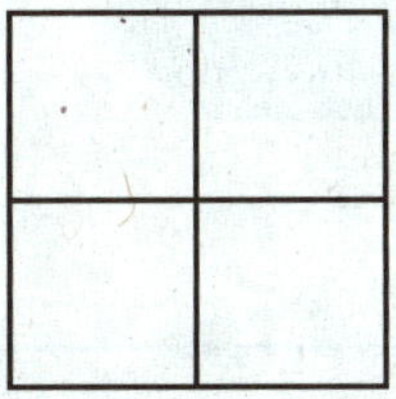
Top

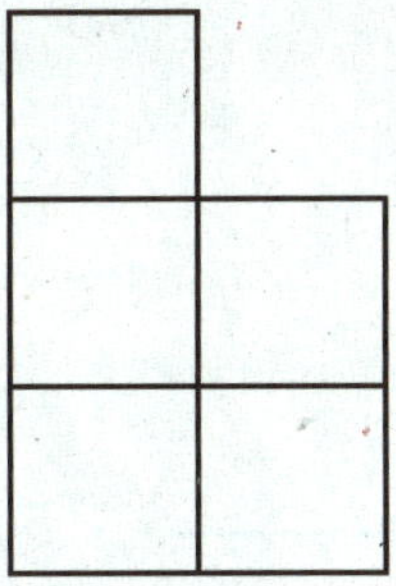
Front

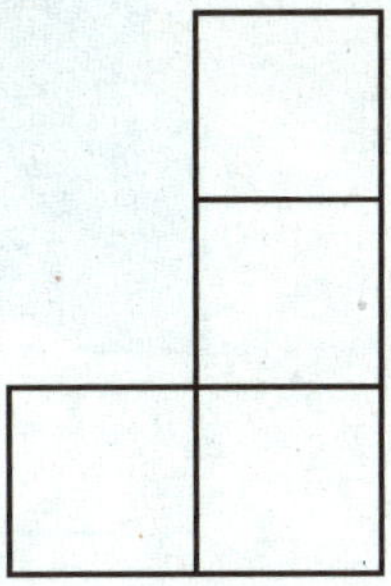
Right

12–2 Going Further

Name ____ Date ____

Vocabulary
volume
cubic units

▶Volume of 3-D Objects

The **volume** of a three-dimensional figure is the number of cubic units that fit inside it.

Find the volume of each figure in cubic units. Build them with cubes if you need to do so.

1 cubic unit

1. 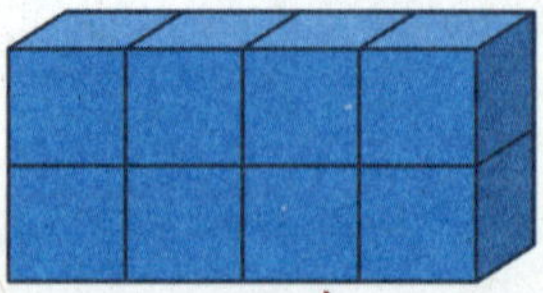

______

2. 

______

3. 

______

4. 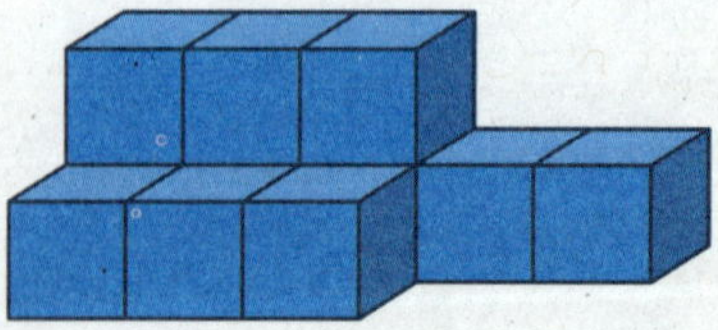

______

5. 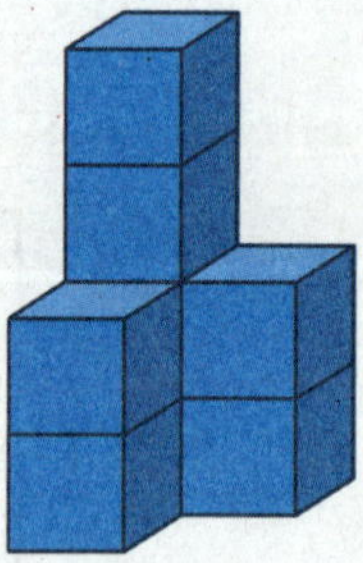

______

6. 

______

12–3 Class Activity

Name ______________________ Date ______________

► Prism Nets

Cut out each net and form the solid figure.

1.

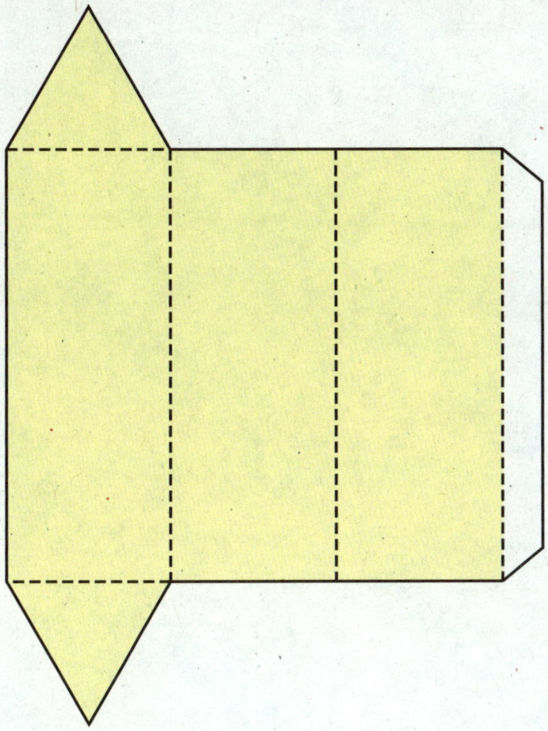

2.

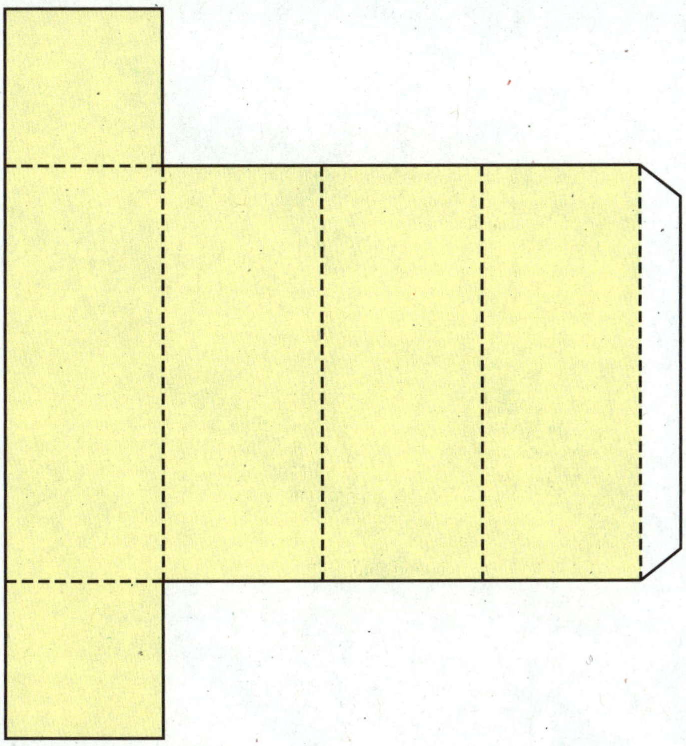

Name ______________________ Date ______________

Cut out each net and form the solid figure.

3.

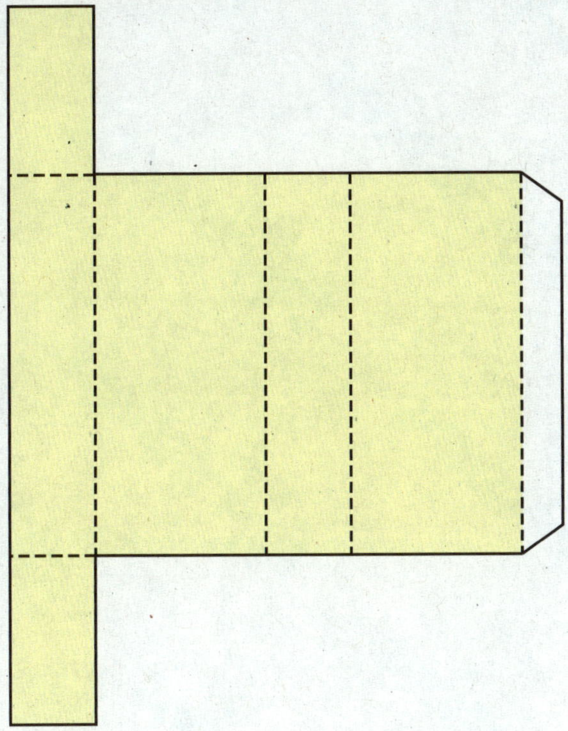

4.

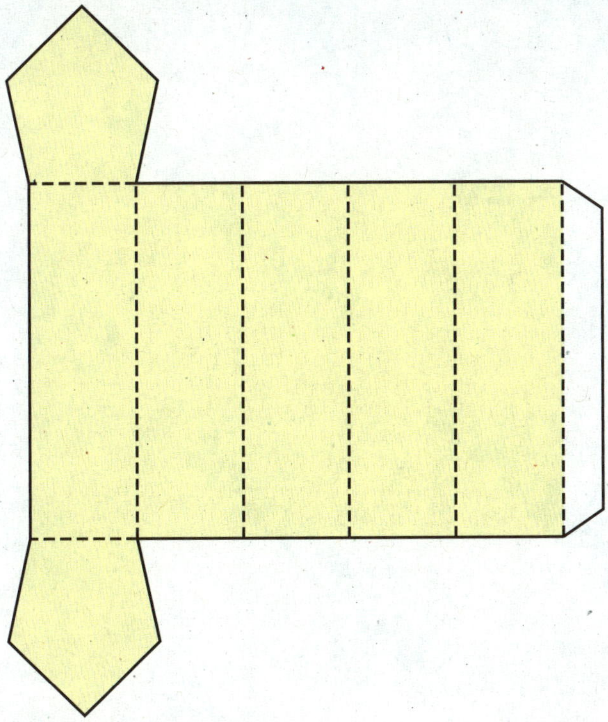

12–3 Class Activity

Name ____________________ Date ____________

►Cylinder Net

Cut out each net and form the solid figure.

5.

►Square Pyramid Net

6.

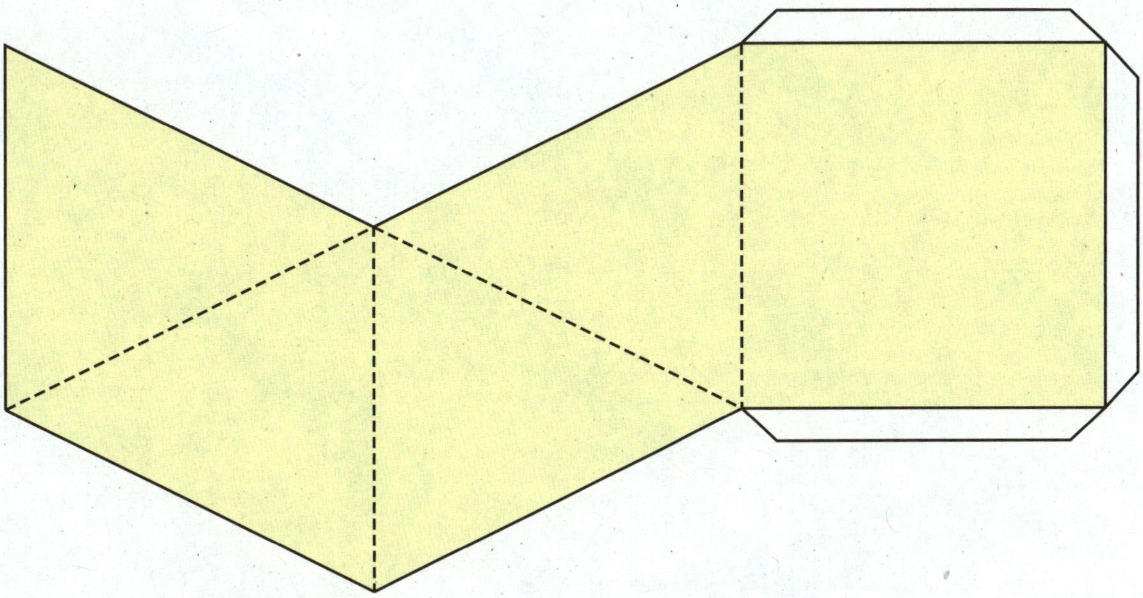

12–4 Class Activity

Name Date

►Build a Cone

Cut out the net and form the solid figure.

1.

12–4 Class Activity

Name ____________________ Date ____________

Vocabulary
edge   face
vertex   vertices

▶ Sort 3-D Figures

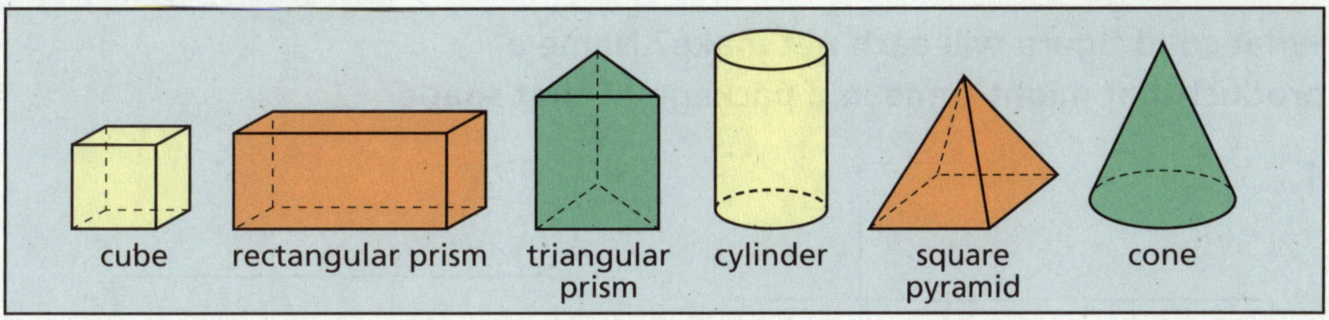

Use the figures above to complete exercises 2–3. Use the words edge, face, and vertex (or vertices).

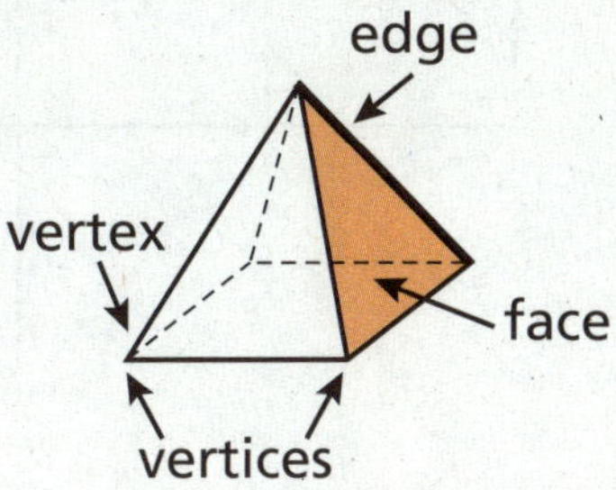

2. Choose your own sorting rule to sort the solid figures shown into two groups.

My sorting rule is ______________________________

______________________________.

The figures in one group are ______________________________

______________________________.

The figures in the other group are ______________________________

______________________________.

3. Choose a different sorting rule to sort the solid figures shown into two groups.

My sorting rule is ______________________________

______________________________.

The figures in one group are ______________________________

______________________________.

The figures in the other group are ______________________________

______________________________.

______________________________.

12–4 Class Activity

Name ______________________ Date __________

▶ Packages

What solid figure will each net make? Name a product that might come in a package of that shape.

4.

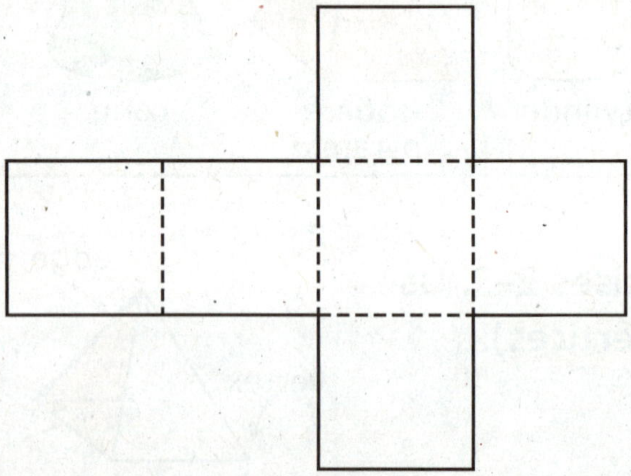

____

5.

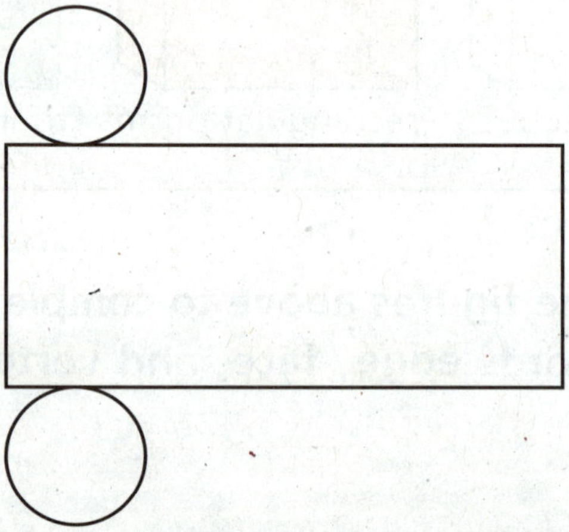

____

6.

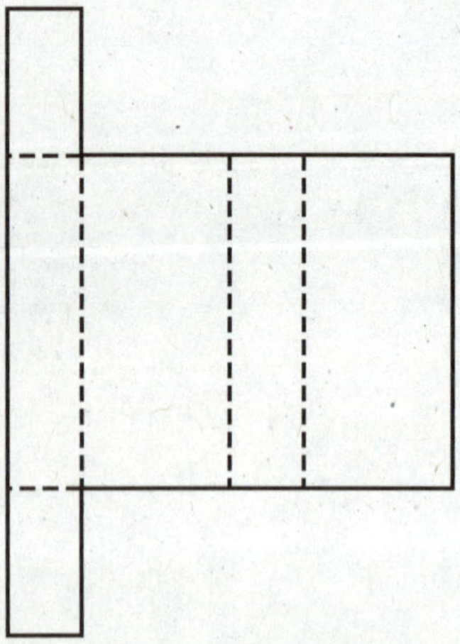

____

7.

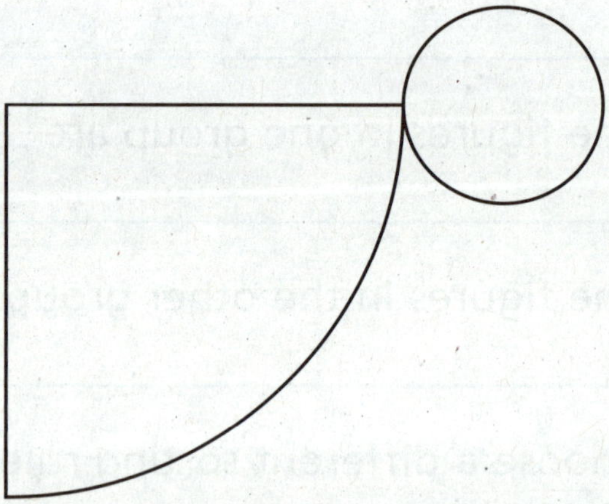

____

8. Choose a product and design a package for it. You can copy one of the nets above onto inch grid paper or create your own net for your package. Include your product's name and information on the net, color it, and then fold it to create your package.

12–5 Class Activity

Name ______________________ Date ____________

Vocabulary
circle
radius
diameter
circumference

► Characteristics of a Circle

1. Place a pencil inside one end of a paper clip. Hold the pencil point in place on a sheet of paper. Place another pencil inside the other end of the paper clip. Ask a partner to hold your paper still while you draw a **circle** by moving the second pencil.

2. Draw and label a **radius** on your circle.

3. How does the length of the radius compare to the length of the paper clip?

____

4. Draw and label a **diameter** on your circle.

5. How does the length of the diameter compare to the length of the paper clip?

____

____

6. Find the **circumference** of this circle. Describe your method.

____

____

____

____

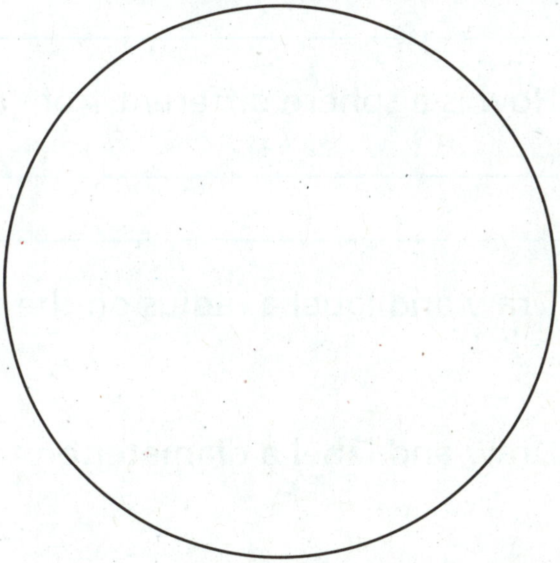

12–5 Class Activity

Name _______________ Date _______________

Vocabulary
sphere

► Characteristics of a Sphere

This is a **sphere**.

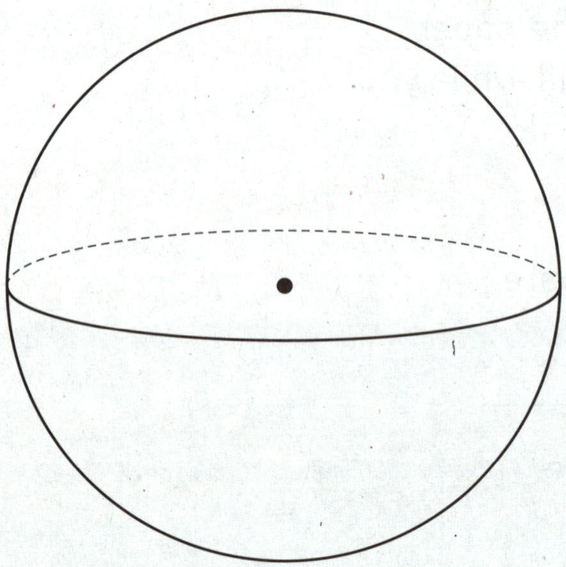

7. How is a sphere similar to a circle?

____

____

____

8. How is a sphere different from a circle?

____

____

9. Draw and label a radius on the sphere.

10. Draw and label a diameter on the sphere.

12 Unit Test

Name ______________________ Date ______________

1. Draw a net that will form a cube when folded.

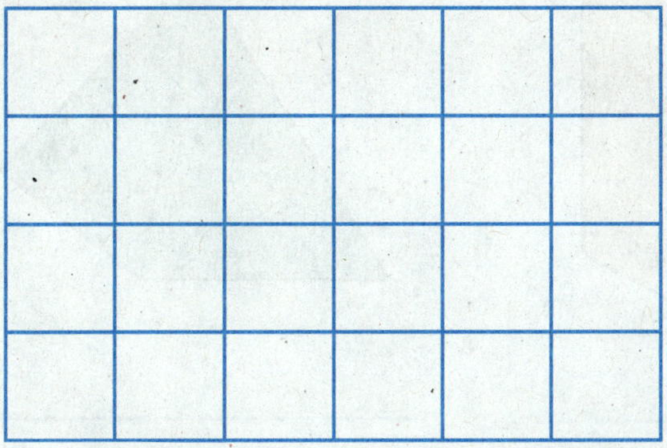

2. Study the model below. Draw the front, back, right, left, and top views.

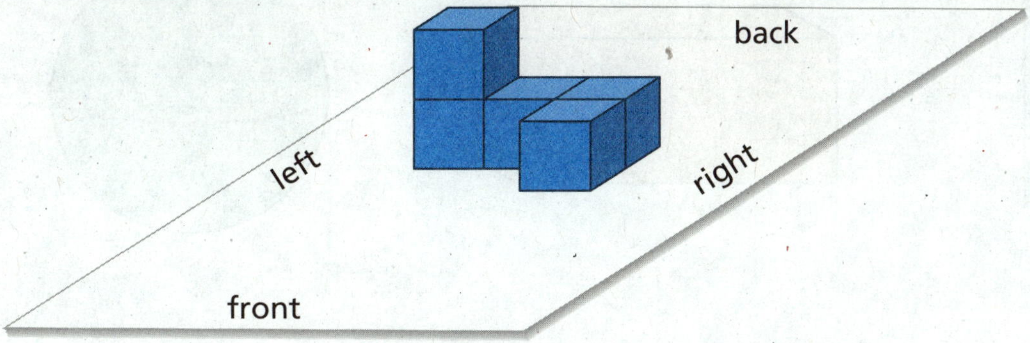

12
Unit Test

Name ____________________ Date ____________

Name the solid figure.

3.

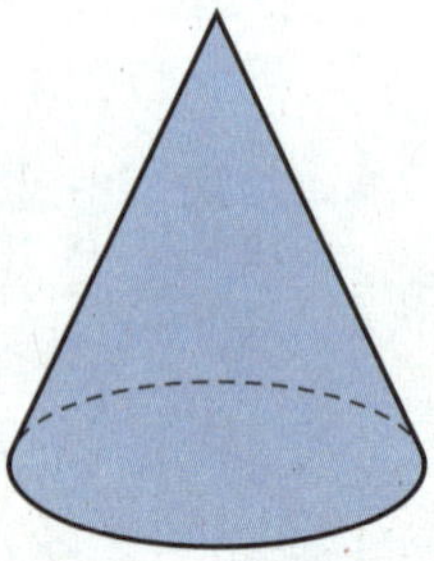

____

4.

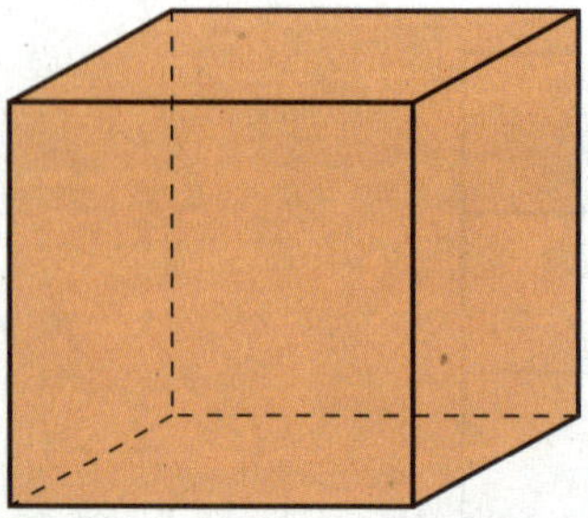

____

5.

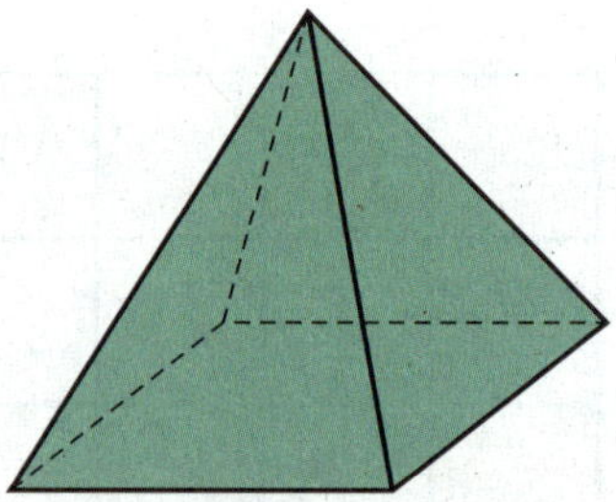

____

6.

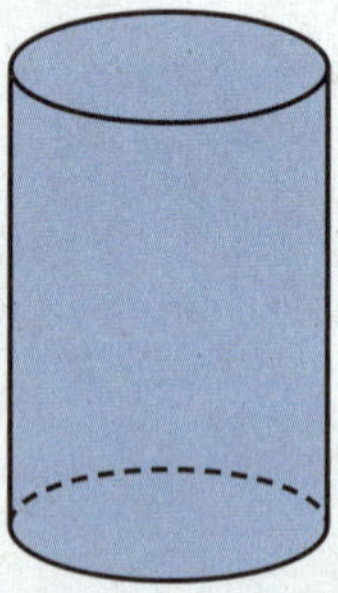

____

7.

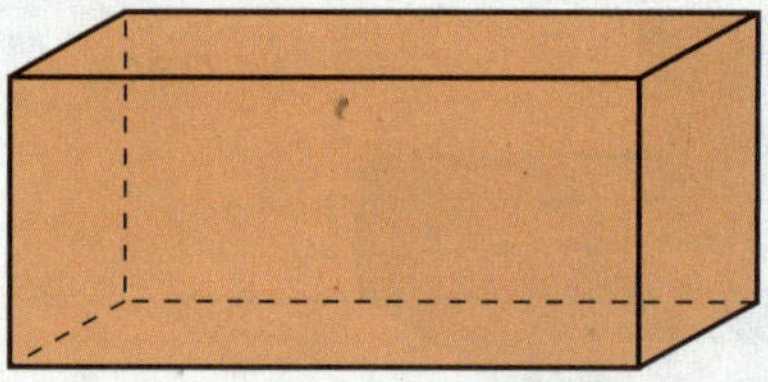

____

8.

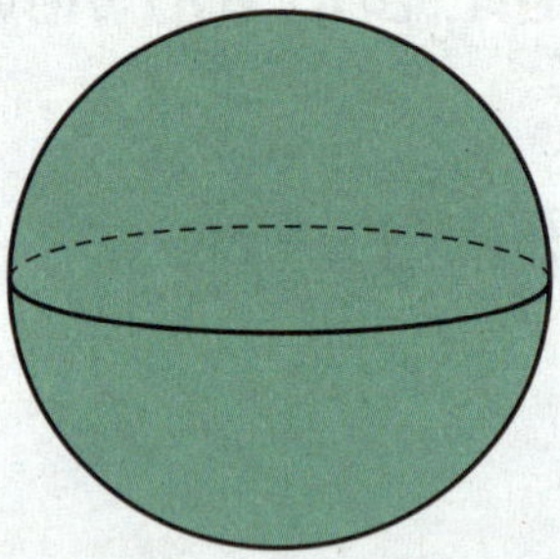

____

9. Name the solid figure that the net will form.

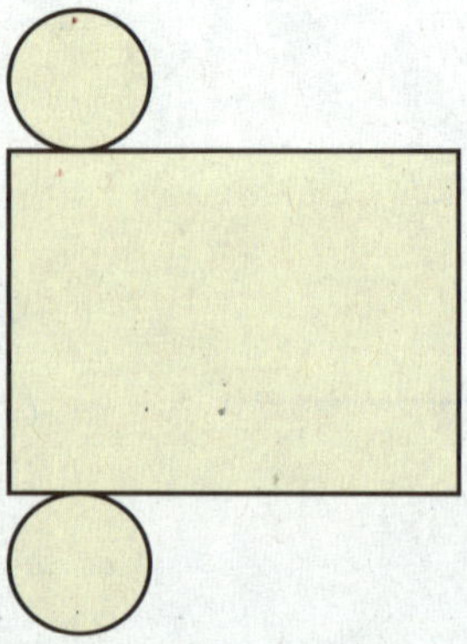

____

10. Extended Response
Name and describe this prism. Tell what you know about its faces, edges, and vertices.

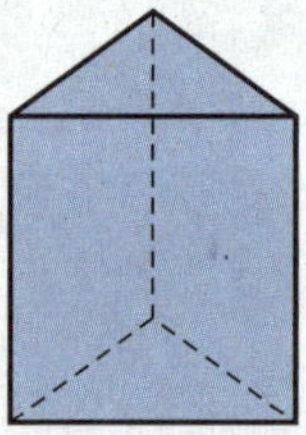

____
____
____
____
____

13–1 Class Activity

Name ____________________ Date ____________

Vocabulary
inch (in.)

► Estimate and Measure Length

Estimate the length of each line segment in inches. Then measure it to the nearest inch.

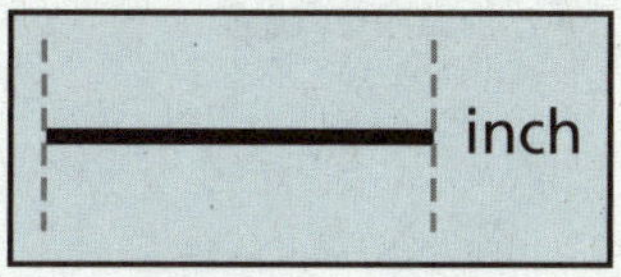

1. 

Estimate: ____________ Actual: ____________

2. 

Estimate: ____________ Actual: ____________

Estimate the length of each line segment in inches. Then measure it to the nearest $\frac{1}{2}$ inch.

3. 

Estimate: ____________ Actual: ____________

4. 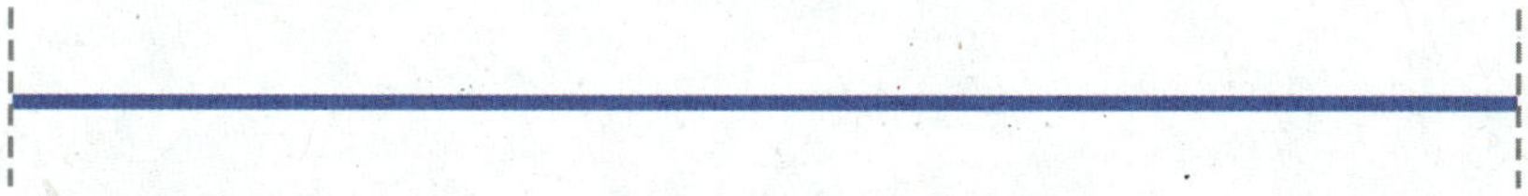

Estimate: ____________ Actual: ____________

Estimate the length of each line segment in inches. Then measure it to the nearest $\frac{1}{4}$ inch.

5. 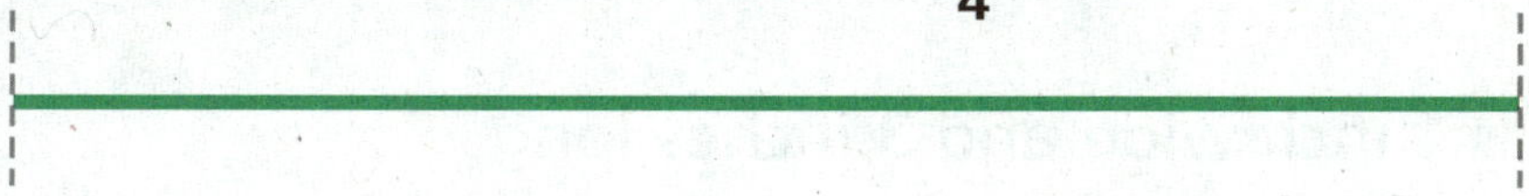

Estimate: ____________ Actual: ____________

6. 

Estimate: ____________ Actual: ____________

13–1 Class Activity

Name ______________________ Date ____________

▶ Draw Line Segments

Draw a line segment that has the given length.

7. 5 inches

8. $4\frac{1}{2}$ inches

9. $4\frac{3}{4}$ inches

10. $3\frac{1}{4}$ inches

11. 2 inches

12. $1\frac{1}{4}$ inches

13. $1\frac{1}{2}$ inches

14. $3\frac{3}{4}$ inches

15. Draw a rectangle that is 1 inch wide and 3 inches long.

Family Letter

Dear Family,

In this unit, students explore ways to measure things using the customary and metric systems of measurement.

The units of measurement we will be working with include:

U.S. Customary System

Length
1 foot (ft) = 12 inches (in.) 1 yard (yd) = 3 feet (ft) 1 mile (mi) = 5,280 feet (ft)
Capacity
1 cup (c) = 8 fluid ounces (oz) 1 pint (pt) = 2 cups (c) 1 quart (qt) = 2 pints (pt) 1 gallon (gal) = 4 quarts (qt)
Weight
1 pound (lb) = 16 ounces (oz)

Metric System

Length
1 meter (m) = 10 decimeters (dm) 1 meter (m) = 100 centimeters (cm) 1 decimeter (dm) = 10 centimeters (cm)
Capacity
1 liter (L) = 1,000 milliliters (mL)
Mass
1 kilogram (kg) = 1,000 grams (g)

Students also read, write, and compare temperatures in degrees Fahrenheit and degrees Celsius.

You can help your child become familiar with these units of measurement by working with measurements together. For example, you might estimate and measure the length of something in inches and convert the measurement to feet. You might use a measuring cup to explore how the cup can be used to fill pints, quarts, or gallons of liquid. From inside, you could read the temperature on an outdoor thermometer and decide if it is hot, warm, cool, or cold outside.

Thank you for helping your child learn important math skills. Please call if you have any questions or comments.

Sincerely,
Your child's teacher

Carta a la familia

Estimada familia:

En esta unidad los estudiantes descubren cómo medir cosas utilizando tanto el sistema medidas usuales como el sistema métrico decimal.

Las unidades de medida con las que trabajaremos incluirán:

Sistema usual

Longitud	
1 pie (pie) = 12 pulgadas (pulg)	
1 yarda (yd) = 3 pies (pies)	
1 milla (mi) = 5,280 pies (pies)	
Capacidad	
1 taza (taza) = 8 onzas líquidas (oz)	
1 pinta (pt) = 2 tazas (tazas)	
1 cuarto de galón (ct) = 2 pintas (pt)	
1 galón (gal) = 4 cuartos de galón (ct)	
Peso	
1 libra (lb) = 16 onzas (oz)	

Sistema métrico decimal

Longitud	
1 metro (m) = 10 decímetros (dm)	
1 metro (m) = 100 centímetros (cm)	
1 decímetro (dm) = 10 centímetros (cm)	
Capacidad	
1 litro (L) = 1,000 mililitros (mL)	
Masa	
1 kilogramo (kg) = 1,000 gramos (g)	

Los estudiantes también leen, escriben y comparan temperaturas en grados Farenheit y en grados centígrados.

Puede ayudar a su niño a que se familiarice con estas unidades métricas trabajando juntos con las medidas. Por ejemplo, pueden estimar y medir la longitud de algo en pulgadas y convertir la medida a pies. Podrían usar una taza de medidas para aprender cómo se pueden llenar pintas, cuartos de galón o galones con la taza y un líquido. Desde el interior de la casa podrían leer la temperatura en un termómetro exterior y decidir si la temperatura exterior es caliente, cálida, fresca o fría.

Gracias por ayudar a su niño a aprender destrezas matemáticas importantes.

Si tiene alguna duda o comentario, por favor comuníquese conmigo.

Atentamente,
El maestro de su niño

Name _______________________________________ Date _______________

► Convert Customary Units of Length

> 1 foot (ft) = 12 inches (in.)
> 1 yard (yd) = 3 ft or 36 in.
> 1 mile (mi) = 5,280 ft or 1,760 yd

Complete.

1. 1 foot 3 inches = _____ inches
2. 1 yard 3 inches = _____ inches
3. 2 feet 5 inches = _____ inches
4. 1 yard 1 foot = _____ inches
5. 1 yard 9 inches = _____ inches
6. 2 feet 7 inches = _____ inches
7. 1 yard 2 feet = _____ inches
8. 2 feet 11 inches = _____ inches
9. 1 foot 10 inches = _____ inches
10. 2 yards = _____ inches
11. 3 feet = 1 _____
12. 6 feet = _____ yards
13. 27 feet = _____ yards
14. 2 feet = _____ inches
15. 32 feet = _____ yards _____ feet or _____ yards
16. 16 feet = _____ yards _____ foot or _____ yards
17. 29 feet = _____ yards _____ feet or _____ yards
18. 25 feet = _____ yards _____ foot or _____ yards

Solve.

19. Marcus has 27 feet of rope to make rope swings. He needs 6 yards of rope for each swing. How many rope swings can he make? How many feet of rope will be left over?

    ____

20. Cassidy has 50 inches of ribbon. She wants to divide it equally among her 6 nieces. How many inches of ribbon can each niece have? Give the answer as a mixed number.

    ____

13–2 Class Activity

Name ______________________ Date ____________

Vocabulary
inch
foot
yard
mile

▶ Find Benchmarks

Write the answer.

21. This line segment is 1 **inch** long. Put two fingers on the line segment. Then hold up your fingers. Write the name of an object that is about 1 inch (or two finger widths) long.

____

22. One **foot** is equal to 12 inches. Spread both hands on a ruler to show 1 foot. Write the name of an object that is about 1 foot (or both hands) long.

____

23. One **yard** is equal to 3 feet or 36 inches. How many 12-inch lengths are in 1 yard? Write the name of an object that is about 1 yard long.

____

24. One **mile** is 5,280 feet or 1,760 yards. In describing a long distance, why would it make sense to use miles instead of feet or yards?

____

▶ Choose Appropriate Units

Choose the unit you would use to measure each. Write *inch, foot, yard,* or *mile.*

25. the width of a piece of notebook paper ______________

26. the length of a classroom board ______________

27. the height of the school ______________

28. the distance you travel to school ______________

13–3 **Class Activity**

Name ______________________ Date ____________

Vocabulary
centimeter (cm)

► Estimate and Measure Length

Estimate the length of each line segment in centimeters. Then measure it to the nearest centimeter.

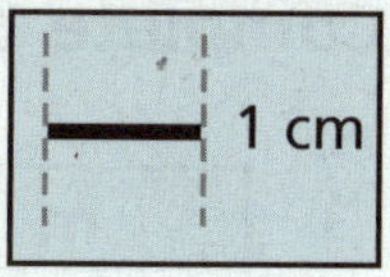

1. 

Estimate: ____________ Actual: ____________

2. 

Estimate: ____________ Actual: ____________

3. 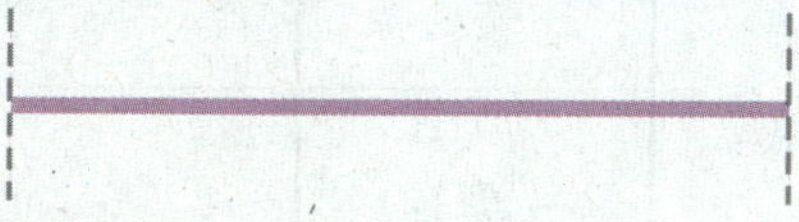

Estimate: ____________ Actual: ____________

4. 

Estimate: ____________ Actual: ____________

5. 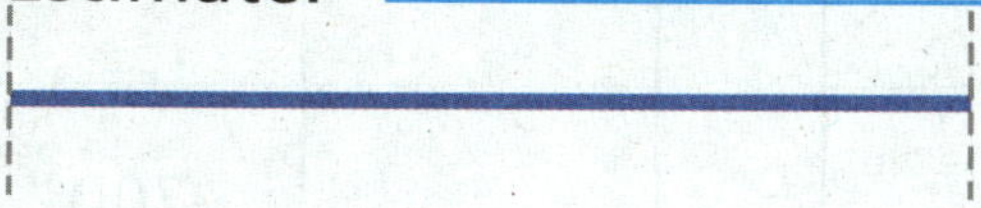

Estimate: ____________ Actual: ____________

6. Estimate the length of these items in your classroom. Then measure to the nearest centimeter. Record your information in the chart.

	Estimate (cm)	Actual (cm)
pair of scissors		
gluestick		
pencil		
marker		

13–3 Class Activity

Name ______________________ Date ______________

Vocabulary
centimeter (cm)
decimeter (dm)
meter (m)

▶ Convert Metric Units of Length

Complete the tables.

7.

m	cm
1	100
2	
	300
	400
5	
	600
7	
8	
	900
	1,000

8.

m	dm
1	10
2	
	30
	40
5	
6	
7	
	80
	90
10	

9.

dm	cm
10	100
20	
	300
40	
50	
	600
	700
80	
	900
	1,000

Compare. Write >, <, or = in the ◯.

10. 120 cm ◯ 1 m

11. 10 dm ◯ 100 cm

12. 3 m ◯ 3,000 cm

13. 6 m ◯ 600 dm

13–3 Class Activity

Name _______________ Date _______________

Complete the tables.

14.

cm	dm
10	1
20	
30	
40	
	5
	6
	7
80	
	9
	10

15.

cm	m
100	1
	2
	3
400	
500	
600	
	7
	8
900	
1,000	

16.

dm	m
10	1
20	
	3
	4
50	
	6
70	
80	
	9
	10

Compare. Write >, <, or = in the ◯.

17. 30 dm ◯ 2 m

18. 200 cm ◯ 2 m

19. 70 cm ◯ 70 dm

20. 1 m ◯ 50 cm

21. 800 cm ◯ 7 m

22. 5 dm ◯ 60 cm

13–3 Class Activity

Name ______________________ Date ____________

Vocabulary
centimeter (cm)
decimeter (dm)
meter (m)
kilometer (km)

▶ Find Benchmarks

23. This line segment is 1 **centimeter** long. Use your little finger to show 1 centimeter. Write an object that is about 1 cm (or your little finger width) long.

____

24. One **decimeter** is equal to 10 cm. This line segment is 1 decimeter long. Spread your hand to show 1 decimeter. Write an object that is about 1 dm (or your hand spread out) long.

____

25. One **meter** is equal to 100 cm. How many decimeters are in one meter? Write an object or distance that is about 1 meter long.

____

26. One **kilometer** is 1,000 meters. It takes you about 10 minutes to walk a kilometer. Write the name of a place that is about 1 km from your house.

____

▶ Choose the Appropriate Unit

Choose the unit you would use to measure each. Write *centimeter, decimeter, meter,* or *kilometer.*

27. the width of your classroom _______________________

28. the distance you fly on an airplane _______________________

29. the length of a pencil _______________________

30. the length of your fingernail _______________________

Name Date

► Estimate and Find the Perimeter

Estimate the perimeter in inches. Then measure each side to the nearest $\frac{1}{4}$ inch and find the perimeter.

1. 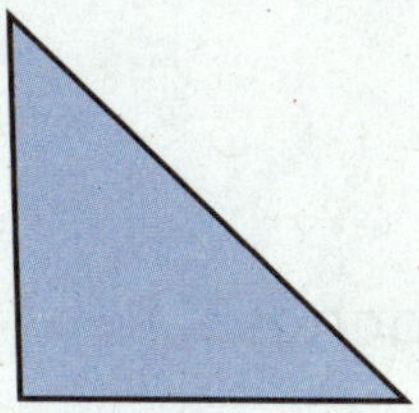

2. 

3. 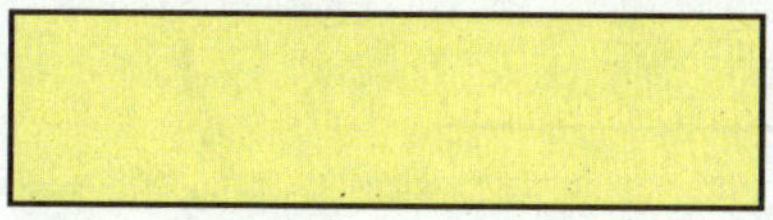

4. 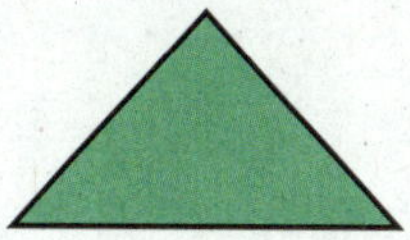

5. 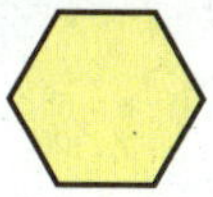

6. 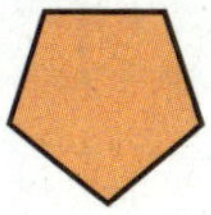

7. 

8. 

13–4 Class Activity

Name ______________________ Date ____________

▶ Add Customary Units of Length

Add.

9. $3\frac{1}{2}$ inches + 4 inches

____

10. $8\frac{1}{4}$ inches + $2\frac{1}{4}$ inches

____

11. $5\frac{1}{2}$ inches + $8\frac{1}{2}$ inches

____

12. $3\frac{1}{4}$ inches + $2\frac{3}{4}$ inches

____

13. $4\frac{1}{2}$ inches + $5\frac{1}{4}$ inches

____

14. $7\frac{1}{4}$ inches + $\frac{1}{2}$ inches

____

15. $4\frac{1}{2}$ inches + $5\frac{3}{4}$ inches

____

16. $5\frac{1}{2}$ inches + $5\frac{3}{4}$ inches

____

17. $3\frac{3}{4}$ inches + $5\frac{3}{8}$ inches

____

18. $4\frac{5}{8}$ inches + $6\frac{3}{4}$ inches

____

Solve.

19. Mia wants to make a friendship bracelet. She needs three pieces of string that are each $9\frac{3}{4}$ inches long. How many inches of string does she need in all?

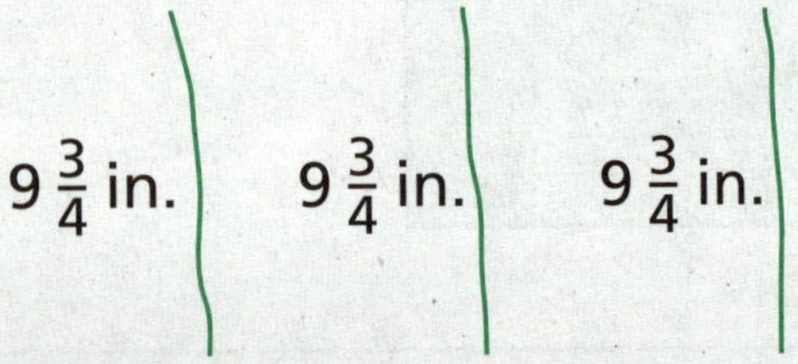

____

20. Larry measured his living room. Then he wrote down the measurements. What is the perimeter of his living room in feet?

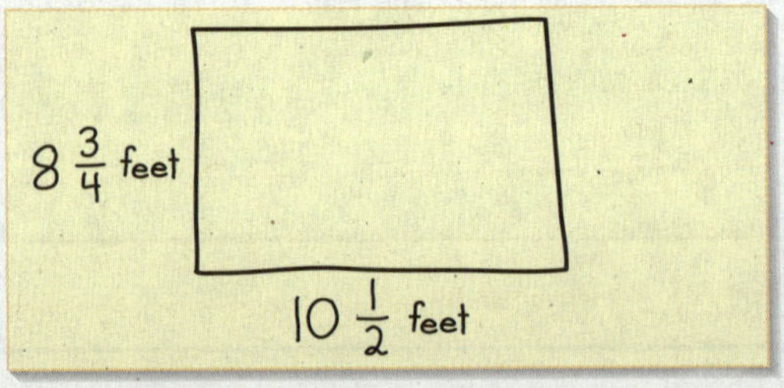

____

13–5 Class Activity

Name ____________________ Date ____________

Vocabulary

cup (c)
fluid ounce (fl oz)
quart (qt)   gallon (gal)

► Units of Capacity

1 **cup**  = 8 **fluid ounces**

4 cups  = 1 **quart**

2 cups  = 1 pint

4 quarts = 1 **gallon**

Solve.

1. Regina drank 2 cups of milk. Rex drank 8 fluid ounces of milk. Who drank more milk?

   ____

2. Fran spilled a half-gallon of water. Mark spilled 3 quarts. Who spilled more water?

   ____

3. Would you rather have a pint and a half of your favorite drink or 4 cups?

   ____

4. Would you rather have a cup or a fourth of a pint of a drink you don't like?

   ____

5. There are 2 quarts of tomato juice in the refrigerator. Mrs. Chavez needs $\frac{3}{4}$ of a gallon to make a stew. Does she have enough? Explain.

   ____

   ____

6. Juana has a 12-cup punch bowl. She uses a 1-quart container to fill it. How many times must she pour a quart into the bowl to fill it? Explain.

   ____

   ____

13–5 Class Activity

Name ______________________ Date ______________

▶ Convert Units of Capacity

Complete the table.

1 cup (c) = 8 fluid ounces (fl oz)
2 cups (c) = 1 pint (pt)
4 cups (c) = 1 quart (qt)
16 cups (c) = 1 gallon (gal)

	Number of cups	Number of pints	Number of quarts	Number of half-gallons	Number of gallons
Cup					
Pint					
Quart					
Half-Gallon					
Gallon					

Complete.

7. 8 cups = _____ pints

8. $\frac{1}{2}$ cup = _____ fluid ounces

9. 9 pints = _____ quarts

10. _____ pints = 18 quarts

11. _____ quarts = 4 gallons

12. 8 quarts = _____ gallons

13. 16 fluid ounces = 1 _____

14. 8 pints = 1 _____

15. _____ cups = 3 pints

16. 5 pints = _____ quarts

17. _____ fluid ounces = $\frac{1}{2}$ gallon

18. _____ quarts = $8\frac{1}{4}$ gallons

Name ____________________ Date ____________

► Establish Benchmarks

Complete.

19. This container holds 1 cup. Write the name of another container that holds about 1 cup.

____

20. This container holds 1 pint. Write the name of another container that holds about 1 pint.

____

21. This container holds 1 quart. Write the name of another container that holds about 1 quart.

____

22. This container holds 1 gallon. Write the name of another container that holds about 1 gallon.

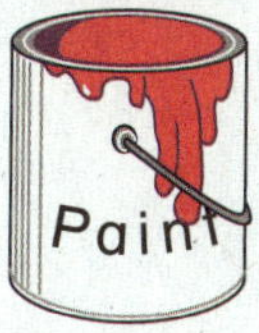

____

► Choose Units

Choose the best unit to use to measure how much each item can hold. Write *cup, pint, quart,* or *gallon.*

23. a carton of heavy cream ____________

24. a swimming pool ____________

25. a flower vase ____________

26. a wash tub ____________

27. **Math Journal** Think of a container. Choose the unit you would use to measure its capacity. Draw the container and write the name of the unit you chose. Explain why you chose that unit.

13–5 Class Activity

Name ____________________ Date __________

▶ Estimate Customary Units of Capacity

Ring the better estimate.

28.

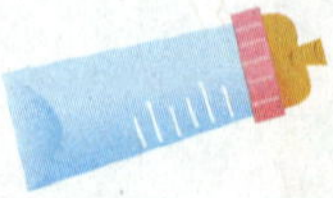

2 cups

2 quarts

29.

5 gallons

5 cups

30.

1 pint

1 gallon

31.

1 cup

1 pint

32.

1 cup

1 gallon

33.

5 gallon

30 gallon

Solve.

34. Jamie makes a shopping list for a picnic with his four friends. He estimates that he'll need a pint of lemonade for the group to drink. Do you think his estimate is reasonable? Explain.

____

____

____

13–6 Class Activity

Name ______________________ Date ______________

Vocabulary
liter (L)
milliliter (mL)

▶ Convert Metric Units of Capacity

1 liter (L) = 1,000 milliliters (mL)

Complete.

1. 2 L = ______ mL
2. 15,000 mL = ______ L
3. $\frac{1}{2}$ L = ______ mL
4. ______ L = 250 mL
5. ______ L = 4,000 mL
6. 4,000 mL = ______ L

▶ Benchmarks for a Liter and a Milliliter

Write the answer.

7. This bottle holds 1 **liter**.

Name another container that holds about 1 liter.

____

8. This eyedropper holds 1 **milliliter**.

Name another container that holds about 1 milliliter.

____

▶ Choose the Appropriate Unit

Choose the unit you would use to measure the capacity of each. Write *mL* or *L*.

9. a kitchen sink ______
10. a soup spoon ______
11. a teacup ______
12. a washing machine ______

Circle the better estimate.

13. a juice container 1 L 1 mL
14. a bowl of soup 500 L 500 mL

13–6 Class Activity

Name ____________ Date ____________

▶ Solve Problems Involving Capacity

Solve.

15. Diane has 39 cups of lemonade to divide equally among 4 tables. How much lemonade should she put at each table?

16. A recipe calls for 3 pints of milk. How many times must you fill a 1-cup measuring cup to make 3 pints?

17. Mr. Valle made 26 cups of barbeque sauce. He wants to divide it equally among 3 friends. How much sauce will each friend get?

18. Rebecca has 33 cups of ice. Each pitcher of iced tea needs 4 cups of ice. How many pitchers can Rebecca fill? How much ice will be left over?

19. One bottle of water has a red label and holds 2 liters. Another bottle of water has a blue label and holds 1,500 milliliters. What color is the label on the larger bottle?

20. Camilla poured 2,300 milliliters of punch into a punch bowl. Then José poured 3 more liters of punch into the bowl. How many milliliters of punch are in the bowl altogether?

21. A bowl of punch has 2L of lemon-lime soda and 600 mL of lemonade. How many more mL of lemon-lime soda does the punch have?

22. A pudding recipe makes 6 cups of pudding. Will a 1-quart container be large enough to hold the pudding? Why or why not?

23. Would you rather have 500 milliliters of your favorite drink or $\frac{1}{4}$ liter?

24. A bottle holds 750 mL. How many liters will 2 bottles hold?

13–7

Class Activity

Name ____________________ Date ____________________

▶ Use Improper Fractions and Mixed Numbers in Measurements

Write the improper fraction or mixed number for each measurement.

1. $\frac{7}{2}$ c = ____

2. $\frac{9}{5}$ L = ____

3. $\frac{18}{4}$ m = ____

4. $1\frac{3}{8}$ qt = ____

5. $1\frac{3}{4}$ ft = ____

6. $3\frac{2}{3}$ gal = ____

7. $4\frac{1}{2}$ in. = ____

8. $\frac{16}{7}$ pt = ____

9. $3\frac{7}{8}$ c = ____

10. $2\frac{5}{6}$ mi = ____

11. $3\frac{1}{3}$ yd = ____

12. $\frac{19}{12}$ ml = ____

13. $\frac{17}{9}$ km = ____

14. $2\frac{1}{4}$ in. = ____

15. $\frac{21}{5}$ qt = ____

13–7 Class Activity

Name ________________________ Date ____________

▶ Fractions as Lengths

Write the length of each line segment using a fraction.

16.

______

17.

______

18.

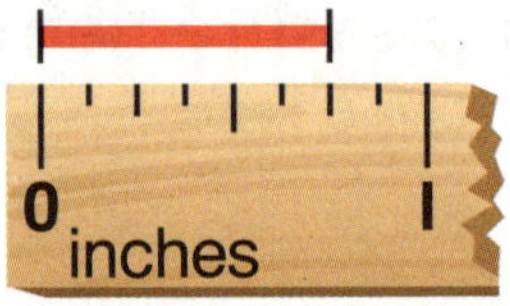

______

Write the length of each line segment using an improper fraction and a mixed number.

19.

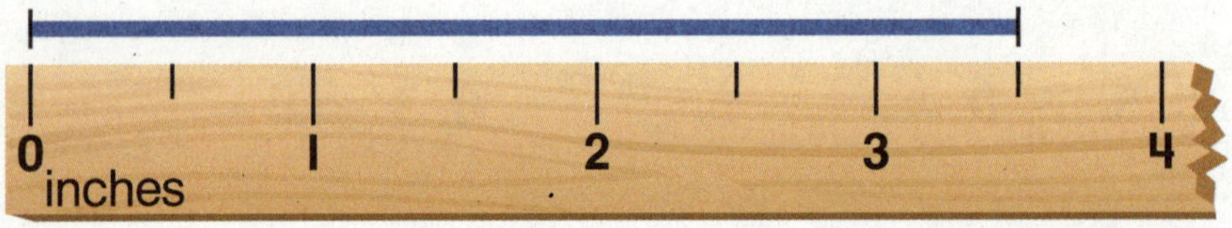

______

20.

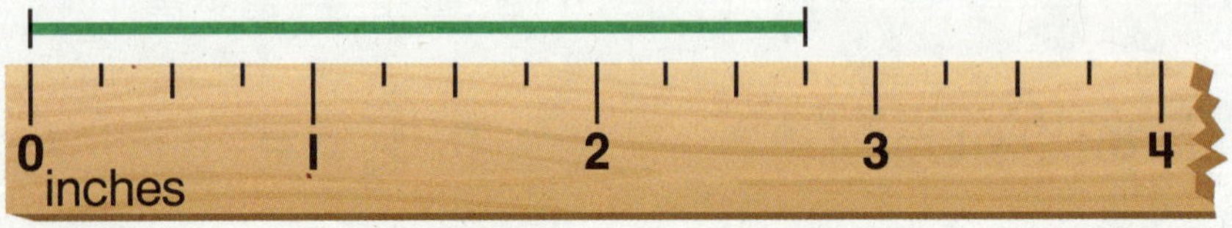

______

21.

______

22.

______

13–8 Class Activity

Name ______ Date ______

►Review Measurement Equivalencies

Complete.

1.

Inches	Feet
12	1
1	$\frac{1}{12}$
2	
4	

2.

Feet	Yards
	1
1	
2	
4	

3.

cm	m
	1
1	
87	
158	

4.

Cup	Pint
	1
1	
	2
3	

5.

Pint	Quart
	1
1	
6	
	$1\frac{1}{2}$

6.

Quart	Gallon
4	1
1	
2	
	$1\frac{1}{2}$

7. 1,500 mL = ______

8. 7L = ______

9. 16 cups = ______ pints = ______ quarts = 1 gallon

10. 1 cup = ______ pint = ______ quart = ______ gallon

11. 6 c = ______ pt = ______ qt = ______ gal

12. 48 c = ______ pt = ______ qt = ______ gal

13. **Math Journal** Seth wants to make a rectangular garden. He has 20 feet of fence. Draw two possible rectangular gardens that Seth could make with the fence. Label the gardens in both feet and inches.

Name Date

13–9 Class Activity

Name ______________________ Date __________

Vocabulary
pound (lb)
ounce (oz)

▶ Ounces or Pounds

Complete.

1.

Ounces	Pounds
16	1
1	
	2
	3
8	
4	

2.

Pounds	Ounces
$1\frac{1}{2}$	
$2\frac{3}{4}$	
4	
	68
$4\frac{1}{2}$	
	76

3. 2 lb = ________ oz

4. 60 oz = ________ lb

5. 10 lb = ________ oz

6. ________ lb = 12 oz

7. 2 oz = ________ lb

8. 40 oz = ________ lb

▶ Establish Benchmarks for a Pound and an Ounce

9. This weighs about 1 **ounce**.

Name another item that weighs about 1 ounce.

____

10. This weighs about 1 **pound**.

Name another item that weighs about 1 pound.

____

13–9 Class Activity

Name ______ Date ______

▶Choose the Appropriate Unit

Choose the unit you would use to measure the weight of each. Write *pound* or *ounce*.

11. a backpack full of books ______

12. a couch ______

13. a peanut ______

14. a pencil ______

Circle the better estimate.

15. a student desk	3 lb	30 lb
16. a television	20 oz	20 lb
17. a hamster	5 oz	5 lb
18. a slice of cheese	1 lb	1 oz

Solve.

19. Kiko bought 2 pounds of peaches, 8 ounces of cherries, 12 ounces of plums, and $1\frac{1}{4}$ pounds of apples. What was the total weight of her purchases?

______

______

20. A pound of potatoes was used to make some soup. If the soup is divided evenly among 8 people, how many ounces of potatoes will each person get?

______

21. Would you rather have a pound and a half of your favorite nuts or 20 ounces?

______

22. Gregory bought $1\frac{1}{4}$ pounds of nails at 10¢ an ounce. How much did he pay?

______

13–9 Class Activity

Name ______ Date ______

Vocabulary
gram (g)
kilogram (kg)

▶ Grams and Kilograms

Complete.

23.

Grams	Kilograms
1,000	1
1	
	2
	3
500	
40	

24.

Kilograms	Grams
$1\frac{1}{2}$	
$\frac{200}{1,000}$	
	250
$5\frac{3}{4}$	
6	
$6\frac{1}{2}$	6,500

25. 2 kg = ______ g

26. 750 g = ______ kg

27. 10 kg = ______ g

28. ______ kg = 500 g

▶ Benchmarks for a Gram and a Kilogram

Write the answer.

29. A paper clip has a mass of about 1 **gram**.

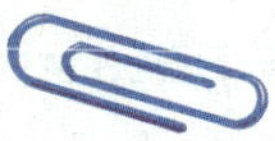

Name another item with a mass of about 1 gram.

______

30. A math book has a mass of about 1 **kilogram**.

Name another item with a mass of about 1 kilogram.

______

13–9 Class Activity

Name ____________________ Date ____________

▶Choose the Appropriate Unit

Choose the unit you would use to measure the mass of each. Write *gram* or *kilogram*.

31. an elephant

____

32. a crayon

____

33. a stamp

____

34. a dog

____

Circle the better estimate.

35. a pair of sunglasses	150 g	150 kg
36. a horse	6 kg	600 kg
37. a watermelon	40 g	4 kg
38. a quarter	500 g	5 g

Solve.

39. The mass of a small penguin is 1 kilogram 800 grams. How many grams less than 2 kilograms is that?

____

40. Would you rather have $\frac{1}{2}$ kilogram or 400 grams of your favorite candy?

____

41. Rolls of coins are sometimes weighed to check how many are inside. A penny weighs about 3 g. About how many grams would a dollar's worth of pennies weigh?

____

42. Jenna wants to put 200 grams of peanuts in each of 5 small cups for party favors. Would a 1-kg bag of peanuts be enough to fill the cups? Explain.

____

____

____

13–9 Class Activity

Name _______________ Date _______________

► Choose the Better Estimate

Ring the better estimate.

43.

200 grams

200 kilograms

44.

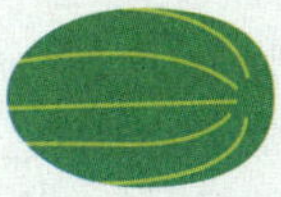

10 kilograms

10 grams

45.

1 ounce

1 pound

46.

100 pounds

10 ounces

47.

100 pounds

1 ton

48.

1 kilogram

10 kilograms

Solve.

49. Suzie estimated the weights of objects and ordered them by the estimates of their weights. She explained that estimating them was easy since the smallest objects weighed the least and the largest objects weighed the most. Do you agree with Suzie?

____

____

13–9 Name ______________________ Date ______

Going Further

▶Add and Subtract Measurements

Dear Math Students,

Today my teacher asked me to add 2 feet 6 inches and 3 feet 8 inches. Here is how I solved the problem. Is my calculation right?

```
  2 ft 6 in.
+ 3 ft 8 in.
-----------
  6 ft 4 in.
```

If not, please correct my work and explain below.

Thank you,

The Puzzled Penguin

50. ____

____

Solve.

51. 3 ft 5 in. + 4 ft 9 in.

52. 4 yd 1 ft − 1 yd 2 ft

53. 6 lb 8 oz + 3 lb 7 oz

54. 3 pt 1 c + 5 pt 1 c

55. 6 h 20 min − 4 h 30 min

56. 5 days 17 h + 3 days 12 h

57. Carlie jumped 48 dm, 340 cm and 4 m on her third triple jump. What is the total distance she jumped in centimeters?

____

58. Aaron made 4 lb of potato salad. He put 2 lb 6 oz in take-out containers. How much potato salad is left?

____

13–10 Class Activity

Name _______________________________ Date ______________

▸Temperature in Fahrenheit

Circle the better estimate of the temperature.

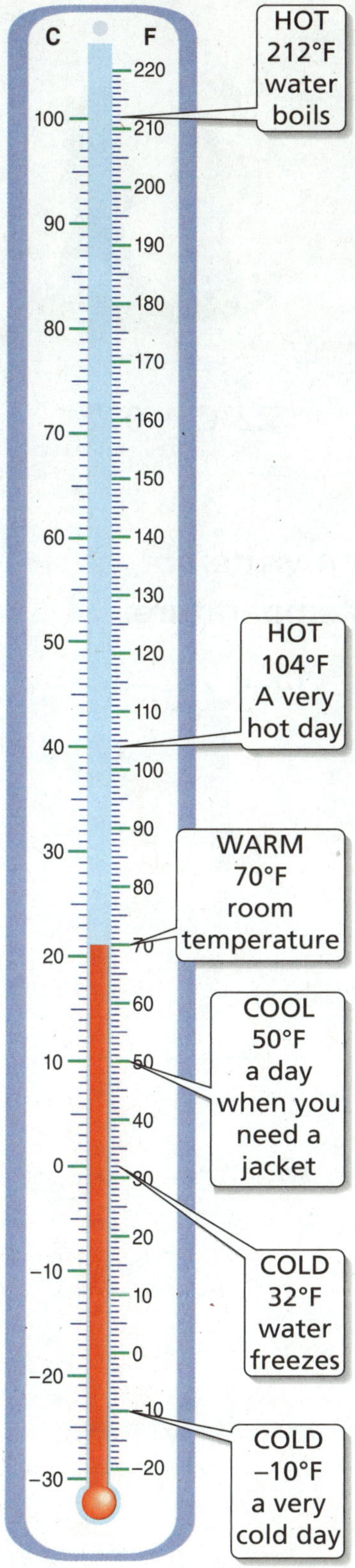

1.

20°F 80°F

2.

32°F 84°F

3.

0°F 53°F

Write the temperature using °F. Then write *hot, warm, cool,* or *cold* to describe the temperature.

4.

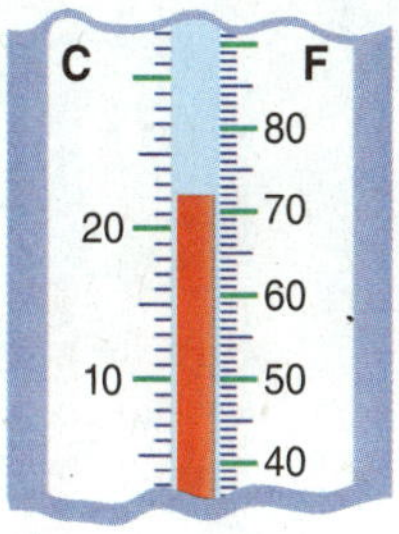

____

5.

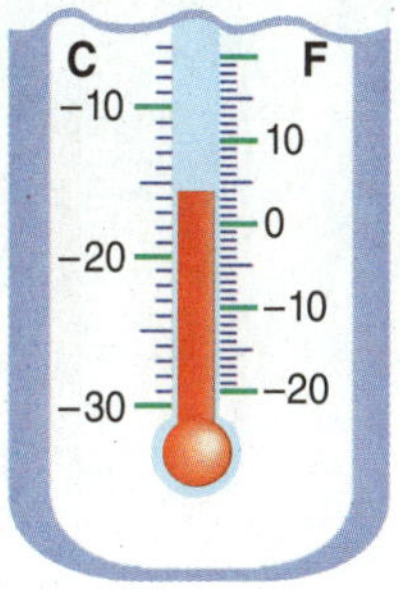

____

6.

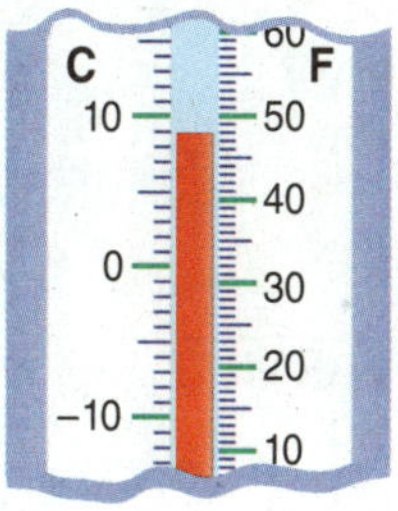

____

7.

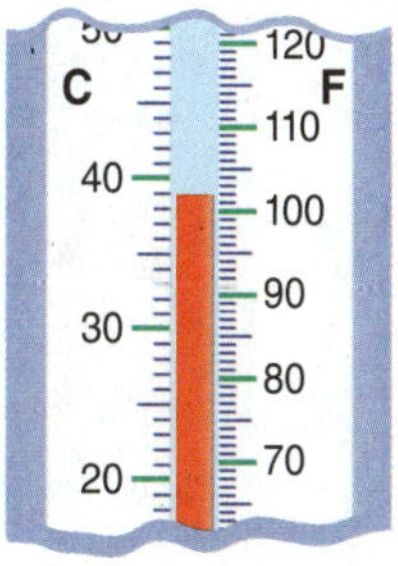

____

8.

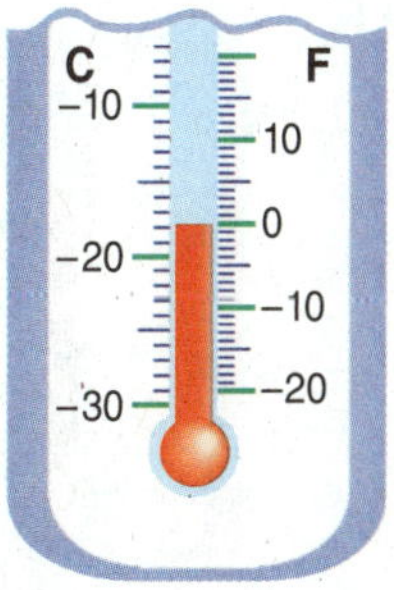

____

9.

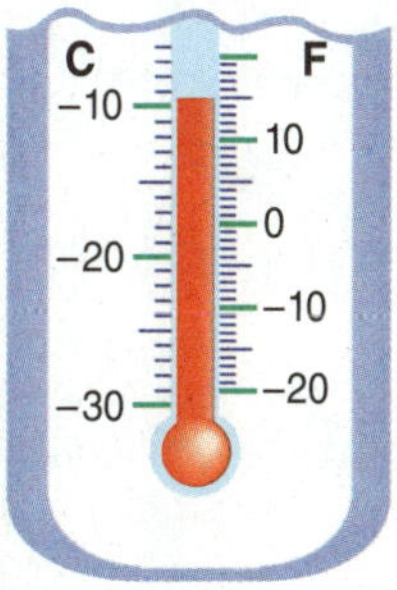

____

13–10 **Class Activity**

Name ______________________________ Date ______________

▶Temperature in Celsius

Circle the better estimate of the temperature.

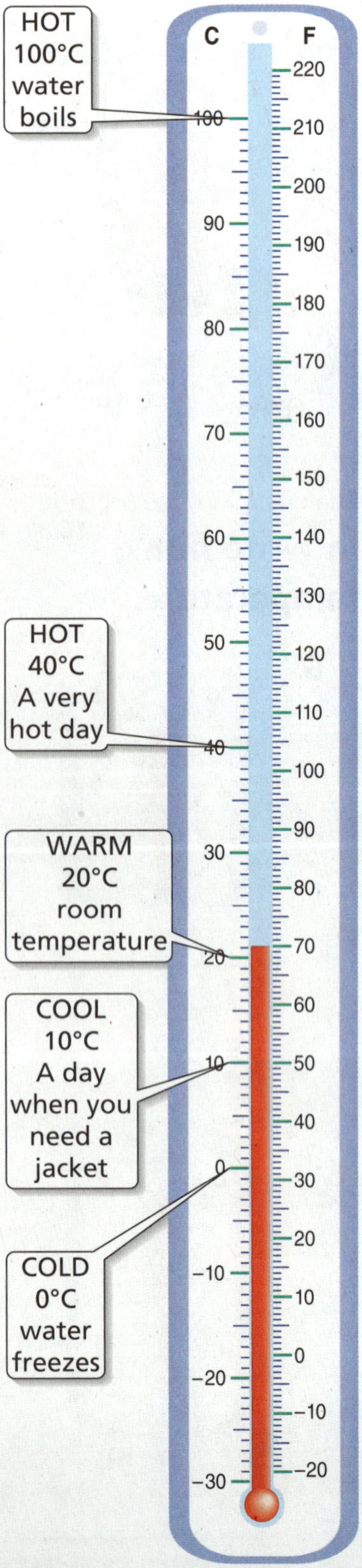

10.

50°C 11°C

11.

30°C 100°C

12.

22°C 0°C

Write the temperature using °C. Then write *hot, warm, cool,* or *cold* to describe the temperature.

13.

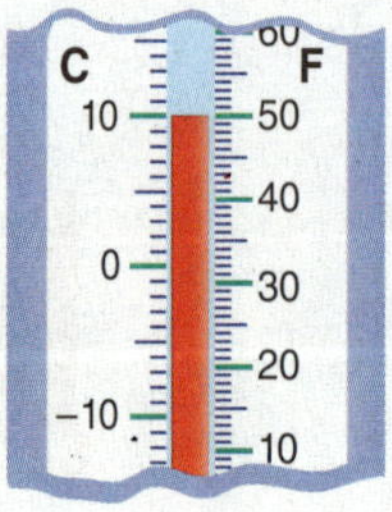

____

14.

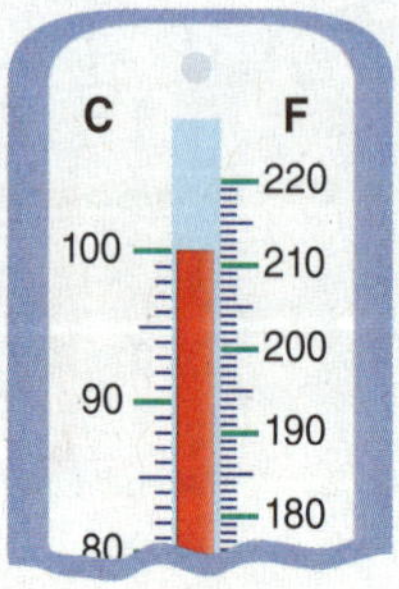

____

15.

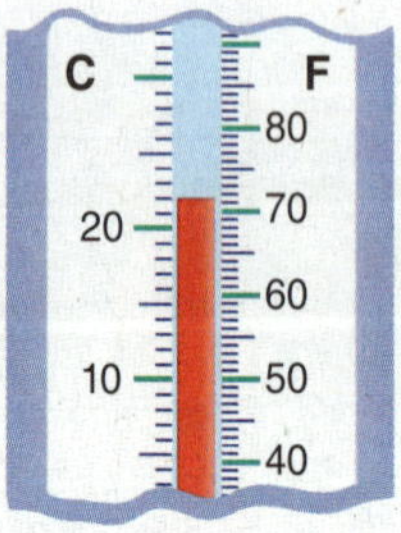

____

16.

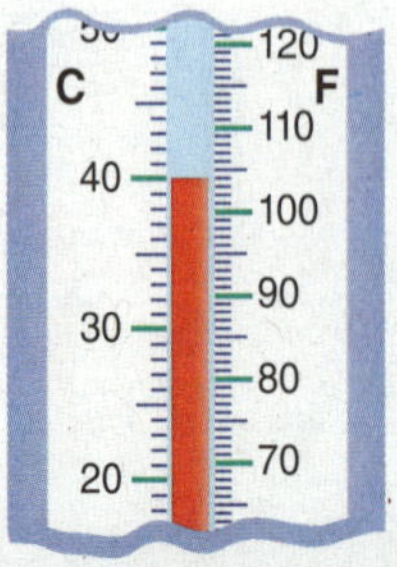

____

17.

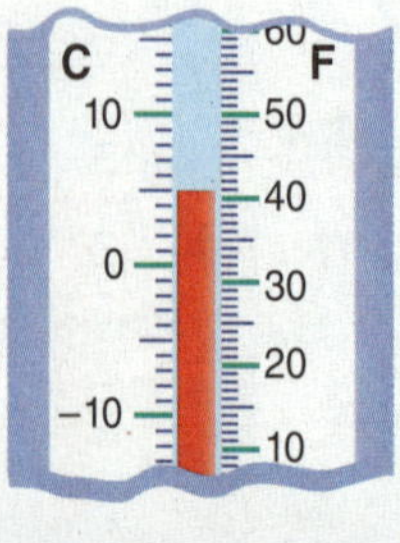

____

18.

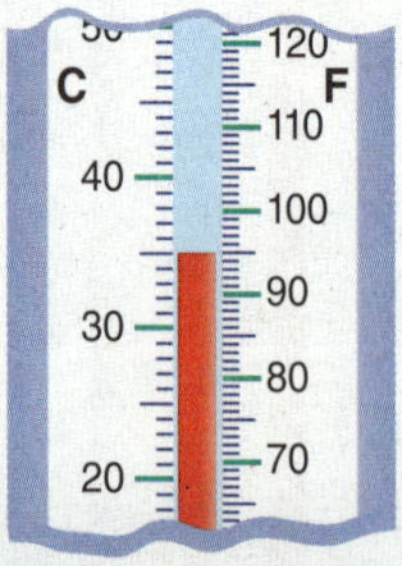

____

Name ____________________ Date ________

▶ Math and Science

Bees store the honey they make in a structure called honeycomb. The bees need the honey that is stored for food during the winter. The best thing for the bees is to have as much space as possible to store the honey.

1. Cover a piece of paper with circular counters. Cover the same size piece of paper with pattern block hexagons. Do the circles cover the page completely?

   ____

   Do the hexagons cover the page completely?

   ____

2. The honeycomb is made out of hexagons. Why does the hexagon work better for the bees than the circle?

   ____

   ____

   ____

3. You can surround 1 hexagon with 6 hexagons and there won't be any holes. Use pattern blocks to support or disprove the statements.

   ____

   ____

Name ______________________ Date ______________

▶ Shadows

4. If you measured the shadow of a yardstick at different times of the day, do you think the shadow would always be the same length or would it be different? Make a prediction.

____

____

5. Measure the length of the shadow of a yardstick at four different times of the day. Put the yardstick at the same spot each time. Record the shadow lengths in the table below.

Time of Day	Length of Shadow of Yardstick

6. On a separate piece of paper, make a bar graph that shows the length of the shadow at different times of the day.

7. Write about what you found out. Compare what you found out to what you predicted in exercise 4.

____

____

____

____

13 **Unit Test**

Name ______________________ Date ______________

1. Estimate the length of the line segment in inches. Then measure it to the nearest $\frac{1}{4}$ inch.

Estimate: ______________________

Actual: ______________

2. Estimate the length of the line segment to the nearest centimeter. Then measure it to the nearest centimeter.

Estimate: ______________________

Actual: ______________

Complete.

3. 2 feet 3 inches = _____ inches

4. 24 feet = _____ yards

5. 1 yard 2 feet = _____ inches

6. 2 meters = _____ centimeters

7. 400 centimeters = _____ meters

8. 5 pints = _____ cups

9. 13 quarts = _____ gallons

10. 8 quarts = _____ pints

11. 1 liter = _____ milliliters

12. 24 ounces = _____ pounds

13. 2 pounds = _____ ounces

14. 2,000 grams = _____ kilograms

15. Ring the better estimate.

a.

2 gallons

2 cups

b.

12 ounces

12 pounds

c.

30 milliliters

3 liters

Name ______________________ Date ______________

16. **Write the temperature. Then write *hot, warm, cool,* or *cold* to describe the temperature.**

a.

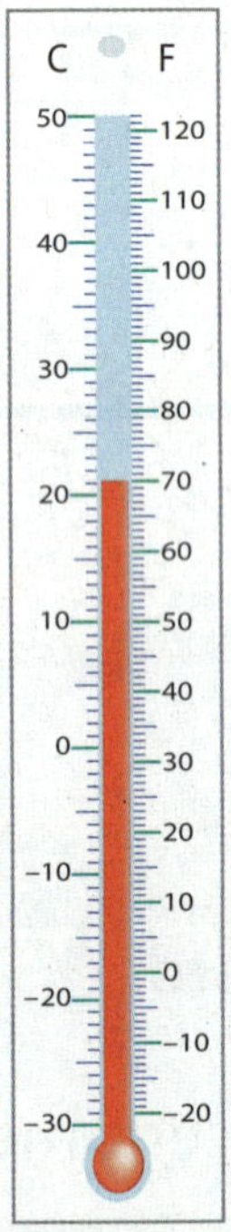

_____ °F _______

b.

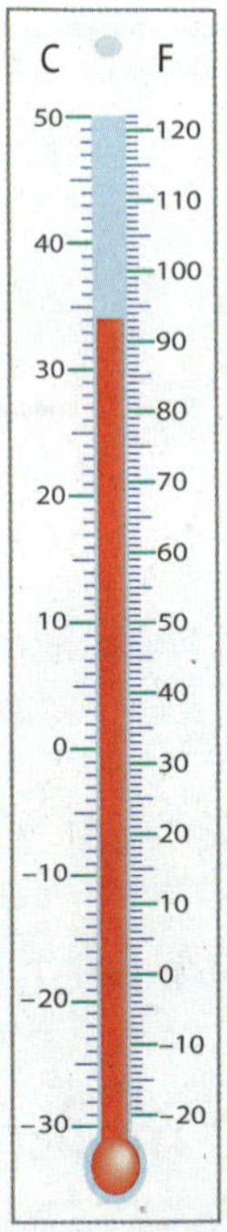

_____ °C _______

17. **Use the rectangle around 17a.–c. to complete 17a.–c.**

a. Estimate the perimeter in inches. __________

b. Find the actual perimeter in inches.

____

c. Estimate the area in square inches.

____

Solve.

18. Bert has 56 gallons of water for the pet shop's fish tanks. Each tank holds 6 gallons of water. How many tanks can Bert fill? How much water will be left?

____

19. A ten-gallon fish tank needs to have half of its water replaced every two weeks. How many quarts of water need to be replaced every two weeks?

____

20. **Extended Response** A loaf of bread has 40 slices. Each slice weighs 1 ounce. How many pounds does the loaf of bread weigh? Explain how you found the answer.

____

____

14–1 Class Activity

Name ____________________ Date ____________

Vocabulary
map

▶Read a Map

Each square on the **map** is 1 block. You can travel up, down, right, or left along the lines on the map.

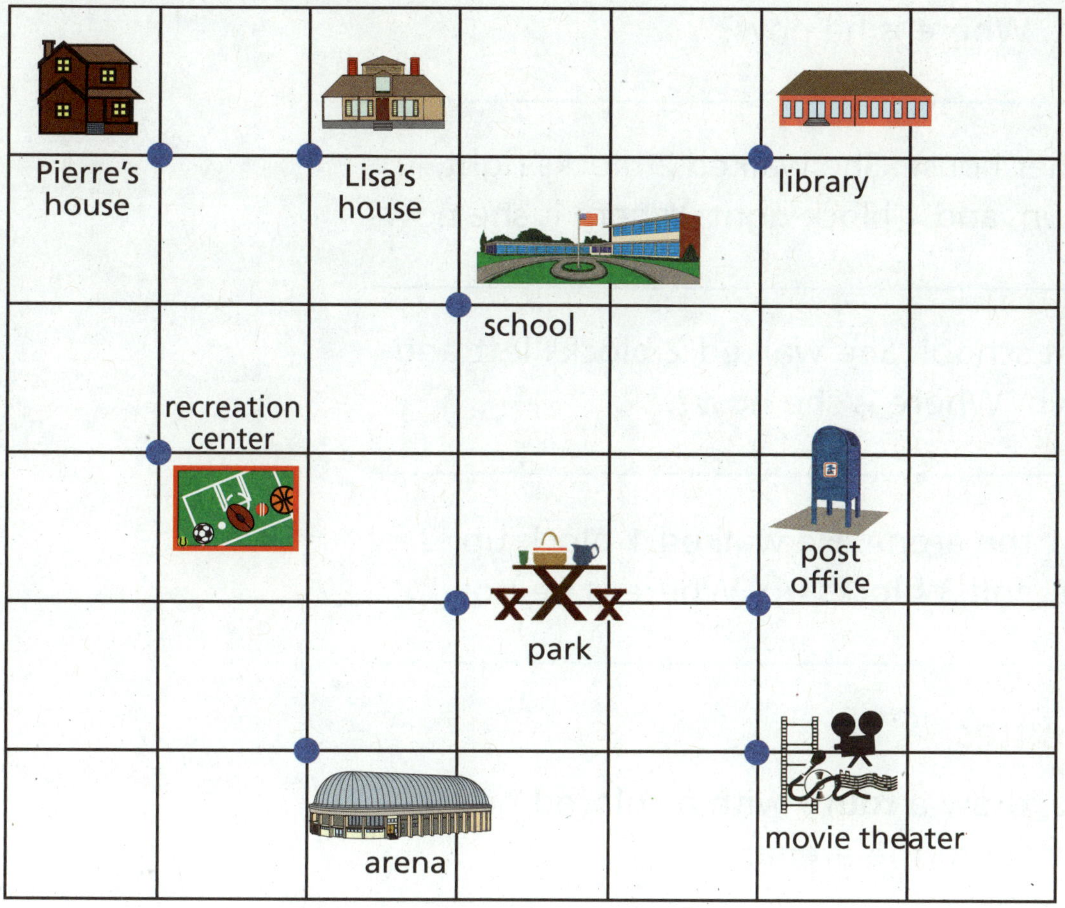

1. How many blocks is the school from the park?

____

2. How many blocks is the library from the post office?

____

3. Whose house is closer to the library, Pierre's or Lisa's?

____

By how much? _______________

14–1 Class Activity

Name ____________________ Date ____________

Vocabulary
route

▶ Follow Directions

Use the map on page 509 to answer the questions.

4. Pierre was at the park. He walked 1 block up and 2 blocks left. Where is he now?

____

5. Lisa was at her house. She walked 2 blocks right, 3 blocks down, and 1 block right. Where is she now?

____

6. Sarah was at school. She walked 2 blocks left and 1 block down. Where is she now?

____

7. Lucio was at the arena. He walked 1 block up, 3 blocks right, and 3 blocks up. Where is he now?

____

▶ Describe Routes

8. On the map, draw a **route** with a colored pencil from the school to the arena.

9. Describe your route.

____

10. How many blocks long is your route?

____

11. On the map, draw another route with a different colored pencil from the school to the arena.

12. Describe your route.

____

13. Which of your routes is longer?

____

Name Date

▶ Make a Map

14. Draw a map of an amusement park. Include a waterfall, treasure chest, bumper cars, a snack bar, and other places such as raging rapids, scrambler, pirates cove, or sunken ship. Place each point for the place where two grid lines intersect on the map.

14–1 Class Activity

Name ______________________ Date ____________

▶ Use Your Map

Use the map you created on page 511 to complete the following.

15. Draw a route on your map with a colored pencil from the snack bar to the bumper cars.

16. Describe this route.

____

____

17. Draw a route on your map with a different colored pencil from the snack bar to the water fall.

18. Describe this route.

____

____

19. Which place is further from the snack bar, the bumper cars or the waterfall?

____

Choose two places on your map.

20. Name the two places and describe a route from one to the other.

____

____

21. Describe a different route from one place to the other.

____

____

22. Is the second route longer, shorter, or equal in distance to your first route?

____

Family Letter

Dear Family,

Your child is working on a geometry unit about coordinate grids.

Students first work on grids without number labels. Then they make a map by adding features (places or objects) where two grid lines intersect. They describe routes on the map as up, down, right, and left in blocks or units.

Students then progress to coordinate grids — grids with number labels for each horizontal and vertical line. They describe locations on grids using ordered pairs. For example, this coordinate grid shows the point (2, 3). The first number in the ordered pair shows how far to the right the point is from 0. The second number shows how far up the point is from 0.

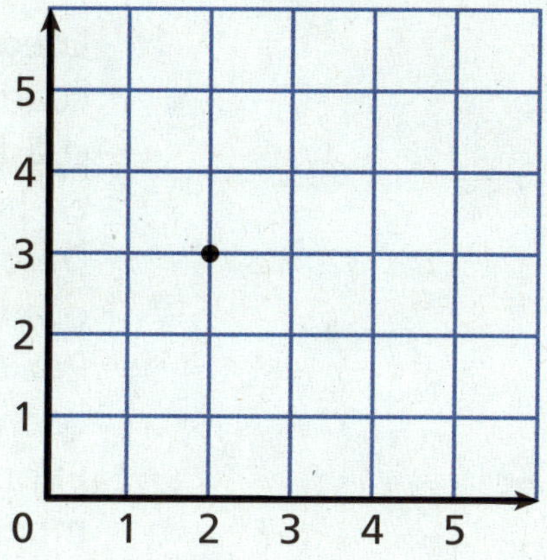

In the last lesson, students draw triangles and quadrilaterals on coordinate grids. They also use grid lines to measure the length of line segments and to draw rectangles from specific descriptions. The rectangle shown here is a possible response to the following description: The width of the rectangle is 3 units shorter than its length.

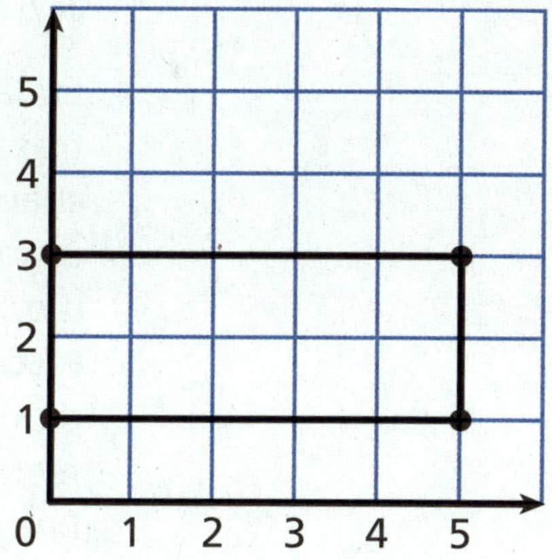

If you have any questions or comments, please call or write to me.

Sincerely,
Your child's teacher

Carta a la familia

Estimada familia:

Su niño está trabajando en una unidad de geometría sobre las cuadrículas de coordenadas.

Al principio, los estudiantes trabajan con cuadrículas que no están rotuladas con números. Agregan puntos (que representan lugares u objetos) donde se cruzan dos rectas para hacer un mapa. Describen las rutas en el mapa en términos de bloques o unidades hacia arriba, hacia abajo, hacia la derecha o hacia la izquierda.

Luego, los estudiantes usan cuadrículas de coordenadas, o sea, cuadrículas rotuladas con números en la recta horizontal y vertical. Describen ubicaciones en las cuadrículas usando pares ordenados. Por ejemplo, esta cuadrícula de coordenadas muestra el punto (2, 3). El primer número del par ordenado muestra a qué distancia a la derecha de 0 está el punto, y el segundo número muestra a qué distancia vertical está de 0.

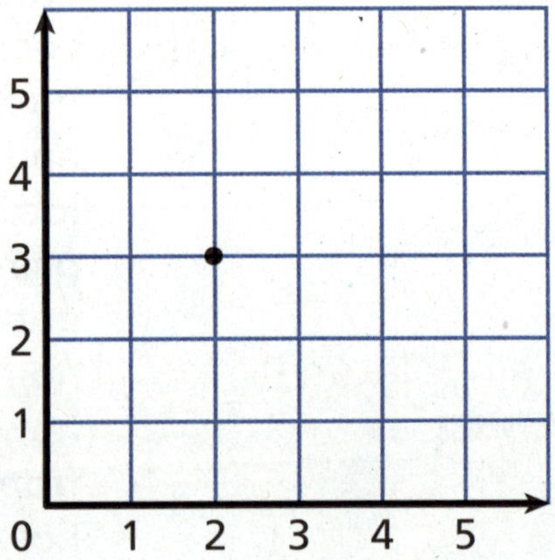

En la última lección los estudiantes trazan triángulos y cuadriláteros en cuadrículas de coordenadas. También usan las rectas de la cuadrícula para medir la longitud de segmentos de recta y trazan rectángulos a partir de descripciones específicas. El rectángulo que se muestra aquí es una respuesta posible a la siguiente descripción: el rectángulo tiene 3 unidades menos de ancho que de largo.

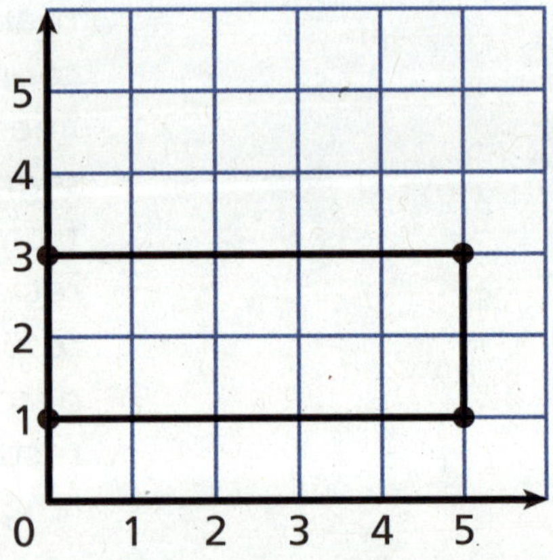

Si tiene alguna duda o pregunta, por favor comuníquese conmigo.

Atentamente,
El maestro de su niño

14–2 Class Activity

Name ______________________ Date ______________

Vocabulary
ordered pair
coordinate grid

►Coordinate Grids

You can use **ordered pairs** to find and name points on a **coordinate grid**.

Hector's Backyard

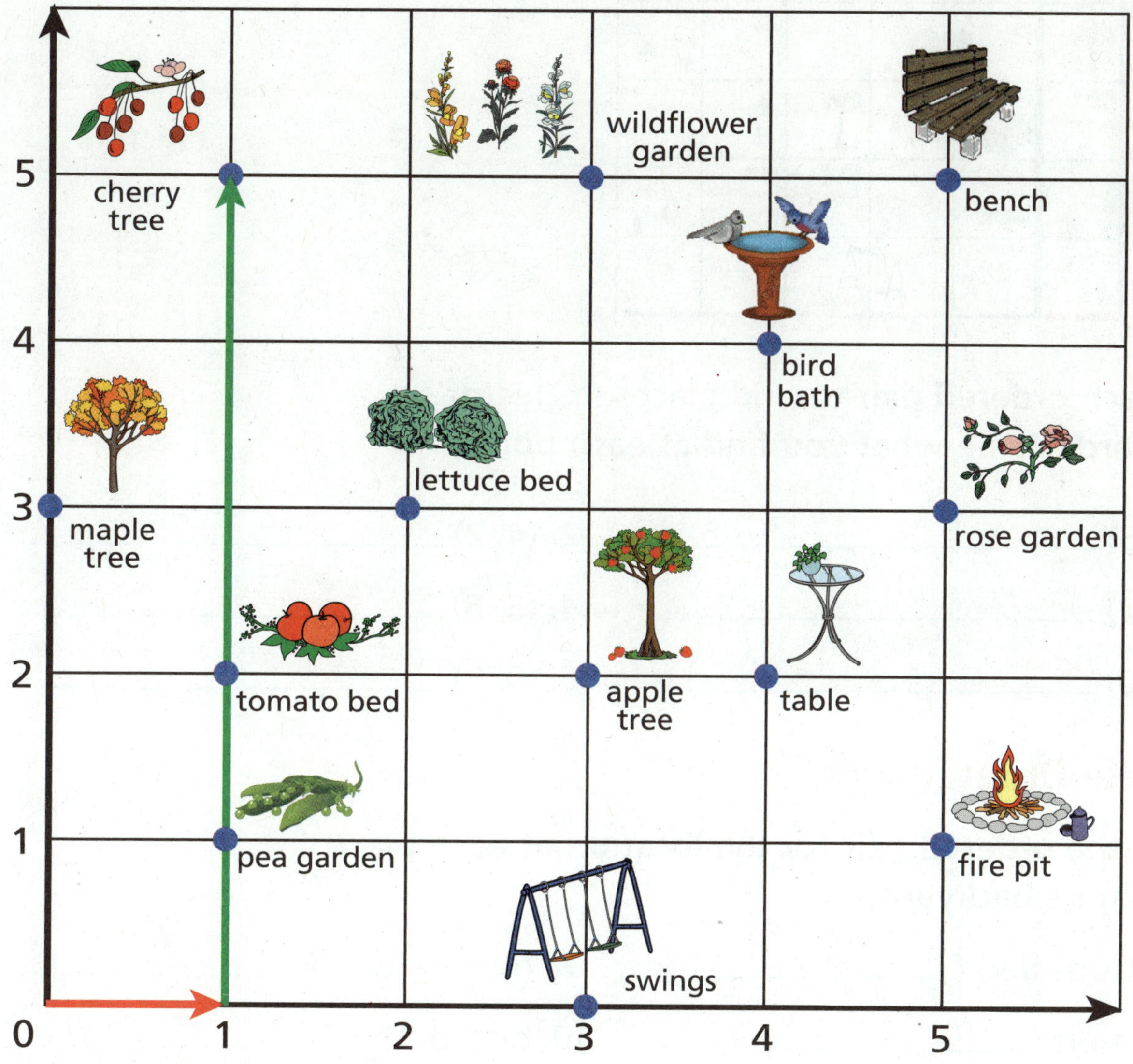

The cherry tree is located at (1, 5). To find (1, 5), start at 0. The first number tells how many spaces to the **right**, so move 1 space to the right. The second number tells how many spaces **up**, so move 5 spaces up.

(right, up)

14–2
Class Activity

Name ______________________ Date ____________

▶Locate Points

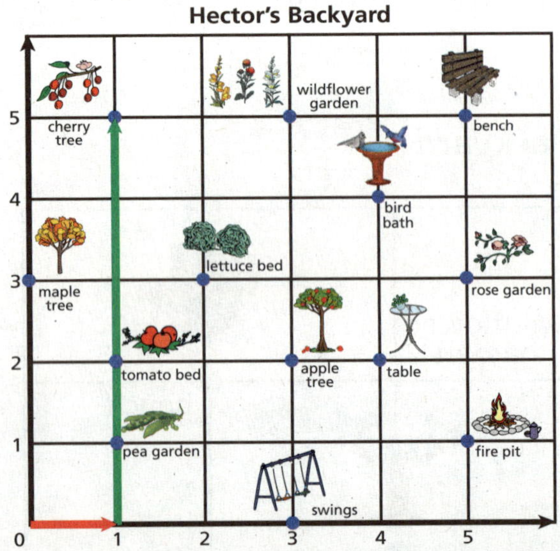

Use each ordered pair to find places in Hector's backyard. Name what you find at each point.

1. (3, 5) ____________
2. (4, 2) ____________
3. (1, 2) ____________
4. (5, 5) ____________
5. (3, 0) ____________
6. (0, 3) ____________

▶Write Ordered Pairs

Write the ordered pair for the location of each place in Hector's backyard.

7. lettuce bed (____, ____)
8. rose garden (____, ____)
9. fire pit (____, ____)
10. bird bath (____, ____)
11. apple tree (____, ____)
12. maple tree (____, ____)
13. Draw a new place at the intersection of two grid lines on the map of Hector's backyard. Write the ordered pair for its location. (____, ____)

Name ______________________ Date ____________

► Solve Problems With Ordered Pairs

Use the coordinate grid below for exercises 14–18.

Fair Ground

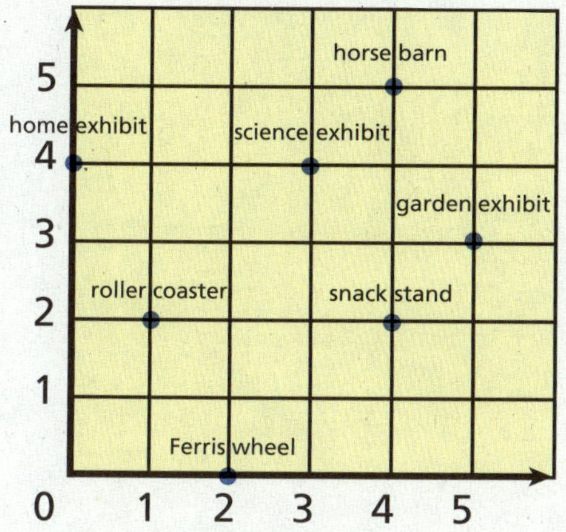

14. Larry went to the fair with his sister, Marissa. First they went to (1, 2). Where did they go first?

____

15. Larry and Marissa went to (3, 4). What is located at (3, 4)?

____

16. In the afternoon, Larry went to the home exhibit and Marissa went to the Ferris wheel. Write the ordered pairs for each location.

home exhibit (_____, _____) Ferris wheel (_____, _____)

17. What do the points for the Ferris wheel and home exhibit have in common?

____

18. Larry said he would meet Marissa at the horse barn at (5, 4). What mistake did he make? What is the correct ordered pair?

____

Name Date

▶Figures on Grids

Use the coordinate grid below for exercises 19–22.

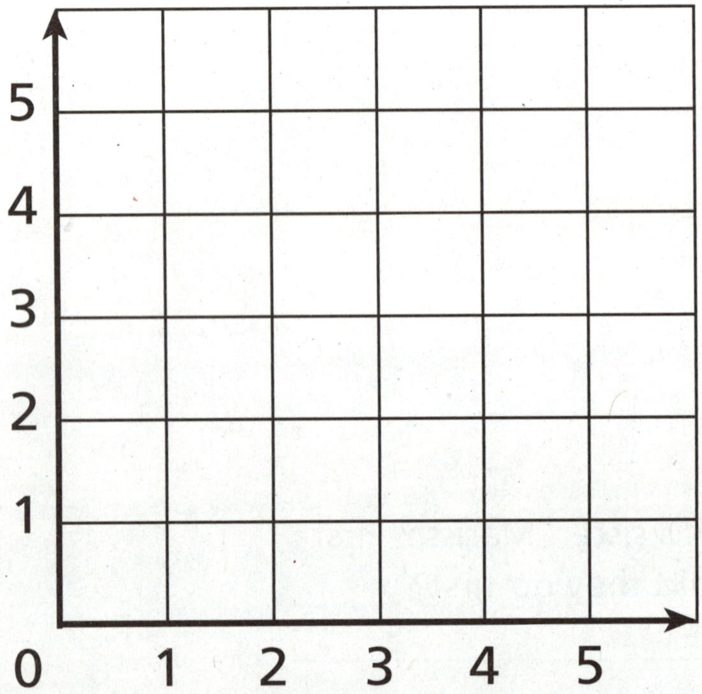

19. Graph each ordered pair. Label the point with the given letter.

Point *A* (1, 1), Point *B* (1, 4), Point *C* (2, 4), Point *D* (2, 1)

20. Draw a line segment to connect the points in order that you marked for exercise 19. Name the figure you drew.

____

21. Graph each ordered pair. Label the point with the given letter.

Point *E* (3, 3), Point *F* (3, 5), Point *G* (5, 5), Point *H* (5, 3)

22. Draw a line segment to connect the points in order that you marked for exercise 21. Name the figure you drew.

____

14–3 Class Activity

Name ____________________ Date ____________

▶ Triangles on Coordinate Grids

1. Mark a point on this coordinate grid to form the third vertex of a right triangle. Join the three points with line segments to make a right triangle.

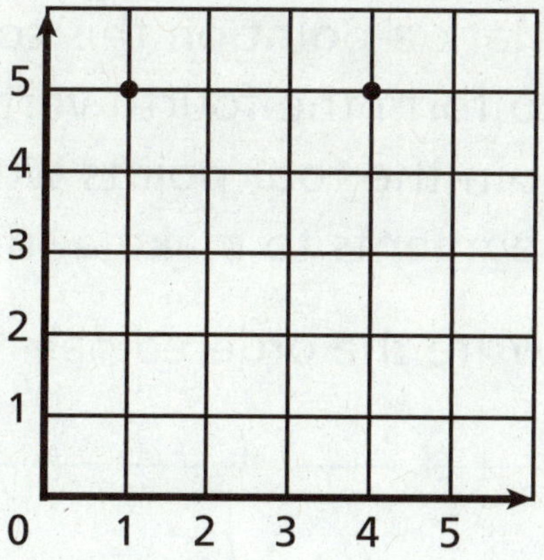

2. Write the ordered pair for each vertex.

(____, ____) (____, ____) (____, ____)

3. Mark a point on this coordinate grid to form the third vertex of an obtuse triangle. Join the three points to make an obtuse triangle.

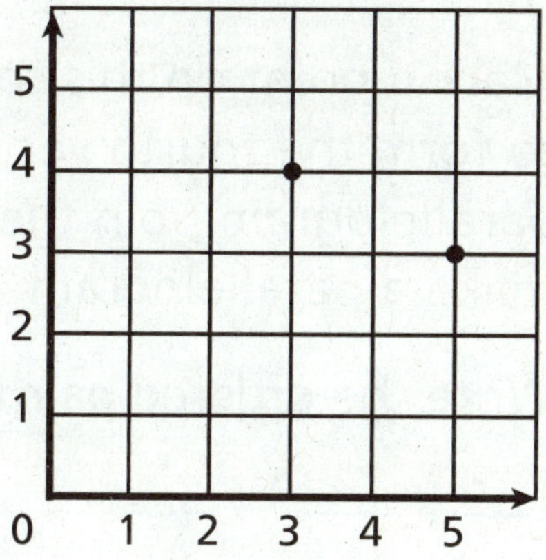

4. Write the ordered pair for each vertex.

(____, ____) (____, ____) (____, ____)

5. Draw a triangle on this coordinate grid. Place each vertex at the intersection of two grid lines.

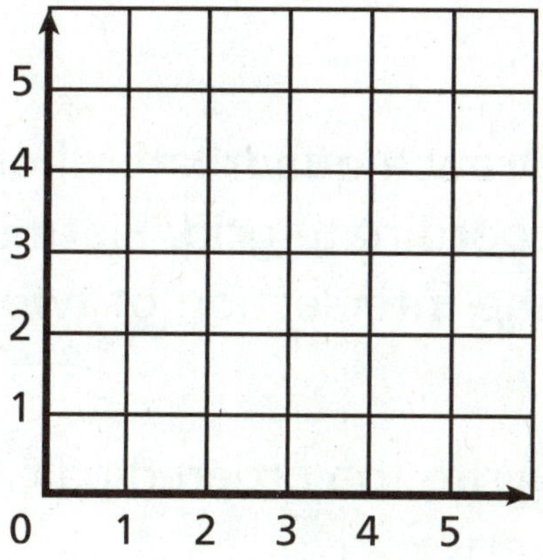

6. Write the ordered pair for each vertex.

(____, ____) (____, ____) (____, ____)

14–3 Class Activity

Name ______________________ Date ______________

▶ Quadrilaterals on Coordinate Grids

7. Mark a point on this coordinate grid to form the fourth vertex of a square. Join the four points with line segments to make a square.

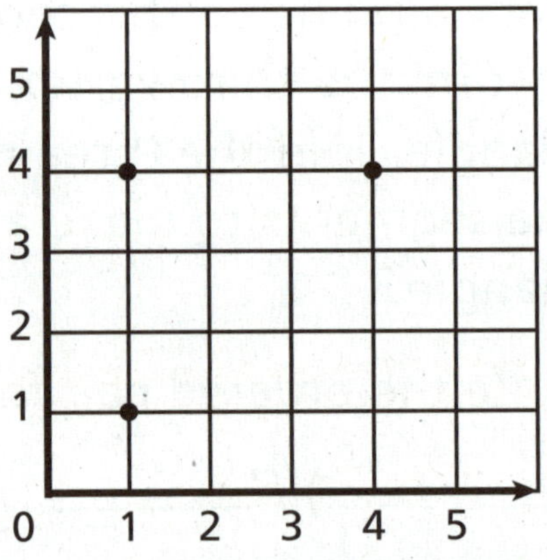

8. Write the ordered pair for each vertex.

(____, ____) (____, ____)

(____, ____) (____, ____)

9. Mark a point on this coordinate grid to form the fourth vertex of a parallelogram. Join the four points to make a parallelogram.

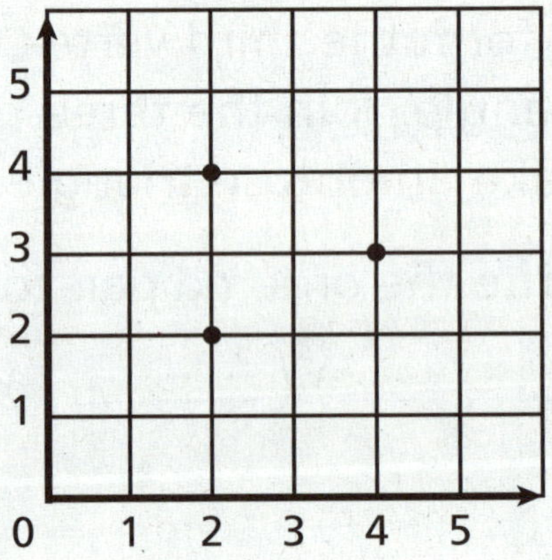

10. Write the ordered pair for each vertex.

(____, ____) (____, ____)

(____, ____) (____, ____)

11. Draw a quadrilateral on this coordinate grid. Place each vertex at the intersection of two grid lines.

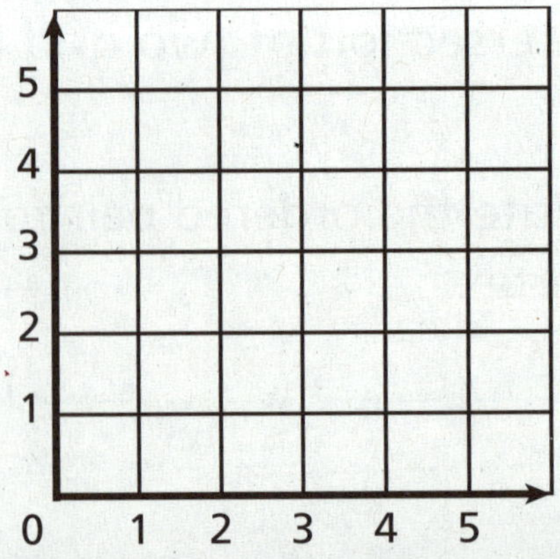

12. Write the ordered pair for each vertex.

(____, ____) (____, ____)

(____, ____) (____, ____)

14–3 Class Activity

Name ______________________ Date ______________

▶ Distance Between Points

The distance between two parallel line segments on a grid is 1 unit.

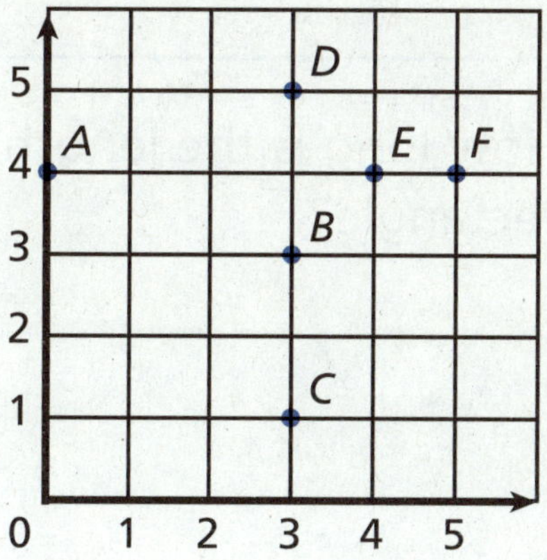

13. Draw a horizontal line segment from *A* to *E*. How long is the line segment?

____

14. Draw a horizontal line segment from *E* to *F*. How long is the line segment?

____

15. How long is the line segment from *A* to *F*?

____

16. Draw a vertical line segment from *D* to *B*. How long is the line segment?

____

17. Draw a vertical line segment from *B* to *C*. How long is the line segment?

____

18. How long is the line segment from *D* to *C*?

____

19. Draw a horizontal line segment with endpoints at the intersection of grid lines.

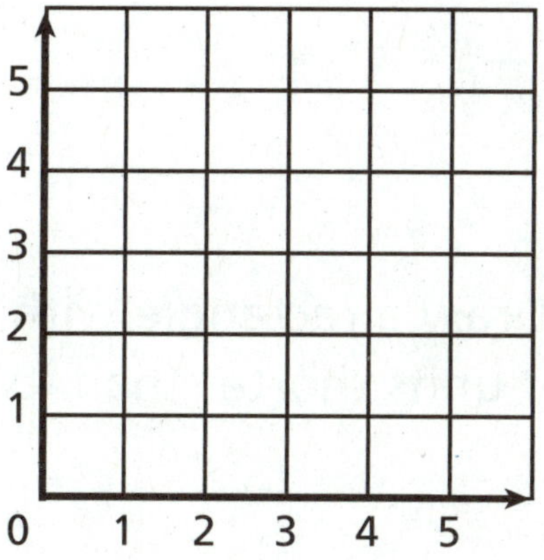

20. How long is your horizontal line segment?

____

21. Draw a line segment that is perpendicular to your horizontal line segment with endpoints at the intersection of grid lines.

22. How long is your vertical line segment?

____

14–3 Class Activity

Name ____________________ Date ____________

▶Dimensions of Rectangles

23. How long is the width of this rectangle?

____

24. How long is the length of this rectangle?

____

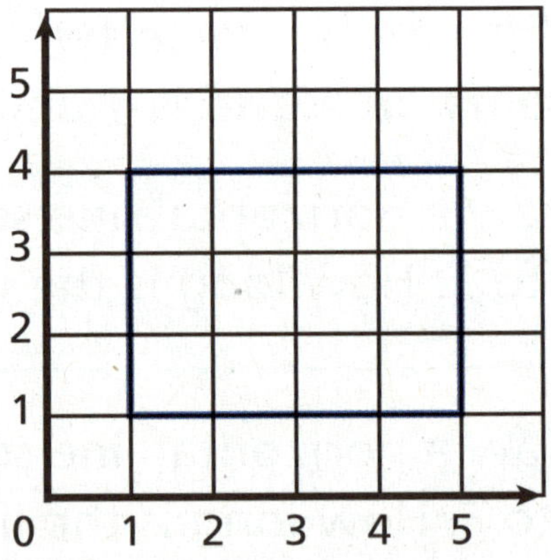

25. Draw a rectangle with a length that is 2 units longer than its width.

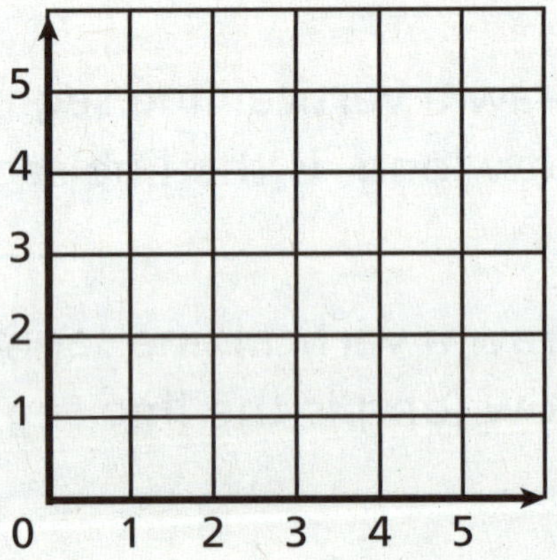

26. Draw a rectangle with a width that is 3 units shorter than its length.

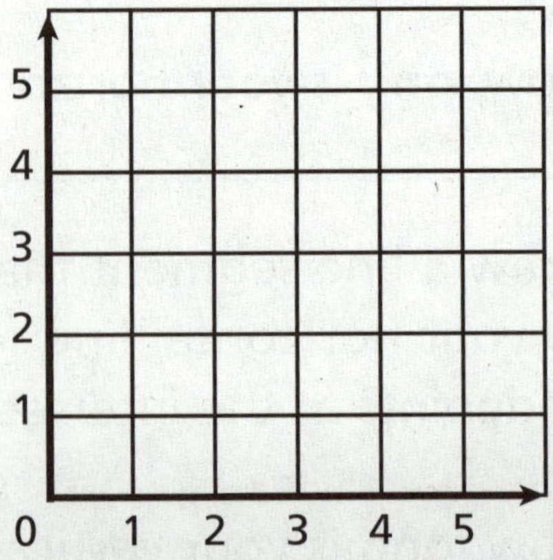

14 Unit Test

Name ______________________ Date ______________

Use the coordinate grid below to complete exercises 1–4.

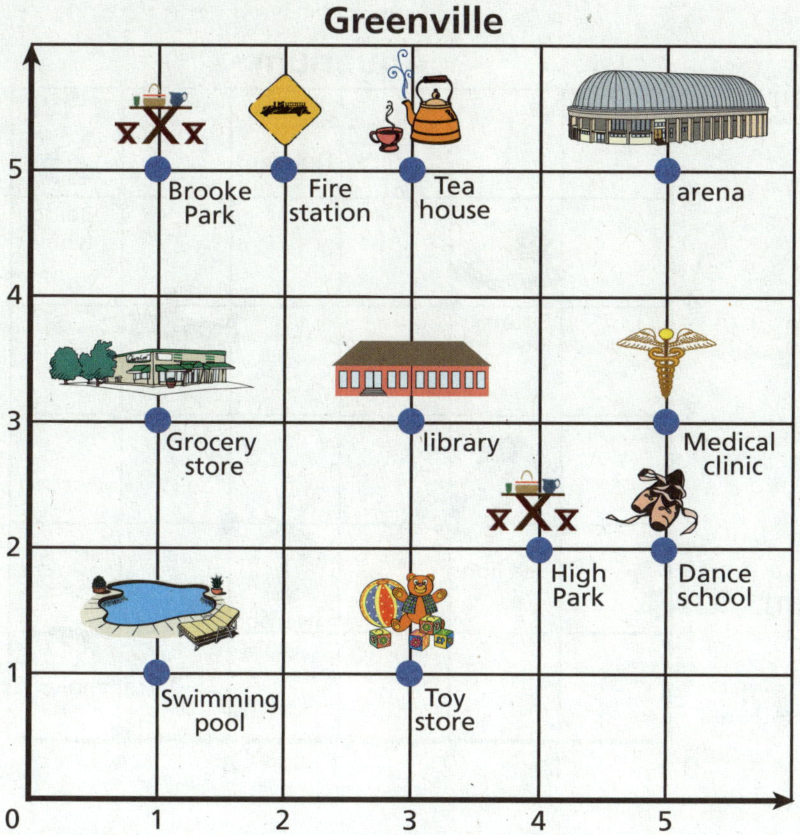

1. Lita started at the toy store. She walked 2 blocks right and 1 block up. Where is she?

____

2. Lyle was at Brooke Park. He walked 1 block down, 3 blocks right, and 2 blocks down. Where is he?

____

3. Chen was at the arena. He walked 1 block down, 3 blocks left, 3 blocks down, and 1 block left. Where is he?

____

4. Michaela wants to go from Brooke Park to the Dance school. Describe a route that she can take.

____

14 Unit Test

Name ______________________ Date ______________

Use the coordinate grid below to complete exercises 5–10.

Name the animals you find at the point for each ordered pair.

5. (1, 2) ______________

6. (5, 0) ______________

Write the ordered pair for the location of the animals.

7. Sharks (_____, _____)

8. Dolphins (_____, _____)

9. Mato went to the aquarium. The first place he went to was at (5, 5). Which place did he go to first?

____

10. **Extended Response** After watching the sea lions being fed, Mato went to see the otters and the harbor seals. Write the ordered pair for each animal.

otters (_____, _____) harbor seals (_____, _____)

What is the order of the numbers in an ordered pair? Why does the order matter? Use the example of the otters and harbor seals in your explanation.

____

____

____

____

____

E–1 Class Activity

Name ____________________ Date ____________

Vocabulary
place value
standard form
word form

▶ Identify Place Value Through Hundred Thousands

To read and write numbers you need to understand **place value**.

1. What are the names of the places of a three-digit number?

____

Hundreds	Tens	Ones
2	3	5

2. How do we read and write 235 with words?

____

Hundred Thousands	Ten Thousands	Thousands	Hundreds	Tens	Ones
1	6	8	2	3	5

Write the value of the underlined digit.

3. 1<u>3</u>,456 ________ **4.** 190,<u>7</u>65 ________

5. <u>8</u>8,763 ________ **6.** 4,5<u>6</u>7 ________

▶ Write Numbers Different Ways

Standard form: 15,678 **Word form**: fifteen thousand, six hundred seventy-eight

Write each number in standard form.

7. six thousand, one hundred eight ________

8. six thousand eight ________

9. one hundred sixty six thousand, eighty ________

Write each number in word form.

10. 17,893 ____________________

11. 175,635 ____________________

E–1

Class Activity

Name ____________________ Date ____________

Vocabulary

- greater than >
- less than <
- equal =
- greatest
- least

► Compare and Order Numbers to 10,000

Discuss the problem below.

Jim has 24 trading cards and Hattie has 42 trading cards. Who has more trading cards? How do you know?

Write greater than (>), less than (<), or equal (=) to make each statement true.

12. 4,008 ◯ 4,108
13. 2,356 ◯ 2,563
14. 8,567 ◯ 9,567
15. 3,989 ◯ 3,899
16. 2,385 ◯ 2,385
17. 3,235 ◯ 2,350

Write each group of numbers in order from greatest to least.

18. 8,456 4,567 4,675

____

19. 3,465 3,654 3,546

____

► Add, Subtract, and Estimate with Large Numbers

Solve using any method. Use estimation to check that your results are reasonable.

20.
$$\begin{array}{r} 73{,}608 \\ +\ 9{,}729 \\ \hline \end{array}$$

21.
$$\begin{array}{r} 33{,}756 \\ -\ 13{,}897 \\ \hline \end{array}$$

22. Bob's town has a population of 13,226 people. Mia's town has 11,867 people. Tani's town has 33,569 people. How many people live in the three towns?

____

23. How many more people live in Tani's town than Bob's town?

____

E-2 Class Activity

Name ______________________ Date ______________

Vocabulary
array
area

▶ Model a Product of Ones

The number of unit squares in an **array** of connected unit squares is the **area** of the rectangle formed by the squares. We sometimes just show the measurement of length and width.

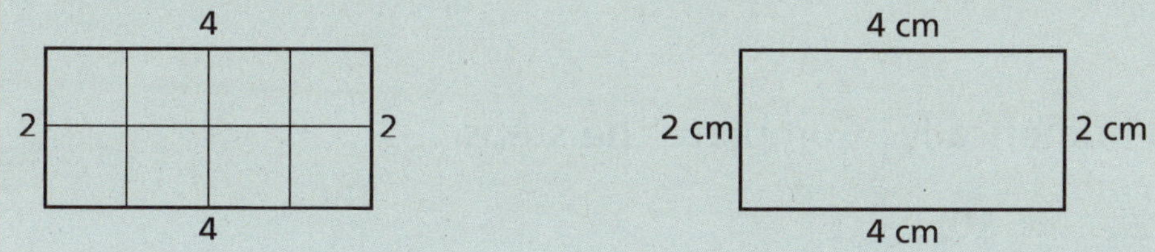

You can draw a rectangle for any multiplication. In the real world, we use multiplication for finding both sizes of arrays and areas of figures.

A 2×4 rectangle has 8 unit squares inside, so $2 \times 4 = 8$.

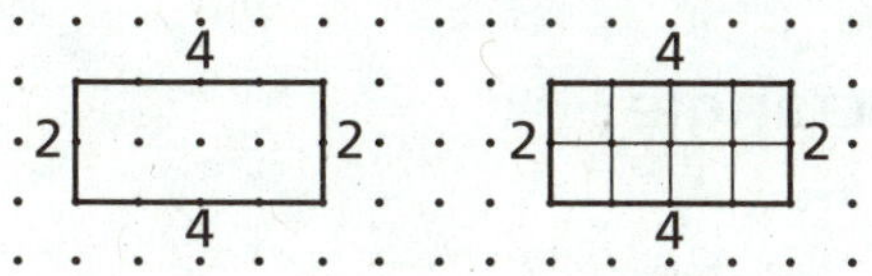

1. On your MathBoard, draw a 4×2 rectangle. How is the 4×2 rectangle similar to the 2×4 rectangle? How is it different?

____

____

____

____

2. How do the areas of the 2×4 and 4×2 rectangles compare?

____

____

E–2 Class Activity

Name ______________________ Date ______________

▶ Factor the Tens to Multiply Ones and Tens

This 2 × 40 rectangle contains 8 groups of 10 square units, so its area is 80 square units.

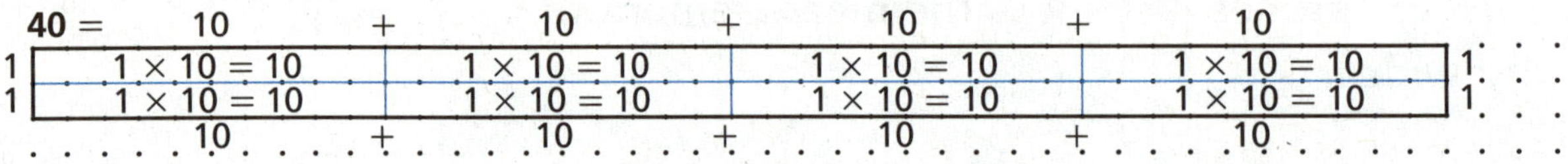

3. How can we show this numerically? Complete the steps.

$2 \times 40 = (2 \times 1) \times (\_\_\_\_\_ \times 10)$

$= (\_\_\_\_\_ \times \_\_\_\_\_) \times (1 \times 10)$

$= \_\_\_\_\_ \times 10 = 80$

4. On your MathBoard, draw a 40 × 2 rectangle and find its area.

____

5. How is the 40 × 2 rectangle similar to the 2 × 40 rectangle? How is it different?

____

____

____

____

6. Write out the steps for finding 4 × 20 by factoring the tens. Use your MathBoard if you need to.

____

____

____

E–2 Class Activity

Name ______________________ Date ______________________

▶ Model a Product of Tens

7. Find the area of this 20 × 40 rectangle by dividing it into 10-by-10 squares of 100.

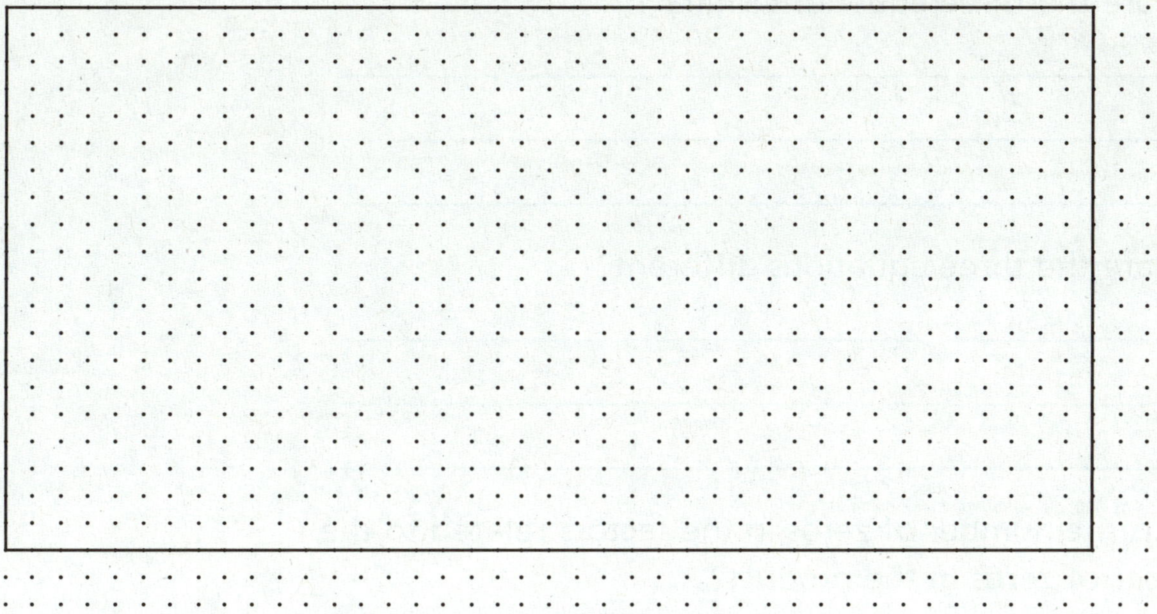

▶ Factor the Tens

8. Complete the steps to show your work in problem 7 numerically.

20 × 40 = (______ × 10) × (______ × 10)

= (______ × ______) × (10 × 10)

= ______ × 100

= 800

9. Is it true that 20 × 40 = 40 × 20? Explain how you know.

____

10. Write out the steps for finding 40 × 20 by factoring the tens. Use your MathBoard if you need to.

____

____

Name ____________________ Date ____________

▶ Compare Equations

In this lesson, you looked at these three equations.

$2 \times 4 = 8 \qquad 2 \times 40 = 80 \qquad 20 \times 40 = 800$

11. How are the three equations similar?

12. How are the three equations different?

13. How is the number of zeros in the factors related to the number of zeros in the product?

E-3 Class Activity

Name ________________ Date ________

Vocabulary
factors
product

▶ Look for Patterns

Multiplying large numbers in your head is easier when you learn patterns of multiplication with tens.

Start with column A and look for the patterns used to get the expressions in each column. Complete the table.

Table 1

	A	B	C	D
	2×4	$2 \times 1 \times 4 \times 1$	8×1	8
1.	2×40	$2 \times 1 \times 4 \times 10$	8×10	____
2.	20×40	$2 \times 10 \times 4 \times 10$	____	____

3. How are the expressions in column B different from the expressions in column A?

____

____

____

4. In column C, we see that each expression can be written as a number times a place value. Which of these **factors** gives more information about the size of the **product**?

____

5. Why is 8 the first digit of the products in column D?

____

6. Why are there different numbers of zeros in the products in column D?

____

____

E–3 Class Activity

Name ______________________ Date ______________

▶ Compare Tables

Complete each table.

Table 2

	A	B	C	D
	4 × 3	4 × 1 × 3 × 1	12 × 1	12
7.	4 × 30	4 × 1 × 3 × 10	12 × 10	______
8.	40 × 30	4 × 10 × 3 × 10	______	______

Table 3

	A	B	C	D
	5 × 8	5 × 1 × 8 × 1	40 × 1	40
9.	5 × 80	5 × 1 × 8 × 10	40 × 10	______
10.	50 × 80	______________	______	______

11. Why do the products in Table 2 have more digits than the products in Table 1?

____

____

12. Why are there more zeros in the products in Table 3 than those in Table 2?

____

____

E–4

Class Activity

Name ________________ Date ________

Vocabulary
area
square units

▶ Explore the Area Model

Copy this rectangle on your MathBoard.

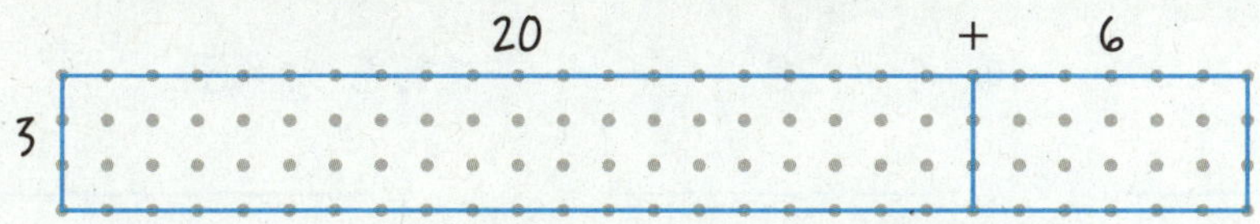

1. How many **square units** of **area** are there in the tens part of the drawing? ____________

2. What multiplication equation gives the area of the tens part of the drawing? ____________ Write this equation in its rectangle.

3. How many square units of area are there in the ones part? ____________

4. What multiplication equation gives the area of the ones part? ____________ Write this equation in its rectangle.

5. What is the total of the two areas? ____________

6. How do you know that 78 is the correct product of 3×26?

____

____

7. Read problems A and B.

   A. Brad's photo album has 26 pages. Each page has 5 photos. How many photos are in Brad's album?

   B. Nick took 5 photos. Haley took 26 photos. How many more photos did Haley take than Nick?

   Which problem could you solve using the multiplication you just did? Explain why.

____

____

____

E–4
Class Activity

Name ____________________ Date ____________

▶ Use Rectangles to Multiply

Draw a rectangle for each problem on your MathBoard. Find the tens product, the ones product, and the total.

8. 8×38
______
______
______

9. 3×29
______
______
______

10. 4×28
______
______
______

11. 5×46
______
______
______

12. 2×38
______
______
______

13. 3×28
______
______
______

14. 5×30
______
______
______

15. 5×28
______
______
______

Solve each problem.

Show your work.

16. Claudia's father planted 8 rows of tomatoes in his garden. Each row had 12 plants. How many tomato plants were in Claudia's father's garden?

____

17. The bakery can ice their cakes with chocolate, strawberry, or vanilla icing. The bakery has a total of 67 different ways to decorate iced cakes. How many different combinations of icing and decorations can the bakery make?

____

18. Complete this word problem. Then solve it.

________ has ____ boxes of ________.

There are ____ ________ in each box.

How many ________ does ________

have altogether? ______________

E–5 Class Activity

Name Date

▶ Numeric Multiplication Methods

You have used the area model to help you multiply. In this lesson, you will learn some numeric multiplication methods that are related to this area model.

Expanded Notation Method

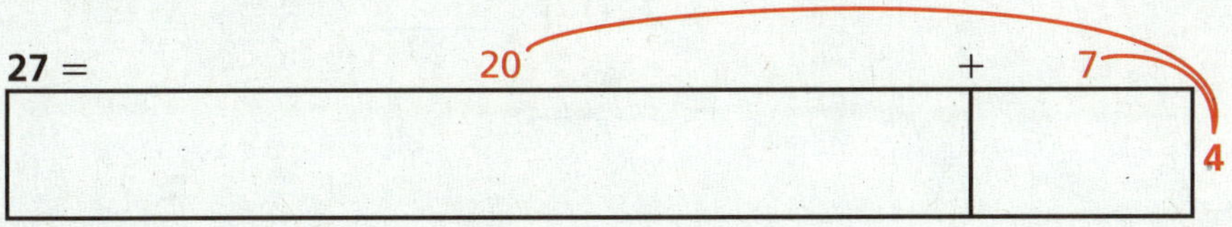

$$\begin{array}{r} 27 \\ \times\ 4 \\ \hline \end{array} \qquad \begin{array}{r} 27 = 20 + 7 \\ 4 \\ \hline 4 \times 20 = \ 80 \\ 4 \times \ 7 = \ 28 \\ \hline 108 \end{array}$$

Algebraic Notation Method

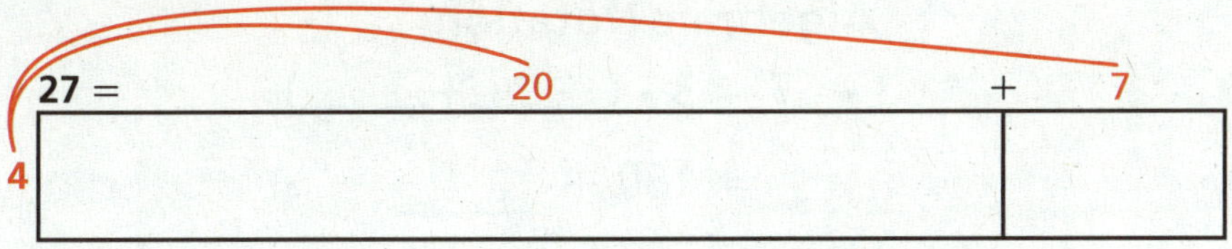

$$\begin{aligned} 4 \times 27 &= 4 \times (20 + 7) \\ &= 80 + 28 \\ &= 108 \end{aligned}$$

▶ Connect the Multiplication Methods

Refer to the examples above.

1. What two values are added together to give the answer in the Expanded Notation Method?

____

2. What two values are added together to give the answer in the Algebraic Notation Method?

____

3. Choose one of the numeric methods and explain how it relates to the Rectangle Sections Method.

____

____

____

____

____

E–5 Class Activity

Name ____________ Date ____________

▶ Practice Different Methods

Fill in the blanks in the following solutions.

4. 3 × 76

Expanded Notation

76 = ____ + 6
× 3 = ____
3 × ____ = ____
____ × 6 = 18
____

Algebraic Notation

3 • 76 = ____ • (70 + 6)
= 210 + ____
= ____

5. 3 × 67

Expanded Notation

67 = ____ + 7
× 3 = ____
3 × ____ = ____
____ × 7 = 21
____

Algebraic Notation

3 • 67 = 3 • (____ + ____)
= 180 + ____
= ____

Solve using a numeric method. Sketch a rectangle if necessary.

6. 8 × 53 = ____

7. 6 × 72 = ____

8. 6 × 27 = ____

9. 5 × 64 = ____

10. 5 × 46 = ____

11. 7 × 92 = ____

E–6

Class Activity

Name ______________________________ Date ____________

▶ Compare Multiplication Methods

Compare these methods for solving 7×23.

Method A	Method B	Method C	Method D	Method E
$23 = 20 + 3$	$23 = 20 + 3$	23	23	$^{2}23$
$\times\ 7 = \quad 7$	$\times\ 7 = \quad 7$	$\times\ 7$	$\times\ 7$	$\times\ 7$
$7 \times 20 = 140$	140	140	21	161
$7 \times 3 = 21$	21	21	140	
161	161	161	161	

1. How are all the methods similar? List at least two similarities.

____

____

____

2. How are the methods different? List at least three differences.

____

____

____

▶ Analyze the Shortcut Method

Method E can be broken down into 2 steps.

Method E:	Step 1	Step 2
	$^{2}23$	$^{2}23$
	$\times\ 7$	$\times\ 7$
	1	161

3. Where are the products 140 and 21 from methods A–D?

____

____

____

E–6

Class Activity

Name ____________________ Date ____________

▶ Practice Multiplication

Solve using any method. Sketch a rectangle if necessary. Check your answer by rounding and estimating.

4. $4 \times 68 =$ ______

5. $8 \times 72 =$ ______

6. $47 \times 9 =$ ______

7. $6 \times 54 =$ ______

8. $6 \times 23 =$ ______

9. $98 \times 2 =$ ______

10. $4 \times 82 =$ ______

11. $4 \times 86 =$ ______

Name ______________________ Date ______________

►Compare the Three Methods

You can use the **Rectangle Sections Method** to multiply a one-digit number by a three-digit number.

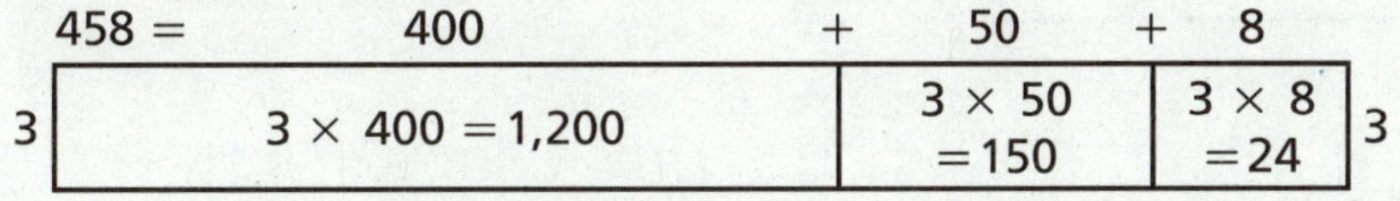

$$\begin{array}{r} 1{,}200 \\ 150 \\ +\quad 24 \\ \hline 1{,}374 \end{array}$$

1. What are the two steps used to find the product of 3 × 458 using the Rectangle Sections Method?

____

The **Expanded Notation Method** uses the same steps as the Rectangle Sections Method.

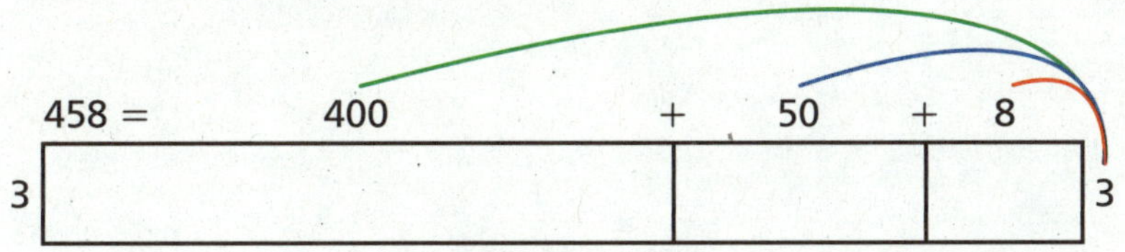

$$\begin{array}{rcr} 458 & = & 400 + 50 + 8 \\ \times\ 3 & & 3 \\ \hline 3 \times 400 & = & 1{,}200 \\ 3 \times 50 & = & 150 \\ 3 \times 8 & = & 24 \\ \hline & & 1{,}374 \end{array}$$

2. What is the last step in the Expanded Notation Method and the Rectangle Sections Method?

____

The **Algebraic Notation Method** uses expanded notation just like the other two methods. Even though the steps look different, they are the same as in the other methods.

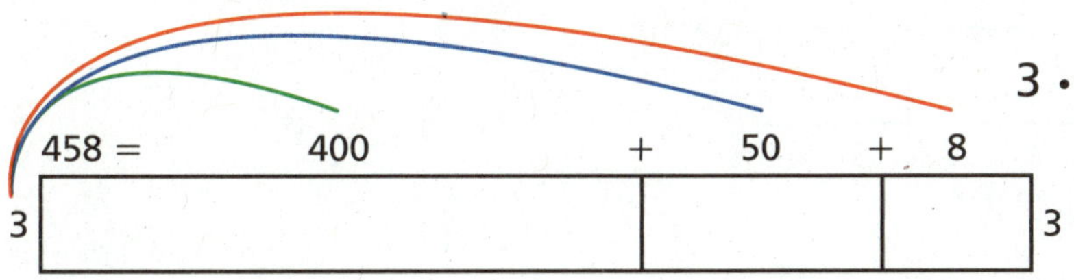

$$\begin{aligned} 3 \cdot 458 &= 3 \cdot (400 + 50 + 8) \\ &= (3 \cdot 400) + (3 \cdot 50) + (3 \cdot 8) \\ &= 1{,}200 + 150 + 24 \\ &= 1{,}374 \end{aligned}$$

3. What is the first step in all three methods?

____

E–7 Class Activity

Name ______________________________ Date ______________

Use the rectangles to help you solve the multiplication problems.

1. = + +

2. = + +

3. = + +

4. = + +

E–8 Class Activity

Name ______________________ Date ______________

► Compare Multiplication Methods

Look at the drawing and the five numeric solutions for 437 × 6.

	437 = 400	+ 30	+ 7
6	6 × 400 = 2,400	6 × 30 = 180	6 × 7 = 42

Method A	Method B	Method C	Method D	Method E
				2 4
437 = 400 + 30 + 7	437 = 400 + 30 + 7	437	437	437
× 6 = 6	× 6 = 6	× 6	× 6	× 6
6 × 400 = 2,400	2,400	2,400	42	2,622
6 × 30 = 180	180	180	180	
6 × 7 = 42	42	42	2,400	
2,622	2,622	2,622	2,622	

1. How are the solutions similar? List at least two ways.

____

____

____

2. How are the solutions different?
List at least three comparisons between methods.

____

____

____

____

3. How do Methods A–D relate to the drawing? List at least two ways.

____

____

____

Name ____________________ Date ____________

▶Analyze the Shortcut Method

Look at this breakdown of solution steps for Method E.

Step 1	Step 2	Step 3
$\begin{array}{r} {\scriptstyle 1} \\ 363 \\ \times \quad 5 \\ \hline 5 \end{array}$	$\begin{array}{r} {\scriptstyle 3\,1} \\ 363 \\ \times \quad 5 \\ \hline 15 \end{array}$	$\begin{array}{r} {\scriptstyle 3\,1} \\ 363 \\ \times \quad 5 \\ \hline 1{,}815 \end{array}$

4. Describe what happens in Step 1.

5. Describe what happens in Step 2.

6. Describe what happens in Step 3.

Practice the Shortcut Method on these problems.

7. $\begin{array}{r} 415 \\ \times \quad 3 \\ \hline 1{,}245 \end{array}$

8. $\begin{array}{r} 768 \\ \times \quad 9 \\ \hline 6{,}912 \end{array}$

9. $\begin{array}{r} 632 \\ \times \quad 7 \\ \hline 4{,}424 \end{array}$

10. $\begin{array}{r} 349 \\ \times \quad 6 \\ \hline 2{,}094 \end{array}$

E–9 Class Activity

Name ________________________ Date ____________

Vocabulary
dividend
divisor
quotient

▶ Divide Hundreds

In mathematics, special words are used to describe parts of a problem.

Discuss these multiplication and division words.

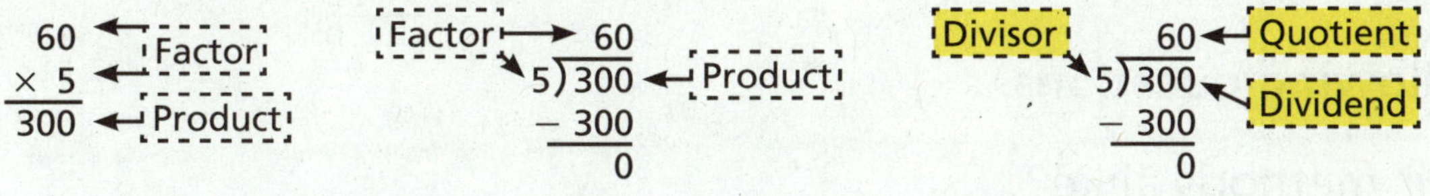

1. Describe the relationships among these 5 words in rectangles.

____

____

▶ Three Division Methods

The sidewalk crew knows that the sidewalk is 330 square feet. The sidewalk is 5 feet wide. How long is the sidewalk? Brianna, Carlos, and Michelle each use a different method to find the answer.

Brianna's Rectangle Sections Method

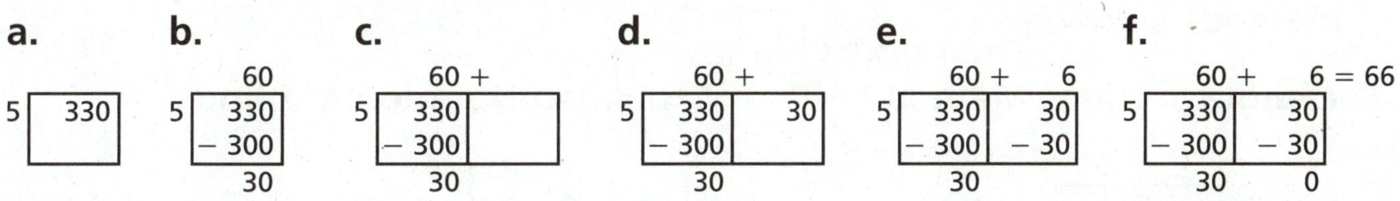

Carlos's Expanded Notation Method

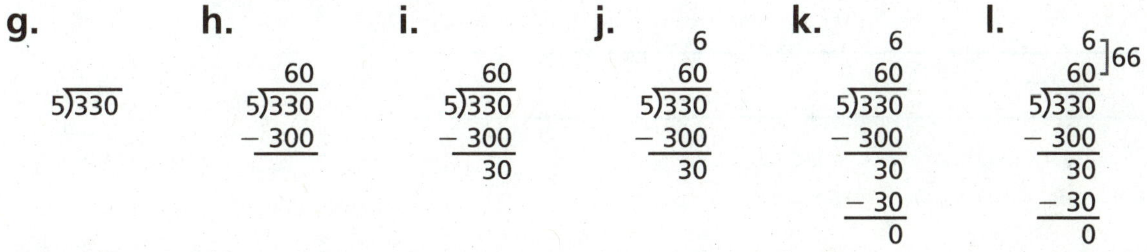

Name ____________________ Date ____________

▶ Three Division Methods (Continued)

Michelle's Digit-by-Digit Method

m.	n.	o.	p.	q.	r.
	6	6	6	66	66
5)330	5)330	5)330	5)330	5)330	5)330
	– 30	– 30	– 30	– 30	– 30
		3	30	30	30
					– 30
					0

Answer the following questions.

2. How are their methods alike?

____

____

3. How are their methods different?

____

____

4. What other methods do you know that could solve this problem?

____

____

5. How do the division methods relate to the multiplication methods below?

Rectangle Sections Method

	60 +	6
5	60 × 5 = 300	5 × 6 = 30

300
+ 30
330

Expanded Notation Method

66 = 60 + 6
5 = 5
5 × 60 = 300
5 × 6 = 30
330

____

____

E–10 Class Activity

Name ______________________ Date ______________

Vocabulary
estimate
rounding

▶ Estimate Products

It is easier to **estimate** the product of a two-digit number and a one-digit number when you think about the two multiples of ten close to the two-digit number. This is shown in the drawings below.

1. In each drawing, find the rectangles that represent 3×70 and 3×60. These rectangles "frame" the rectangles for 3×63 and 3×68. Find the values of 3×70 and 3×60.

$3 \times 70 =$ ______________ $3 \times 60 =$ ______________

2. Look at the rectangle that represents 3×68. Is 3×68 closer to 3×60 or to 3×70? So is 3×68 closer to 180 or 210?

____

3. Look at the rectangle that represents 3×63. Is 3×63 closer to 3×60 or to 3×70? Is 3×63 closer to 180 or 210?

____

4. Explain how to use **rounding** to estimate the product of a one-digit number and a two-digit number.

____

____

____

E-10 Class Activity

Name ________________ Date ________

Use compatible numbers to estimate each quotient.

5. 177 ÷ 3

☐ ÷ ☐ = ☐

6. 915 ÷ 8

☐ ÷ ☐ = ☐

7. 196 ÷ 5

☐ ÷ ☐ = ☐

8. 124 ÷ 6

☐ ÷ ☐ = ☐

9. 564 ÷ 7

☐ ÷ ☐ = ☐

10. 384 ÷ 4

☐ ÷ ☐ = ☐

Solve.

11. A teacher needs to order 5 book sets for her class. The total cost of the book sets were $276. About how much was each book set? Explain your thinking.

___

___

___

E–11 Class Activity

Name Date

▶ The Puzzled Penguin

Dear Students,
Today I had to solve this problem.

Barron counts 37 tiles across the floor and 6 tiles down one side. How many floor tiles are there in the room?

$$\begin{array}{r} 37 \\ +\ 6 \\ \hline 43 \end{array}$$ floor tiles

Is my answer correct? If not, please help me understand why it is wrong.

Thank you,
The Puzzled Penguin

1. Is the Puzzled Penguin correct? Explain your thinking.

2. Use a drawing to show could you use a rectangular array to help you solve the problem.

3. Which two operations can you use to solve this problem?

4. How can you use estimation to check if your answer is reasonable?

E–11 Class Activity

Name ______________________ Date ______________

▶The Puzzled Penguin

Dear Students,

Today I had to solve this problem.

> Ariana works at her family 's fruit stand. She was asked to bag 32 grapefruits. Each large bag can hold 4 grapefruits. How many large bags will Ariana need to fit all the grapefruits?

32 - 4 = 28	28 - 4 = 24	24 - 4 = 20	20 - 4 = 16
16 - 4 = 12	12 - 4 = 8	8 - 4 = 4	7 bags

Is my answer correct? If not, please help me understand why it is wrong.

Thank you,

The Puzzled Penguin

5. Is the Puzzled Penguin correct? Explain your thinking.

____

____

____

____

6. Use a drawing to show how could you use counters to help you solve the problem.

7. Which two operations can you use to solve this problem?

____

8. How can you use multiplication to check if your answer is correct?

____

E–12

Class Activity

Name _______________ Date _______________

►Explore Change Over Time

Look at the function table and answer the questions.

Money in Savings Account

Week	Amount of Money
1	$210
2	$225
3	$240
4	$255
5	$270

1. What information does this function table show you?

____

____

2. How does the money amount change in the savings account from week to week?

____

3. Predict how much money there would be in the savings account after week 10.

____

4. Explain how you found the answer to exercise 3.

____

____

____

____

5. Do you think the same pattern and function rule will continue over time? Explain.

____

____

Name ______________________ Date ______________

Sam kept track of an animal's weight at the zoo.
Here is the data he collected to the nearest pound.

Month	Weight (pounds)
January	48
February	56
March	64
April	72
May	80

▶ Practice with Change Over Time

6. Make a line graph with the data above.

7. What do you notice about the data over time?

____

8. What was the change in weight between February and March?

____

9. Predict what the weight of the animal will be in June?

____

10. Explain your thinking for exercise 9.

____

____

Glossary

A

acute angle An angle whose measure is less than 90°.

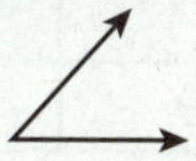

acute triangle A triangle in which the measure of each angle is less than 90°.

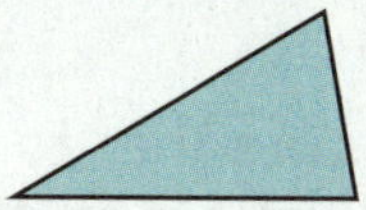

addend A number to be added.

Example: 8 + 4 = 12

addend   addend

addition A mathematical operation that combines two or more numbers.

Example: 23 + 52 = 75

addend   addend   sum

adjacent (sides) Two sides that meet at a point.

Example: Sides *a* and *b* are adjacent.

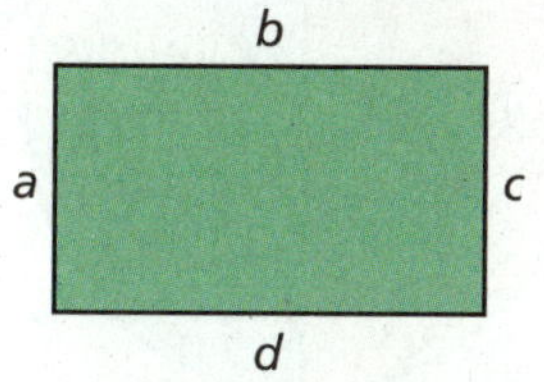

A.M. The time period between midnight and noon.

angle A figure formed by two rays or two line segments that meet at an endpoint.

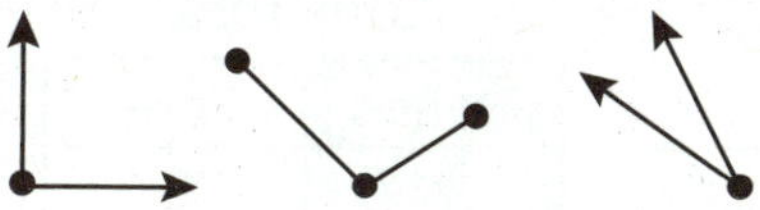

area The number of square units in a region

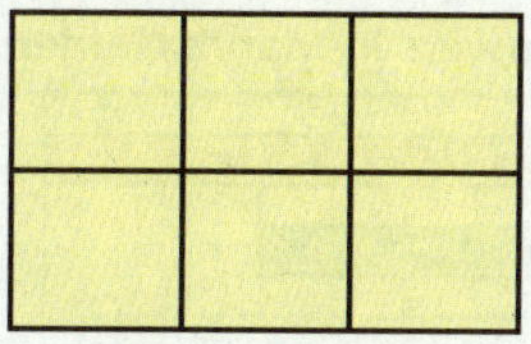

The area of the rectangle is 6 square units.

array An arrangement of objects, pictures, or numbers in columns and rows.

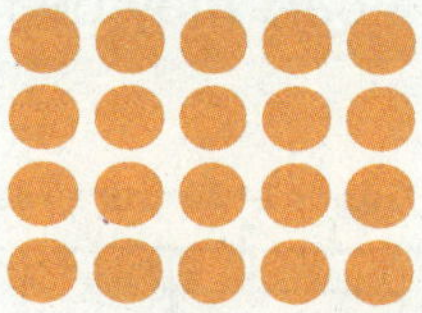

Associative Property of Addition (Grouping Property of Addition) The property which states that changing the way in which addends are grouped does not change the sum.

Example: (2 + 3) + 1 = 2 + (3 + 1)

5 + 1 = 2 + 4

6 = 6

Associative Property of Multiplication (Grouping Property of Multiplication) The property which states that changing the way in which factors are grouped does not change the product.

Example: (2 × 3) × 4 = 2 × (3 × 4)

6 × 4 = 2 × 12

24 = 24

axis (plural: **axes**) A reference line for a graph. A bar graph has 2 axes; one is horizontal and the other is vertical.

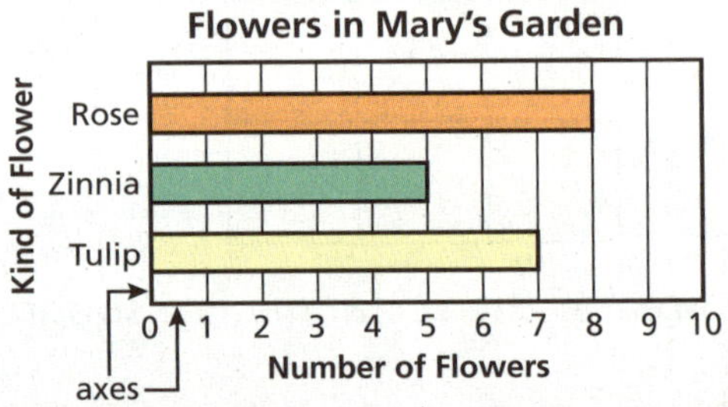

B

bar graph A graph that uses bars to show data. The bars may be horizontal or vertical.

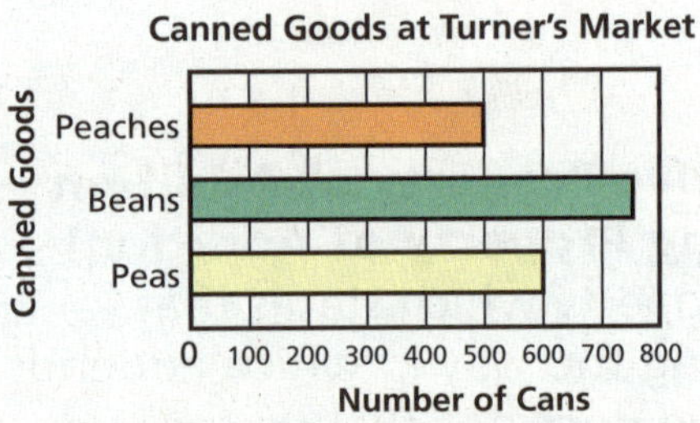

base (of a geometric figure) The bottom side of a 2-D figure or the bottom face of a 3-D figure.

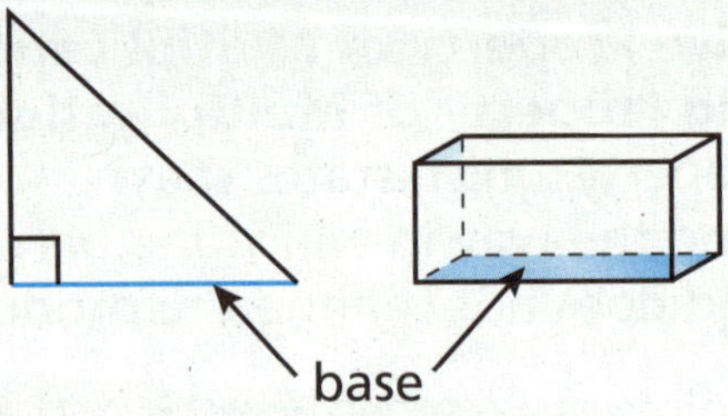

C

calculator A tool used to perform mathematical operations.

capacity The amount a container can hold.

cell A rectangle in a table where a column and row meet.

Coin Toss

	Heads	Tails
Sam	11	6
Zoe	9	10

} cell

centimeter (cm) A metric unit used to measure length.

100 cm = 1 m

circle A plane figure that forms a closed path so that all points on the path are the same distance from a point called the center.

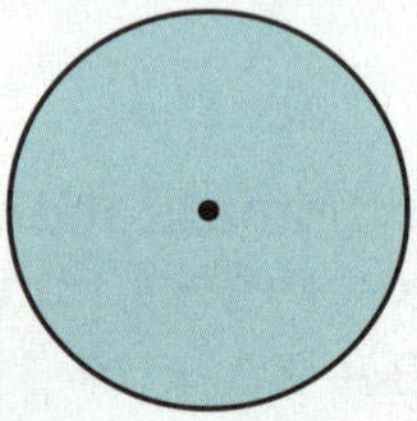

circle graph A graph that represents data as parts of a whole.

Jacket Colors in Ms. Timmer's Class

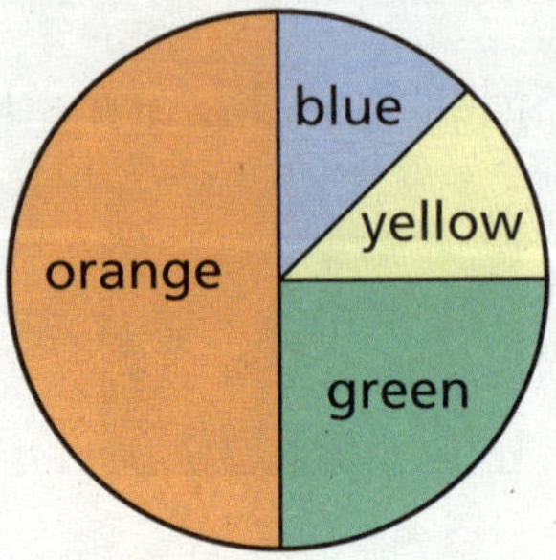

circumference The distance around a circle, about $3\frac{1}{7}$ times the diameter.

column A vertical group of cells in a table.

Coin Toss

	Heads	Tails
Sam	11	6
Zoe	9	10

column

Commutative Property of Addition (Order Property of Addition) The property which states that changing the order of addends does not change the sum.

Example: $3 + 7 = 7 + 3$

$10 = 10$

Commutative Property of Multiplication (Order Property of Multiplication) The property which states that changing the order of factors does not change the product.

Example: $5 \times 4 = 4 \times 5$

$20 = 20$

comparison bars Bars that represent the larger amount, smaller amount, and difference in a comparison problem.

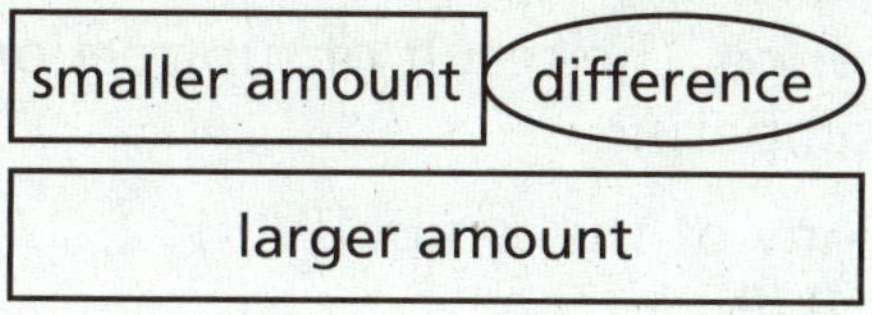

In Volume 2, we use comparison bars for multiplication.

cone A solid figure that has a circular base and comes to a point called the vertex.

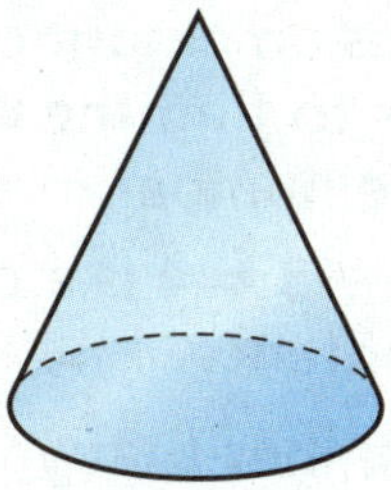

congruent figures Figures that have the same size and shape.

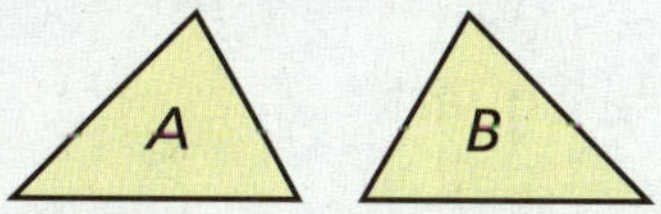

Triangles A and B are congruent.

coordinates The numbers in an ordered pair that locate a point on a coordinate grid. The first number is the distance across and the second number is the distance up.

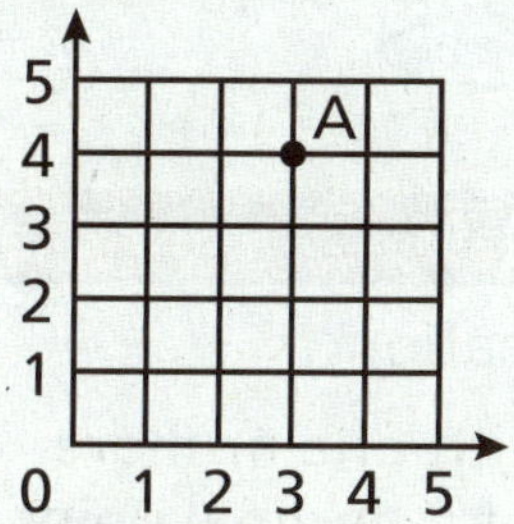

The coordinates 3 and 4 in the ordered pair (3, 4) locate Point *A* on the coordinate grid.

coordinate grid A grid formed by two perpendicular number lines in which every point is assigned an ordered pair of numbers.

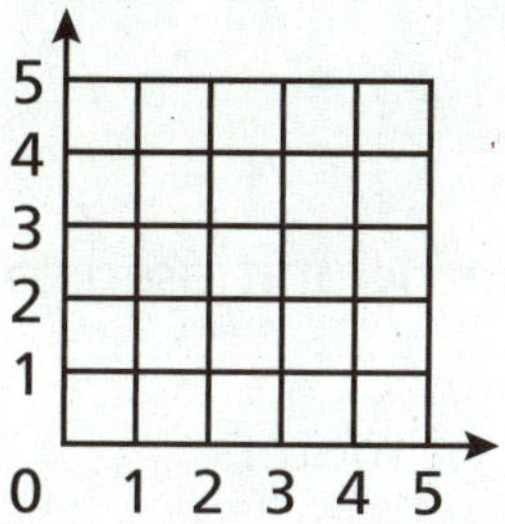

cube A solid figure that has six square faces of equal size.

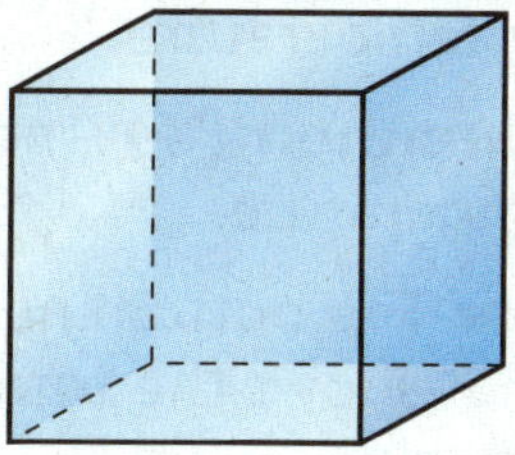

Glossary (Continued)

cup (c) A customary unit of measurement used to measure capacity.

2 cups = 1 pint
4 cups = 1 quart
16 cups = 1 gallon

cylinder A solid figure with two congruent circular or elliptical faces and one curved surface.

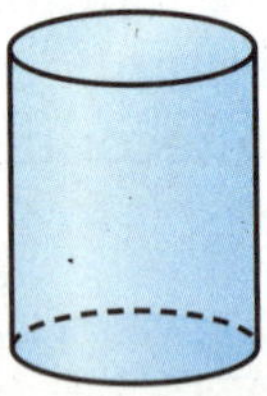

D

data Pieces of information.

decimal A number with one or more digits to the right of a decimal point.

Examples: 1.23 and 0.3

decimal point The dot that separates the whole number from the decimal part.

1.23
↑
decimal point

decimeter (dm) A metric unit used to measure length

1 decimeter = 10 centimeters

degree (°) A unit for measuring angles or temperature.

degrees Celsius (°C) The metric unit for measuring temperature.

degrees Fahrenheit (°F) The customary unit of temperature.

denominator The bottom number in a fraction that shows the total number of equal parts in the whole.

Example: $\frac{1}{3}$ ← denominator

diagonal A line segment that connects two corners of a figure and is not a side of the figure.

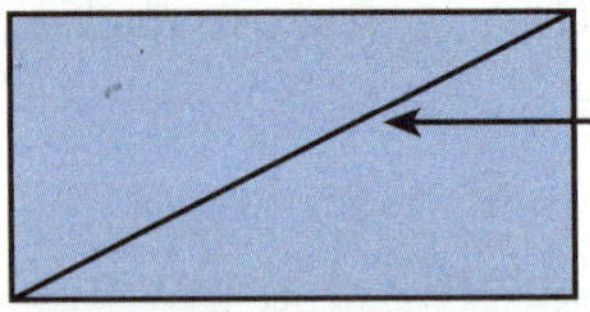

diameter A line segment that connects two points on a circle and also passes through the center of the circle. The term is also used to describe the length of such a line segment.

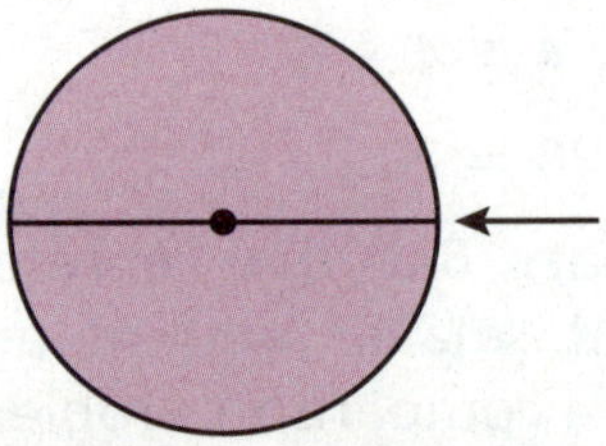

difference The result of subtraction or of comparing.

digit Any of the symbols 0, 1, 2, 3, 4, 5, 6, 7, 8, 9.

dividend The number that is divided in division.

Examples:

$12 \div 3 = 4$ (12 ↑ dividend) $\quad 3\overline{)12}$ with quotient 4 (12 ↑ dividend)

division The mathematical operation that separates an amount into smaller equal groups to find the number of groups or the number in each group.

Example: 12 ÷ 3 = 4 is a division number sentence.

divisor The number that you divide by in division.

Example: $12 \div 3 = 4$ (3 ↑ divisor) $\quad 3\overline{)12}$ with quotient 4 (3 ↑ divisor)

E

edge The line segment where two faces of a solid figure meet.

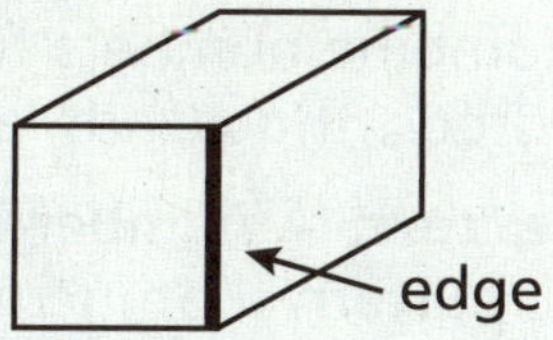

elapsed time The time that passes between the beginning and the end of an activity.

endpoint The point at either end of a line segment or the beginning point of a ray.

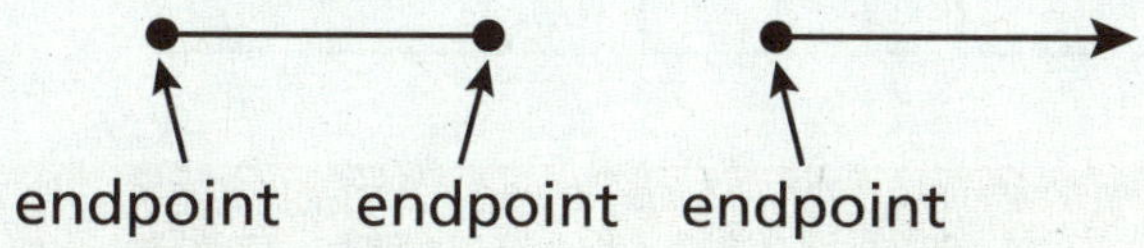

equation A mathematical sentence with an equals sign.

Examples: $11 + 22 = 33$
$75 - 25 = 50$

equilateral triangle A triangle whose sides are all the same length.

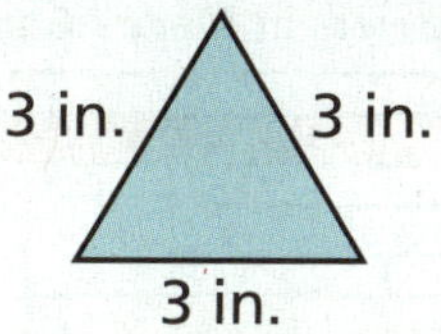

equivalent Equal, or naming the same amount.

equivalent fractions Fractions that name the same amount.

Example: $\frac{1}{2}$ and $\frac{2}{4}$

equivalent fractions

estimate About how many or about how much.

even number A whole number that is a multiple of 2. The ones digit in an even number is 0, 2, 4, 6, or 8.

event In probability, a possible outcome.

expanded form A number written to show the value of each of its digits.

Examples:
$347 = 300 + 40 + 7$
$347 = 3$ hundreds $+ 4$ tens $+ 7$ ones

expression A combination of numbers, variables, and/or operation signs. An expression does not have an equals sign.

Examples: $4 + 7$ $\quad a - 3$

F

face A flat surface of a solid figure.

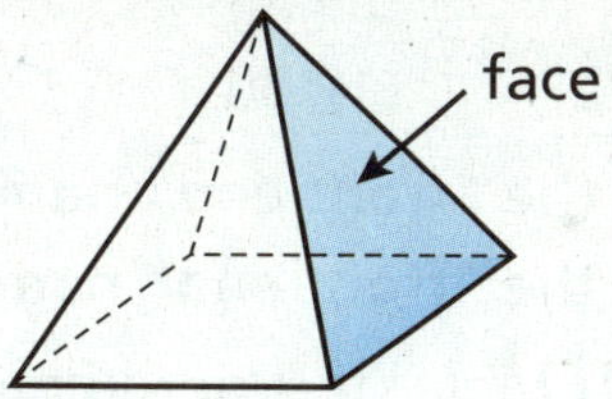

factors Numbers that are multiplied to give a product.

Example: $4 \times 5 = 20$

factor factor product

flip To reflect a figure over a line. The size and shape of the figure remain the same.

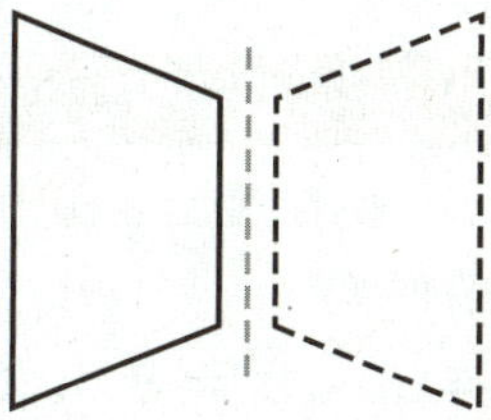

foot (ft) A customary unit used to measure length.

1 foot = 12 inches

formula An equation with variables that describes a rule.

The formula for the area of a rectangle is:

$A = l \times w$

where A is the area, l is the length, and w is the width.

fraction A number that names part of a whole or part of a set.

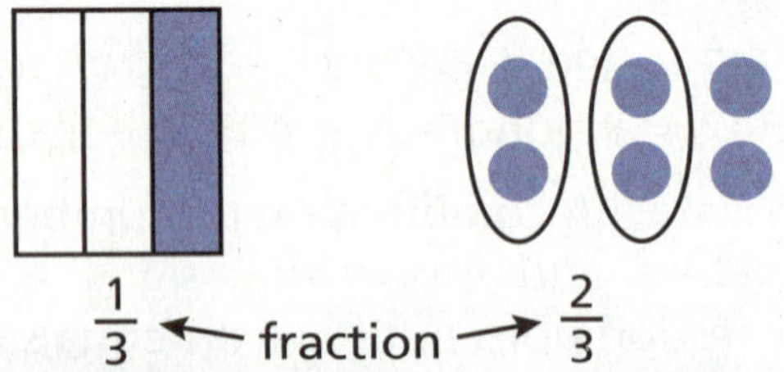

front-end estimation A method of estimating that keeps the largest place value in a number and drops the rest.

Example:

527	→	500
+ 673	→	+ 600
		1,100

The 5 in 527 is the "front end" number

The 6 in 673 is the "front end" number

function table A table of ordered pairs that shows a function.

For every input number, there is only one possible output number.

Rule: add 2	
Input	Output
1	3
2	4
3	5
4	6

G

gallon (gal) A customary unit used to measure capacity.

1 gallon = 4 quarts = 8 pints = 16 cups

gram (g) A metric unit of mass, about 1 paper clip.

1,000 grams = 1 kilogram

greater than (>) A symbol used to compare two numbers.

Example: $6 > 5$
6 is greater than 5.

group To combine numbers to form new tens, hundreds, thousands, and so on.

growing pattern A number or geometric pattern that increases.

Examples: 2, 4, 6, 8, 10...
1, 2, 5, 10, 17...

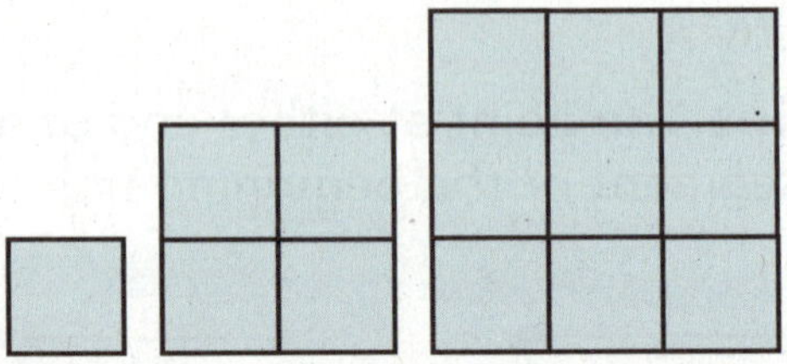

H

height A measurement of vertical length, or how tall something is.

horizontal Extending in two directions, left and right.

horizontal bar graph A bar graph with horizontal bars.

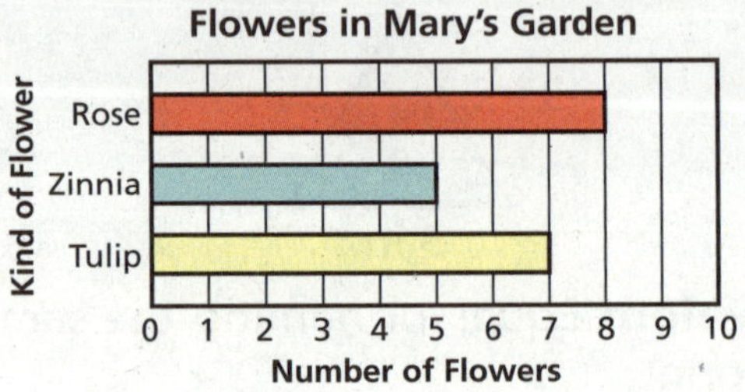

hundredth One of the equal parts when a whole is divided into 100 equal parts.

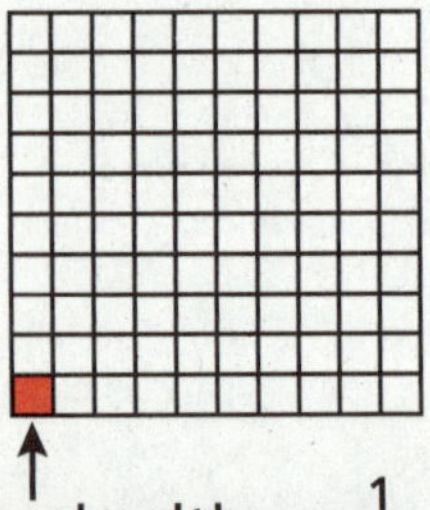

one hundredth = $\frac{1}{100}$ = 0.01

I

improper fraction A fraction in which the numerator is equal to or is greater than the denominator. Improper fractions are equal to or greater than 1.

$\frac{5}{5}$ and $\frac{8}{3}$ are improper fractions.

inch (in.) A customary unit used to measure length.

12 inches = 1 foot

isosceles triangle A triangle that has at least two sides of the same length.

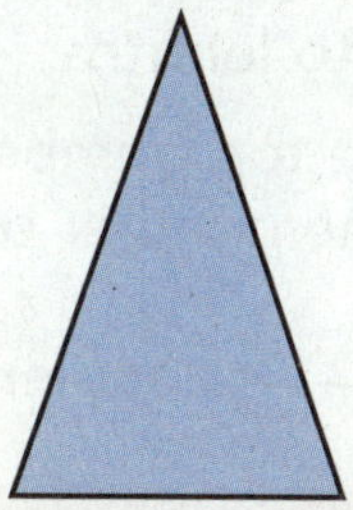

K

key A part of a map, graph, or chart that explains what symbols mean.

kilogram (kg) A metric unit of mass.

1 kilogram = 1,000 grams

kilometer (km) A metric unit of length.

1 kilometer = 1,000 meters

L

less than (<) A symbol used to compare numbers.

Example: $5 < 6$

5 *is less than* 6.

line A straight path that goes on forever in opposite directions.

line graph A graph that uses a straight line or a broken line to show changes in data.

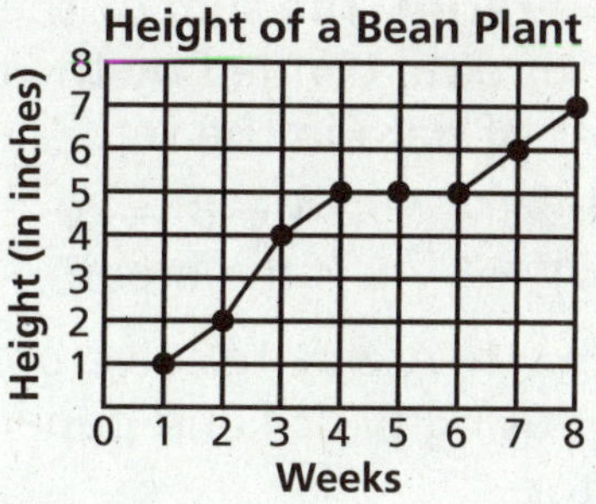

line of symmetry A line on which a figure can be folded so that the two halves match exactly.

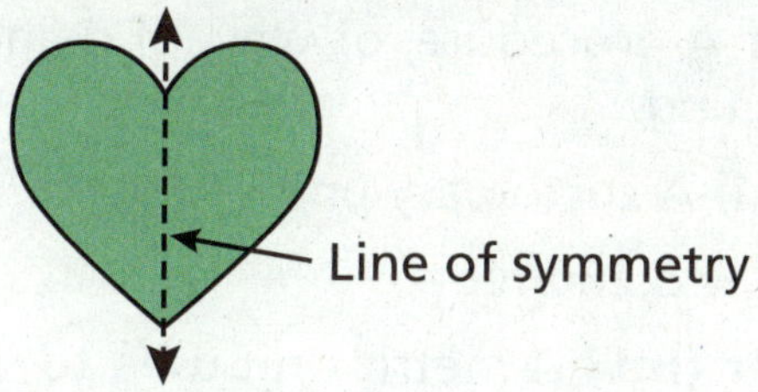

line plot A way to show data using a number line.

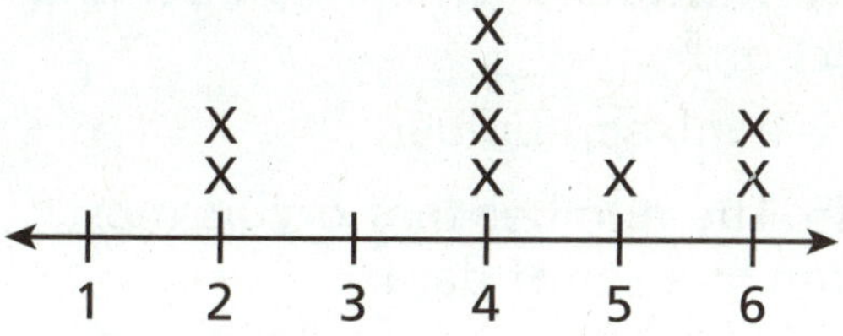

line segment A part of a line. A line segment has two endpoints.

liter (L) A metric unit used to measure capacity.

1 liter = 1,000 milliliters

M

mass The amount of matter in an object.

mean (average) The sum of the values in a set of data divided by the number of pieces of data in the set.

Example: $3 + 5 + 4 + 8 = 20$
$20 \div 4 = 5$ 5 is the mean

mental math A way to solve problems without using pencil and paper, or a calculator.

meter (m) A metric unit used to measure length.

1 meter = 100 centimeters

method A procedure, or way, of doing something.

mile (mi) A customary unit of length.

1 mile = 5,280 feet

milliliter (mL) A metric unit used to measure capacity.

1,000 milliliters = 1 liter

mixed number A whole number and a fraction.

$1\frac{3}{4}$ is a mixed number.

mode The number that occurs most often in a set of data.

In this set of numbers {3, 4, 5, 5, 5, 7, 8}, 5 is the mode.

multiple A number that is the product of the given number and another number.

multiplication A mathematical operation that combines equal groups.

Example: $4 \times 3 = 12$
factor factor product

$3 + 3 + 3 + 3 = 12$
4 times

N

net A flat pattern that can be folded to make a solid figure.

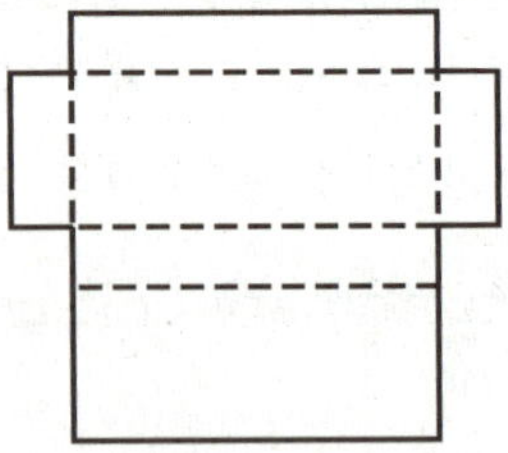

This net can be folded into a rectangular prism.

number line A line on which numbers are assigned to lengths.

numerator The top number in a fraction that shows the number of equal parts counted.

Example: $\frac{1}{3}$ ← numerator

O

obtuse angle An angle that measures more than 90° but less than 180°.

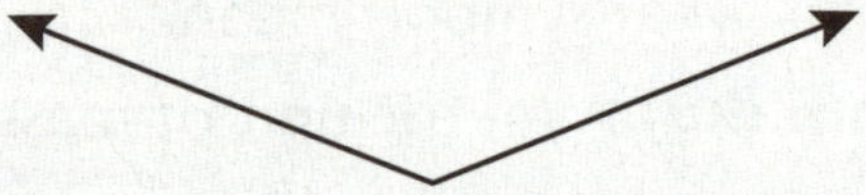

obtuse triangle A triangle with one angle that measures more than 90°.

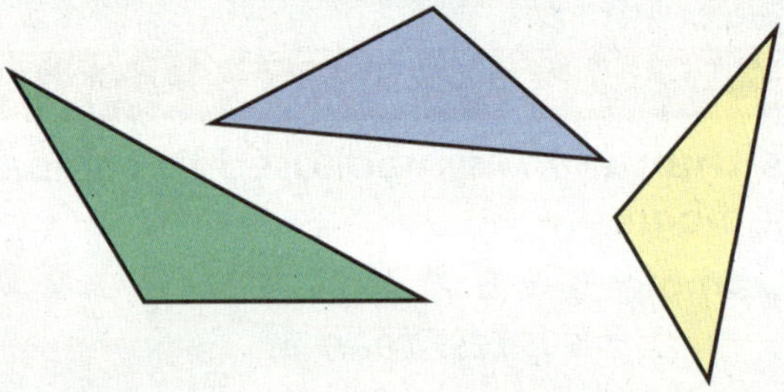

odd number A whole number that is not a multiple of 2. The ones digit in an odd number is 1, 3, 5, 7, or 9.

opposite sides Sides that are across from each other; they do not meet at a point.

Example: Sides *a* and *c* are opposite.

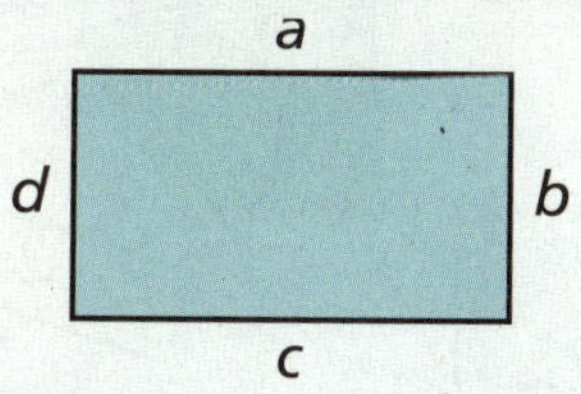

ordered pair A pair of numbers such as (3, 4) in which one number is considered to be first and the other number second. They can name a point on a coordinate grid.

ordinal numbers Numbers used to show order or position.

Example: first, second, fifth

ounce (oz) A customary unit used to measure weight.

16 ounces = 1 pound

P

parallel lines Two lines that are everywhere the same distance apart.

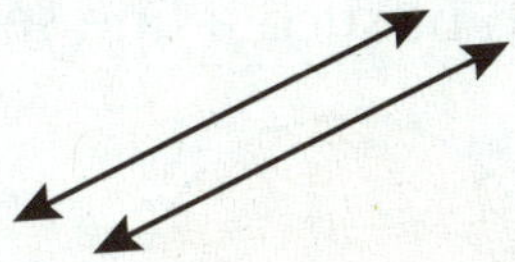

parallelogram A quadrilateral with both pairs of opposite sides parallel.

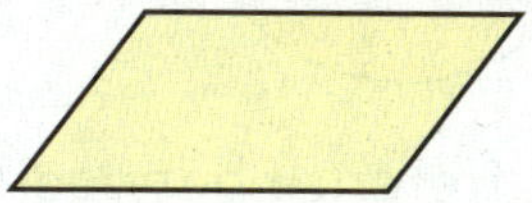

partner One of two numbers that add to make a total.

Example: 9 + 7 = 16 ← total *sum*

partner *addend* (9), partner *addend* (7)

perimeter The distance around the outside of a figure.

perpendicular Two lines or line segments that cross or meet to form right angles.

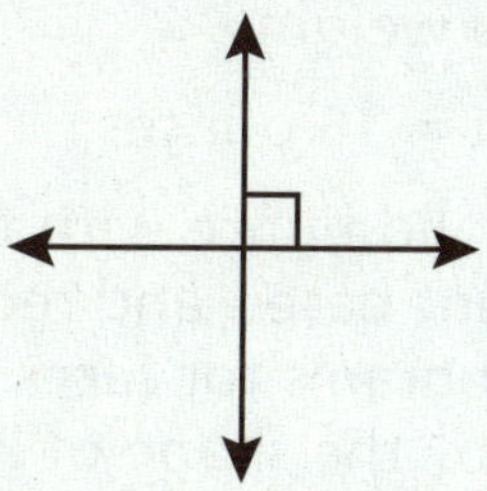

pictograph A graph that uses pictures or symbols to represent data.

pint (pt) A customary unit used to measure capacity.

1 pint = 2 cups

place value The value assigned to the place that a digit occupies in a number.

9 ↑ hundreds, 6 ↑ tens, 2 ↑ ones

place value drawing A drawing that represents a number. Hundreds are represented by boxes, tens by vertical lines, and ones by small circles.

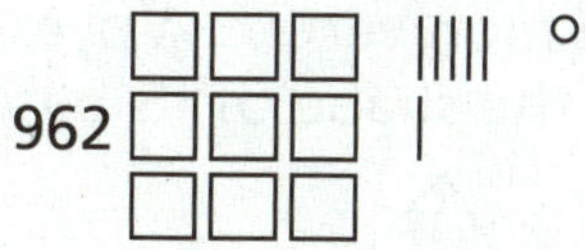

plane figure A closed figure that has two dimensions.

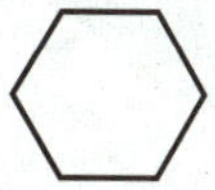

P.M. The time period between noon and midnight.

pound (lb) A customary unit used to measure weight.

1 pound = 16 ounces

prism A solid figure with two parallel congruent bases, and rectangles or parallelograms for faces. A prism is named by the shape of its bases.

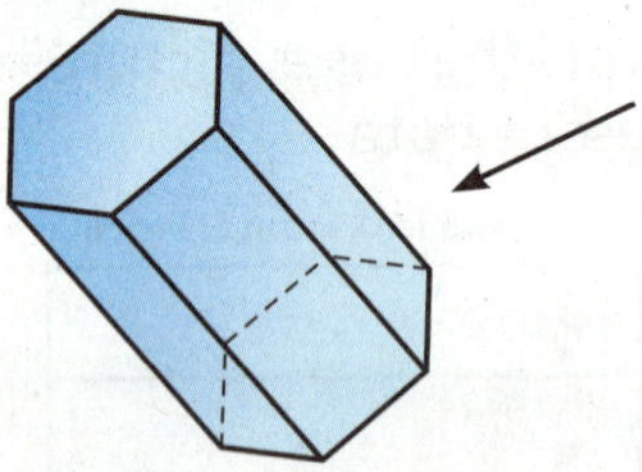

probability The chance of an event occurring.

product The answer when you multiply numbers.

Example: $4 \times 7 = 28$

factor factor product

proof drawing A drawing used to show that an answer is correct.

$$\begin{array}{r} 249 \\ +\ 386 \\ \hline 635 \end{array}$$

(carried digits: 11)

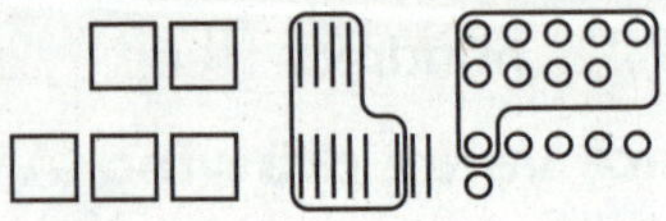

pyramid A solid figure with one base and whose other faces are triangles with a common vertex. A pyramid is named by the shape of its base.

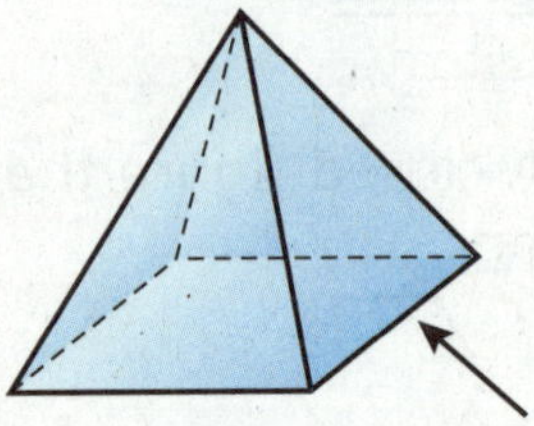

Q

quadrilateral A figure with four sides.

quart (qt) A customary unit used to measure capacity.

1 quart = 4 cups

quotient The answer when you divide numbers.

Examples:

$35 \div 7 = 5$ ← quotient (5)

$7\overline{)35}$ with 5 ← quotient

R

radius A line segment that connects the center of a circle to any point on the circle. The term is also used to describe the length of such a line segment.

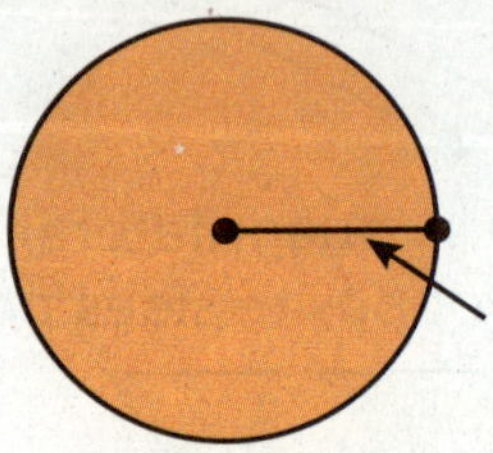

range The difference between the greatest number and the least number in a set of data.

In this set of numbers {12, 15, 18, 19, 20}, the range is 20 − 12 or 8

ray A part of a line that has one endpoint and goes on forever in one direction.

rectangle A parallelogram that has 4 right angles.

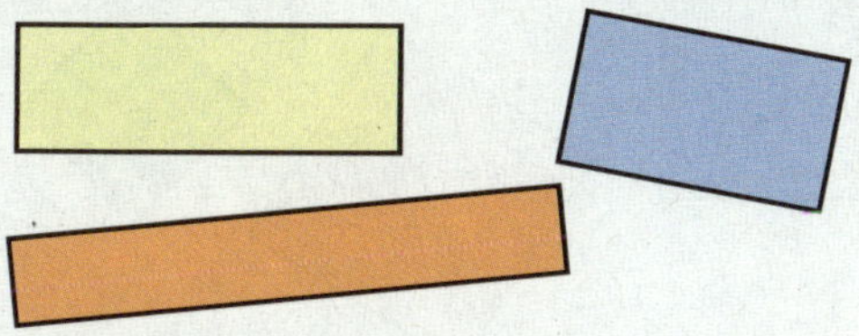

rectangular prism A prism with six rectangular faces.

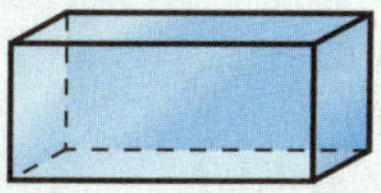

rectangular pyramid A pyramid with a rectangular base and four triangular faces.

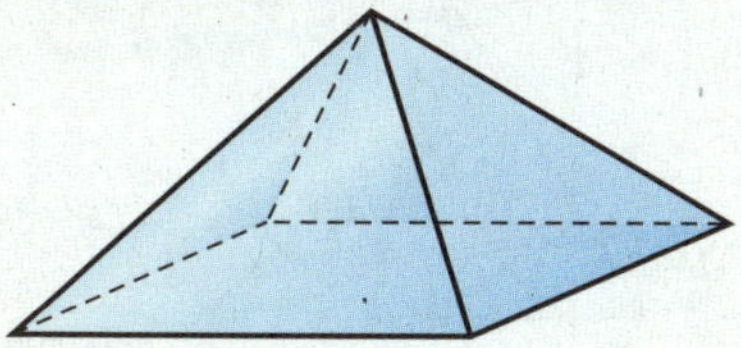

repeating pattern A pattern consisting of a group of numbers, letters, or figures that repeat.

Examples: 1, 2, 1, 2, …
A, B, C, A, B, C, …

rhombus A parallelogram with congruent sides.

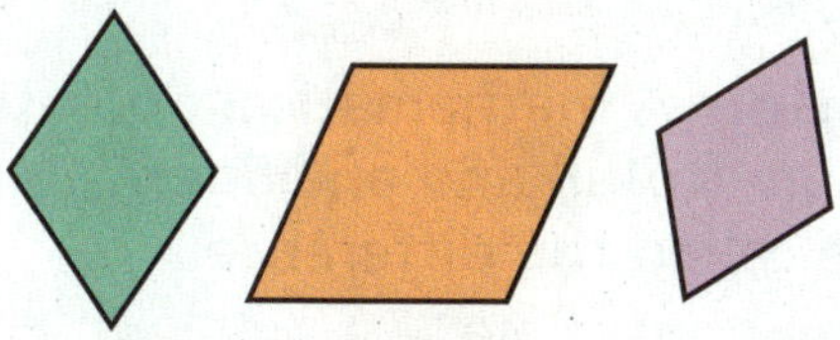

right angle An angle that measures 90°.

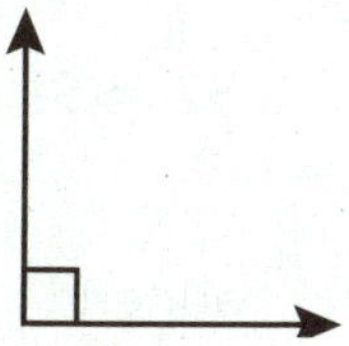

right triangle A triangle with one right angle.

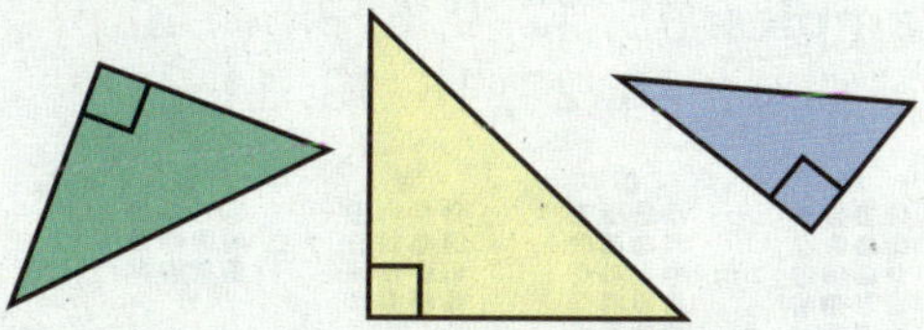

round To find about how many or how much by expressing a number to the nearest ten, hundred, thousand, and so on.

route The path taken to get to a location.

row A horizontal group of cells in a table.

Coin Toss

	Heads	Tails	
Sam	11	6	
Zoe	9	10	} row

S

scale An arrangement of numbers in order with equal intervals.

scalene triangle A triangle with sides of three different lengths.

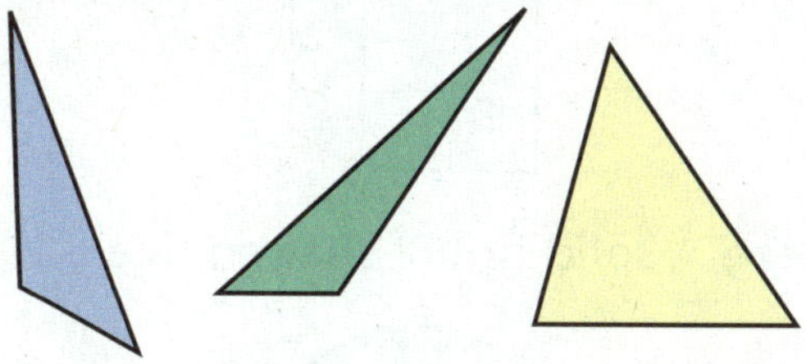

shrinking pattern A number or geometric pattern that decreases.

Examples: 15, 12, 9, 6, 3,...
25, 20, 16, 13, 11,...

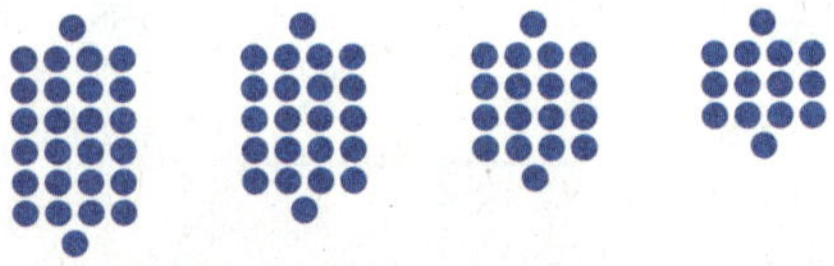

side (of a figure) A line segment that makes up a figure.

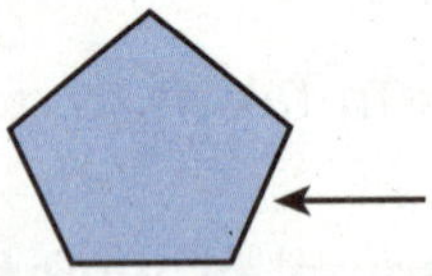

simplify To write an equivalent fraction with a smaller numerator and denominator.

slide To move a figure along a line in any direction. The size and shape of the figure remain the same.

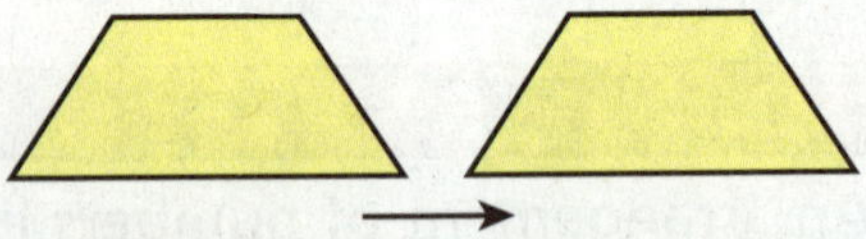

solid figure A figure that has three dimensions.

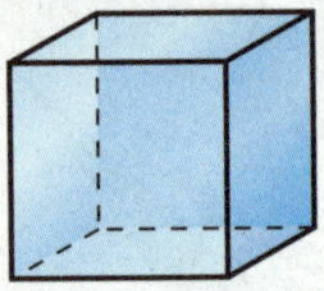

sphere A solid figure shaped like a ball.

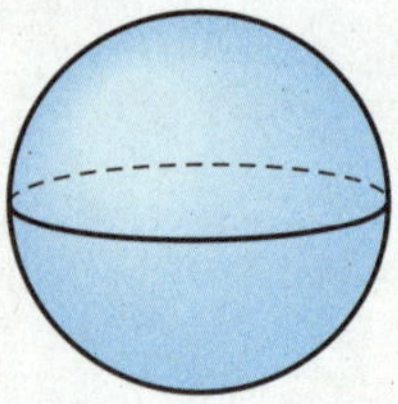

square A rectangle with four sides of the same length.

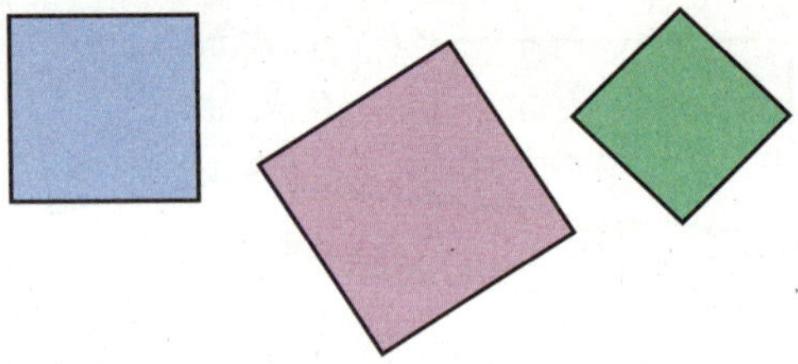

square number A product of a whole number and itself.

Example: $4 \times 4 = 16$
↑
square number

square pyramid A pyramid with a square base and four triangular faces.

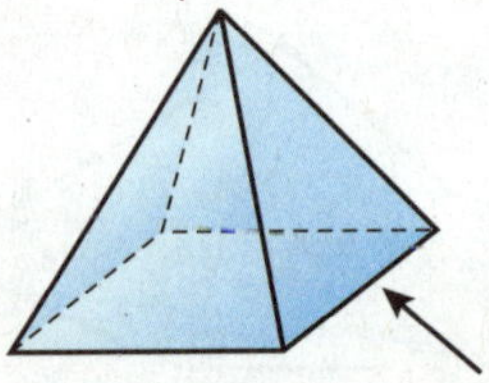

standard form The name of a number written using digits.

Example: 1,829

straight angle An angle that measures 180°.

subtract To find the difference of two numbers.

Example: $18 - 11 = 7$

subtraction A mathematical operation on a sum (total) and an addend, which can be called the difference.

Example: $43 - 40 = 3$

sum The answer when adding two or more addends.

Example: $37 + 52 = 89$

37	52	89
addend	addend	sum
partner	*partner*	*total*

survey A method of collecting information.

symmetry A figure has symmetry if it can be folded along a line so that the two halves match exactly.

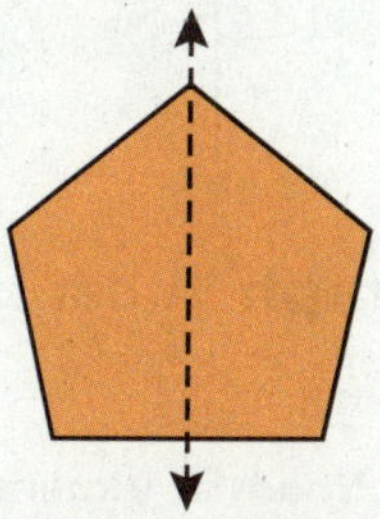

T

table An easy to read arrangement of data, usually in rows and columns.

Coin Toss

	Heads	Tails
Sam	11	6
Zoe	9	10

tally marks Short line segments drawn in groups of 5. Each mark including the slanted marks stands for 1 unit.

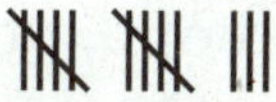 means 13

5 5 3

tenth One of the equal parts when a whole is divided into ten equal parts.

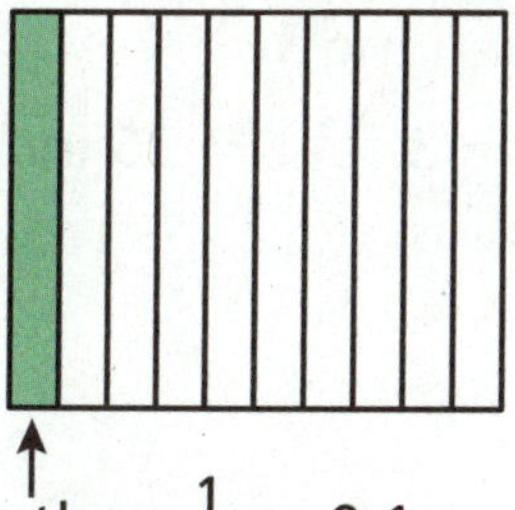

one tenth = $\frac{1}{10}$ = 0.1

thermometer A tool for measuring temperature.

total The answer when adding two or more addends. The sum of two or more numbers.

Example: 672 + 228 = 900

partner *addend* (672), partner *addend* (228), total *sum* (900)

trapezoid A quadrilateral with exactly one pair of parallel sides.

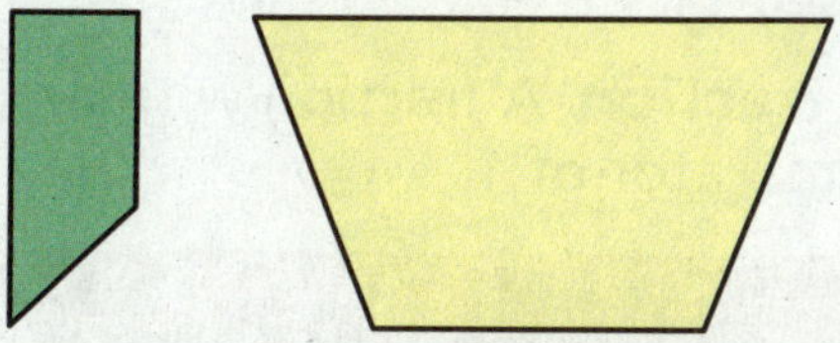

triangular prism A solid figure with two triangular faces and three rectangular faces.

Example:

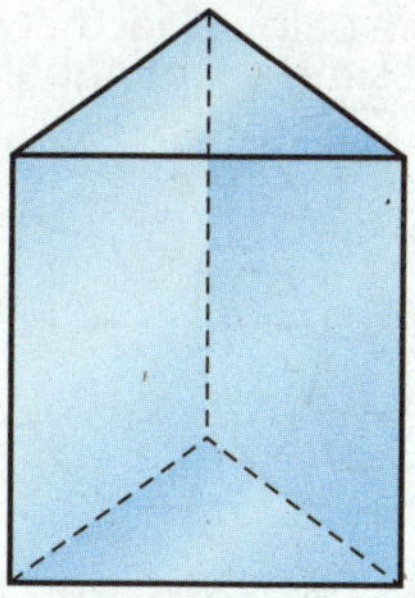

triangular pyramid A pyramid whose base is a triangle.

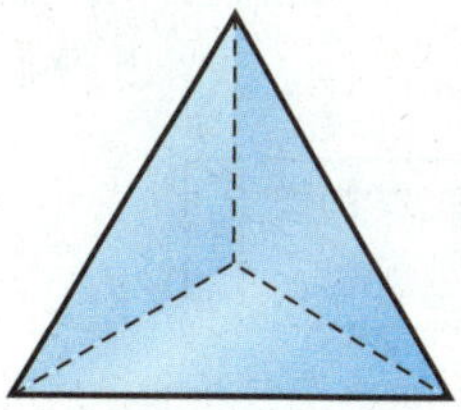

turn To rotate a figure around a point. The size and shape of the figure remains the same.

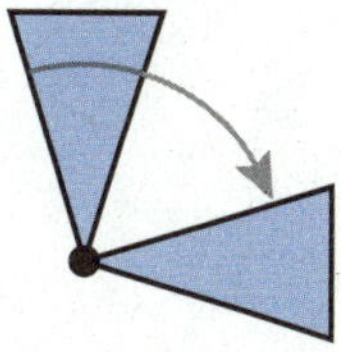

U

ungroup To open up 1 in a given place to make 10 of the next smaller place value in order to subtract.

unit fraction A fraction with a numerator of 1.

V

Venn diagram A diagram that uses circles to show the relationship among sets of objects.

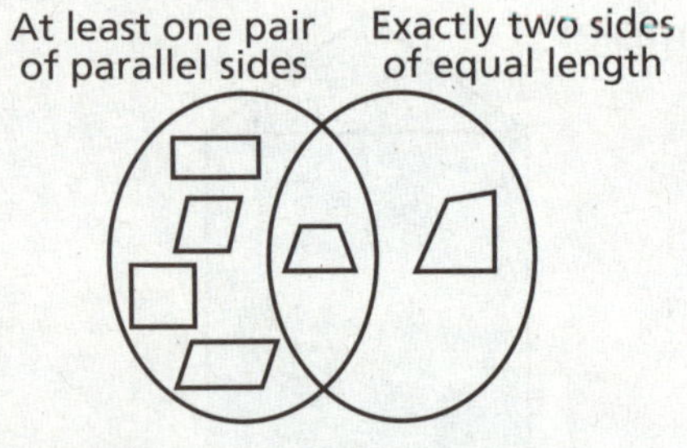

vertex A point where sides, rays, or edges meet.

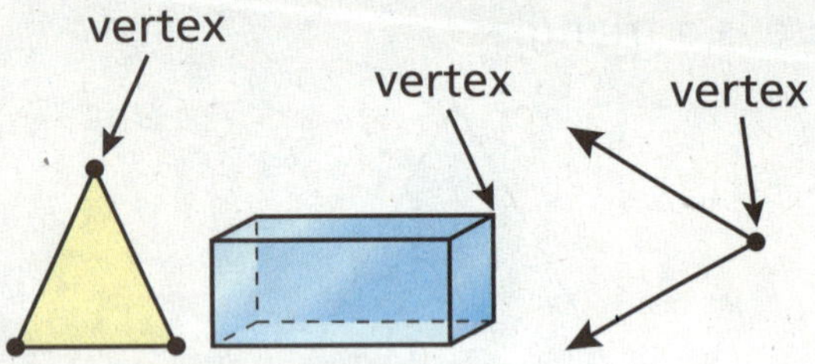

vertical Extending in two directions, up and down.

vertical bar graph A bar graph with vertical bars.

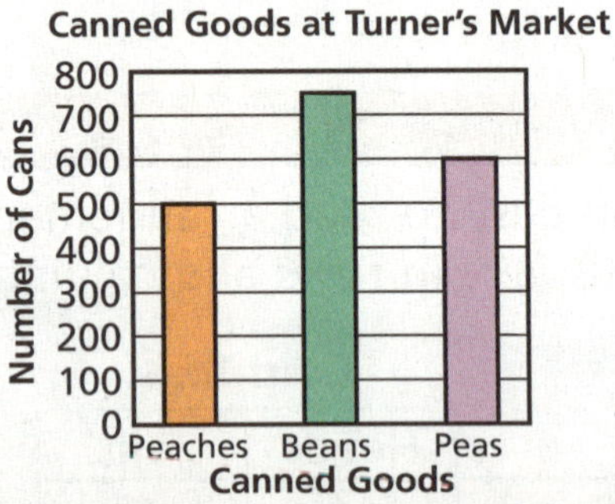

W

weight The measure of how heavy something is.

word form A name of a number written using words instead of digits.

Example: Nine hundred eighty-four

Y

yard (yd) A customary unit used to measure length.

1 yard = 3 feet = 36 inches